Wide praise for *Trudeau and Our Times*

"In prose that is lucid and gripping, the authors of **Trudeau and Our Times** have brought the public and private selves of Pierre Trudeau together, illuminating in the process his overwhelming impact on the country's political life. Trudeau 'haunts us still' but the authors go a long way toward explaining that mystery. Their book is an antidote to amnesia."
– Citation by the Canada Council Jury for the Governor General's Literary Award, 1990, in Non-Fiction

"With evident scholarship and lively prose . . . the authors focus on three decades of individual and national development through a startlingly clear lens . . . " – Chris Wood, *Maclean's Magazine*

"Intensive research, admirable writing skills and the careful thought Clarkson and McCall bring to this project provide the reader with an insightful look at the man who 'haunts us still.' . . . Pierre Trudeau has been our magnificent obsession. This is a work worthy of him and the special place he holds in our [national] psyche." – Harvey Schachter, *Kingston Whig-Standard*

"**Trudeau and Our Times** is full of fine scholarship, but it is never dull . . . Clarkson and McCall invest familiar events with sharp insight and a storyteller's gift . . . Easily the best work to date on Trudeau's life and career." – Satya Das, *Edmonton Journal*

"This is not your usual stuffy political biography . . . The authors succeed in making interesting reading . . . out of Trudeau's most important political achievements . . . [but] there is also enough titillating, gossipy material here to match any of the sex scandal tabloids on the supermarket racks."
– Gordon Henderson, *Windsor Star*

"Trudeau and Our Times provides by far the best explanation to date of the forces that shaped and drove the fascinating man who led the country for fifteen years." – Geoffrey Stevens, *Toronto Star*

"A first-rate book . . . a fruitful collaboration . . . Everyone should read Clarkson and McCall." – Terry Morley, *Victoria Times-Colonist*

"Trudeau and Our Times stands out as a clearly written, sensitive and engaging account of Trudeau's origins and character; it is a work replete with psychological insights, sophisticated in its analysis of the shifting political currents of the era, and objective in its treatment both of the former prime minister and of the party and politics he was to dominate for so long." – Description read at the ceremony for the 1990 Governor General's Literary Awards, January 22, 1991.

STEPHEN CLARKSON
& CHRISTINA McCALL

Trudeau
and Our Times

Volume 1: The Magnificent Obsession

An M&S Paperback from
McClelland & Stewart Inc.
The Canadian Publishers

An M&S Paperback from McClelland & Stewart Inc.

First printing August 1991
Cloth edition printed 1990

Canadian Cataloguing in Publication Data

Clarkson, Stephen
Trudeau and our times

"An M&S paperback."
Contents: v. 1. The magnificent obsession.
Includes bibliographical references and index.
ISBN 0-7710-5416-5 (v. 1)

1. Trudeau, Pierre Elliott, 1919- . 2. Canada - Politics and government - 1963-1984.* 3. Prime ministers - Canada - Biography.
I. McCall, Christina II. Title.

FC626.T7C58 1991   971.064'4'092   C91-094076-2

Quoted material on pages 43-44: from *Cyrano de Bergerac* by Edmond Rostand, translated by Brian Hooker. Copyright © 1923 by Henry Holt and Company. Reprinted by permission of Henry Holt and Company, Inc.

Quoted material on pages 176-77: from *Consequences* by Margaret Trudeau. Copyright © 1982 by Margaret Trudeau Enterprises Limited. Reprinted by permission of Seal Books.

Quoted material on page 180: *The Poetry of Robert Frost* edited by Edward Connery Lathem. Copyright 1923, © 1969 by Holt, Rinehart and Winston. Copyright 1951 by Robert Frost. Reprinted by permission of Henry Holt and Company, Inc.

Cover illustration by Mark Summers

Printed and bound in Canada

McClelland & Stewart Inc.
The Canadian Publishers
481 University Avenue
Toronto, Ontario
M5G 2E9

This book is for
Alice Helene Mannaberg Clarkson
who in so many ways made it possible

CONTENTS

FOREWORD

He haunts us still. Six years after he resigned as prime minister, a quarter of a century after he first sought office, Pierre Elliott Trudeau and his ideas remain dominant in the northern attic of the continent, a standard against which other political actors, thinkers, theorists, and hopefuls – past and present – measure themselves and are measured.

Trudeau's central place in the national consciousness is all the more remarkable when his present situation is considered. He has lived out his three-score-years-and-ten. He has retired to the city of his birth, to a perch in a minor law firm. His party is out of power, debt-ridden, and divided. His entourage has shrunk to a few loyalists, men who shared power with him and who now share his exile from it. His liberal interventionist ideas have been out of fashion for at least a decade. His vision of a Canadian federalist Utopia has been shattered. And his connections in the élites of both Quebec and English Canada are remarkably few.

There is no big money backing him and there never has been. In a country where politicians and businessmen have traditionally been in lockstep, both the old and the new money have always regarded him with deep suspicion. He was independently rich and a radical when he went into politics, and he remains independently rich and, according to his lights, radical still. He is a statesman who likes to think of himself as being on the side of ordinary people but who has rarely done anything ordinary in his life. He is an intellectual who has consistently shown contempt for the timidity of the Canadian academic community, which has just as consistently displayed its anger at him in return.

And yet whenever he reappears in public life – and as a romantic with an acute political intelligence, he knows just when, and when not, to be seen and heard – his impact is immediate, powerful, surprising. He co-edits a book of earnest essays and it outsells every other book on the market for months. He appears at a party convention called to choose the successor to his own successor and the cameras lovingly and ceaselessly seek him out. A major constitutional initiative of the current government – which was elected to succeed his with the largest majority ever accorded a federal administration and then re-elected on the basis of its influence in his own backyard in Quebec – fails spectacularly. But the present prime minister is not blamed for the failure. Pierre Trudeau is.

This is a book about the Trudeau phenomenon, an attempt to analyse his impact on the Canadian reality written by two people who watched it from front-row seats, one as an academic analyst and sometime political activist, the other as a magazine editor and political journalist. It started out as something quite different – a study of the Liberal Party in the 1980s, intended as a sequel to *Grits*, a book by Christina McCall published in 1982, which was a portrait of the Pearson-Trudeau party in its heyday. Under scrutiny, the Liberal Party at the end of the Trudeau era turned out to be little more than a shell, the franchised name for a governing formula that had worked for generations but had lost its fizzle. The Grits were an agglomeration of the ambitious, dependent on one man who cared very little about the party's past and even less about its future. The Liberal Party had become the Trudeau Party, and when he retired, it fell apart. What was interesting was not its militants but its leader, not its past but his impact on our present.

Although centred on Trudeau, *Trudeau and Our Times* is not intended to be strictly a biography (the book that half the academics and journalists concerned with Canadian politics would like to write but that probably should await the opening of his archives or the publication of his memoirs, or both). Instead, it is a look at the relationship between the politician and the polity, the leader and the led, that focuses on Trudeau's last five years in office, when the issues with which he had struggled throughout his career came to a climax in a ministry that tested the limits of state power.

The Magnificent Obsession is the first volume of this two-part study. It deals with his socio-cultural and intellectual background and how it led him and the country to constitutionalism – the attempt to resolve through legalistic formulations Canada's contradictions as a nation, an effort that absorbed Trudeau's interest and energy for most of his public life and that has continued to absorb the country long after his retirement as its leader.

Part I

Trudeau in Crisis, Trudeau in Triumph

CHAPTER 1

THE MIRACULOUS YEAR

The notion that political power in a democracy is open and attainable, that it is vested in people everybody knows and has claims on – after all, we elect them, they have to please us, we recognize their faces from a thousand television shows, their views from a hundred interviews – is never more acute than on a general election day, when there is a possibility that power will move, that it might be snatched from one group of politicians and bestowed on another, according to the collective electoral will.

May 22, 1979, was that kind of day in Canada. The federal campaign whose climax it marked had been talked of for months as one of the most important in the nation's history. In every part of the country people thought it might signal the end of the Liberal era that had begun in 1935, before the majority of citizens casting their votes in this election were born. The Progressive Conservative Party, which had been in decline most of that time – having held power federally for only six of the previous forty-four years – was expected to come into its own. In the capital city of Ottawa, the election's possible outcome was discussed with a particular urgency all day long and all over town, outside polling booths in residential districts in the early morning, over drinks in restaurants downtown at noon, in the corridors of government buildings as the civil servants prepared to go home at five o'clock. Careers could be ruined or inflated within the next few hours, policies doomed, files become dangerous, friends alienated, offices commandeered, whole lives changed.[1]

By the time the clock on Parliament Hill struck eight that night and the polls were closing across Ontario and Quebec, the city was in the grip of an excitement that was an anomalous mixture of fear, hope, and longing. The incumbent prime minister, Pierre Elliott Trudeau, was closeted with his closest political advisers in his official residence at 24 Sussex Drive. Diplomats and senior bureaucrats were making clever, restless jokes at elegant dinner parties before settling down to coffee, *eau-de-vie*, and the prognostications of the CBC. In campaign committee rooms, suburban family rooms, and neighbourhood bars, people were gathering to await the returns.

Downtown in the old Château Laurier hotel, the Liberal Party had once again taken over the ballroom where it had celebrated election victories for decades. At this early hour in the evening, everything was in place for the festivities: The security guards posted at the door to check the invitations. The television cameras that would transmit the leader's speech to the waiting nation once the election's outcome was known. The bar. The band. The video screens that were beginning to flash the early returns from the Maritimes. Even a handful of attractive people, standing around the walls like movie extras, many of them young party workers who hadn't realized that they should have waited until the results were coming in from the west before showing their faces downtown.

Older, wiser, more important Liberals were either still in their home-away-from-home apartments and hotels or drifting in and out of the suite on the Château's fifth floor reserved by the party in the name of a prominent senator. Half a dozen of them were expecting phone calls that would summon them "if things look good" to join the prime minister at his house for a while before he was driven down to the hotel to make his thank-you speech.

At eight o'clock their spirits were high. "The weird thing was," one of them said later, "that we were feeling feisty. Even though the polls had been bad for over a year and the press was set against us, and we had run hard and scared for more than two months in what was one bitch of a campaign, we somehow had the feeling that we might pull it off, that we still had the kind of political savvy the Tories never dreamed of. We figured we might get a minority, but hell, we could handle that. When the first results came in from the Maritimes and we were holding strong, and then we heard from Quebec and things looked even better there than we had hoped, our confidence took a leap. Whew! we were saying, figuring on drinking champagne at 24 Sussex before the night was done. Then we began to hear the bad news from Ontario and by eight-thirty it began to dawn on us. *We could lose. We really could lose.* Crazy as it sounds, that simple truth was just so hard to accept. I mean, we were Liberals. *Trudeau* Liberals. And Trudeau couldn't lose. That was part of his myth."[2]

By the time Trudeau came to the Château sometime around midnight, slipping in by a side door in order to concede his defeat, the simple truth had taken hold in the crowd: the Liberals had won only 114 seats to the Conservatives' 136. Wilting in the heat of the television lights, exhausted by this long night at the end of a hard campaign, the party militants, as Trudeau liked to call them, stood muted, their earlier optimism an embarrassing memory. Many of them watched in tears as their leader leapt onto a small platform and began to give one of his remarkable performances. The great man in defeat. The hero falls from grace.[3]

His speech was one of four texts prepared by his staff to meet every contingency: Liberal majority, Liberal minority, Tory majority, Tory minority, the last possibility having become the reality. The text had been handed to Trudeau at 24 Sussex once the last returns had come in from the west. After asking the small band of faithful Liberals gathered in his drawing room whether they could think of a good reason why he shouldn't concede his defeat, he had climbed the staircase to his private quarters on the second floor, memorized the salient points in the suggested text for his concession speech, changed from an old T-shirt and pants into an elegant suit, and indulged himself in one of his customary conceits, a fresh rose from the governor general's greenhouse, which he fixed in his lapel. Now under the lights in the Château ballroom, his eyes were alive with emotion, his face curiously luminous, like that of a martyr going to the stake. He proceeded to deliver his speech-writer's partisan sentiments ("The Liberal Party has fought a great fight and will fight many great fights in the future") as though they were articles of faith. "As for me, I will be a good leader of the opposition," he declared, ". . . and this country will need us in the future as it has in the past." Then he ended his oration with an extemporaneous recital of some lines from a favourite poem of his speech-writer's: "For all its sham, drudgery and broken dreams, it's still a beautiful world."[4]

Despite these moist promises, Trudeau was to prove a dismal leader of the opposition. But May 22, 1979, was no ending, no broken dream of a night. It was the beginning of the most extraordinary year of Trudeau's extraordinary public career, a miraculous year when fortune would turn so dramatically in his favour that by the following May, he would find himself catapulted from the nadir of this moment to a new apogee. He would struggle with and surmount the serious problems with his marriage that had plagued his public life for years. He would resign as leader of the Liberal Party and then quickly return to lead it again. He would win his fourth election victory and with it a second chance to realize his political goals. And he would take on his political arch-enemy, René Lévesque, the premier of his home province and the chief proponent of Quebec separatism, and defeat him in a referendum whose outcome would be interpreted for a time to mean that it was Trudeau's view of Canada that would prove to be the nation's destiny.[5]

These events would be widely described as a series of almost magical acts, perpetrated by a superhuman who was either the god/hero or demon/villain of Canadian life, depending on the commentator's visceral response. This role – in which Trudeau had been cast and re-cast ever since he became nationally prominent in the 1960s – encompassed many of the contradictions and inaccuracies that had been part of his political persona from the beginning of his public career.

The facts of Trudeau's life had been packaged into a formula version that went something like this: He had been born rich in Montreal to a Scottish-Canadian mother and a French-Canadian father, who had died when he was in his teens. He had been a brilliant student who had travelled the world, taking classes at great universities, seeking adventures on every continent. He had come back home to live a dilettante's life, writing occasionally for a small radical magazine, travelling intermittently, practising a little labour law, taking part in the occasional dramatic protest against the religious repressions and political inequities that marked his home province at the time. He was generally described as having entered the Canadian political mainstream reluctantly when he was forty-five, in company with other, more prominent French Canadians who were concerned about the increasing strength of Quebec separatism, to have become prime minister – again reluctantly – by virtue of a mysterious force called Trudeaumania that had something to do with sexuality and had roused among the populace high expectations that were subsequently deflated by his transformation from a playboy/dilettante in politics into an arrogant iron man/leader. He had run the country for eleven years to distinctly mixed reviews. His detractors, who by now included most of the country's businessmen, political commentators, and academic élite, despised him and predicted Canada's ruin if he continued to govern. His supporters, who included the entire French-Canadian wing of the Liberal Party, as well as the left-leaning faction of its English-Canadian wing, the upper reaches of the federal bureaucracy, and a still-significant segment of the electorate in both French and English Canada, believed that although the achievement of his noble goals had been prevented by adverse circumstances, he had striven valiantly in the cause of Canadian unity.[6]

This over-simplification of Trudeau's life was due in part to his own secretiveness about himself, which was evident before he went into politics and became compulsive afterwards. Following a flurry of revelatory articles that appeared after he first became a contender for the prime ministership in 1968 and were based on details about his past provided by relatives and friends, he set about convincing his intimates that they should be secretive too. Anyone thought to have divulged private information about him was distanced from his presence. When he did talk to the journalist George Radwanski, who wrote the biography that Trudeau's staff had urged him to co-operate on in the mid-1970s as part of a plan to recoup his already waning popularity, he was cautious in his answers, very much in control of the interpretation of his life's events. Of most other anglophone commentators who tried to penetrate his façade he was dismissive. "Why did they make up all that nonsense?" he asked in studied puzzlement years afterwards. "Why did they think they were qualified to analyse my life when they couldn't even get the facts straight and they knew so little about Quebec?"[7]

Trudeau could only rarely be persuaded to meet journalists or analysts in order to "get the facts straight." He was so intent on preserving his privacy that he did not even like entertaining his cabinet colleagues unless some state occasion demanded it. It was as though he had learned Charles de Gaulle's dictum that a political leader gains by keeping his distance, revealing judiciously only what he wants to reveal. This opacity served to protect a powerful element of his effectiveness as leader, the "otherness" that English-Canadian commentators had ceaselessly remarked on and that he himself had fostered as an essential part of his political appeal.[8]

Far from being a magician or a solitary outlaw or a Machiavelli reincarnated as his own Prince or a dove with falcon's claws – all descriptions attached to him by writers trying to penetrate the romance of his calculated mysteriousness – Trudeau had managed to dominate Canadian life for eleven years by the time he lost the election of 1979 (and would continue to dominate it for several more) because he was an unusually gifted, wilful, and shrewd political leader. He had achieved a symbiosis with his society based on a lifetime devoted to trying to understand its history and to affect its future.[9]

Trudeau chose Canada and Canada chose Trudeau –
and continued to choose him again and again – for complex reasons resulting from complementary needs. Trudeau as an individual had striven obsessively to become a
hero from the days of his youth, and in 1968, Canada, as
an anxious but hopeful collective still incompletely
formed as a state, was ready to accept a visionary leader
to guide it into its second century. Between these two
entities there was a fateful attraction. Their needs met and
clashed and met again to produce one of the most interesting eras in Canada's history.

CHAPTER 2

The Formative Decades

That after so many years in the public eye, Pierre Trudeau could still be perceived as mysterious in 1979 was a classic symptom of Canada's two solitudes. Quebec, its history and its culture, was still only dimly understood among English-speaking Canadians as the 1970s ended, some twenty years after the Québécois had begun their concerted attempts to achieve social and political equality through a quiet revolution. Outside his home province, Trudeau remained vaguely foreign, however often Canadians saw his face, heard his voice, experienced his supple reasoning. Inside it, he fitted into an intense struggle that his compatriots instinctively understood. To the Québécois, Trudeau was never mysterious. He was complex. A privileged, self-possessed, combative, driven intellectual-turned-politician now on the edge of oblivion.

Their responses to his electoral loss in May 1979 were complex as well. Even his opponents could feel the poignancy of his situation. After his concession speech had been broadcast, Pierre de Bellefeuille, a Montreal writer and editor not noted for his sympathy to Trudeau's ideas, commented on CBC Television, "Trudeau's weaknesses are sophistry and arrogance. There was a little sophistry [in his speech tonight] but we were spared the arrogance. In the final analysis, he is a great man."

Few people watching Trudeau that night, either in the Château ballroom or on the television screen, would have known from his demeanour that he was in the midst of what the psychologist Erik Erikson famously described as an identity crisis. It was Erikson's theory that such crises occur throughout life when the persona, the mask the individual presents to the world, no longer fits the self. In the late spring of 1979, Pierre Trudeau was suffering – at the advanced age of fifty-nine – a long-delayed identity crisis of humiliating proportions. Shortly before his electoral defeat, in wrangling about their marriage with his estranged wife, Margaret Sinclair Trudeau, he had insisted that he had "never lost in my life and I'm not losing you." Now, at the same time that his political career was being described as having come to an ignominious end, the spectacular nature of his marital breakdown was being commented on all over the world. Margaret Trudeau, who had run away from her husband and family two years before to "find herself," was cavorting for the media in Canada and the United States as part of the promotion for a book about her life with Pierre that had been put together by a British ghost-writer. For weeks, Canadian newspapers had been full of stories about her international exploits as she described her inflated ambitions, her sexual encounters with the rich and famous, and her experiences with drugs in the capitals of the world, in an exhibitionistic display of self-engrossment that shamed her husband and their young children repeatedly.[1]

Trudeau was at his nadir. The carefully constructed life, which had been seen for so long as perfectly realized, was shattered. The mask of self-containment and complete control no longer fit the man suffering inside.

• • •

Everything that had gone wrong for Pierre Trudeau politically and personally in 1979 had its roots in the complexities of his intellectual and psychological background and
in the nature of his relationship with his society.

He had grown up in a family that was prototypical of
the new French-Canadian bourgeoisie then emerging in
post-World War I Montreal, a still-weak capitalist class
trying to establish a foothold in an economy whose main
industrializing energy had been provided by British,
Anglo-Canadian, and American entrepreneurs, who had
been exploiting Quebec's resources since the Conquest in
1759. When Trudeau's parents, Charles-Émile Trudeau
and Grace Elliott, married in 1915, they were bent on
moving upwards in a society where the French-speaking
majority had been kept in its inferior place for more than
a hundred and fifty years.

At the time, Charles-Émile Trudeau was a struggling
young lawyer, the ambitious son of an illiterate Quebec
farmer named Joseph Trudeau, who after half a lifetime
of relentless toil had sold his land on the south shore of the
St. Lawrence, where his family had farmed for nine
generations, and moved to the nearby town of Saint-Rémi
so that his younger sons could be educated at a Jesuit
classical college in Montreal and reap the consequent
social and financial benefits. The Trudeau family was
driven on by the steely will of Joseph's wife, whose own
father had been the mayor of his village and whose
brother was a doctor. Malvina Trudeau was determined
that her children would not have to live as she and her
husband had, wringing a living out of selling their vegeta-
ble crop and the maple syrup harvest from their sugar
bush at the Marché Bonsecours in Montreal. Of her eight
surviving children (five others died in infancy), four sons
went to a classical college, two becoming lawyers and a
third a dentist; one daughter married a lawyer, another

the owner of a general store. "Charlie" Trudeau was her eighth child and her most ambitious, liveliest son.

The woman he chose for his wife, Grace Elliott, was the daughter of a widower named Philip Armstrong Elliott, who had grown prosperous keeping a saloon and speculating in real estate in downtown Montreal. Philip Elliott had been born into a family of Scottish origin who had settled in New England in the eighteenth century and then, as British loyalists, made their way north after the American Revolution to settle in Quebec. His forebears were struggling farmers and lumberjacks, but Philip Elliott proved to have a talent for making money. By the time he was middle-aged, he could afford to send his only daughter to Dunham Ladies' College in the Eastern Townships, where, although an ardent Catholic, she went to be "finished" along with the daughters of Quebec's Anglo-Protestant establishment. (Grace's mother was a French Canadian named Sarah Sauvé, whose two sons, Allan and Gordon Elliott, were raised as Protestants like their father but whose daughter was baptized in the Catholic church, a practice that was not uncommon in mixed marriages.) Grace's acquired gentility was tempered by a practicality learned from living in the flat above her father's tavern, The Captain's Saloon on Aylmer Street, after her mother died, and from working as a secretary in a Montreal office when she left the ladies' college. She met Charlie Trudeau at mass in the chapel of the Collège Sainte-Marie in downtown Montreal when they were both still in their teens and he was a student there. When the Elliotts moved to Longueuil on the south side of the St. Lawrence after a fire destroyed their tavern, Charlie Trudeau used to walk across the frozen river from Montreal to keep company with Grace on winter nights. They courted for nearly a decade before they could afford to marry in 1915. By all accounts it was a match of striking opposites. Charlie was a dynamo, gutsy, gregarious, extravagant, and loud. Grace was contemplative, devout, frugal, forbearing, and resolutely refined. They belonged to racial groups that were at loggerheads over Canada's role in World War I. Gordon Elliott, Grace's brother, went to war as a pilot and was shot down and severely wounded. Charlie Trudeau, though eminently eligible (he was single and only twenty-seven when war broke out), stayed home and tended to his law practice in order to build the good life his mother expected for her children rather than fighting England's imperial battles abroad.[2]

Once the war was over, Charlie grew impatient with the three-man law office he had set up with his brother and brother-in-law. On the lookout for ways to make more money than any small-time lawyer could expect to acquire in a city where French-speaking people were excluded from big business, he dreamed up the idea of establishing an Automobile Owners' Association that offered, for a $10 membership, discounts on gasoline, towing, and repair costs. It was an imaginative, risky venture, based on a shrewd recognition of the emerging importance of the automobile in middle-class life. The American Way was seeping into the consciousness of sleepy Quebec and Charlie Trudeau was determined to make his fortune from it.

Pierre Trudeau was born just as this business was in the start-up stage. The formative years of his childhood were spent not in boundless affluence but in a household charged with the tensions of adults living on the financial edge, striving to transcend formidable class barriers and cultural constraints. The AOA ran on Charlie's raw energy and money borrowed from his friends and his somewhat reluctant father-in-law. For several years it was uncertain whether he could make a go of it, and Grace Trudeau had to be penny-pinching and bravely optimistic in the face of her relatives' doubts and the demands of her growing family. She had given birth to four children in rapid succession, a daughter (Suzette, born in 1918) and three sons (the first, born in 1916, died in infancy; the second was Joseph Philippe Pierre Yves Elliott, born in 1919; and the third, Charles Elliott, was born in 1922).

By this time, Grace Trudeau was living in a largely French-Canadian milieu and had come to terms with the free-wheeling behaviour of her husband, who brought a formidable temper as well as a formidable zest to the task of running a new business in the wide-open Montreal of the 1920s. Political corruption, blind pigs, brothels, street gangs, and mobsters were part of the teeming street life in a city where the politics was French Canadian but the economy was dominated by the English with their banks, their big department stores, their railroads, their country estates, their collections of European art, their mock-English clubs and hunt balls. The French-Canadian bourgeoisie lived quite separate lives, scrambling to make a living as accountants, lawyers, doctors, and shopkeepers, in thrall to the Catholic church, their view of temporal power filtered through the clergy, who were almost as ignorant of the larger world as they were themselves. Resentment of their position was only beginning to stir. There was still some anti-English bitterness left over from the conscription crisis of World War I and a growing apprehension, fed by the nationalist historian the Abbé Groulx, that the post-war influx of American capital would threaten French Canada's survival. But the prosperity of the 1920s dissipated these feelings and, on the surface, there was general racial harmony.[3]

The Trudeau family lived modestly at 5779 Rue Durocher, a solid yellow-brick structure that was part of a row of six dwellings built in 1913 with a ten-foot yard in front and a lane at the back where garbage was picked up and schoolboys congregated to play games and make mischief. It was a partly mixed neighbourhood, with a smattering of Irish Catholics and Jews living side by side with French Canadians, just inside the boundaries of Outremont, a new middle-class suburb now swallowing up the farmland that had stretched for miles only a decade before. Nearby was an imposing church, Saint Viateur, where the Trudeaus went to mass, and a few blocks away, the Académie Querbes, an impressive new school that had been opened in 1916 by the premier of the province, Sir Lomer Gouin, in the presence of the archbishop of Montreal. Intended for the children of the upwardly mobile French and Irish Catholic bourgeoisie, Querbes held classes in both French and English. Attention was paid to sports and other extracurricular activities and the educational tone was resolutely forward-looking and remote from the style of the village schools where simple curés had taught French Canadians to read, write, figure, and say their catechisms in the nineteenth century. The Trudeau boys were enrolled at Querbes, first in the English section and then in the French, and instructed to appreciate its wonders: the swimming pool, the bowling alley, the stone façade that gave it an aura of architectural splendour and made it the equal of Lower Canada College and Bishop's, the important schools for the English Protestants.[4]

The Durocher house was also close to Charlie's main AOA garage, where he went early and worked late, leaving the upbringing of the children largely to his wife. Under the pressure of turning his small business into a large success, Charlie Trudeau had developed into a curser and a shouter who had been known to get into fist-fights with his mechanics, who had no qualms about crawling under a car or pumping gas and changing oil if he was short-handed. As his business thrived, he abandoned his law practice and began to consort with a crowd of French-Canadian entrepreneurs whose zest for business matched his own.[5]

"Charlie could be brutal," an old acquaintance of the family remarked years later. "His noisy self-confidence may have been entertaining for his poker-playing pals at the Club Saint-Denis [a club founded by French Canadians who were excluded from the English men's clubs]. But for his family, his vivacity had a dark side. When he was in a rage or got roaring drunk it was hard to stand up to him."[6]

Charlie knew how difficult it was for French Canadians to thrive and he wanted his sons to grow up tough and smart, attributes he encouraged by insisting they take boxing lessons, compete fiercely in all kinds of sports, and excel academically. In early childhood, Pierre had been frail and sensitive, a condition that worried his mother and irritated his father. In order to meet Charlie's demands Pierre learned to discipline himself rigorously, to overcome his weaknesses – to do calisthenics outdoors in winter, to take part in lacrosse and hockey, team sports that his agile, gregarious father had excelled at but where he might be the smallest player on a team, to conquer his natural shyness by forcing himself to ask challenging questions of adults in authority, to fight back when street toughs accosted him on the way to school, and to suppress an embarrassing tendency to cry, which he had displayed in public more than once when he was younger and weaker.

By the time he was twelve and ready for enrolment at Collège Jean-de-Brébeuf, the Jesuit classical college on Côte Sainte-Catherine, the Trudeaus had bought a new house on McCulloch Avenue that cost $23,000, a hefty sum for the period. A three-storey brown-brick building with a large backyard deep in the heart of Outremont, it was a more substantial property than the house on Durocher, which had been sold for only $11,000, but it was an unpretentious place nevertheless. It suited the discreet gentility of the middle-aged woman who was its mistress and the three children she was bringing up with the help of a country girl, who acted as a maid of all work, and a handyman-driver named Grenier, who worked for the Trudeaus for forty years. Certainly, it was a far cry from the kind of opulent mansions that the English had built in the Square Mile in downtown Montreal in the previous century or the grandiose structures they were building now in their own ghettoized suburb of Westmount.

The Trudeaus continued to live there even after Charlie sold his service stations to Imperial Oil for just over a million dollars and moved on to other enterprises that suited his swaggering temperament: an amusement park, a mining investment portfolio, apartment houses, a share in the Montreal Royals baseball club. Inflated by his business prowess, he spent money freely on promoting the careers of promising boxers, on travelling with his friends to sporting events all over the continent, on eating and drinking well, and in gambling with gusto at stud poker and contract bridge. The Jesuit priests who taught Pierre at Brébeuf remembered the elder Trudeau's largesse more than thirty years after his death. He would offer to buy them Havana cigars to pass around at a college dinner in honour of a visiting papal delegate or to send them a case of whisky for their own pleasure any time they liked. "Just put it on my account," he would say grandly in acknowledgement of his own and the Jesuits' worldliness. "There is no reason why you shouldn't have the best." This kind of display was looked on disapprovingly by his frugal wife and seems to have been a source of embarrassment to his sensitive son Pierre, whose classmates recalled

that he was reluctant to tell them he had travelled to
Europe in 1933 with his family for a summer holiday in
celebration of their new wealth. Even among the bour-
geois families who sent their sons to Brébeuf, few French
Canadians could afford such an extravagance in the early
Dirty Thirties.[7]

Instead of being ruined by the Depression, Charlie
Trudeau had grown richer through a combination of
audacity, a refusal to speculate in stocks, and a natural
shrewdness inherited from his own father and mother,
who had been quick to understand what kind of farm
produce would fetch the most at market and what sort of
profession would give their sons a chance to get ahead in a
socio-economic milieu that was stacked against them. In
politics Charlie had remained Conservative or *bleu*, as his
parents were before him. He supported the flamboyant
mayor of Montreal, Camillien Houde, for the leadership
of the provincial Conservative Party in 1929 and then
raised money for Maurice Duplessis, who had been a contemporary at law school, when he took over the Conservative Party and combined it with dissident Liberals and
nationalists to form the Union Nationale in 1936. Associates of Duplessis later told his biographer, Conrad
Black, that if Charlie Trudeau had lived long enough,
Duplessis would have appointed him to his legislative
council after he was elected premier of Quebec in 1936,
out of gratitude for Trudeau's help. Despite Charlie's
close involvement with two of the prototypical political
leaders of French Canada in his time, all the adult Pierre
Trudeau could remember about Quebec politics in this
period was that on election nights, his father always
"cursed the Liberal machine" whenever it rolled in a
majority of seats for *les rouges*, federally or provincially.[8]

By this time, Pierre had grown into a wiry adolescent.
A photograph of his family taken on the steamship *Cham-*

plain on their transatlantic voyage in 1933 shows him looking fiercely proud, a compelling boy with intense eyes and clenched fists. In contrast, his older sister, Suzette, who was fifteen, looked modest and withdrawn, his younger brother, Charles (called Tip), like a sweet-faced, acquiescent ten-year-old.

The foothold the adolescent Pierre was establishing in his father's world was knocked awry by Charlie Trudeau's death two years later at the age of forty-seven. He died in April 1935, after catching pneumonia on a visit to his baseball club's spring training camp in Florida. This loss was to prove pivotal in Pierre Trudeau's life, an event that profoundly changed the course of his development. The trauma he suffered ultimately turned him into a very different kind of adult from the rich businessman he might have become if Charlie Trudeau had lived another thirty years and Pierre had grown up under his influence.

His early response to his bereavement was marked by the kind of erratic behaviour that often occurs when an adolescent is prevented from resolving normal conflicts with his father – conflicts aggravated in Pierre Trudeau's case by the fact that he and Charlie Trudeau were so different in temperament, the boy naturally introverted and shy, the father extroverted, demanding, and earthy to the point of coarseness but at the same time demonstrative and tactile. "He was a great hugger," Trudeau remembered forty years after Charlie's death.

On another occasion he said to an astonished acquaintance, "Actually, I didn't like him very much. You never knew what to expect." These contradictory attitudes reflect the ambivalence he must have felt when suddenly the most powerful presence in his life, the gigantic figure the adolescent Pierre was just starting to confront on his way to a separate adult existence, disappeared, leaving him in a state of psychic imbalance. He was never going to be able to prove conclusively that he was just as smart as Charlie if not smarter, just as tough if not tougher. The day would never come when he could successfully challenge the "lickings" he describes his father as having given him when he disobeyed, when paternal dominance would be replaced by the father's acknowledgement of the son's achievements as a grown man.[9]

Abruptly, at the age of fifteen, there had occurred in his life a calamity that would significantly disrupt his emotional formation, turning him into the kind of man who evolves outside the normal patterns of growth. His early confrontation with death would force him to develop great strengths but at the same time leave him prey to crippling weaknesses.[10]

Maurice Sauvé, who went to Charlie Trudeau's funeral as part of a Boy Scout guard of honour, never forgot the intensity of the family's grief. "I didn't know Pierre then. I am four years younger," he remembered, "but he was a Boy Scout too, which is why we went to the funeral, and in Outremont the Trudeaus' grief was often remarked on. Their house looked dark for years, shut down by tragedy."[11]

What went on behind that dark façade the adult Trudeau was at pains to avoid revealing, other than admitting that his reaction to his father's death was so profound and so far-reaching that he still cried uncontrollably at funerals when he was a grown man. What was noticed by their neighbours and friends was that the Trudeau family became withdrawn, muted, and even more refined in its tastes. Gone were the days when the Trudeau children went to their paternal grandparents' house in Saint-Rémi for big family gatherings and Pierre and Tip got their white sailor suits dirty chasing chickens with their country cousins, the days when boxers, ballplayers, and Charlie's hard-drinking buddies arrived in a swarm at the house on McCulloch Avenue, telling crude jokes, talking pro sports, scheming big schemes. Gone was the uneasy balance of the family's extreme mother–father polarity.

Travelling to Florida to her husband's deathbed, Grace Trudeau had expressed to her daughter, Suzette, great apprehension about how she would raise her sons without their father. She turned to the Church for solace and advice. Having always been devout, she became even more strictly observant in her mourning, a deepened involvement with religion that directed her children even further away from the high-flying world that Charlie Trudeau had revelled in during the last flamboyant years of his life. The family continued to live comfortably, if unpretentiously, in the house on McCulloch Avenue with their loyal household help, and the same Victorian sofas and chairs with *petit point* seats, the same prized Dresden china standing unused in the cupboard. But now they spoke English almost exclusively to one another since Charlie was no longer there to question them about their schoolwork, sports, friends, ambitions. Pierre responded to his mother's religiosity by going with her frequently to early-morning mass, developing the engrossment in spiritual matters that would persist throughout his life. He also took on her disdainful attitude towards emotionalism. "When my father was around, there was a great deal of effusiveness and laughter and kissing and hugging. But after he died, it was a little bit more the English mores which took over, and we used to even joke about, or laugh at, some of our cousins or neighbours or friends – French Canadians – who'd always be very effusive within the family and towards their mothers and so on," he remembered.[12]

The unhappy confluence of his widowed mother's desolation with his own adolescent turmoil reinforced his tendency to withdraw from intimacy with others, which was to mark his behaviour ever afterwards. He rarely brought his school friends to McCulloch Avenue. A wide gulf separated his private and public selves. At home with his mother or in public with her friends, he was quiet, shy, non-communicative, polite, "English" in his attitudes.

And yet, with his *copains* at school and on the streets of Montreal he still played at being like his ebullient father, a lippy boy, street-smart and outrageous, deliberately provoking strangers into fist-fights. It was as though he was emulating Charlie Trudeau's exaggerated machismo and at the same time acting out an inner rage at his father for having abandoned him forever by dying, the kind of anger that is often associated with the early stages of grief but that he would never be able to outgrow fully.[13]

André Lussier, a Montreal psychiatrist, told the *New Yorker* writer Edith Iglauer, whose remarkable profile of Trudeau was published in 1969, that his adolescent ambivalence about his father's death was probably accompanied by irrational fears and guilts that fostered his compulsion to become unique, to be "un original," as he himself expressed this urge. Acting out was not unusual for an adolescent in search of an identity separate from his parents; in young Pierre's case what was remarkable was the extremes to which he went. Throughout his adolescence and adulthood, the carefully controlled Pierre would be subject to sudden outbursts of rage or displays of sarcasm that would have a devastating effect on his victims and on himself. It was as though another powerful shadow personality would always be lying in ambush waiting to sabotage with sudden displays of aggression or combativeness what he was trying to accomplish with modesty, reason, and calm detachment.[14]

In this period of his adolescence, he made a show of repudiating Charlie Trudeau as a model. He stopped using his father's rough French, the slangy patois of the

Québécois, and set about learning to speak the classical French of Molière and Racine, taking diction lessons after school to perfect his accent. He experimented with changing his name, calling himself first Pierre-Philippe Trudeau, then Pierre Esprit Trudeau (in the manner of Pierre Esprit Radisson, the explorer), and finally, Pierre Elliott-Trudeau, with a hyphen linking the surnames of his ethnic duality. He turned his back on the populist sports his father had revelled in (baseball, hockey, lacrosse, boxing) and boasted that he would compete henceforth only with himself in activities like diving, skiing, and canoeing. He practised these largely solitary athletic skills relentlessly, developing the individualism and displaying the perfectionism that later marked his behaviour in other areas. He began to express an intense dislike for people who drank to excess, an attitude he still held forty years afterwards. "I always thought that one of the reasons Pierre so disliked the business world," said a French-Canadian social scientist who came to know him well in the early 1960s, "was that many businessmen of his generation drank heavily, as his own father had, and he clearly hated alcohol's effect on people's behaviour."[15]

As part of the gentrification process that the Trudeaus underwent in the late 1930s, Pierre was sent to the Taylor Statten camp in northern Ontario, where the sons of the English-Canadian élite were dispatched for summer holidays. The private-school boys gathered there were astonished by this thin kid from Montreal who vied with them at diving and canoeing while quoting Baudelaire at the same time. For Trudeau, it was his first protracted encounter with the world of the Canadian upper middle class, a society that still aped the style of the English as it had since colonial times.[16]

At home in Montreal, he saw next to nothing of Anglo-Canadians. The milieu he lived in was intensely French despite his family's preference for speaking English. His priests, his teachers, his own friends – and those of his mother, sister, and brother – were mostly francophones. At Brébeuf, the Jesuits prided themselves on being the educators of Quebec's French-speaking élite and reminded their pupils constantly that they were *la crème de la crème*. What mattered was the disciplined study of the classics, the development of a capacity for ordered reasoning, and a sense of belonging to a privileged few. French-Canadian moral superiority was a given, a countervailing force to their very evident economic inferiority. The young Trudeau obviously found the pride that this attitude encouraged a useful disguise for his general unease and his mounting ambivalence about being a French Canadian. Running with a cheeky crowd who called themselves "les snobs," he was sometimes brazenly obstreperous, getting himself thrown out of class for disobedience.

It was during these formative years of his late adolescence, particularly under the tutelage of a broad-minded young priest, Father Robert Bernier – a Franco-Manitoban intellectual of eclectic interests who fixed in the young Pierre's mind forever the view that as a French Canadian one did not have to be parochial – that he experienced the pleasure of playing with abstract ideas and found in intellectualizing a way to cope with the frightening uncertainties with which his father's death haunted his life. The Cartesian postulate that the way to certain truth lay through rejecting all previous beliefs and starting with a clean intellectual slate appealed to Pierre's antipathy to authority and desire for certainty. He used his intellect like a weapon, competing aggressively for top marks in a class of students remembered at Brébeuf as unusually brilliant, arming himself for verbal combat with the Jesuitical tricks of sophistry and rhetoric, scoring knockout blows against classmates who were intellectually less agile. His compulsion to contradict whatever others were saying was aggravating – "He always had to have the last word," his brother, Tip, told an acquaintance later – and a further means of insulating himself from intimacy.[17]

Outside the Brébeuf fortress the miseries imposed by the Depression were taking their toll on Quebec. In 1932 a quarter of a million people were on the relief rolls in Montreal, many of them migrants from farms and small towns where American branch plants had cut back their operations or closed them down in the wake of the Wall Street crash in 1929 and the world-wide depression that followed. As social dislocation spread, Quebec nationalism was rising again, fed not just by economic problems but by revived fears that the gradual dismantling of the British Empire after World War I – signalled in Canada by the passing of the Statute of Westminster in 1931 – might mean a swallowing-up of French Canada by the United States. Disdain for English Canada's capacity to survive without the protection of the *pax britannica* began to be expressed in newspaper editorials, accompanied by a new-found attraction to the Latinate ideologies of Mussolini and Franco. In the corporatism that these European fascists espoused lay a possible route for the Roman Catholic church in Quebec to preserve its hegemony while "civilizing" capitalists and keeping labour quiescent at the same time. In the midst of this mid-1930s swirl of discontent, Maurice Duplessis was elected premier as leader of the Union Nationale, the upstart reform party that promised to defend Quebec's integrity against the centrist welfarism taking hold in Ottawa under the new Liberal government of Mackenzie King.

At Brébeuf politics was usually distanced or discussed largely in high-flown historical terms. In the debates within the staff and student body between the pan-Canadians of the Henri Bourassa mould and the Laurentian nationalists embracing the ideas of the Abbé Groulx, Pierre Trudeau would sometimes expound a pro-federal position, cheering for Wolfe's victory over Montcalm at the Conquest, for instance, or suggesting that everybody sing "Rule Britannia" and drift off home instead of continuing a nationalist discussion he found tedious. On another occasion, he took the opposite tack and ganged up with some Brébeuf boys who burned the Union Jack. Among his teachers, these stances were seen less as expressions of anglophilia or anglophobia than as efforts to attract attention and show off his uniqueness.

This behaviour, which was in direct contrast to the way he acted with his mother, could be attributed partly to the usual quest of the late adolescent looking for a place in society by trying on various identities. But in Pierre's case, as he came to the end of adolescence, no easy resolution to this normal developmental task was in sight. He was still demonstrating unusually high levels of internal conflict apparently derived from being unable to resolve the profound differences between the values of his mother and father and his own grief and guilt over his father's death.[18]

After his graduation from Brébeuf in 1940, Trudeau entered the law school at the Université de Montréal, where his father had studied thirty years before, but it was a decision he soon regretted. "The law school was abysmal," he said later. "The courses consisted entirely of parochial instruction in petty law with none of the large issues addressed." His father's advice – to the effect that if you had a law degree, you were ready for anything you might aspire to – was obviously misguided. He decided that the study of law in Quebec in the 1940s readied one for nothing nobler than "a two-bit life among unthinking people."[19]

His unhappiness was deepened by the fact that World War II, then raging in Europe, meant that he could not escape getting personally involved in the intense racial conflicts over military service that were obsessing French-speaking Quebeckers, most of whom saw the war as another British conflict that was none of their affair. Rather than bow to his English side and enlist, Pierre did the legal minimum by enrolling in the Canadian Officers Training Corps at the university, a ploy that many middle-class Canadians used to avoid combat overseas.

At a COTC summer training camp, he staged a scene that vividly expressed his ambivalent attitude towards war, authority, and his racial duality. Charles Lussier, a fellow cadet who was Trudeau's contemporary at law school and later a distinguished public servant, remembered, "One day our cadet captain marched us over to a depot where we were to move some shells. The officer in charge was English and gave instructions entirely in that language, [and] even though all eight of us were French Canadians . . . we just naturally obeyed. Well, seven of us did. Not Pierre. He didn't budge. When the cadet captain asked what was wrong, he answered, in his flawless French, 'I didn't understand a word he said.' The cadet captain explained this to the officer and the latter repeated the order in faltering French. Pierre stood by quietly while the officer stumbled through the instructions and then said, in his impeccable English, 'Good, now I understand you. Remember that here in Canada, we are entitled to be commanded in two languages.'" Only then did Trudeau go to work, leaving his confrères both proud and nervous. "After all," Lussier summed up, "the country was at war and we were soldiers in a military camp, and there he was, defying the orders of an officer in defence of language rights!" And, coincidentally, showing himself to be superior one more time – superior to the French, superior to the English, superior, above all, to the colonial mentality that defined both Canadas at the time.[20]

Arguments for and against participation in the war raged throughout its duration in Quebec. Camillien Houde, the mayor of Montreal whose campaigns Charlie Trudeau had supported financially, was incarcerated for urging his compatriots not to register for enlistment. Two years later, when Mackenzie King held his famous referendum on conscription, English Canada voted overwhelmingly for it and French Canada voted overwhelmingly against, an outcome that further exacerbated racial tensions. Trudeau himself espoused the anti-conscription cause, attending marches and meetings, publicly aligning himself with his generation of French Canadians. In the autumn of 1942, during a federal by-election in Outremont, he was a featured speaker at a public meeting supporting the anti-conscription candidacy of the young lawyer Jean Drapeau against a distinguished soldier, Major-General Léo LaFlèche, the candidate put forward by the Liberals. Trudeau's acerbic pun "Finie la flèche du conquérant, vive le drapeau de la liberté!" was striking enough to become Le Devoir's headline the next day. Now in his early twenties, Trudeau seemed finally to be embracing the racial identity over which he had vacillated in his teens. Even so, for such a combative young man there must have been something ignominious in taking a pacifist position during a war that was seen among the English-speaking as a noble fight against a monstrous tyranny; later on, Trudeau was called upon to justify this decision.[21]

Trudeau finished his law degree in 1943 and then spent a year articling in a downtown firm only to realize that practising law interested him even less than studying it. In the summer of 1944, while the controversy over the war still preoccupied French Canadians – this time the dispute was over replacement recruiting for the final campaigns that were to end the conflict in Europe – Trudeau sought a way to escape the legal profession, his own confusions, and the claustrophobia of Quebec. Now twenty-four, he still nourished larger ambitions and saw himself as a heroic loner. "I remember hearing someone recite one of Cyrano de Bergerac's famous 'tirades', the conclusion of which is, 'Ne pas monter bien haut peut-être, mais tout seul' and suddenly, I found there an expression of who I was and what I wanted to be," he remarked.[22]

It is revealing of Trudeau's contradictions that he, the ardent rationalist, carried with him into adult life the dream of emulating Cyrano, the arch-romantic. Every educated French Canadian of Trudeau's generation knew intimately the exploits of de Bergerac, a seventeenth-century French nobleman and swordsman of great prowess, as mythologized in the sentimental drama about him by Edmond Rostand. De Bergerac was portrayed by Rostand as a brilliant wit and poet, a protector of the weak, enemy of the pompous and powerful, a fighter against tyranny, capable of taking on a hundred bullies and winning against all odds, a man who refused compromise, fripperies, and flattery. The tirade or declamation that so affected the young Trudeau that he was still talking about it when he was over sixty begins with the protagonist's vigorous and eloquent refusal to seek favours from the powerful and ends with his declaration that he wants:

> To sing, to laugh, to dream,
> To walk in my own way . . .
> Free to cock my hat where I choose . . .
> To fight or write. To travel any road
> Under the sun or the stars . . .

And if my nature wants that which grows
Towering to heaven like the mountain pine,
I'll climb, not high perhaps, but all alone![23]

In identifying with Cyrano, Trudeau was appropriating a mythic model for his life, formulating the dream in which every young adult wraps his goals. Like those of other would-be heroes, his life dream took on a particularly dramatic form: he would perform amazing feats and win special honours. He would yearn – as he openly admitted – to climb alone to the heights.[24]

What made Trudeau's case special was that he had the money to pursue his dream, however impractical or improbable it might have seemed to his contemporaries in wartime Montreal. After fifteen years of depression and war, his family was seen in Outremont as indisputably rich even though Grace Trudeau still refused to live ostentatiously. In the three years before he died, her husband had nearly tripled the money he had been paid for his gas stations, leaving a fortune estimated at $3 million. After his death, his estate was professionally managed to ensure its continued growth.

"In those days, when everybody in the middle class had to count nickels and dimes, three million dollars was a lot of money," said Jean de Grandpré, who was a classmate of Trudeau's at Brébeuf and remained a friend of Trudeau's sister, Suzette, after de Grandpré had become a powerful symbol of success in Quebec's legal and business circles. "It set Pierre apart. It meant he had choices the rest of us didn't have. He could afford to search for his identity. People like me – my father managed the Montreal offices of two American insurance companies but had to take a one-third cut in salary during the Depression – were forced by economic necessity to get on with our careers, to go to McGill to improve our English because English was the language of business, to get a law degree and enter a practice immediately. Most of us married fairly early and started to raise a family, and you had to earn money for that. As a rich bachelor, Pierre was able to spend years 'finding himself.' "[25]

De Grandpré was identifying what many men who measured themselves against Trudeau were to point out enviously throughout his career: his refusal to be tied down by convention, an attitude characteristic of men with grandiose aspirations and an intense need to deny their own mortality.[26]

This nonconformity had a cost. In rejecting an ordinary career, Trudeau was at the same time avoiding the normal emotional development that comes with a commitment to love, marriage, and family. As a law student still living at home in his twenties, he conducted pallid, "correct" romances with genteel young French-Canadian women his mother approved of, romances that always stopped short of marriage (though he was once engaged briefly) and rarely, if ever, involved the intimacy that grows out of self-revelation. In the world of bourgeois Outremont he was seen by women at this stage of his life as not particularly attractive, in part because of his own self-consciousness about his appearance. (He had the remnants of adolescent acne and was unhappy that he was not tall and brawny; later on, the faintly scarred skin was to add to his appeal to women, and the muscled body he developed seemed supple and youthful in comparison with his more corpulent contemporaries.) Socially he was still immature, displaying a severe shyness that he sometimes masked with manic stunts like doing handstands in the middle of crowded parties or by indulging in sarcastic remarks that distanced him further from women. (He once said to a girl he had invited home for tea, "If I had hips like yours, I'd give up cake.")[27]

In September 1944, a month before his twenty-fifth birthday, Trudeau left Montreal to enrol in a master's program at Harvard University in Cambridge, Massachusetts. His troubled extended adolescence was over. But it was to prove just the prelude to a prolonged and difficult quest – emotional, intellectual, and vocational – that would take most of the next two decades.[28]

As if to shake the memory of wartime Quebec from his mind, a sign on Trudeau's door at Harvard proclaimed him to be "Pierre Trudeau, citizen of the world." To his chagrin, he soon discovered his preparation for world citizenship had been inadequate. Whatever the pretensions of the Jesuits at Brébeuf, most of the American students knew more about the world than he did. They had spent their undergraduate years immersed in the social sciences, not practising debating techniques and spinning theories about the nature of Art and the existence of God.

In his search for excellence, he had gravitated to the intellectual centre of the United States, which was then coming into its own as the post-war world's dominant political, economic, and cultural force in a period that the writer Gore Vidal once described as "America's high imperial noon." At Harvard, the august professor of government Carl Friedrich was teaching that written constitutions were the bulwark democratic societies needed to guarantee individual liberties and protect themselves from the threats of political extremism. The challenging theories of the British economist John Maynard Keynes, about the prevention of cyclical economic depressions by technocratic management techniques, were being debated by economists who alternated between teaching courses in Cambridge and shaping government policy for the Roosevelt Democrats in Washington. The aesthetic of modernism was being preached by leading architects and missionaries of the movement such as Walter Gropius, with whom the English-Canadian architect John C. Parkin and Pierre's own brother, Tip Trudeau, came to spend their architectural novitiates.[29]

It was heady stuff for a young man who only the year before had been trying to cope with the tedium of working in a Montreal law office by finding a new place to eat lunch every day. Trudeau buckled down to his work like a man with an enormous thirst. By the time he had completed four semesters in the master's program in political economy and government he had acquired a solid formation in positivist, American social science. Of the eight economics courses he studied, two were on economic theory with Wassily Leontief, the Russian émigré who was to win a Nobel prize for his input–output modelling of the American economy; two were under Alvin Hansen, the principal American apostle of Keynesianism who shaped post-war Washington's fiscal policies; one was on central banking with the seminal analyst of business cycles, Joseph Schumpeter.

These courses were balanced by eight more in political science, of which two were taught by the great constitutionalist Carl Friedrich and another by the leading historian of political thought, Charles McIlwain, who preached the liberal doctrine that there are some individual rights so sacrosanct that even a government should not be able to touch them. According to Louis Hartz, who was in Trudeau's cohort at Harvard and later became the leading historian of American liberalism, Pierre was captivated by the basic premises of liberal political theory. The discovery that an impressive tradition of Western thought supported his instinctive and passionate individualism was tremendously exciting to this intellectual refugee from collectivist Quebec. It marked a milestone in his intellectual itinerary, which, at this stage, had passed nowhere near the political left.[30]

With his Harvard degree in hand, Trudeau then sailed for France to enrol at the École libre des sciences politiques, an élite institution where places were much sought after by the offspring of the French bourgeoisie. It was 1946 and Paris was alive with political and intellectual ferment. Trudeau sat in on lectures by two of the dominant intellectual figures of the post-war French academy, the economist François Perroux and the conservative sociologist Raymond Aron, who was locked in a bitter debate with such Marxist sympathizers as Jean-Paul Sartre, whose extreme ideological positions and far left-wing political causes seem to have had little impact on the religious young liberal from Quebec.[31]

Trudeau also set about having what he called a bloody good time. Far from the restraints of Outremont, he concocted elaborate practical jokes for the entertainment of other students at the Maison des étudiants du Canada, most of whom had come to Paris without much money, driven on by a passion for seeing and understanding the post-war world. They roamed Paris together, talking in the bistros, planning for the holiday breaks when they could travel to feast on the music, art, and architecture of Europe. Trudeau's maternal uncle Gordon Elliott lived in a village in the south of France and introduced him to his famous neighbour, the modernist painter Georges Braque. When Trudeau roared down on his Harley-Davidson motorcycle with his friend Roger Rolland to visit for the weekend, Madame Braque baked a cake with a maple leaf outlined in icing to celebrate the young Canadians' arrival.

At the end of the university year, Trudeau decided to quit Paris. His undergraduate courses at "Sciences Pô" were academically inferior to the graduate work he had done at Harvard, and he decided to move on to the London School of Economics, where he made a surprisingly sharp turn to the left. At the LSE, he attached himself to the school's towering intellectual figure, Harold Laski, the political theorist who had become Great Britain's most powerful spokesman for socialism. As a senior officer in the British Labour Party, Laski was constantly pushing the government to introduce a far more radical program of social and economic reforms than the cautious prime minister, Clement Attlee, felt able to countenance. Under Laski's aegis, Trudeau began work on a thesis to be called "Liberties in the Province of Quebec" and positioned himself for the first time decidedly on the political left, according to a Canadian contemporary, Robert McKenzie.[32]

What was unusual about these peregrinations was not Trudeau's run around the great graduate schools of the Western world but the way he used his years abroad. The normal practice would have been to seek training for a specific profession, learn its shibboleths, master its vocabulary, acquire its diplomas, and then proceed to tackle its hierarchy. Instead, he engaged in a search not for credentials that would lead to the bureaucratic career in international affairs that his choice of institutions and courses might have indicated, but for something more ambitious: a basic understanding of the world and how it works, and what his destiny within it might be.

"In a way, I should have been a philosopher. I was always looking for the answers to the large questions," he said reflectively one day forty years later over lunch in Montreal. "In the Depression it was, 'Where did all the money go?' Later on, I wondered, 'What makes people obey?' These are central questions for the study of economics and politics and constitutional law as well as philosophy, and it was in those disciplines that I began to look for answers."[33]

Beyond these temporal questions, Trudeau was struggling with even more puzzling spiritual ones about the relationship between God and man, and the obligation of the religious to their society – questions that grew out of new attitudes that were being expressed by educated Catholics in North America and Europe towards the intellectual control wielded by the hierarchy of the Roman Catholic church. He took these concerns with him from Europe to the Middle East and Asia, where he went as part of a *Wanderjahr* in 1948–49 when he was purportedly taking notes for the doctoral thesis he never really worked on in earnest. This long journey gave him the chance to confer with Buddhist priests and Hindu gurus as well as to observe other political cultures and to involve himself in self-imposed tests of meditation, strength, and endurance. As he moved eastward, he grew a beard, affected turbans, flowing robes, and sandals, and began to use the Eastern mannerism of inclining his head with his hands pressed together when meeting others, signifying, "I salute the divine within you."

He was as far away from home as he could get but the conflicts in his personality continued. One week he was contemplative, the next aggressive. His father was not with him to force him to ask hard questions of those in authority, but Pierre asked questions anyway of any official who might say him nay, issuing challenges that sometimes provoked the kind of incidents that his need for swagger still demanded. He was thrown in jail on a couple of occasions, chased by police, stopped by border guards.

By this time, Trudeau was nearly thirty years old. In an experience common to those who venture away from home to find themselves, he had accomplished – in a characteristically self-dramatizing way – the essential task of deciding what he was *not*. He had already rejected the kind of career in law or business that his father had embraced and that he, with his inherited capital, could easily have matched or outdone. He could not become a citizen of the world, however bravely declarative the sign on his door at Harvard may have been. No matter how many countries he visited and revolutionary wars he observed while wearing native dress, he still had to have a nationality. Though he had eradicated all traces of patois from his perfected French, he did not want to live in exile in France in emulation of his uncle Gordon. In Paris at Sciences Pô he had discovered that the French were patronizing to French Canadians, an attitude they were to display and he was to loathe for the rest of his life. He had fallen in love with English political thought but he could not visualize himself as a quasi-Englishman, a tutor at the LSE looking forward to a life as a don, like his contemporary Robert McKenzie.

In the spring of 1949, nearly five years after he had left home determined to think great thoughts and experience great events, he came back to Montreal still undecided about what to do with his life. He had absorbed and appropriated as his own the world-view of the idealistic post-war generation just coming into full maturity in the Western democracies, a generation that was internationalist in its reaction to the horrors of the recent war, rationalist in its approach to democratic politics, modernist in its cultural vision, Keynesian in its economic thinking, and generally dedicated to social egalitarianism. He was returning home if not in triumph, nevertheless intellectually transformed.

CHAPTER 3

SEARCHING FOR A CAUSE

The Quebec of 1949 seemed to Trudeau even more regressive than he remembered. It was a place of startling contrasts. The province had attained a measure of prosperity and social calm under the firm hand of Maurice Duplessis, who was now in his third term in office. The premier was directing the Quebec economy towards a dependent industrialization by courting Anglo-Canadian and American investment and at the same time fostering the myth that Quebec was still a pastoral society, a Catholic Eden dedicated to God and the enduring values of family life.[1]

Born into a prominent Conservative family in Trois-Rivières and imbued from childhood with political ambition, Duplessis had perfected during his apprenticeship years as a lawyer the fervid style of the demagogue. After a rocky first term as premier in the late 1930s, he had been defeated only to be returned to power in 1944. He was to remain in office for the next fifteen years and to prove so formidably adept at governing that while he lived, his party seemed invincible. His success was due in no small part to the political machine he built out of his visceral understanding of how to manipulate his compatriots into consenting to his ideas. Through an ingenious and insidious reward system, he was able to decree not just who would get riding nominations, cabinet portfolios, and government jobs, but who would be granted scholarships, teaching posts, pensions, and short-term relief, as well as where bridges, hospitals, and roads were to be built and which contractors would build them. In a cleverly contrived and astutely managed complicity with the Roman Catholic hierarchy, the press, and the English-Canadian business barons of Montreal, he had made himself "le Chef" of a backward society by teaching the people, who kept re-electing him, to love their myths and accept their lot.[2]

To enforce social peace after the end of the war, Duplessis had introduced strict anti-strike legislation, which created rumblings of discontent in the labour force. In the winter of 1949, just before Trudeau came home from travelling the world, workers' grievances about pay and working conditions had precipitated a strike in the mining town of Asbestos that the government had been trying for weeks to settle, first through arbitration and then by force. Trudeau went to take a look at the situation in the company of his friend Gérard Pelletier, who was covering the events at Asbestos as a reporter for *Le Devoir*. They drove out together to Asbestos in a battered sports car one day in April for a three-week adventure that was to turn into a catalytic event in Trudeau's life. His short stay there became part of his legend later on: how he and Pelletier were detained briefly by the police; how Trudeau addressed a church-hall meeting of miners in a style so inflammatory it alarmed the union leader, Jean Marchand, who was organizing the strike; how the strikers called Trudeau "Saint Joseph" in response to his beard and his oratorical zealotry.

Besides serving as a dramatic episode in Trudeau's heroic odyssey, Asbestos brought into intellectual focus for him Quebec's contemporary reality. It was an arresting illustration of what he had been studying at the LSE: class formation in an emerging capitalist society. The workers' liberty was being suppressed by the same forces that had created their jobs: foreign capital and the Quebec state. Even though the government's brutal assault on the miners did not actually spark a social revolution – and even though his own participation in the struggle fell somewhat short of John Reed's in *Ten Days That Shook the World* – Trudeau was able to observe at Asbestos what he later described in print as "a turning point in the entire religious, political, social and economic history of the Province of Quebec."[3]

In view of his interpretation of what was happening in his home province, it was small wonder that Trudeau, with his passion for liberty and his interest in politics, turned to the federal government at Ottawa as an alternative locus of action. While he was still at Brébeuf, he had adopted as one of his certain truths the belief that democracy was the noblest form of government and then had added the precept, taken from his readings in Lord Acton at Harvard and the LSE, that federalism was the highest form of democracy. Now these views were bolstered by the fact that in Quebec at mid-century, progressives involved in social action were affirming the value of the central government as a balancing force that could mitigate the worst excesses of Duplessisism.[4]

To test these ideas – and to familiarize himself with the realities of government – Trudeau found a job through an academic acquaintance as a junior civil servant in the Privy Council Office in Ottawa. Afterwards all Gordon Robertson, his immediate superior, could remember about the hiring of Trudeau was that the PCO was "desperately poor in terms of Quebeckers," so when this impressively bilingual French Canadian with a background in law, economics, and political science appeared in the summer of

1949, he was quickly taken on staff. Despite his eclectic education and his relatively advanced age, Trudeau was "a very junior guy" in the bureaucratic hierarchy, as he described it later, who found himself stashed away in a garret of the East Block and put to work on "a whole lot of demanding tasks for which nobody else had time."[5]

The government experience Trudeau gained over the next two years would prove valuable in his political life, but at the time he found the job oddly humiliating. It involved beavering away at tedious, eye-straining, anonymous work of the kind that he had been avoiding for years. Jack Pickersgill, the public servant who ran the Prime Minister's Office – and, some said, the country itself – did not even know who Trudeau was at the time. When Trudeau spoke with other French Canadians in the federal bureaucracy about events in Quebec and Ottawa, they often referred to themselves in code as "les Grecs," a response to the fact that even under Louis St. Laurent, the first French-Canadian prime minister in nearly forty years, French Canadians were still treated in the capital as an inferior caste. They had to struggle to survive as *vendus* in the civil service or to behave as MPs in the House of Commons like "trained donkeys" under the whips of their English-Canadian masters, as Trudeau was later to describe them. By late 1951 he had come to the conclusion that his future lay in Quebec, however restricted political conditions there might make it.[6]

His decision to return home to Montreal was closely linked to a powerful revelation. Many years later, he said publicly that this epiphany "sometime in my late twenties or early thirties" was *the* most exhilarating and important thing that ever happened to him – more exhilarating and important than his election as prime minister, than his marriage, than the birth of his sons, than the achievement of constitutional reform or any of the other significant events of his eventful career. What he had undergone was in effect a kind of spiritual transfiguration that marked the critical age-thirty transition in his life. It involved coming to the realization that he was "a whole person . . . my own judge and my own master." He called this a recognition and acceptance of "the concept of incarnation . . . as the personalists put it." In short, he had embraced the precepts of personalism, a radical Catholic doctrine that had become a formidable post-war ideological rival to existentialism in France.[7]

That Trudeau's behaviour throughout his life was tied up with his religiosity was usually unfathomable to those who were taken in by his public mask. It was easy to forget in the resolutely secular atmosphere of the post-war era in Canada that Trudeau had grown up in Quebec when the Catholic church was at the pinnacle of its power. During his youth and early manhood, the clerical hierarchy still dominated the lives of French Canadians from conception to grave. The Church was inseparable from the political system. It ran the educational institutions. It dispensed social welfare through its hospitals and charities. It controlled cultural and intellectual life right down to what kind of books could be published, what sort of paintings and sculpture exhibited, what kind of plays performed.[8]

Trudeau's friend and near contemporary Jean Le Moyne explained this pervasive control when he wrote in a series of perceptive essays that the clergy had come to dominate Quebec because the Catholic church was the only entrenched institution left after the Conquest, when the colony's political, military, commercial, and religious leaders returned to France, abandoning the colonists to their British fate. It was the selfless clerics who had saved the *habitants* from assimilation into the English-speaking continent that surrounded them. "Having once saved us from the perils of extinction . . . [they] kept up the habit but thereafter tended to save us from life." By the twentieth century, the clergy's control over intellectual as well as spiritual life, and its concomitant insistence on the separation of the spirit and the flesh, created a dangerous dualism that led to guilt, fear, and self-alienation, emotions that Le Moyne believed accounted for a morbid, neurotic strain in Quebec life and literature. In Le Moyne's analysis, it was a Catholicism that despised women and ignored the joyful aspects of Christianity, that denounced sensuous love, earthly happiness, and freedom of thought as sins.[9]

For decades there had been quiet resentment of clerical repression among intellectuals and artists in the province. Le Moyne's father, who had studied in Paris before World War I, had brought home with him ideas about liberty that greatly influenced his son and the talented group of writers who were his friends. But for these young people, who had grown up in the 1920s and 1930s and were clustered around the literary periodical they founded, *La Relève*, "the only freedom was in contemplation and in discussion." Because the clergy was so powerful, dissenting opinions were expressed only in private, rebellion was cloaked in theorizing and in poetry; the only real escape was to leave Quebec.

The artist who wanted to be free was doomed to exile – an internal exile of the kind that Le Moyne accepted for himself or an external exile like that of so many Quebec writers and artists who fled Canada to live abroad. The most famous of these exiles was the great modernist painter Paul-Émile Borduas, who rejected the conventional realism in art demanded by the Catholic church. When Borduas published his pungent manifesto *Refus global* in 1948, calling for opposition to authority at all levels, he was fired from his job as an art teacher and went to work abroad, first in New York and then in Paris. Not long after Trudeau came home from Europe, he was taken to see Borduas by their mutual friend Roger Rolland. They found him in his studio, packing his belongings in tears, facing the loneliness and financial vicissitudes of starting again in a foreign city when he was already deep into middle age.

Trudeau's own response to the authoritarianism of the Church hierarchy had always been different. As part of his adolescent combativeness he had pushed back at ecclesiastical as well as every other kind of authority. At Brébeuf the teachers had called him "un catholique protestant" because of his habit of constantly challenging their dicta in the name of his right to freedom of thought. At the same time Catholic faith and practice had been bred in his bones by his mother at home, so in rebelling against the priests' authority he did not – as did so many in his generation and those immediately following it – reject the dogma of the Church. What he wanted was to maintain both the certainties of his faith *and* the obsession with personal freedom that had taken hold of his imagination.

Personalism suggested a way to reconcile these seemingly contradictory needs. It was an intellectually vigorous, revivalist Christianity that had its beginnings in France in the 1930s as an attempt to find a third way between capitalism and communism. By the end of the war, it had become a militant left-wing Catholicism that had gained a substantial following among the French intellectual élite. As interpreted by its chief post-war exponent, Emmanuel Mounier, personalism was openly antagonistic to the sentimentality of old-fashioned, middle-class Catholicism, its depiction of Christ as a cloying sweet Jesus, its sheep-like believers, its rigidity – the kind of Catholicism that was practised in Quebec.[10]

Mounier exhorted young Catholics to rethink their faith in terms of its implications for personal commitment and social reform, to be tough rather than meek in their spirituality. Such injunctions spawned the phenomenon of the worker-priests in post-war France, who shed their clerical robes and went into the factories in an attempt to bring a radical Christian praxis to a working class increasingly estranged from the bourgeois Church. The personalists believed that lay Catholics could interpret Christian ideals for themselves in their own lives without having to kowtow to the Church hierarchy. It was a militant response to the frightening societal contradictions of the mid-twentieth century and the inadequacy of old doctrines to deal with them.

In these ideas, Trudeau found the rationale for a way of being that released him from many of the problems that had plagued him for years. By embracing the almost Protestant belief that he could incarnate the Divinity in his own person, he could channel his conflicting feelings – his difficulties with intimacy, his guilt about his wealth, his scorn for capitalists, his hostility to authority, his ambivalence about his French-Canadian identity – into practical action. He went back to live in Quebec in 1952 with a streak of the almost messianic fervour that is implicit in the personalist idea of incarnation. As a militant embodying the Christian credo, he would return to his people and call them into the twentieth century from the pre-Enlightenment obscurantism in which he considered them to have languished since the Conquest. He would transcend their cultural parochialism, their political backwardness, even their "lousy French," through the loftiness of his motives and the clarity of his mind. He could be an intellectual worker-priest among the *habitants* of French North America, pitting himself against the élites of the province – the Church hierarchy, the English-Canadian business class, and, above all, the government of Duplessis, whose name had become a symbol among

Quebec progressives for all that was wrong with their society. By taking on Duplessis, this devil incarnate, he could play a very special kind of hero, an intellectual Cyrano. He would not have to conform to anyone's standards or bend his will to a boring job, an overbearing boss, a circle of petty-minded colleagues. He could fight for noble ideals.[11]

In deciding to apply the precepts of personalism to the socio-political situation at hand, Trudeau was plunging into the ferment that characterized Quebec in the 1950s. The power of reaction may have "seemed eternal," as the writer Alec Pelletier once remarked, but the Duplessis regime was actually under siege from a motley array of social forces, mostly outside the party system. Chief among these were the major trade unions, which, under the prodding of Gérard Picard and Jean Marchand and along with the teachers' associations, were just beginning to reject obedience to Church authority in favour of the self-directed solidarity of organized working people; the social science faculty at Laval University, animated by the Dominican priest Father Georges-Henri Lévesque, who had inspired the co-operative movement; the *caisses populaires*, which gave the working people of Quebec a sense of new possibilities to be achieved by pooling their individual savings; the newly established television network of Radio-Canada, whose commentators, notably René Lévesque, were breaking down French Canada's isolation by bringing news and images of the outside world straight into the living rooms of the province; the influential newspaper *Le Devoir*, then a Catholic but anti-Duplessis, left-leaning publication directed by its scrappy publisher, Gérard Filion, and inspired by its personalist editor, André Laurendeau; and a persistent if tiny group of English-speaking Quebeckers who were intent on reform, most notably F.R. Scott, the poet, social activist, and professor of law at McGill who was brilliant at using the courts to undermine Duplessis and at acting as a tireless champion of civil liberties and artistic freedom.[12]

Insignificant as a factor at first, the provincial Liberal Party gradually became a force to be reckoned with as well, under its leader Georges-Émile Lapalme. Lapalme had been parachuted into the job from the caucus of the federal Liberal Party but proved an unwilling puppet. He soon distanced himself from the federal Liberals and in 1955 restructured the provincial party as the Féderation libérale du Québec, a mass-based organization with a democratic constitution. Although he lost both the 1952 and 1956 elections and resigned the leadership disheartened in 1958, Lapalme left his successor, Jean Lesage, a party that was open to practical reformers eager to oppose Duplessis.[13]

For years, these varied reform groups struggled to bring light into what was later called the "Great Darkness." They were taking part in the early stages of a phenomenal intellectual and artistic flowering in Quebec that would take a full decade to reach political fruition.[14]

Trudeau eventually came to know almost everybody in the loose coalitions that made up the 1950s reform movement. But he was most closely identified with a group of personalists with whom he allied himself openly on the publication of the first issue of the Montreal magazine *Cité libre*, dated June 1950.[15]

Several members of the magazine's first editorial board had belonged to Jeunesse étudiante catholique, the student arm of Action catholique canadienne, a spiritual revival movement that had flourished in Quebec since the 1930s. Most "Jécistes" were recruited as adolescents by priests or teaching sisters who had noticed their intelligence and devotion. Jeanne Sauvé, who as Jeanne Benoit was a prize pupil of the Grey Nuns in Ottawa during the Depression, remembered that deciding to work full-time as a *propagandiste* at the movement's central office in Montreal in the early 1940s when she was barely twenty was almost as serious a life decision for her as going into a nunnery. It meant giving up her family life and her work as a federal government secretary and living communally with other Jécistes in order to proselytize in Quebec high schools about the need for students to turn their faith into practical action in daily life.[16]

The Jécistes were usually seen as a prissy lot by outsiders. "I loathed their piety," said Maurice Sauvé later. "They were a chapel of do-gooders, a Catholic Salvation Army, and they seemed to run their lives according to ideas that were anti-life, anti-fun, anti-everything. When I got to know Jeanne [who was later his wife] I realized this was far from the truth, but it was the general impression among my contemporaries."[17]

By the time *Cité libre* was founded, the sometime Jécistes on its board were in their early thirties, now living "civilian" lives, with middle-class jobs and young families. But they were still idealistic, committed Catholics, concerned with social equity and the welfare of the working class. They were convinced that the conservatism of the Quebec clergy and its condoning of the abuses of the Union Nationale had to be challenged by frontal attack. They decided to publish a magazine modelled on *Esprit*, the journal Mounier edited in Paris, whose purpose would be to defy the Church establishment and help "break the silence" by creating among French Canadians a new awareness of Quebec's problems. In Trudeau they found an ally who was markedly unlike them in background and style but whose concerns were close to theirs and whose intellectual brilliance they frequently found amazing.

Gérard Pelletier, the driving force behind the founding of the magazine, was the bridge between Trudeau and his old Jéciste colleagues, who at first thought Trudeau epitomized the kind of snobbery that could be expected from the graduate of a Jesuit college. Pelletier had met Trudeau briefly when he was a student in Montreal and had got to know him better in Europe after the war, when he discovered that they shared a high esteem for both Mounier and *Esprit*. It was in the activist spirit of personalism that Trudeau went with Pelletier to Asbestos. It was also Pelletier who helped Trudeau decide, while he was working in Ottawa, that his place as a Christian activist committed to political and social change was in Quebec.[18]

Pelletier was to prove perhaps the closest and most enduring friend of Trudeau's life. There was something about the combination of gentleness and fierce social commitment in Pelletier, who had grown up as a station agent's son in Victoriaville, that turned off Trudeau's compulsive competitiveness. Trudeau admired Pelletier for his commitment and his activism. Pelletier admired Trudeau for his learning, his elegance, his intellect. Of the lasting associations he formed in the late 1940s with Trudeau and Jean Marchand, who was to prove important in their political endeavours, Pelletier wrote, "Friendship, like love, is always slightly miraculous." Mutual friends believed that throughout Trudeau's public career, Pelletier's advice served to bring out the altruist in him, to get him to put away the combative behaviour that often served as his social mask, to help him return to the personalist principles they both espoused, to be his best, most humane self.[19]

Among his social peers, there was some surprise at Trudeau's decision to leave the public service and make common cause with the *Cité libre* crowd. Its earnest goals were at odds with the contradictory images that Trudeau was still projecting. In the English-Canadian Ottawa world, he had been seen as work-obsessed and withdrawn, a shy and capable young man who was obviously "sound" (the bureaucrats' preferred adjective of praise) and destined for a solid career. In Outremont, he was still playing the daring-young-man-on-the-motorbike, a pose he had adopted in the 1940s, and was seen as a romantically unorthodox figure.[20]

Decades later, Jean Le Moyne could still recall his bafflement at the contrast between Trudeau the rich, debonair bachelor and Trudeau the committed personalist. He had encountered him often in the landscape of Montreal in the 1940s, escorting "les jeunes filles ou sa maman ou toutes les deux" to dances and concerts attended by the French-Canadian bourgeoisie. But Le Moyne had never sustained a serious conversation with Trudeau until he and Pelletier came to his house one day in the early 1950s to persuade him to let them publish in *Cité libre* an article criticizing the clergy that they had heard he had written but had been advised by his priest not to publish. They invited him to one of the meetings they held regularly as part of their communal approach to editing the magazine.

"There were eighteen people gathered in the basement of Charles Lussier's house with everybody seated at a long table," Le Moyne remembered. "In the dim light I could see two small bottles of wine at each end and a Dominican priest, a man both austere and paternalistic, sitting in their midst. At *La Relève* we would never have had such a person present. The discussion was extremely mature but it was so solemn and ponderous I wanted to escape. Our meetings were very different. We would have a wonderful dinner with much laughter and talk about books. The end of the evening would find us under the table replete with good wine and great ideas. I was thinking about this [contrast] when the Dominican suddenly asked me where I was coming from, and I answered him facetiously, 'From under the table, Father.' Nobody knew what I was talking about, of course. But if they had known, I had the feeling they wouldn't have laughed."[21]

What attracted Trudeau to *Cité libre* was Pelletier's rallying cry that their generation did not have to go abroad to find freedom or fulfilment but could "stay home and change the place." In the magazine's pages, he could tweak the noses of the Quebec authorities he had provoked into rejecting him. Trudeau's association with Laski at the LSE, his involvement with the strikers at Asbestos, his open-minded reporting in *Le Devoir* of a conference he had attended in Stalin's Moscow, and his fierce criticism of the government in *Cité libre* soon came to the notice of the Quebec religious and political élites, who decided that somehow Charlie Trudeau's son had gone very, very wrong. His behaviour was seen as deliberately inflammatory in a political atmosphere where Red Scare tactics were intrinsic to the Union Nationale's hold on the electorate. Godless communism was out there waiting, Duplessis told his credulous flock. It would destroy the Church, the social order, the whole beloved way of life that had made Quebec a safe haven in a frightening world. And the faithful must remember that communism – like other manifestations of the Devil's work in the world – could appear in many guises. The provincial Liberal leader, Georges-Émile Lapalme, was "soft" on it, for instance. *Le Devoir*, the crusading newspaper, was spreading its pernicious ideas. Even the Liberal regime of Louis St. Laurent in Ottawa was unable to understand how communist infiltration of democratic societies worked; its centralizing ambitions and its new social welfare laws might weaken Quebec's ability to resist. Those who had been subject to foreign influences were dangerous carriers of seditious ideas. In his rhetoric, Duplessis yielded nothing to the American senator Joseph McCarthy; if anything, he was more eloquent and more convincing.[22]

The general acceptance of these attitudes in Quebec meant that throughout the 1950s Trudeau was denied the teaching job he wanted at the Université de Montréal, where the government controlled academic appointments through the Church hierarchy. In this highly charged atmosphere Trudeau had an impact in Quebec over the next few years, through his association with *Cité libre*, that no tame professor could possibly have had, an impact far greater than the magazine's tiny circulation and irregular publishing schedule would suggest. As issue followed issue, a coherent analysis of Quebec society emerged that was based on clearly worked-out premises. While each member of the magazine's collective brought his special interests to the regular editorial discussions, the end product of their collegial self-criticism was a journal so remarkably consistent in both thought and style that its writers and supporters came to be known as "Citélibristes," as though they were members of a political movement. The implication was not far off the mark. Their articles spoke for their generation's impatience with the intellectual bankruptcy of the province's ruling élites. In the prime of their young adulthood, they were banging on the locked doors of their society's controlling institutions.[23]

That it took audacity to publish their ideas in Duplessis's Quebec was soon evident. Pelletier and Trudeau were summoned to explain themselves to the archbishop, Paul-Émile Léger, at his official residence in Montreal shortly after *Cité libre* began to appear. What ensued was a kind of medieval dispute, with Léger claiming that if he were to condemn the magazine, it would be with great regret, and Trudeau, ever the protestant Catholic, interrupting him to say that the magazine's editorial board would appeal such a ruling to the Mother Church in Rome "as is our right."[24]

Trudeau's pugnacious self-confidence enraged Léger and Duplessis. According to Duplessis's biographer, Conrad Black, the premier "particularly detested Pierre Elliott Trudeau whom he considered lazy, spoiled and subversive." At one point in 1954, Léger wrote to Duplessis, thanking him for his "energetic intervention . . . on the occasion of the 'Trudeau scandal'." When Black asked Léger years afterwards just what the scandal and the intervention comprised, the illustrious churchman could not remember but suggested that it was Trudeau's general opposition to the government and the Church that so irritated him.[25]

What Trudeau brought the *Cité libre* collective – besides the audacity that his temperament and financial security allowed – was the knowledge of democratic theory that he had absorbed at Harvard and the LSE and a reputation as a man who understood the mysteries of economics. The Citélibristes soon got over their unease in his company, although he always seemed a little aloof, a man "who simply dropped into our milieu every once in a while."[26]

Over the next decade – mostly in *Cité libre* but also in Jacques Hébert's reform weekly *Vrai*, in *Le Devoir*, in contributions to books, and in the occasional scholarly paper – Trudeau assembled a political-economy analysis of French Canada's problems that grew out of the Citélibristes' collective critique of Quebec as well as out of certain principles about Canadian federalism being articulated by F.R. Scott in his lectures and writings on constitutional law. Trudeau's superbly written essays and articles added up to a devastating analysis of the Quebec he had grown up in, the world he had decided neither to reject nor to comply with, but to transform.

His work made it plain that he was intent on identifying a complete agenda for change. For years he had laboured to transcend his own backwardness as a French Canadian, but personal redemption was not enough. He wanted to cause his whole society to transcend what he saw as the ignominy of its past. He meant to drag his people "out of the wigwam," as he described their collective inwardness.

He depicted the Church hierarchy and the politicians as forming a repressive élite that kept itself powerful by denying the modern world and fostering a regressive ideology. The industrialization of Quebec by foreign capital that had been going on for most of the century was causing the proletariat that it had created great hardship, a suffering the élites refused to address. Trudeau believed strong unions were the social vanguard that would demand a remedy for these ills from a system that was too undemocratic to respond to the parliamentary opposition. He preached the need for "functionalism," a *tabula rasa* approach to be taken to redesigning the federal system by dividing powers between the central and provincial levels of government according to which functions each performed best. Above all, he wanted to see the nurturing of a genuine democracy free of corrupt electoral practices and dedicated to the basic goals of collective social justice and individual self-realization.

These largely liberal ideas would hardly have seemed provocative anywhere else in Canada in the 1950s, and a few years later they had become a commonplace in Quebec as well. But in that place and time, expressed by a man who could have belonged so easily to the establishment he was attacking, Trudeau's individualism, anticlericalism, and egalitarianism were radical indeed. They contained the rationale for his whole political career and motivated his public actions for the rest of his life.

Throughout the 1950s, the Duplessis government precipitated a series of civil liberties infringements and political scandals – the Padlock Law uproar, the Roncarelli case, the Trois-Rivières bridge collapse, the Natural Gas scandal, the Murdochville strike, the Wilbur Coffin trial – that provided Trudeau with ample material for analysis and activism. Besides his work in *Cité libre*, he experimented with other outlets for protest and engagement. As a qualified lawyer he occasionally practised civil law, taking on human rights cases that interested him, particularly on behalf of trade unions, often waiving a fee. As a self-styled economist and consultant, he drafted policy positions, again generally for trade unions. As a social activist, he joined in establishing public-educational institutions such as the Institut canadien des affaires publiques, and he was a founding organizer of the Rassemblement provincial des citoyens, a coalition that tried to mould a coherent electoral force out of the various groups opposed to the Duplessis juggernaut in the provincial election of 1956.[27]

Widespread praise that same year for his brilliant introduction and conclusion to the book he edited on the strike at Asbestos, *La grève de l'amiante* – an analysis that owed something to F.R. Scott's perceptive views of French Canada's contradictions – led to invitations to speak at conferences and to comment in the media. The next year he wrote a series of limpid essays for *Vrai* on the nature of political authority, turning his graduate readings of Hobbes, Locke, and Rousseau into an attack on the clergy's claim to temporal authority, a polemic against Duplessis's abuse of power, and an argument for real democracy in Quebec. Further recognition for his writing came in 1959 in the form of a major prize, the President's Medal of the University of Western Ontario, for the best scholarly article of the year.[28]

• • •

Despite his impressive displays of reformist zeal, many of Trudeau's political allies remained puzzled about the nature of his commitment. He had an odd way of remaining emotionally detached as though he were afraid of losing his personal independence. He was involved in almost every important reformist cause that came up, but he developed a reputation as someone who might escape to Europe or Asia on some new odyssey whenever an organizational job turned tedious or a group's infighting became emotionally demanding.[29]

"There was something not quite mature in him in those days, something too boyish for a man in his thirties. For most of us, commitment to reform affected us in the essentials of our everyday lives. But for Pierre, it seemed like an intricate game that he applied himself to fiercely on occasion and then moved away from," one of the Citélibristes said afterwards. Even the labour organizer Jean Marchand, who first encountered Trudeau at Asbestos and then saw him often to discuss union matters in the 1950s, found him young for his age. He and Trudeau were born only ten months apart but it sometimes seemed there was a generation between them.[30]

Trudeau's contemporaries were detecting in him characteristics of a Jungian psychological archetype, the *puer aeternus*, or eternal youth, the kind of person who "remains too long in adolescent psychology . . . all those emotional characteristics that are normal in a youth of seventeen or eighteen are continued into later life coupled in most cases with too great a dependence on the mother." Most people of Trudeau's generation were now engrossed in the normal responsibilities of early middle age: mortgages, adolescent children, burgeoning careers. But he continued to live with his mother on McCulloch Avenue and to play the attentive son, escorting Grace Elliott Trudeau to concerts and parties, holidaying with her in Europe, or arranging to have friends such as Thérèse Casgrain invite her to accompany them abroad. His siblings, Suzette and Tip, had long since married and since neither of them was interested in business, Pierre oversaw the management of the family fortune and generally looked after his mother's welfare.[31]

It wasn't that Grace Trudeau fit the mother-as-devouring-ogre stereotype. She was soft-spoken and lively and had many friends and interests. After Charlie Trudeau died, she had begun to indulge her passion for the arts, sitting on the Montreal Symphony board and collecting paintings, pastimes that suited her temperament as well as her status as a prosperous matriarch. But her early bereavement and loneliness clearly affected her elder son deeply, and his devotion to her was touching to her contemporaries – and dismaying to his friends, who had begun to worry when he dismissed the possibility of teaching at Laval in the 1950s because Quebec City was too far from Outremont. They saw the cosiness of McCulloch Avenue as an imprisonment for Trudeau, no matter how much he protested that his mother always encouraged him to do what he wanted.

A friend remembered vividly being invited for drinks to the Trudeaus' house in company with several intellectuals who were in Montreal to attend meetings of the Learned Societies. One of the guests was Donald Creighton, the doughty University of Toronto historian and notorious francophobic curmudgeon, who was rambling on with unctuous emphasis about how kind he thought it was of these *French* Canadians to entertain with such grace the *English*-speaking strangers in their midst. Trudeau caught the patronizing note in Creighton's voice and said witheringly, "We've been civilized here for some time, you know." At that awkward moment, Grace Elliott came into the room. Trudeau took her arm and introduced her with great charm to everyone present, including Creighton. "It was a transformation," said his friend in recollection. "He went from bristling sarcasm to tender concern. It was a Trudeau I had never seen before. Obviously, he adored her and I remembered a mutual friend saying, 'His mother is the love of his life.' "[32]

As a bachelor deep into his thirties, Trudeau was still dating girls in their teens. In his efforts to overcome his earlier reputation as socially withdrawn, he had turned himself into a man about town, sought after by *les jeunes filles de bonne famille*, who would giggle about him in the corridors of the convents where the burghers of Outremont sent their daughters. "We lived two blocks from the Trudeaus," an Outremont matron remembered, "and my older brother had gone to school with him. I can remember my teenage friends saying that they knew when he was home from his travels because they had seen his motorcycle or his sports car on the streets; it gave them a delicious *frisson*. They were always plotting foolishly how they might 'catch' him. He was like a movie star and we probably knew at some level that he wasn't going to be 'caught.' But he fed our fantasies by dancing with sixteen-year-olds at parties and by telling their mothers he hadn't settled down yet because he hadn't found the 'right girl.' "[33]

In describing such behaviour, the Jungian psychologist Marie-Louise von Franz has noted, "The two typical disturbances of a man ... [with] a mother complex are homosexuality and Don Juanism. In the latter case, the image of the mother – the perfect woman who will give everything to a man and who is without shortcomings – is sought in every woman. He is looking for a goddess so that each time he is fascinated by a woman he has later to discover that she is an ordinary human being [and] ... the whole fascination vanishes and he turns away disappointed, only to project the image anew onto one woman after another." According to von Franz, the Don Juan displays "the romantic attitude of the adolescent" long after such behaviour has become inappropriate to his age.[34]

When Trudeau became more publicly prominent in the 1960s, he was accused of being both a homosexual and a Don Juan in vicious gossip campaigns mounted by his political adversaries. The former charge always irritated him. "I have had many homosexual friends in my life in both the artistic and intellectual communities," he said in 1986. "But I never was one myself. And I always found it distasteful when my political enemies tried to use that as a calumny against me." His wife, as well as many close women friends, vigorously rejected the whole idea of his widely rumoured homosexuality. "His sentimental interests always lay with women," said one of them, "even when he was young and shy. He was my first lover and in my experience beyond compare. No French Canadian who knew him well ever thought he was a homosexual – that was used by the English as a canard and his separatist enemies picked it up."[35]

Trudeau was not a true Don Juan either. He dated many women both before his marriage at the age of fifty-one and after his separation and divorce when he was almost sixty. But with most women he was very correct and gallant; certainly he was not a voracious seducer. Still, the guise of swashbuckling sexual adventurer obviously appealed to him sufficiently for him to try it on with increasing frequency as the 1950s wore on. Dating became another sport at which he could publicly excel. He began to appear in the bistros and coffee-houses of Montreal with actresses, models, journalists, and university students, women who were far showier than the well-bred girls who had met with his mother's approval when he was younger. None of these liaisons was exclusive although in the mid-1950s, when he was almost forty years old, he formed a close romantic friendship with a young university student named Madeleine Gobeil, whom he continued to see on a fairly regular basis for the next fourteen years. It was far more usual for Trudeau to go out with a woman a few times, fail to call her for several weeks or months, and then turn up casually on her doorstep again, ready for another round. Even as the dance-away lover, he still alternated in social situations between extreme shyness and devastating sarcasm. Both attitudes were distancing to others and true to the *puer* type, whose contradictory behaviour indicates a deep-seated reluctance to make any kind of commitment while at the same time insisting that such commitments will be made at some indefinite time in the future. Sometime soon he will choose his life's work and his life partner and settle down to raise a family and make a name and a fortune. Meanwhile, he lives "the provisional life" as though there were a glass between him and present reality.[36]

For the remarkable man of this type – and Trudeau was always remarkable – there are positive aspects to the *puer* condition. His emotional disengagement allows him to develop, according to the Jungian analyst Daryl Sharp, "a wealth of religious feelings and a spiritual receptivity which makes him responsive to revelation." Encouraged by his mother's belief in his possible greatness, he may strive after the highest goals and display a willingness to make sacrifices for what is regarded as "the good" or "the truth." He can show perseverance, toughness of will, a healthy curiosity, and, as Carl Jung himself wrote, "a revolutionary spirit which strives to put a new face upon the world."[37]

Trudeau was displaying all these attributes while he was crusading for democracy in Quebec and waiting to discover what to do with his life. But by 1959, the year he turned forty, it began to look even to his associates as though he would never settle down, never find a permanent job or a lasting relationship but would continue to "fritter away his unusual intellectual gifts in aimless bohemianism" and endless travel.[38]

CHAPTER 4

FEDERALISM FOREVER

Suddenly everything changed – for Quebec and for Trudeau. In September 1959, Duplessis died on one of his routine tours of his fiefdom, a visit to the Iron Ore Company's mines at Sept-Îles. Four months later, his successor as premier, Paul Sauvé, also suffered a fatal heart attack; and the following June, the Union Nationale was narrowly defeated at the polls by the Liberals under their new leader, Jean Lesage.[1]

That watershed election of June 22, 1960, opened a new chapter in Quebec's development by ushering the postwar reform generation into bureaucratic and political power. At the same time, it closed a chapter in Pierre Trudeau's life by apparently depriving him of his cause. The ouster of the Union Nationale – if only by a hair's breadth – made Trudeau's crusading role obsolete. There was nothing stopping him from carrying on his fight against continuing abuses of power by the Church hierarchy or from editorializing about the need for true democrats to agitate in order to keep the Liberals on a left-leaning path. He could and he did. But the tone of his short political commentaries in Cité libre in 1960 and 1961 suggested that the fight had lost its savour. Fencing on the sidelines was tame sport now that the magazine was backing the government party.[2]

As an occasionally acid critic of the Liberals, Trudeau had not been offered a place on the new premier's team although ridings were found for other reformers, such as the lawyers Paul Gérin-Lajoie and Pierre Laporte and the broadcaster René Lévesque. Instead, Trudeau was appointed associate professor of law by the Université de Montréal – "with almost indecent haste," as he described it – once it was clear which way the political winds were blowing.[3]

In 1961 he settled into his office at the university's new Institut de recherches en droit public and began to lecture on constitutional law and to attend the institute's planning meetings. His colleagues and students were soon telling stories about Trudeau turning up for academic meetings in the afternoons, calling for coffee as though he had just rolled out of bed; Trudeau being stopped by the U.S. Coast Guard while rowing a boat from Florida to Castro's Cuba; Trudeau being asked for a quick comment on a scholarly paper and sending a reply back from somewhere in Sardinia; Trudeau at a disco with a blonde he had "stolen" from one of his law students, dancing with greater panache than anybody else even though he was older by twenty years than most of the people in the *boîte*. While Trudeau was caught up in his *vie bohème*, changes were taking place all around him as various sectors of Quebec society became obsessed with *rattrapage* – catching up with the rest of the modern world.[4]

The Liberals' electoral victory had released an enormous outburst of energy. The talented generation whose idealistic reformism *Cité libre* had articulated in the 1950s were determined to use the newly captured state machinery to modernize Quebec society. The new premier, Jean Lesage, egged on by his impatient cabinet ministers and their aggressive allies in the bureaucracy, had embarked on a host of reforms. In their first two years in office, the

Liberals brought in a new labour code that granted public servants the right to organize and strike, opened up the government policy planning process to labour and business groups, enfranchised younger voters by lowering the voting age from twenty-one to eighteen, reformed the electoral system and legislature, created a new ministry of cultural affairs with a special bureau responsible for defending the French language, and introduced universal health insurance.[5]

With these changes under way, René Lévesque, now the audacious minister of hydroelectric resources and public works who was spoiling for a fight with Quebec's Anglo-Canadian electricity companies, persuaded Lesage to call a snap election in late 1962. The Liberals swept the province, running on the nationalist slogan "Maîtres chez nous." They then proceeded to nationalize the private power companies and consolidate them into Hydro-Quebec, a Crown corporation that would soon become one of the provincial economy's main engines of growth, exploiting its water resources, encouraging its engineering talent, and providing managerial and labouring jobs for francophones. This second electoral victory also emboldened the government to establish a ministry of education, a dramatically symbolic act that finally broke the authority of the Church hierarchy by secularizing the school system.[6]

Several of Trudeau's close allies were now powerful figures in the new Quebec. Gérard Pelletier had been appointed editor of La Presse, the Montreal daily; André Laurendeau, as editor-in-chief of Le Devoir, had become an even more influential voice; and Jean Marchand, presiding over the newly secularized Confédération des syndicats nationaux, was a force to be reckoned with as the province's most important labour leader. Trudeau began meeting regularly in Montreal in the company of these three old friends for discussions with René Lévesque.

Important changes were also under way in Quebec's universities. The social sciences – economics and political science, sociology, and psychology – were displacing the classical curriculum. In this new intellectual context Trudeau, as a Harvard and LSE graduate, might have been expected to be in his element, but he was moving from the ideological left towards the political centre. His espousal of federalism and liberal constitutional theory was of little interest to the students who were crowding the lecture halls of the Université de Montréal, their minds alive with socialist theories and the new nationalist euphoria. Trudeau took to engaging in verbal jousts with the more radical among them in and out of the classroom. He became a target for attack by these students, which depressed him, he confided in his friend Charles Taylor. On one occasion, he grabbed a nationalist tract from a student who was engrossed in reading it and demanded to know whether he had read Plato and if not, why would he waste his time with such drivel – an action that was audacious in commission but oddly conservative and censorious in style.[7]

It was beginning to look as though the dream of being a hero that Trudeau had formulated in his youth might turn out to mean driving his sports car a little too fast or wearing his hair a little too long. Now in his early middle age, he was a law professor among law professors and not even the most accomplished or the most authoritative at that. These accolades still belonged to Frank Scott, who had been appointed dean of law at McGill, on the other side of Montreal's mountain. Trudeau was in danger of becoming a rebel without a purpose, his heroic goals substantially unfulfilled, his future apparently a tame one. That he was saved from this fate – the dreaded fate of being ordinary – was due to the unexpected reappearance of an old enemy in a new guise. The enemy was still

French-Canadian nationalism, and the fight against its new manifestations in post-Duplessis Quebec was to become the great cause of his life.[8]

In the 1950s, Trudeau the polemicist had been at pains to show that the parochial Quebec nationalism of the previous half-century had been generated by a petty bourgeois class: the lawyers, merchants, small businessmen, and prosperous farmers who, along with the Church hierarchy, felt threatened by the forces of industrialization. This group's ideology of political autonomy and cultural *survivance* was preached in the schools, on the hustings, and from the pulpits, using the spectre of an English-Protestant threat to Roman Catholic French Canada to justify its hegemony. The populace was frightened by the élites into believing that without their protection, the cursed English or the marauding Americans would destroy French Canada's way of life.[9]

Now in the charged atmosphere of the early 1960s, Trudeau the professor was alarmed to hear similar nationalistic calls for Quebec autonomy from the kind of student radicals, intellectuals, and artists who used to be *Cité libre* readers but who were now finding its analysis old hat compared with what they read in *Parti pris*, a rival journal that was avowedly socialist. Where *Cité libre* had been critical of the Church hierarchy but remained Catholic, the new nationalist intelligentsia was militantly secular. Where the Citélibristes had embraced liberal-democratic politics as the route to reform, the new nationalists saw the Quebec state as the salvation of the "Québécois," a term that had come into vogue and was loaded with symbolic meaning. Trudeau decided he was hearing the insistently selfish voice of a new bourgeoisie, the emerging urban class that feared its rise would be blocked by the continuing dominance of Anglo-Canadians and Americans in the business world, where English was the language of the workplace and a WASP background an important qualification for the boardroom. He saw the Liberal government in Quebec City as pandering to the self-aggrandizing attitudes of this new bourgeoisie.[10]

The Lesage Liberals had gained power in 1960 by making a broad appeal to a number of elements in the electorate. Their reform agenda had gained them support from the urban professional and working classes. But they had also courted the traditional nationalist groups that had kept Duplessis in power in the 1950s. Once in office, they found that the "national question" was becoming more, not less, acute. Modernization was starting to make Quebec's social institutions and practices more like those of the rest of North America, and French Canadians were discovering that their progress was constrained within their own society by the fact that anglophones still dominated the economy and held the best jobs. The Lesage government quickly found itself responding to a new nationalism that had become assertive rather than defensive and decided to consciously embrace it in dealing with Ottawa.

More public funds were needed if Quebec was to have all the trappings of the modern welfare state that the Liberals had promised. Rather than increase provincial taxes and suffer a loss of popularity, they decided to go after Ottawa for a greater share of the national tax pie. At the same time, they began to call for greater powers for Quebec within the Canadian federation, including the right to make its own foreign policy, particularly in its relations with France.[11]

Encouraged by the provincial government's assertiveness, the new nationalists began to escalate their demands, proclaiming the need for, at the very least, a special constitutional status for Quebec within Canada, with the most vigorous of their number calling for full sovereignty.

The Quebec separatist movement – which was to dominate the Canadian political agenda for decades – was fast becoming a serious political force.

These developments evoked Trudeau's scorn. Far from bringing rationalism to politics, the Quiet Revolution – the phrase that was being used everywhere to describe the tumultuous changes going on in Quebec – was arousing French Canadians to fresh displays of the emotionalism he so despised. "Let us be coldly intelligent," he had urged his compatriots in his very first *Cité libre* article, and cold intelligence was what he now heatedly demanded of them. Prodded by Jean Marchand, he set out to mount an intellectual counter-attack. Over the next few years he produced half a dozen powerful essays that directed against the new nationalists the arguments he had developed to counter Duplessisism during the previous decade. They were a mixture of devastating invective and magisterial theory, a style that Trudeau had made his specialty.[12]

For him, nationalism was historically regressive, a force that was responsible for the worst wars in history. It was unacceptable, in his view, to exalt collective political claims at the cost of individual human rights. Calling nationalism a wasteful alienation of precious political energy and a reactionary throwback to the state-of-siege mentality of Quebec's Church-dominated days, Trudeau reaffirmed the individualist position of *Cité libre*, saying that in a post-colonial society like Quebec, personal freedom should have priority over such collective rights as those being claimed by the neo-nationalists. Furthermore, nationalism was logically untenable since every group that considered itself a "nation" contained even smaller ethnic minorities that could themselves claim independence. If the nationalist trend were followed to its logical conclusion, human societies would become hopelessly fragmented. The solution lay in broader, not narrower, definitions of community.[13]

For the annual meeting of the Canadian Political Science Association in Charlottetown in 1964 he embellished these ideas in a scholarly paper on federalism. Expanding on his view of the British North America Act as a wise compromise between central and provincial jurisdictions, he put forward the almost Hegelian thesis that federalism represented reason and will in politics whereas nationalism expressed ethnic chauvinism in action. Federalism was far better suited to promoting the full development of French Canadians' capabilities than linguistic isolationism. By erecting a nationalist state on the territorial limits of an ethnic Quebec, separatism would return French Canadians to the wigwam and prevent the modernization that was necessary for Quebec's evolution. "Open up our borders," he scribbled. "Our people are being asphyxiated to death!"[14]

The nature of the Canadian federation meant Quebec could easily escape this asphyxiation. Under the British North America Act, he argued, the province already had all the power it needed to achieve its legitimate cultural, social, and economic goals. At a time of growing interdependence among world nations, it would be irresponsible to destroy federalism, which he saw as a brilliant prototype that Canada could offer humankind – a significant and successful experiment in governing a polyethnic society.

The essays and scholarly papers Trudeau produced in the early 1960s showed him at the height of his form as a writer and made him *the* Quebec theoretician of federalism – not just a member of the *Cité libre* collective but a distinct voice. In the course of writing them, he turned federalism and its corollary, anti-nationalism, into fixed principles from which he would not budge. Federalism was to be his lodestar. Anti-nationalism was his new crusade. He would save his compatriots from the follies of the new nationalism just as he had helped save them from the repressions of the old.

The logic of Trudeau's attack on French-Canadian nationalism – which he equated with parochialism – was so powerful that it mesmerized him for the rest of his public life. He was unable to consider the positive changes Quebec nationalism had already brought about and the potential value it had in this new form. However much the Quiet Revolution was being mythologized as the flowering of a new age, the seeds for it had actually been planted during the 1940s and the 1950s. Rather than being a revolution, the reforms of the 1960s constituted an evolution – and a noisy one at that – that built on Maurice Duplessis's defence of the Quebec state's *autonomie*. While resisting Ottawa's interventions, Duplessis had also strengthened his power by controlling the flow of provincial funds to Church-run institutions such as schools and hospitals. This eroded the relative power of the Church by making it dependent on rather than directive of the state.[15]

These changes were a prerequisite for achieving the massive social reforms that Trudeau had called for in *Cité libre* and that the provincial Liberals were now bringing into force. Nevertheless, Trudeau blindly attacked as retrograde any linking of social reform with nationalism. Leaning heavily on the pan-Canadian positions advocated by Henri Bourassa during the first half of the century, he began to speak out with increasing force against the xenophobic direction Quebec was taking. Nationalism was a heresy. Good men must stamp it out. In confronting the ideologues of neo-nationalism, Trudeau was becoming an ideologue himself.

. . .

As the 1960s wore on, the political atmosphere in Quebec was further agitated by random bombings perpetrated by the Front de libération du Québec, a small terrorist group modelled on Third World anti-imperialist movements, notably the Algerian Front de libération nationale. While English Canadians were gradually being made aware that the country's post-war calm had been shattered, French-Canadian federalists were increasingly alarmed by the potential that their province's noisy evolution had for turning into a real revolution that would explode the federal structure. In March 1963, the disaster-ridden Conservative regime of John Diefenbaker was squeezed out of power in Ottawa by the Liberals under the leadership of Lester Pearson. A former diplomat and Nobel laureate, Pearson formed a minority government with a clear plan for reform that had been developed and refined while the Liberals were in opposition by his policy advisers, the newspaperman Tom Kent and the Toronto management consultant Walter Gordon. But despite the strengths of these ideas and the efforts of an energetic cabinet to bring them about, Pearson's government soon developed a reputation for bumbling ineptitude, because of the vigour of the Conservative opposition's attacks on it and the government's seeming incapacity to cope with the new Quebec. Fears began to be expressed across the country that the Canadian governmental system was breaking down.[16]

In response to the federal Liberals' difficulties, Marc Lalonde, a young French-Canadian lawyer practising in Montreal, began to describe to some of his friends his deep concerns about relations between Quebec and Ottawa. Lalonde was a farmer's son, committed, as a personalist Catholic, to social action. He had worked full-time for Action catholique after graduating from a classical college in 1950, then had completed a law degree in

Montreal before studying Modern Greats on a scholarship at Oxford. After returning to Canada he had spent an instructive year in Ottawa working as an assistant to the minister of justice. "In those years, *Cité libre* was my bible," he remembered. But unlike most of the magazine's original personalist supporters, who were a decade older and had grown up thinking that politics was "a carbuncle on society," Lalonde believed in direct involvement in the political arena. The modern state played a crucial role in people's lives and the committed were required to engage with it. Lalonde feared that despite the Pearson government's high-minded intentions, it was stymied by Quebec. Pearson's experience in Canadian politics was limited. He had spent most of his working life as a diplomat concerned with international, not national, issues. He could not speak French, his Quebec advisers were either too weak or too old-fashioned to give him proper advice, and his decision to set up a Royal Commission on Bilingualism and Biculturalism, to which André Laurendeau had been appointed as co-chairman with the English Canadian Davidson Dunton, was a commendable but cumbersome way to seek solutions to urgent problems. Lalonde decided to gather together a group of intellectuals to discuss the situation.[17]

Trudeau was a natural for the group, even though he was ten years older than its other members, who were all under thirty-five. His ideas were well known to Lalonde through his writing in *Cité libre*, and they had mutual friends in personalist circles. They had met briefly in 1950 when Lalonde was trying to decide on a course of postgraduate study and was sent to ask advice from Trudeau while he was still working in Ottawa. Now Trudeau's tough federalist position was attracting wider attention. He had become a favourite interview for the Quebec press when they wanted to stir up the nationalist/federalist debate, and his fluent English made him an important focus for anglophone journalists who were crowding into Montreal trying to find the answer to the question that was perplexing the rest of Canada: "What does Quebec want?"[18]

The Lalonde group met on a weekly basis throughout the winter of 1963–64 and in the spring decided to produce an appeal for political action. Calling themselves the Comité pour une politique fonctionnelle, they were shrewd enough to get their manifesto into the mainstream by having it published simultaneously in English as well as French, and in large daily newspapers as well as in *Cité libre* and *The Canadian Forum*, its counterpart in English Canada. The most important men connected with the committee from Trudeau's point of view were Albert Breton, an economist whose ideas on nationalism buttressed his own; Lalonde himself, whose experience in Ottawa was more recent than Trudeau's and whose progressive Catholic ideas, strength of character, and internationalist leanings were highly compatible with Trudeau's; and Michael Pitfield, another Montreal lawyer who had served in the Justice Department at the same time as Lalonde and was now working in Ottawa for the Royal Commission on Taxation. Out of this group's intense discussions emerged key members of the enduring band of committed federalists who would stick with Trudeau for the next twenty years in the unswerving belief that his view of the Canadian state was The Truth.[19]

After the publication of the committee's manifesto in May 1964, Trudeau's allies began to speak with greater urgency about the need for partisan action to counter separatist agitation. Trudeau himself began to think about "jumping into the mêlée again." The question was when and how to jump. He had never made the kind of commitment to party politics that other federalists of his generation, such as Maurice Lamontagne and Maurice Sauvé, had decided on years before. Charles Taylor, the political philosopher who came to know Trudeau in the late 1950s, saw him as a man who believed that his role was to provide intellectual leadership, but because of his shyness he did not have the easy capacity with people that politicians need. Other friends saw Trudeau's spurning of the partisan arena as part of his proclivity for living the deferred life: just as the ideal woman or ideal job had not yet been found, neither had the ideal political party.[20]

Along with several of his friends in the labour movement, notably Pelletier and Marchand, Trudeau had been attracted in the 1950s to the largely anglophone social democratic movement the Co-operative Commonwealth Federation, because he hoped it might become electorally viable as a labour party in the British style. The attraction had never been much more than a mild flirtation despite the efforts of two enlightened social democrats, Thérèse Casgrain and F.R. Scott, to draw him into more active involvement. Peter Scott, a poet, critic, and F.R.'s only son, remembered afterwards with amusement that he and Trudeau campaigned for Casgrain when she was running for office in the early 1950s as leader of the Parti social démocratique du Québec, the French-Canadian wing of the CCF. Their efforts consisted of driving recklessly around Montreal in Trudeau's open sports car with a bullhorn. They regaled passers-by with CCF slogans in two languages, vying with each other in a public display of witty bilingualism, with Scott concocting the French sentences and Trudeau embellishing the English.[21]

In her memoirs, Casgrain describes the Trudeau of those days as a somewhat unreliable ally. "Trudeau had the reputation of being rather a dilettante and despite his first-rate intelligence, lacking in perseverance. He was fond of launching ideas or movements only to lose interest and turn to something else. This attitude . . . probably had something to do with the collapse of the *Rassemblement* [the anti-Duplessis coalition put together in 1956]. While he was president he took a trip overseas and when he returned the *Rassemblement* no longer existed."[22]

The fundamentally anglophone and Protestant CCF was never able to make any headway in francophone and Catholic Quebec in any case. In the early 1960s, when its successor, the New Democratic Party, came out with a two-nations-in-the-bosom-of-a-single-state policy on the Quebec–Canada question, Trudeau was disgusted by what he regarded as a dangerous decision that played into the hands of the separatists. In view of the retrogressive attitudes of the other main parties, the Progressive Conservatives and the Créditistes, it began to look as though the only possible vehicle for him and his allies was the federal Liberal Party, that collection of compromisers he had previously so despised. After all, he and his confrères told one another, the party had radical roots in nineteenth-century Quebec and had fostered openness in its attitude towards French Canadians throughout the twentieth century when its success had been equated with winning seats in Quebec. Whatever its ideological shortcomings, the Liberal Party had produced two French-Canadian prime ministers in Sir Wilfrid Laurier and Louis St. Laurent, and its English-Canadian leaders had consistently courted and heeded Quebec lieutenants.[23]

Trudeau's path to Liberalism was smoothed by his friendship with Jean Marchand. Because of his status in the union movement, Marchand had been approached repeatedly in the late 1950s and early 1960s by the Lesage Liberals in Quebec City and the Pearson Liberals in Ottawa to stand for election under their respective banners. At first he refused to join Lesage because he felt the union movement still needed him; later he was dismayed by the provincial Liberals' nationalism. He was equally wary of the federal party because of the compromises it had made with Duplessis during the St. Laurent regime and his own experience as a unilingual unionist leading deputations to St. Laurent's Ottawa. But once activists like Lévesque and Laporte had shown the party's reform capacity at the provincial level, and once Marchand had accepted Trudeau's belief that the separatist threat had to be countered by political action at the federal level, the Liberal Party in Ottawa began to be attractive to him because of its potential for power. René Lévesque had warned Marchand several times to be sure to bring allies into the party with him so he would not suffer from isolation among the professional politicians, and in late 1962 there had been talk of a dozen of the anti-Duplessis reformers, including Trudeau, running as Liberals to bolster Marchand's position.[24]

This prospect was sabotaged for the purposes of the 1963 election by Lester Pearson's precipitous decision in January of that year to make the acceptance of U.S. nuclear warheads for Canadian weapons part of his election platform, an action that infuriated many Canadians, including Marchand, who felt that the decision showed Pearson to be a far less principled man than his reputation indicated. Trudeau's response to Pearson's nuclear flip-flop took the form of campaigning for his NDP friend Charles Taylor and publishing a scathing polemic in Cité libre. In it he vilified the "anti-democratic reflexes of the spineless Liberal herd" and eviscerated its leader: "Power beckoned to Mr. Pearson. He had nothing to lose but honour. He lost it. And his whole party lost it too."[25]

Once again, Trudeau was stuck in the role of the gadfly inveighing against the establishment. Nuclear war was indeed a horrifying spectre, but by staying out of the political action, he could do nothing about it – or about any other public issue. True to form, he was resisting a commitment to a real-life situation and castigating Pearson for being caught in a dilemma that he needed to confront himself. Power beckoned to him as well. The worsening situation in Quebec, his advancing middle age, and the young federalists in the Lalonde group who were looking to him for leadership were pushing him towards it inexorably. Compromises would have to be made.

By the summer of 1965 it had become evident that if Trudeau was ever going to commit himself to political action, the time had come. Throughout that year, his old friend Jean Marchand had been holding intense discussions with the federal Liberals about his own future. Marchand had been appointed to the Laurendeau–Dunton commission on bilingualism and biculturalism at its inception in 1963 but had grown impatient with its deliberations. His experience in reforming the Quebec labour movement had convinced him that the Liberal Party could be reformed too. He knew Pearson was being urged by his finance minister and chief political adviser, Walter Gordon, to call an election for the autumn of 1965 in order to achieve the majority Gordon was convinced the Liberals needed to control the House of Commons and the political agenda.[26]

To win a majority, the party desperately needed a new team from Quebec. Not only had Pearson's Quebec lieutenants, Lionel Chevrier, Maurice Lamontagne, and Guy Favreau, proved inadequate, his Quebec caucus was caught up in a series of damaging scandals, which the Conservative leader John Diefenbaker was playing up in order to discredit the Liberals and their French-Canadian contingent. With his populist reputation, his gift for oratory, and his consummate skill at handling people, Marchand looked like a saviour to Gordon and Pearson. Marchand was adamant that he would not come to Ottawa without friends to accompany him. By this time, the Marchand team that might have been a dozen strong in 1963 had shrunk to two: Pelletier and Trudeau, neither of whom had a reputation calculated to endear them to Liberal organizers. Despite the strength of his bargaining position, it took all of Marchand's wiles to convince the Liberals to accept his friends as candidates. Their objections had been expected, and he was adept at countering them. What he did not expect was the difficulty he would have with Trudeau himself.

During the spring and summer of 1965, while Marchand was talking to the Liberals and then assessing their proposals in private sessions with Pelletier and Trudeau, Trudeau was firm about his commitment. He had made up his mind. It was time to enter the arena. After convoluted negotiations, the three men finally announced their intentions in a widely publicized press conference held at the Windsor Hotel in Montreal in early September 1965: they would be candidates for the Liberal Party of Canada in the federal election that had already been called for November 5.

In response to the shocked disapproval of some of their friends, Pelletier and Trudeau wrote jointly an elaborate explanation for this decision that was published in the October 1965 edition of *Cité libre*, the last piece either of them would write for the magazine. It set out to provide a rationalization for their conversion to Liberalism with a big L, "using my ideas and Pelletier's writing skills," as Trudeau modestly described it later. Quoting Plato's aphorism that the price for those who stay out of politics is "to be governed by people worse than themselves" and reminding their readers they had preached a personalist conception of society for fifteen years, the two men painted their decision as pure pragmatism. The threat to Canadian federalism represented by neo-nationalism

needed to be corrected by strengthening federal power in
Ottawa. Trudeau and Pelletier had given up none of their
ideals. For them, "the political party is not an end but a
means." They concluded that "for Quebeckers inspired
by the dual concern for a dynamic federalism and a progressive social policy the Liberal option [is] today the
most realistic and most constructive [one]."[27]

Despite this very public and altogether logical apologia, something in Trudeau still balked at commitment.
Even though the safe Liberal riding of Mount Royal had
been grudgingly made available to him after Marchand
strong-armed the backroom Liberal organizers, and an
efficient campaign had been mounted on his behalf, he
tried twice to back out of the race. At one point, Marchand came to Montreal and spent six hours with him
convincing him he had to continue. "I talked like a father
to him," said Marchand. "He had got himself into an
overwrought state [about running against his old friend
Charles Taylor, who was once again the NDP candidate]
and needed a lot of reassurance."[28]

Not long after he was elected in November, Trudeau
buzzed off to Europe to ski, as though to affirm that his
life had not changed very much; he was as fancy-free as
ever. Early in 1966 when Lester Pearson telephoned him in
London, where he had travelled from Switzerland to celebrate the New Year, and asked if he would like to serve as
the prime minister's parliamentary secretary, Trudeau
tried to duck the honour and the responsibility. Marchand
heard about his non-committal response and was on the
Ottawa–London long distance line within minutes, insisting that Pierre grow up and take the job. He dismissed
Trudeau's explanation that he was going to Ottawa not in
pursuit of power but because he wanted a platform for his
ideas, telling him that power was what was needed to put

his ideas into effect. Once Marchand convinced him that
accepting Pearson's offer was important to their cause,
Trudeau threw himself with zest into parliamentary politics, a game at which he would shortly prove the most
adept practitioner of his generation.

CHAPTER 5

COMING TO CHARISMA

The Ottawa that Trudeau confronted in his first term as a member of Parliament was a city in turmoil, the troubled capital of a country suffering the strains of transition. The old Canada, the colonial Canada that had been under the protection (and at the beck and call) of the British, had long since ceased to exist, a fact that was being acknowledged reluctantly even in the anglophile small towns and rural areas of the Maritimes and the west. The highly charged debate in the previous parliament over whether Canada should fly its own distinctive flag had shown how much fear and anger the simple fact of the country's growing distance from its British past had caused many older English Canadians whose political loyalties were Conservative and whose sense of national identity was still tied to the Union Jack.

At the same time, the generation of Canadians who had brought the country through the important colony-to-nation transition were experiencing a crisis of authority. This was the anti-imperialist, pro-American governing élite made up of the politicians, bureaucrats, and businessmen clustered around the Liberal Party, who had combined to run the country in the 1930s and 1940s and had reached the height of their influence in the 1950s. Their formula for success – having Canada act as a middle power and peacekeeper internationally while riding along on the coattails of American prosperity continentally – was not working very well any more.[1]

Canada's good offices as mediator were no longer as much in demand as they had been in the immediate post-war years. Abandoning diplomatic politeness, the Egyptian president, Gamal Abdal Nasser, had unceremoniously suggested a decade after the Suez Crisis that Canadian peacekeeping troops in the Gaza Strip would find more favour in his eyes if they gathered up their Boy Scout hats and toddled off home. Even worse, there was a growing suspicion that Canada's role in the worsening conflict in Vietnam was less as peacekeeper than as message-carrier, and perhaps even spy, for the United States.[2]

Dismay about Canadian entanglement in American foreign policy was just part of a general domestic concern about Canada's relationship with its neighbour. Ever since the fear of excessive dependence on the American economy had been voiced in 1957 by Walter Gordon in his role as chairman of the Royal Commission on Canada's Economic Prospects, public apprehension had continued to grow despite the scorn for these fears expressed by mainstream economists. Fresh evidence of unchecked American take-overs of Canadian businesses coincided with attempts made by Washington to harness American branch plants abroad to the task of correcting the international payments deficit caused by the U.S. military involvement in Southeast Asia. The sense of social dislocation produced by the assassination of John Kennedy, the civil rights crisis, and the Vietnam misadventure was spilling over into Canada as draft dodgers flowed north, creating new anxieties that were further fuelled by daily television coverage of race riots in urban America's black ghettos. The great democratic society to the south – envied and emulated in Canada for generations – had taken on a darker aspect, and fears that the country might follow the American trend to anarchy amidst affluence were aggravated by the seeming inability of Canada's own élites to deal with serious economic and social problems. As a counterpoint to the pervasive unease that gripped older or more conservative Canadians, there had grown up among the younger or more progressive a defiant optimism that some as yet unidentified change would soon transform the country. Once the old, with their fusty ideas, their antiquated attachments, their foolish fears, had been swept out of power, and the young with their energy and strength had been swept in, love, love, love – or something very like it in the form of a more democratic, more open government and a more equitable, more compassionate, more intellectually alive society – would prevail. Younger academics started questioning the middle-power nostrums of the old Liberal élite, proposing a more independent, less deferential foreign policy.[3]

Younger journalists started writing as though Canada, too, could become a Camelot. "I am part of a generation of Canadians who have grown up without a sense of inferiority," declared the writer Peter Desbarats, and across the country his statement resonated with his peers. These were the post-war Canadians who had come of age during the boom years, who had achieved higher levels of education in greater numbers than their parents and grandparents, who had travelled farther and more frequently and had been influenced by the huge post-war influx of European immigrants – the generation that had absorbed some of the wild hopes for a new social order that were emanating from the young in English Canada's two great mentor countries, the United States and the United Kingdom. Their aspirations and vitality were finding expression in the modernist paintings and sculpture that were being shown in galleries in Toronto and Vancouver, in the poetry and novels reflecting contemporary Canadian realities that were just beginning to be published, in the home-grown plays that were being "work-shopped" in old factories and lofts, and in the brilliance and daring of some of the films that were being produced for the National Film Board and the Canadian Broadcasting Corporation. Reflecting this widespread creative excitement, the CBC-TV Sunday-night public affairs show *This Hour Has Seven Days* was having the kind of explosive effect on English Canada that René Lévesque had set off in Quebec a decade earlier with his program *Point de mire*.[4]

These conflicting responses to societal change – nagging fears and overblown hopes – came together in a confusing crescendo when Canada celebrated its hundredth birthday in 1967. It was the year of Expo 67, the great World's Fair held in Montreal to enthusiastic international notices, the year when Canadians put out more flags, built more auditoriums and hockey rinks, indulged in more fanciful flights of patriotic rhetoric, and greeted more heads of state and other glittering visitors from abroad than the country had seen in the previous century.

While the centennial celebrations were buoying the national mood, the Quebec situation continued to simmer. The Bi and Bi commission had brought down an interim report warning Canadians that the frustrations suffered by Quebec's francophone majority over their inferior linguistic and economic status were causing "the greatest crisis in [Canada's] history." The clamour for new political leadership continued. The opposition Conservatives had begun the brutal process of ousting their leader, John Diefenbaker, and the governing Liberals were beginning to grumble privately that Lester Pearson, however much they admired his past successes, was dragging them down by his present ineptitudes.[5]

In brief, Canada's system of legitimation was in trouble. Canadian society had developed what the great German sociologist Max Weber called an "alienation potential" – the preconditions that made it ready for a dramatic change of leadership. That the change would come about swiftly, that Canada was about to be catapulted into a new era under the leadership of a Quebec intellectual with a maverick's reputation and an intricate, stubborn set of ideas about federalism, would have astonished even the most daring of futurologists in the early months of 1967.[6]

To the extent that his arrival in Ottawa had been noticed, Trudeau was still seen as a political novice in the capital, one of the two lesser "wise men" who had stepped into the federal arena when the Liberals recruited Marchand, the real powerhouse from Quebec. It was a response that Trudeau did little to dispel. Socially he kept out of sight for the most part, living quietly in the Château Laurier hotel, confining his disco dancing and flamboyant womanizing to weekends in Montreal. His job as Lester Pearson's parliamentary secretary and his connections with Marc Lalonde and Michael Pitfield, who both knew Ottawa well, allowed him to brush up the knowledge of governmental procedures he had acquired in the Privy Council Office fifteen years before so that he did not have to endure a period of apprenticeship of the kind Gérard Pelletier was suffering as a backbencher. His political progress continued to be smoothed by Marchand, who protected him from the hostility of old-time Liberals in the Quebec caucus who resented his privileged position in Pearson's office.[7]

The advancement to the parliamentary secretary's job of so strong an opponent of "special status" for Quebec had drawn a direct protest from Jean Lesage, who feared Trudeau would seize the opportunity to articulate at the

very centre of Ottawa's power structure his tough federalist position. Lesage knew Trudeau's views were bolstered by enthusiastic allies in the PMO. Tom Kent,
Pearson's policy adviser, and Gordon Robertson, his clerk
of the Privy Council – as well as the new minister of
finance, Mitchell Sharp – had insisted that Pearson summon up the courage to resist the apparently insatiable
government of Quebec by rebuffing demands that the
province be allowed to opt out of further federal programs, as it had with the Canada Pension Plan in 1964.[8]

The PMO's newfound firmness had not prevented the
Ottawa–Quebec City relationship from deteriorating further. In June 1966 what had seemed from the federal view-
point a dangerously autonomist Liberal government in
Quebec City had been squeezed out of office by the even
more stridently nationalist Union Nationale, revitalized by
its peppery leader, Daniel Johnson. With his slogan
"Égalité ou indépendance," the new premier proclaimed
his intention to ride the twin horses of conservative
nationalism and radical neo-nationalism. Under his aegis,
Quebec would either achieve equality with English Canada or seek complete independence.

Shortly after he was elected, Johnson had travelled to
France to urge its president, Charles de Gaulle, to lend his
towering prestige to the cause. In response, Marcel
Cadieux, the under-secretary of state for external affairs,
had moved to contain this attempt at establishing an international presence based on independent relations with
France. He assigned his most brilliant protégé, a legal
scholar named Allan Gotlieb, to set up an informal committee of review to monitor Quebec's foreign policy
manoeuvres, which Cadieux regarded as a back-door
route to separation. Lalonde and Pitfield, who were by
now working as advisers to Pearson, became members of
the committee, which was chaired by Trudeau. In early

1967 Trudeau went to Africa to assess how Canada's relations with the continent's francophone states, then in the process of loosening their colonial ties with France, could be used to block Quebec's push for international recognition. After years of theorizing and protesting, he was experiencing the excitement of big-league politics for the first time and showing himself to be extraordinarily adept at mastering its intricacies.[9]

Impressed by Trudeau's performance – and urged on once more by Marchand – Pearson appointed him minister of justice in April 1967, only sixteen months after his election to Parliament. To the surprise of his detractors in Quebec, who had been saying that Trudeau would tire of federal politics as he had of other causes in the past, he took to this new job as though he had been preparing for it all his life – as indeed he had. Throughout the spring and summer, while his cabinet colleagues were enjoying the elaborate centennial celebrations that were animating Ottawa and Montreal, he was holed up in the Justice Department, driving himself and his officials relentlessly. His friends began to say they could not remember him ever having been so happy. His shyness was rarely in evidence. He seemed finally to have found through sustained commitment to work the release that is the only way the *puer* type can be freed from his conflicts. In transposing his fight against French-Canadian nationalism onto the federal stage, where he could exploit his mastery of English and his intellectual dexterity, he was transcending his doubts to become at last what he had always longed to be: an effective man of action, a creative intellectual force, a leader both of opinion and of men.[10]

Even though he was avoiding the limelight, his views were attracting insider attention. Constitutional experts – particularly those on the Justice Department committee set up to advise the new minister on how to reform the

British North America Act – expressed respect for the coherence of his federalist vision and the depth of his constitutional knowledge. A few journalists, having interviewed him on the Quebec question and having come away affected by his clarity and certainty, began to write about his unusual gifts. Some bureaucrats were impressed by his analytical skill, his capacity for work once his interest was engaged, and the steely personality under the polite façade. Most of his cabinet colleagues recognized his superiority in discussion, the invincible intellectual arrogance he showed in the Privy Council chamber after just a few months of attending meetings there.[11]

But if he was known at all to the public in English Canada at large, it was mainly because John Diefenbaker, the Conservative leader, had criticized the clothes he wore in the House of Commons. On the occasion in question, Trudeau had hurried into the green chamber for an unexpected vote looking like a Parisian *avocat* with expensive tastes on his way to an alfresco Sunday lunch, clad in leather sandals, slacks, and a sports coat with a foulard tucked into the neck of his shirt. In the eyes of Diefenbaker, who was always dressed like a country lawyer of sober intent on his way to read the lesson in a Baptist church, Trudeau's clothes were clear evidence of foreign influences and God knows what other deviltry. To the marginally more sophisticated professional politicians in his own adopted party, Trudeau was less a devil than an oddity, an egghead with arcane interests, who was altogether unimaginable as a contender for the Liberal succession. Their eyes were on more conventional candidates for Pearson's job, experienced politicians with worthy ambitions who were due to get the shock of their lives.

Although it became a cliché later that Pierre Elliott Trudeau was chosen Canada's thirteenth prime minister because of his innate charisma, not even Max Weber, who

defined the concept, could have been expected to see in
the still somewhat diffident Trudeau of his first two years
in Ottawa a candidate for greatness. Canada's political
crisis had not yet become acute enough for the public to
acknowledge the need for unconventional leadership, and
Trudeau had not yet displayed publicly the audacious persona he had been trying out for years in Montreal and for
which he was later to become famous across the country.
No one knew that the unsettling circumstances Canadian
society was confronting, combined with Trudeau's strikingly appropriate capacities, would turn him within the
year into an authentically charismatic figure of a kind
unknown before to the dogged citizenry of the frozen
North.[12]

For this transformation to occur, Canada's alienation
potential had to turn into a clearly understood crisis. To
absorb the notion that their home and plaintive land was
in danger of disintegrating, Canadians needed more than
the eloquent warning expressed in the Bilingualism and
Biculturalism commission's preliminary report. They
needed proof. It came unexpectedly in the middle of the
centennial summer as a consequence of the interference in
Canadian affairs of the president of France.

As part of his internationalist strategy, Daniel Johnson
had invited Charles de Gaulle to come to Quebec in
advance of his official centennial visit to Ottawa. For
reasons of his own, the general happily agreed. Having
despised French Canadians for their pro-Vichy sympathies
during World War II, he now saw that the nationalist
fervour in Quebec could be turned to the advantage of his
own imperial design for restoring France's *grandeur* by
undermining American hegemony and building a world-
wide *francophonie*. Elaborate preparations for his welcome
were made, and on July 23, 1967, de Gaulle steamed up the
St. Lawrence on the French cruiser *Colbert* and disem-

barked at Quebec City. The next day he was driven in a triumphal cavalcade to Montreal along the old Chemin du Roy on the north shore of the St. Lawrence, through towns and villages festooned with bunting and lined with cheering Québécois. By the time he reached Montreal's city hall at noon an intoxicating excitement had built up. Responding with apparent spontaneity to the huge crowd gathered in front of the municipal centre, de Gaulle asked to address it.[13]

Although no speech had been announced for this site in the official program, a microphone was already in place on the building's balcony, and the general proceeded to seize both the instrument and the moment that history was offering him. After a few sentences invoking the spirit of the liberation of France in 1944 and the affection that France was starting to feel again for "the French of Canada," he raised his long arms to make his familiar "V" gesture and began to intone the kind of litany that characterizes the ceremonial declarations of French officialdom. First came "Vive Montréal!" which elicited a roar from the crowd. Then came "Vive le Québec!" which brought a louder and longer response. The general waited a moment, then detonated his bombshell: "Vive le Québec . . . libre!"

The consternation created by de Gaulle's audacity in uttering the Quebec separatist movement's inflammatory slogan was instantaneous. The crowd, which was liberally sprinkled with separatist placards, went wild. Within minutes, wire services flashed around the world the astonishing news of this provocative intervention in the politics of France's NATO ally and former colony. On the Montreal city hall terrace, Premier Daniel Johnson remonstrated with his guest that he had just endorsed the slogan of Johnson's political opponents. In the throng of officialdom, René Lévesque, who was still a Liberal deputy now moving hesitantly towards separatism, was also dubious. "C'était un mot de trop," he remarked to a French reporter, indicating he felt the intervention was excessive. All the same, he mused, "Ça allait accélérer beaucoup de choses."

The general's deliberately staged gesture did indeed accelerate things. It constituted a pivotal moment in the Quebec crisis of the 1960s. De Gaulle was a monumental figure on the world stage, renowned for his wartime heroism and his epic efforts to rescue the French Republic over the previous decade. Now he was dramatizing the cause of Quebec independence by bringing to the attention of the world the fact that he was committing France's support to the breakup of the Canadian state.[14]

Trudeau was not publicly prominent in the federal government's response to de Gaulle's intemperate act. But on the morning after the general's astonishing speech, he and Lalonde prevailed on Pearson, over the more conciliatory advice offered by his external affairs minister, Paul Martin, to declare de Gaulle's words "unacceptable" and the general himself, by implication, *non grata*. De Gaulle flew back to Paris without ever travelling to Ottawa, obviously pleased with his mischief-making. Blind to the subtleties of Canadian politics, he had provoked a reaction in the federal body politic that was to frustrate his long-term goal. His audacity concentrated Canadians' attention on the crisis in Confederation so dramatically that vast numbers of them, even in Quebec, became receptive to the kind of tough, unrepentant federalism that Trudeau espoused.[15]

Six weeks later, when Trudeau made his first major policy statement as minister of justice at the Canadian Bar Association annual meeting in Quebec City, he had acquired an aura of authority and had begun to look like the prophet of a new order. To an audience of his professional peers, he delivered a reasoned speech about Canada's need to entrench collective linguistic rights along with individual human rights in a patriated constitution with a charter of rights. This was the way to solve the Quebec problem, he said, the way to make Canada a more modern, more egalitarian state. This was the route to the renewed federalism about which he had been proselytizing ever since Quebec separatism had become a possibility.

Later, at a press conference called because reporters wanted him to elaborate on his proposal, he showed that he was not just a skilful political performer mouthing bureaucratic bromides. He was emotionally committed to these ideas to the point of intemperance. In response to journalistic prodding, Trudeau's temper flared. He said his ideological opponents – who had mocked his charter of rights solution in the Quebec press and were seeking the chimera of special status – were perpetrators of a hoax, a gigantic practical joke. When that sally did not silence his questioners, he escalated his scorn, dismissing the whole idea of special status as *une connerie*, a term that struck the English-speaking journalists as so vulgar that they couldn't translate it in their reports. This was one of the first public displays of the paradoxical Trudeau style that would soon become so familiar. One minute, he was a lawmaker, mandarin-like, deliberate, Grace Trudeau's good boy, the very model of a refined and gentle man. The next minute, he was Charlie Trudeau reincarnated, cussing the onlookers like a grease-smeared mechanic ready to punch out any challenger in the crowd.[16]

In Ottawa, Pearson was appalled by Trudeau's behaviour. But his outburst, so foreign to the normal posturings of politicians in Canada, established the intensity of Trudeau's commitment to his ideas. Throughout the autumn, as he repeated his ardently held belief that Quebec's best hope both for survival and for democratic development lay within Confederation, he began to attract more and more press attention. Among political insiders concerned with the Liberal succession, this newsworthiness was noted. A few canny Grits from English Canada started to seek out the coterie of Quebeckers who were already thinking about how to make Trudeau leader.[17]

In late November, Charles de Gaulle obligingly spoke out once more in unwitting aid of the Trudeau cause. At one of his rare but carefully rehearsed press conferences in Paris, the general restated his assurance that France would support "her children" in their "effort of emancipation," which would "necessarily result in the advent of Quebec to the rank of a sovereign state." That Canada was in crisis there could no longer be any doubt.[18]

Then came the breakthrough that marked Trudeau's public emergence as the purveyor of the new, the charismatic figure that a traumatized Canada was seeking. Early in December – only days after Lester Pearson had formally announced his retirement at last – Trudeau brought before the House of Commons a divorce reform bill and several amendments to the Criminal Code liberalizing laws on abortion and homosexuality. This overhaul of social legislation had been under way in the Justice Department for years. But Trudeau made the changes his own by telling the television cameras outside the House, "The state has no place in the bedrooms of the nation." That this idea was borrowed directly from an editorial written by Martin O'Malley that week for *The Globe and Mail* went unnoticed. Delivered by a minister of the Crown wearing a leather coat and sporting a Caesar haircut, it had an electrifying effect on the public imagination. It expressed a widely felt need to bring Canada up to date in a way that everybody could understand. Here was a man who was willing to declare himself in opposition to the established order, a man who was saying that Canada did not have to be a

Victorian backwater, a museum of outmoded ideas. Canadians did not need to accept the condescending interference of once and future imperial masters. Canada should, could, and, if Trudeau had anything to say about it, *would* make a giant leap into a new age.[19]

Almost immediately, Trudeau began to be talked about as a possible dark-horse candidate to succeed Pearson. Over the Christmas parliamentary recess, he went to Tahiti for a diving holiday that got him more press than all the earnest politicking of all the other would-be Liberal leaders combined. When he came back, his march to the leadership of the Liberal Party and the prime ministership of Canada gathered an astonishing momentum. In the early months of 1968 it was as though he had become Fortuna's darling. First he got tacit support from the incumbent prime minister. Lester Pearson was already convinced by his reading of Liberal history, with its established tradition of alternating between French and English leaders, and by his own unhappy experience with the Quebec crisis, that his successor had to be a French Canadian. His preference was his Quebec lieutenant, Jean Marchand. But it soon became apparent that not only was Marchand's health indifferent and his English inadequate, he was unwilling to stand for the leadership and was urging Pearson to endorse Trudeau instead. So was Marc Lalonde, who had gained authority as an adviser on Quebec over the previous year. And so was Maryon Pearson, the prime minister's wife, a lively woman with recherché ideas who was impressed by Trudeau's verve. At seventy, Pearson was exhausted by his difficulties in office and disenchanted by the exigencies of politics. He wanted to be seen as a progressive leader and to leave the Liberal Party in the hands of a francophone with a solution to the separatist threat. He put aside his doubts about Trudeau, telling him obliquely in Marchand's presence

that if Trudeau were chosen as his successor it would
meet with Pearson's approval, and then "let[ting] a few
friends know I was well disposed towards him."[20]

As a result, Trudeau was able, in his role as justice
minister, to travel the country with Pearson's blessing in
mid-January, visiting each of the provincial capitals to
discuss with the premiers Ottawa's reform proposals for a
constitutional conference, which had been called for early
February in acknowledgement of the urgency of the
Quebec problem. At every stop, Trudeau made news and
won converts to his campaign for a one-Canada federalism, an advantage that annoyed the declared candidates
for the succession since they had been instructed to stay in
Ottawa and mind their portfolios because of the government's precarious minority position. This stricture did not
apply to Trudeau's flamboyant cross-country odyssey
since, as he put it, he was not seeking the leadership but
fighting "to take the fuse out of explosive Quebec
nationalism – by making sure that Quebec is not a ghetto
for French Canadians, that all of Canada is theirs."[21]

Later in the month, Trudeau was given star billing,
thanks to Marchand's intervention, at the first policy convention in Montreal of the Quebec wing of the newly
reconstituted Liberal Party of Canada. He again articulated his hard-line federalism and received a standing
ovation from a crowd that chanted, "Il a gagné ses
épaulettes." With his popularity in English Canada rising, Trudeau had won the respect of many of his former
critics in the Quebec wing of the Liberal Party. He was
looking more and more like a winner to *les rouges*, who
were hungry for continued federal electoral success as a
counterbalance to the alarming direction in which a
revived Union Nationale was taking Quebec.[22]

On February 5, when a nervous Pearson opened the
first ministers' constitutional conference in Ottawa with

the admonition to the participants that the very survival of Canada was at stake, he hoped that the situation could be handled delicately, diplomatically, the way he had handled the international conferences at which he had been such a star earlier in his career. Instead, a fight broke out between his minister of justice and the premier of Quebec, in full view of a large national television audience. Johnson rejected Trudeau's charter of rights outright, dismissing it as merely a tool for his leadership ambitions. In his easy sarcasm, the Quebec premier misunderstood that Trudeau's vigorous defence of the federalist principles he had been articulating for years fitted the Canadian public's mood as well as his own still-undeclared leadership aspirations. Trudeau was projecting courage and conviction in his television image because after years of careful thought, he had achieved complete certainty. In response to Johnson's needling, he repeated his arguments, giving back barb for barb until there was general agreement that he had carried the exchange and the conference.

For the historian Jean-Louis Roy, the Trudeau–Johnson encounter was "one of the most spectacular duels in Canadian politics" and made Trudeau "in less than an hour [a sure thing] to succeed Lester Pearson in the minds and hearts of a large number of Canadians." Federalist opinion had been so sensitized to the separatist threat by this time that Trudeau became the public favourite to lead the country.[23]

In mid-February, after a show of reluctance that most of his friends thought was only a momentary regression to his old habit of vacillation, he finally declared himself officially a candidate and began a six-week campaign that was one part sweet modesty ("How much do you want to be prime minister, Mr. Trudeau?" "Oh, not very much") to one part sexy audacity ("I like to get fun out of life," he said insouciantly, after deliberately staging an acrobatic fall down a flight of stairs and then bouncing to his feet with the grace of a tumbler half his age). Liberal delegates, excited by the press attention Trudeau was getting, ignored the stories they had heard about his past disdain for their kind and rallied to his campaign by the hundreds. A virtual unknown to the party's grass roots in November, he went to the April leadership convention in Ottawa as the candidate to beat. In the midst of the excitement there – Trudeau was repeatedly mobbed by delegates who wanted to reach out and touch him as though he were some kind of messiah – one of his opponents, the young minister of consumer and corporate affairs, John Turner, was heard to remark, "What's this guy got anyway?"[24]

What Trudeau had displayed that winter and spring – as projected by the print and television journalists who were presenting him as the answer to the public's hopes and fears – was an impressive number of the attributes that Weberian scholars have isolated as the prerequisites of political charisma: an element of foreignness, some obvious imperfections of feature and character, elevated social station, a sexual mystique, a facility for dramatic self-presentation, an unusual style of living, and, above all, an extraordinary calling or vocation and along with it, the fighting stance of the crusader preaching social change.[25]

Television cameramen photographed him as though he were a male Garbo. His face, with its faint scarring left over from adolescent acne and its high cheekbones hinting at Indian ancestry, became luminescent under their lights. The man who had previously disliked even appearing on television proved to be a natural master of the medium. Reporters wrote about him in orgasmic prose, marvelling at the lucidity of his intellect, the romance of his travels, the aplomb of his athletic feats, the magic of his attraction to women, the courage of his convictions, the mystery of his wealth-cum-asceticism. The superficial elements of his life had become fodder for the media's voracious maw.

At the same time, respected figures began to make extravagant statements about him. John Porter, the premier sociologist of Canada's "vertical mosaic," enthused over his intellectual opus, which Trudeau himself would have admitted readily was considerably less impressive than Porter's own. Ramsay Cook, the most talented historian of his generation and the only English-Canadian academic who knew Trudeau well, was persuaded by his friends Ethel Teitelbaum, a political activist, and her husband, the artist Mashel Teitelbaum, to begin a Trudeau-for-leader movement in Toronto that attracted a swarm of academics and artists from various fields. John Saywell, a prominent colleague of Cook's at York University, introduced an English translation of Trudeau's collected essays with a salute to his "masterful" political writings, which Saywell said were "based on philosophical premises about the nature of man, society, and the state." Marshall McLuhan, the intellectual of the electronic hour, wrote that Trudeau was so effective on television because "the medium [can't] take a real face. It has to have a mask."[26]

McLuhan was shrewder than anyone knew. The real Trudeau was being falsified. What the public saw was indeed a mask, a heroic image it wanted to believe in that sat uneasily on a man whose complexities were unknown to his euphoric admirers. The inflation of his intellectual and physical attributes in the leadership process – in which he was on the whole a willing participant – was the final factor in turning Trudeau into a charismatic figure. But it also sowed the seeds of the trouble that was coming for him in his public and private lives.

A few warning notes had already been sounded. Jean de Grandpré, his old rival from Brébeuf days, now an established lawyer who had recently been appointed a vice-president of Bell Canada, asked to see Trudeau early in 1968 in the hope of dissuading him from running for the leadership. De Grandpré had been a faithful Liberal for many years and he feared a disaster was coming, both for the party, which he saw as a right-of-centre coalition that would be undermined by Trudeau's left-wing bent, and for Trudeau himself, whom he saw as far too shy to bear the invasion of his privacy demanded by public life. He talked at Trudeau for a couple of hours, outlining and elaborating these points diplomatically. Trudeau listened carefully. But his response was strong and clear. If he did not run, he said, he would be denying the validity of everything he had written about French Canadians being responsible for their own powerlessness because of their unwillingness to take the full part in governing the Canadian federation to which they were constitutionally entitled. Marchand's health would not allow him to stand for the leadership, so unless Trudeau responded to the call there would be no French-Canadian contender. Without a strong voice in Ottawa, Quebec would fall prey to the new nationalists, and the noble experiment of the previous two hundred years of two races living within a single state would collapse. Trudeau saw the need in terms of absolute imperatives: the evil of separatism must be overcome; a heroic effort had to be made; circumstance had pointed to him to make that effort. What he did not say, of course, is that circumstance was answering the need to be heroic that had been part of his psychology for at least a quarter of a century and was offering him the chance to meld his French and English components into a psychic unity that spoke to the country's own deep-felt need for an integrating, even visionary leadership.[27]

Trudeau went on to fight the June 1968 election, which was called soon after the leadership race, in a campaign that was cleverly stage-managed by professional politicians who saw the vote-getting value of Trudeau's daredevil persona. In between the philosophical speeches he gave on the need for a just society and a participatory democracy, he was encouraged to do jack-knife dives into swimming pools and back-flips on trampolines, to kiss every girl in sight, to be as provocative in his rhetoric as his need for self-dramatization demanded. No one mentioned to the dazzled onlookers that he was often seized with stage fright before having to go into a roomful of Liberal activists or that he disliked having his privacy invaded, was alarmed by the intensity of his admirers' demands, and was concerned about the ephemeral nature of the mob adoration he was experiencing. On the surface, it was roses, roses all the way, and the decisive victory that came to him on June 25 was almost anticlimactic.

Afterwards, when academic and journalistic analysts became disillusioned with Trudeau, it was said in books and articles that his march to power had been a combination of political trickery and television voodoo, that it took four ballots for him to win the leadership, which showed how much hard-headed opposition there was to him from the start, statements that suggested his charisma was nothing more than a shrewdly calculated political take-over. Some writers even suggested that the charisma had never existed, ignoring its importance as a positive force for democratization and denying as well the Canadian mood of the time.[28]

Canadians were both extraordinarily fearful and extraordinarily hopeful in 1968. Events had made it clear that the country could not hide out from history any longer, clinging to a colonial mentality and a chore-boy role internationally. The British had never been very interested in Canada and had long since abandoned it. The

Americans were proving much less than the white hope of democracy and the benevolent-big-brother neighbour that many Canadians had hoped they would become. De Gaulle's vision of a world-wide *francophonie* offended the English-speaking people and unsettled the French-speaking. As a collective, Canadians knew that the country needed to grow into another stage of nationhood, but they were uncertain about how to proceed. But here was this clearly superior man saying explicitly in his pronouncements – and implying in his person – that he knew the direction in which Canada should proceed. The country no longer needed the identification with or the protection of superpowers. It could be a power in its own right, a modest one to be sure but with an enviable moral base in its realizable dream of becoming a truly bicultural, bilingual federated state – a "Just Society," the label Trudeau had appropriated from Frank Scott and was now using to describe his Utopia. Trudeau believed in these ideas in 1968 and a great many Canadians believed in him. That there was naïveté on both sides became clear enough in due course.[29]

POWER INFLATES,
HUBRIS DESTROYS

As soon as he settled into office in June 1968, Trudeau set out to fulfil his promise to bring the Canadian state up to date. At first it seemed he could do no wrong. His initial exercise in cabinet-making was impressive, knitting together some of the "new guys with new ideas" he had wanted to attract to government with seasoned ministers from the Pearson regime, including most of his rivals for the leadership. (The notable exception was Robert Winters, the Toronto businessman who placed second on the final ballot at the leadership convention but decided to return to the private sector.) For regional balance he was able to draw on his party's strengthened representation from the west, its strong contingent from the heartland of Ontario, and its small band of Liberals from the Atlantic provinces. And of course, his federalist allies from Quebec came into power with him as midwives of the new era, ready to buoy up his administration by their admiration for his winning style and their faith in his clear objectives.[1]

He put Marc Lalonde in charge of a newly strengthened Prime Minister's Office, where he swiftly became Trudeau's alter ego, the terror of anyone foolish enough to stand in the way of progress. Michael Pitfield was promoted to a deputy clerk's position in the Privy Council

Office, where he could keep an expert eye on the reorganization of the cabinet committee system that Trudeau agreed was vital for modernizing the government's decision-making capacity. The legal experts Ivan Head, Barry Strayer, and Carl Goldenberg were kept on from Trudeau's Justice Department constitutional committee to advise the prime minister on that important dossier. Old friends from the intellectual community, Roger Rolland, Jean Le Moyne, and Tim Porteous, a young lawyer from Montreal, were employed as speech-writers and idea men. Young Liberals who had been prominent in his campaign, Gordon Gibson, Eddie Rubin, Jim Davey, and Pierre Levasseur, were given important support-staff jobs.

Conspicuously absent from the new prime minister's circle were the professional politicians from the Pearson era for whose type Trudeau had expressed a general disdain: the campaign organizer, Keith Davey, and his young sidekick, James Coutts, as well as Davey's mentor, the former finance minister Walter Gordon, who were to sit out the next four years in exile with other left-Liberals from English Canada, watching what was going on in Ottawa with impatience and dismay. Despite their progressive beliefs and their hard-won expertise, they were regarded as purveyors of old ideas, baggage from the Pearson era not wanted on the Trudeau voyage.

Exulting in the first Liberal majority in fifteen years, the Trudeauites went into overdrive to put their program into effect. In some key areas, they knew exactly what they wanted to do and moved confidently to execute their plans. On the prime minister's chief concern – French Canada's position in the federation – they moved purposefully on three fronts. The bill to create the Official Languages Act was introduced in October 1968, establishing a language commissioner as a linguistic ombudsman and formally asserting that Canadian citizens were to be served in both French and English by federal institutions across the country. Capable Quebeckers were quickly appointed to positions of importance throughout the governmental machinery, showing that Trudeau and Lalonde were determined that equality of opportunity would exist for French-speaking Canadians in Ottawa. And a constitutional task force set about reviewing each clause of the British North America Act in order to prepare for negotiations with the provincial premiers on a completely revised constitution that would bring about a renewed federalism.[2]

By these dramatic means Trudeau served notice that he was intent on breaking up the encrusted Canadian vertical mosaic where the WASPs were in command. Along with French Canadians, the first beneficiaries of his anti-parochialism were Jews who were sworn into cabinet, named to the bench, appointed to head departments and regulatory agencies, and hired for ministerial staffs in unprecedented numbers. To give concrete content to his Just Society slogan, Trudeau created a new Department of Regional Economic Expansion, with his most trusted political ally, Jean Marchand, as minister and Tom Kent, the Pearson regime's most progressive policy-maker, as his deputy. He assigned the job of radical tax reform to his finance minister, Edgar Benson, and encouraged his friend and secretary of state, Gérard Pelletier, to make community development innovations. His commitment to participatory democracy was translated into an ambitious process designed to involve the Liberal Party's extra-parliamentary wing in policy-making. Members of Parliament were given research budgets so they could perform their functions as riding ombudsmen more effectively. White Papers were commissioned to give the general public access to legislative planning.[3]

In fields where the Trudeauites were not so certain about what they wanted to do, they were confident that their commitment to rationalism would provide the answers. Policy reviews were announced, declaring the basic premises of several areas of governmental activity – such as housing, foreign relations, military commitments, and Indian affairs – to be open to question, as though each of them suddenly had been designated a *tabula rasa* by some Cartesian overlord.

To anyone familiar with his writings, Trudeau appeared to be revamping Canada's political process along the lines laid out in the gospel according to *Cité libre*. All the ideas he had been advocating for half a lifetime were now being put into practice. It was as though he had become the perfect bilingual, bicultural man, the prototypical Canadian of the future. In Quebec he had garnered new respect, not least for his ability to put English Canadians in their place. In English Canada, he was experiencing something like adulation. As his sister, Suzette Rouleau, expressed it, "My goodness, Pierre is like a Beatle!" The retiring intellectual of a few years before had been transmogrified into a Lothario on the public stage. The kind of young women from the WASP establishment who had not been particularly interested in him twenty years before when he was labouring in the PCO as a civil servant – the daughters of judges, diplomats, and cabinet ministers – now flocked to his banner, to the amusement of his staff, who saw his pleasure in his heightened attraction to women as the kind of break-out they had experienced as sophomores.[4]

But this was no collegian's spree. It was the aphrodisiac effect of power. Trudeau had the best job in the country and could use it to demonstrate his superior education in the philosophy and practice of government, his superior linguistic skills, and his superior understanding of the world. This middle-aged man who had never held a full-time job until he was appointed to cabinet in 1967 was now heading up a multi-billion-dollar government machine, being chauffeur-driven in a bulletproof limousine with fluttering flags and outriders, awaited outside his East Block office by admiring crowds, photographed constantly by hovering hordes of professionals and amateurs, cossetted by a staff of servants, briefed by experts for trips to international meetings with queens and shahs and statesmen – conferences where his intellect was admired and his shadow personality's occasional displays of outrageous behaviour commented on for the most part as though they were nothing but the refreshingly unstuffy expressions of a free spirit's whims. Famous entertainers basked in Trudeau's presence: Barbra Streisand thought she was in love with him; Yoko Ono and John Lennon came to call. Famous thinkers sought his company: Marshall McLuhan, J.K. Galbraith, Henry Kissinger, and André Malraux gave and took advice.

Not surprisingly, his situation went to Trudeau's head. The private Pierre – the cultured, contemplative man who was loving and protective of his family, the passionate idealist who was ardent in his faith, generous and witty with his friends – was taken over by his inflated political persona. The new prime minister clearly loved power. And, predictably, he became inflated by it, displaying the hubris that is a commonplace with those who are thrust into positions of supremacy.[5]

While the public was still titillated by reports of his adventures – and was to continue to be so throughout his political life, no matter how angry voters became with him later over Canada's economic decline – the country's political class was soon offended by this new arrogance of power. Within months of taking office, he managed to insult members of the parliamentary press corps, the collective that had so eagerly reported his rise, by calling them "a crummy lot" and ordering his cabinet and staff to resist their requests for information. He slighted progressives by mocking an advocacy group that was pressing him to intervene in the devastating civil war in Nigeria, flinging at them the condescending question "Where is Biafra?" as though they did not know while *he*, of course, did. He slighted his colleagues in the House of Commons by saying that opposition MPs were "nobodies fifty yards from Parliament Hill." And he disparaged the efforts of the earnest participatory democrats in his own party who asked him to pay heed to the work they were doing in his name by saying, "What about Harold Laski?" – an obscure reference to his mentor at the LSE, who had been reprimanded for challenging Clement Attlee in the name of the Labour Party, which apparently meant that the Liberals' efforts, necessarily punier than those of the great Laski, were foolhardy and a bore.[6]

Taken one by one, these were minor displays of irascibility that were readily excused by his staff. The prime minister was beset by a myriad of tasks, the job of modernizing Canada was exhausting, the journalists ill informed, the opposition full of obstreperous obfuscators, the party activists too impatient. But as time wore on, more serious problems developed that were not so easily explained. Major Trudeauite initiatives kept failing in the face of obstinate political realities, and Trudeau proved incapable of responding well even to the considered criticism of serious people. The Department of External Affairs laboured long and hard on its foreign policy review, but the document it brought forth in 1970 failed even to address Canada's relationship with the United States, let alone prepare the government or the public for the shock of President Richard Nixon's attack on Canada's privileged relationship with Washington. Enriching un-

employment insurance benefits in the name of the Just
Society laid the social security system open to abuse by
"ski bums" using "UI" to develop their skills on the slopes
at the expense of ordinary taxpayers and to the fierce
indignation of small businessmen. Efforts to make the
political process more democratic foundered when Liberal Party stalwarts endorsed policies – such as abortion
on demand, the legalization of marijuana, and more
nationalist action to defend cultural and economic sovereignty – that were anathema to Trudeau personally and
went nowhere as a result. White Papers inviting public
participation in the policy process turned out to be easier
for corporations than for citizens to turn to their advantage. The elaborate restructuring of the cabinet committee system, intended to re-establish political control over
the bureaucracy by enhancing ministerial collegiality,
managed to hamstring both bureaucrats and ministers,
several of whom resigned in frustration. The group of
talented men (there were no women in senior posts)
recruited to the Trudeau PMO and PCO as his closest advisers and expediters of his policy ideas began to be seen as
nothing but technocrats, a super-group of the privileged,
in the journalist Walter Stewart's phrase, who knew very
little about politics or the needs of ordinary people and
who had taken on their leader's arrogant style. In trying
to bypass the old Liberal political-bureaucratic combine,
Trudeau had created a parallel government and unwit-
tingly become its captive.[7]

What was worse than any of these failings was the fact
that official bilingualism, haltingly introduced in English-
speaking Canada, coupled with French power in Ottawa
did little, at least in the short term, to allay nationalist
demands in Quebec, demands that came to a crescendo in
the October Crisis of 1970, when FLQ terrorists kidnapped
a British diplomat and murdered the Quebec minister of

labour. Though he anguished in private as a democrat about suppressing civil liberties in favour of military action, Trudeau – the student of Carl Friedrich, the off-spring of the Weimar Republic, which had succumbed to Hitler's terrorism for lack of adequate emergency powers – invoked the War Measures Act to deal with the crisis and then talked to reporters as though he were playing yet another "I'm superior to you guys" game. "Just watch me," he shot back provocatively when asked how far he would go in seeking to put down terrorism. The intellectual community was so outraged by this behaviour that, as a group, they drew away from Trudeau and began to produce books with titles like *Bleeding Hearts, Bleeding Country* and *Rumours of War*.[8]

His tough stance on terrorism nevertheless brought Trudeau an overwhelmingly favourable response from the public in both Quebec and English Canada, and when the opinion polls acknowledged a new spurt in his popularity, members of his entourage were confirmed in their belief that Trudeau was not being arrogant, he was being misrepresented. According to them, criticism of Trudeau's methods in the media and the universities merely demonstrated Trudeau's success: the élites were discomfited because he was effectively bringing power to the people. A few months after the October Crisis, when he unexpectedly married a beautiful young woman who adored him, it looked as though Trudeaumania might be rekindled and the kissing would never stop.

But in the next year and a half, as the Canadian federation continued to be wobbly and the Canadian economy began to show signs of serious strain, the public turned fickle – just as Trudeau had feared it would before he was inflated by power. (In 1968, he had said to a campaign worker who had remarked on the phenomenon of his supporters' high expectations, "The trick will be to do enough quickly enough before people ... are disappointed.") The myth of Trudeau as the national saviour who knew how to deal with Quebec was broken when Robert Bourassa, the Liberal premier of Quebec who was elected in 1970, rejected the constitutional deal that the prime minister and the anglophone premiers cobbled together as a lowest-common-denominator consensus at a conference in Victoria, British Columbia, in June 1971. Widespread grumbling about Trudeau's evident lack of interest in ordinary citizens' concerns about unemployment and inflation added to the decline in his public support, though this too was ignored by the Trudeauites as a media-induced chimera. They seemed to believe that all he would have to do to win a new mandate when the time came in 1972 was to present himself on the hustings, hold a dialogue with Canadians, and wait for the Liberal votes to come pouring into the ballot boxes. Their surprise was palpable on October 22, 1972, when Trudeau found himself clinging to power by a scant two-seat edge over the Progressive Conservatives, whose own unglamorous leader, Robert Stanfield, had conducted a dogged campaign devoted to the economic issues.[9]

Forced to run his second ministry as a minority government requiring NDP support to survive, Trudeau made a startling switch. He became a pragmatic politician. The technocrats in his office were dispersed and replaced by party loyalists. Policies that had caused him problems were downplayed. And a new band of advisers was recruited. Swallowing his pride, Trudeau accepted offers of help from the seasoned Pearsonian Liberals from Toronto, Coutts and Davey and their team, who brought him the professional savvy and a mastery of the politics of compromise and manoeuvre that he, as a resolutely reformist amateur in politics, had formerly reviled. By bowing to their suggestions that he soften his image – and acceding to the demands for progressive legislation of the able

NDP leader, David Lewis – he patched and relacquered his public mask. By the late spring of 1974, he was ready to break his ties with the NDP and provoke another election. With a shrewd campaign whose nationalist promises and go-go style owed far more to the Toronto group's opinion research than to Trudeau's own beliefs, he triumphed once more, receiving on July 8, 1974, a clear majority for his third ministry.

That summer Trudeau seemed to have reached a new apogee. The man who at forty was regarded by many of his contemporaries as a clever idler without serious commitments, either to a career or to a woman, was at fifty-four confirmed as the most powerful figure in the country, a brilliantly successful politician with an apparently ideal family life.

The deflation was about to begin.

The breakdown of Trudeau's carefully fabricated mask showed on the personal level before it was exposed politically. In September 1974, just two months after the election victory that marked a new high in his career, his twenty-six-year-old wife, Margaret Sinclair Trudeau, was admitted to the Montreal General Hospital suffering from what was described in a press release from the Prime Minister's Office as severe emotional stress. A few weeks later, she appeared on the CTV network to talk at length about how hard she had found her role as wife of the prime minister. The hospitalization and Margaret Trudeau's laundered explanation of her difficulties evoked widespread sympathy. It was the first indication that there was trouble in the paradise the public assumed existed in the prime minister's official residence at 24 Sussex Drive.

The details of what was actually going on in that "large, cold grey mansion," as Margaret Trudeau later described her home, were not known for years. But when they were revealed in a series of remarkable interviews she gave in the late 1970s, and in the two books she talked into a ghost-writer's tape recorder, what had happened became clear. Two wilful people, emotionally arrested in adolescence, had contrived to meet and greet and were about to part again in an agonizing marital conflict that would sap Trudeau's political energy for the next five years. For reasons that had to do with their individual needs, they had each gone into marriage harbouring delusions about the other that were to have horrendous consequences, both private and public.[10]

When Trudeau married Margaret Sinclair in March 1971, it was seen as a brilliant match, personally and politically. The bride was presented as very much a child of her time, the mildly, even admirably rebellious offspring of a bona fide member of the old Liberal élite. Her father, James Sinclair, had been an adept and popular minister of fisheries in the government of Louis St. Laurent, and she seemed the perfect embodiment of the kind of well-connected young people who had turned Trudeau into a popular idol in 1968. She was said to be well educated, well travelled, lively, and intelligent but at the same time modest and versed in the womanly arts. She had sewn her own wedding dress and baked the cake for the reception. She loved poetry and dancing and felt herself to be made for motherhood. Who cared that there was a twenty-nine-year age gap between the bride and groom? Her mother, Kathleen Sinclair – who at forty-nine was two years younger than Trudeau – deflected objections by saying on the couple's wedding day, "He may be old but he's a young man at heart." This was a new age. Love, freedom, and putting an end to crippling convention were what mattered. Marshall McLuhan saw the marriage as the act "of a wizard . . . the transformation of the whole political scene into a marriage feast," a sign of Trudeau's playfulness, his creativity, and, best of all, something that

meant "the Americans . . . have begun to envy us." Wow!
English Canadians said to each other, is this some great
guy or what?[11]

What they were saying in Quebec was, as usual, something different. Several of Trudeau's French-Canadian
contemporaries remarked knowingly that he had married
Margaret Sinclair because she was Scottish like his
mother and because she came from a good family, which
was thought to be important to Trudeau, who, for all his
cavorting in bistros and all his agitating on the left, was
still something of an Outremont snob in their eyes. The
French Canadians were only partly right. Margaret's
father, James Sinclair, was indeed the son of a Glasgow
schoolmaster who had brought his family to Vancouver
when "Jimmy" was two and had made sure he had all the
educational advantages the New World had to offer. As a
dynamic adult, Sinclair had achieved a remarkable success, not just in politics but in the business world, where
he was now chairman of the international conglomerate
Lafarge Cement. But Margaret Sinclair, the fourth of his
five daughters, was not a Scot, she was not rich (Sinclair
had a large income but no great fortune for his children to
draw on), and she most certainly was not a lady of Grace
Elliott's Edwardian ilk. She was the product of post-war
British Columbia – boom-time Bee-Cee through and
through – and the possessor of a sensibility best described
as California North. In the early 1960s, she had been a
bright and popular high school student in an affluent district of Vancouver, concerned with clothes, parties, and
the attentions of her peers. At university, she had moved
on from football stars to campus radicals as her preferred
companions, had learned the rhetoric of the Sixties revolutionaries, and had experimented extensively with drugs
and sex in both Vancouver and Morocco, where she had
gone after her graduation in 1968. As a result of her experiences, she was worldly enough by 1970 to know how to

"catch" Pierre Trudeau in a way that no convent girl
from Outremont had ever been able to manage.

Far from marrying a reincarnation of his mother, Trudeau had taken as his bride a woman whose extroverted
temperament was more like Charlie Trudeau's. Margaret
had met Trudeau first in December 1967, when he was
holidaying in Tahiti in order to consider entering the Liberal leadership race and she was spending Christmas at
the same resort with her family. She had seen him again
briefly at the Liberal convention in 1968, at which her
father was a delegate committed to one of Trudeau's
opponents; had been one of his well-publicized dates
when he was on a brief official visit to Vancouver in 1969;
had taken up his offer (given freely to the young and
beautiful in those days) to look him up in Ottawa if she
ever found herself in the capital by moving there purposefully within weeks of their Vancouver encounter and getting a six-month job with a government department
through her father's contacts. After months of dating him
publicly as one of the string of young English-Canadian
women he was seen with during his first years in politics
and staying with him secretly at the prime minister's
country residence at Harrington Lake on weekends, she
had finally talked him into the marriage she had fanta-
sized about since their first kiss on their first date.[12]

Trudeau had been tortured by many doubts and had
raised many concerns about their differences. During
their carefully concealed engagement, when she went
home to Vancouver for a few months to convert to
Catholicism and to get ready for their wedding, he kept
phoning her to ask whether she was having second
thoughts herself. Finally he had succumbed to his strong
desire for a family of his own; to Margaret's certainty
about their suitability as a couple; and to his unexpected
passion for her person. It was the first time, he confided to

an intimate friend, that he had really felt himself to be in love. Obviously, the loneliness of his bachelor life had come home to him. He was over fifty. His mother was dying. (By the time he introduced Margaret to her at Christmas in 1970, Grace Trudeau was bedridden with arteriosclerosis and was only occasionally lucid.) His brother and sister and their families were busy with their own lives in Montreal. His peers were becoming grand-parents while he was still living like a young man and going out on dates.[13]

Trudeau's old friends remarked later that if Margaret Sinclair had been a French Canadian, Trudeau would not have been fooled for five minutes by her outpourings about freedom trips, William Blake, Krishnamurti, and the ardour of her search for the way of the spirit. He would have seen her for what she was: an immature, somewhat exhibitionistic girl who loved luxury and wanted celebrity in order to impress her friends and fam-ily – most particularly her father, whose neglect of his large family during his political days had left her feeling deprived of male parental attention – without having to make any sustained effort of her own to achieve success. "I [was] always too cute for my own good, too sexy," she said later. "I could always get what I wanted." Trudeau's peers thought he was dazzled, as so many middle-aged people were in the late 1960s and early 1970s – before Nixonomics and the OPEC crisis changed the world econ-omy, before the rise of the new conservatism changed the public philosophy of the Western democracies – by what seemed so alive and unfettered about the baby-boom generation. In Margaret Sinclair, that generation's ideal-ism was packaged in one lovely, lively form that was gilded by her apparent adoration for him.[14]

Trudeau seemed entranced by the way Margaret en-hanced his own contradictory image as a nonconformist in power. It was as though he *knew* that real freedom requires discipline, but he *felt*, as did so many older people at the time, a longing for the wonderful Lucy-in-the-sky-with-diamonds world that the young were claiming they inhabited. In marrying her, it must have seemed as though he could have everything that befitted a hero: the power, the sagacity, and the stable family life that comes with middle age along with the optimism and spontaneity of youth. Margaret's admiring response to the Trudeau inflated by power further pumped up his sense of omnipotence.

Despite the couple's bravura beginnings, including the birth of their first son on Christmas Day, 1971, Trudeau soon showed signs of being disenchanted with his enchantress. Even in the early days of their marriage, the Don Juan in him kept competing with younger men to catch the attention of attractive women who crossed his path in the course of his official duties. At the same time his young wife's essential childishness and youthful vacuity began to alarm the serious man under the playboy mask. "Culture for me was rock music," she once said. For him, conversations about culture – or politics or the bloody crossroads where they meet – were intense discussions about Malraux or Canetti or Braque or Schoenberg, usually conducted in French, a language his wife barely understood. "Don't worry about her," he told a perplexed dinner party of his contemporaries early in their relationship. "She wouldn't know what we were saying, even if we were speaking English."[15]

His friends took him at his word and did not worry about her. But they soon began to worry about him, as they found themselves increasingly cut out of his life. "Within a couple of years, Pierre began to show distinct signs of unhappiness," said one of his oldest friends, who had himself married late in life. "He had asked me when he was contemplating marriage what I thought, and I had told him it was a wonderful idea. But I didn't know Margaret and I hadn't considered deeply the real nature of his earlier relationships. There was a reason, I decided later, that he had never had a completely developed relationship with a mature woman. To love someone fully you have to confront her reality. And to confront a mature woman, you first have to confront yourself."[16]

Trudeau had confronted his spiritual and intellectual needs throughout his life but, never having lived with anyone in adulthood apart from his mother, he had not been required to confront himself emotionally in the intimacy of a mutual interdependence between equals. Marriage for him did not seem to involve an undertaking to make real changes in his attitudes or behaviour. He remained inflexible, self-contained, a stern judge of others' behaviour. "One of the best things about mother was that she never disturbed [my work]," he retorted when his wife complained that he was a workaholic. If marriage required adjustment, it was Margaret who was expected to do the adjusting.[17]

Unfortunately for them both, Margaret was nowhere near mature enough to sustain the dislocation her marriage brought with it. She was still a "dizzy, distracted girl," as she described herself. As a woman in her early twenties who had led a largely feckless existence, she was ill prepared to live with a man whose official role put demands on her that she found constraining in the extreme. She had been mesmerized by Trudeau's political power – the power her father had craved – and by exaggerated stories about his style and his wealth. An avid reader of romantic fiction, she wanted the excitement of greeting heads of state and dining with royalty, the drama of photographers crowding around her in public, the pleasure of clothes-buying sprees in Rome, the envy of other women who were excited by her husband's image and

position. She did not want the tedium of talking triviali-
ties to politicians and diplomats at boring receptions and
dinners, of being constantly shadowed by the Mounties, of
keeping her real opinions to herself, of having to live
within the kind of strictly observed routine that an official
household demands.[18]

Furthermore, by her own admission, she had no idea of
how to cope privately with a man who was by nature
solitary, by training an intellectual, and by circumstance
fixated on his work. Once their courtship was over, Trudeau had very little time for her, even in the evenings,
when he spent hours absorbed in the boxes of official
papers connected with his job. After she had lived with
him for a while she said she "found all the stories about
Trudeau the playboy more and more absurd." He turned
out to be disciplined, preoccupied, given to the rigorous
observance of health routines, devout in his religion, and
frugal in a way that first discouraged her, then drove her
to excesses.[19]

As early as the 1972 election campaign, when pregnant
with her second son, she had exclaimed to an astonished
group of journalists that she had become "just Old Mother
Earth" – an alarming phrase for a twenty-four-year-old
to use as a description of herself and one that revealed the
shock of her disillusion. To counter her boredom, frustration, and loneliness, she soon took to hectoring and quarrelling with the household staff, to spending extravagant
sums of money on clothes and decoration, to complaining
bitterly that her official duties were keeping her from self-
fulfilment through a great career in some as yet undefined
profession, to talking incessantly to the small group of
women, mostly officials' wives, who were her "best
friends" about how difficult she found domesticity with
Pierre, how their "basically strong . . . physical attraction
for one another was being seriously undermined."[20]

It was not all black. She revelled in flirting with Prince Charles and Fidel Castro. She loved holidays with Pierre in the Caribbean and on the Mediterranean and in the Middle East in the villas and yachts of the rich and powerful. Motherhood preoccupied and pleased her intermittently; she enjoyed breast-feeding and jam-making as an open display of her "Mother Earth" capacities and her admiration for the back-to-the-land mores of her generation.

Still, the best weeks of her married life were experienced in the election campaign of 1974, when she achieved a measure of stardom in her own right. Until then, the Trudeaus as a couple had maintained a distance from the press as part of Trudeau's insistence on privacy. But in the spring and summer of 1974, Margaret had a six-week turn in the hot limelight of an election campaign that obviously fed the needs of her extroverted personality. The Toronto Liberals who ran that campaign for Trudeau were convinced that her persona as a beautiful and devoted young wife and mother could be exploited to the party's advantage. She herself had wanted to play an active political role ever since the previous election and, after a quavering start, she took to the hustings with gusto, making speeches across the country, shaking hands with local Liberals, chatting to voters in walkabouts, and talking ingenuously and effusively to journalists about her husband, her children, her philosophy, and her dreams.[21]

News reports and analyses began to describe the "Margaret factor" as being of importance in election calculations, and when the Liberals' substantial victory was celebrated at the Château Laurier in Ottawa on election night in 1974, Trudeau gracefully thanked his wife for her help as she stood beside him under the klieg lights, her face radiant in the glow of their joint victory. For once she had the right part in the right drama. She had "become so involved in the political life that I . . . even dreamed of running in the next election for my father's old parliamentary district [*sic*] in north Vancouver.''[22]

The euphoria didn't last. The day after the election Pierre went back to the boxes of briefs to be mastered in his office; the professional politicians slept late before turning their thoughts to questions of policy and patronage in the new ministry; the photographers and reporters went on to other assignments; and nobody called the heroine of the hour – every hour on the hour – to tell her how magnificent she had been. Margaret was left sitting on the porch of her "freedom room" in the "prison" at 24 Sussex, eating the breakfast her heinous servants had prepared for her, watching the boring sailboats on the sparkling river below, and feeling "that I had been used."[23]

"Something in me broke that day," she told her ghostwriter. Her dreams of glory, having been realized momentarily, were being thwarted once more. By whom? By the professional politicians? She blamed them often in print and in private conversation for her miseries although she clearly enjoyed the public exposure their strategies provided. By her husband? She rarely said directly that Trudeau kept her down although later accounts of her exchanges with him seemed to indicate that they had trapped themselves in a kind of competition about who was the most effective public figure, the sort of contention that more often occurs between adolescent lovers who are stuck with being surrogate siblings in rivalry for adult attention. By herself? It was not until later in her life that she was able to face the fact that her troubles were in part of her own making.[24]

In any case, after July 1974 she entered into open combat with her husband to get the attention she craved. First she took off without consultation for a solitary holiday in Europe, where she searched fruitlessly for a former lover. Then she fell in love with an American senator (later revealed to be Edward Kennedy) at a celebrity tennis match in New York and threatened to kill herself with a kitchen knife when questioned by her husband about their encounter, an episode that led to her hospital stay in 1974. As the post-election months sped on, she became more and more outrageous, acting up wildly in public in Canada and abroad. She burst into song at a formal dinner in Venezuela, appeared sans underwear in a see-through T-shirt in Cuba, yelled "Fuck you!" in front of a group of Japanese dignitaries in Tokyo who witnessed one of her increasingly heated disagreements with her husband. At home she took to smoking marijuana heavily, although she knew that Trudeau hated the habit and that the Mounties assigned to security duty at the prime minister's official residence were aware that she was regularly engaging in an illegal activity. "It became so that Pierre on arriving home from the office would come up not to kiss but to sniff me," she said afterwards.[25]

Nothing seemed to help Margaret Trudeau overcome her unhappiness, not the hospitalization or subsequent psychiatric consultations, not professional lessons in photography, not a private phone line or her own car and freedom from the security officers whose presence so revolted her, not the birth of a third son in October 1975, not her husband's agreement that she could travel where she wished or study what she wanted. The Trudeaus became increasingly acrimonious in their private exchanges and increasingly tense in public. Finally, in March 1977, they decided on a trial separation, which began in a spectacular burst of publicity when Margaret impulsively flew to Toronto for a Rolling Stones concert and got involved in some impromptu partying with the rock stars that caused a minor crisis in Trudeau's office.

• • •

While Trudeau's marital conflict was unfolding in all its messy reality, a new round of political problems began to plague him. However hard he tried to separate his public from his private life, he became increasingly disengaged as prime minister, appearing to drift away from his task, but then re-engaging abruptly when issues could not be ignored. During his third term in office – when he commanded a secure majority in the House of Commons and ought to have been at the peak of his form as leader – he was too disturbed to devote his full concentration to the challenges of his job, just at the point when his government fell victim to one crisis after another. Since his pride prevented him from admitting even to his political intimates how beset he was at home, few people realized that what looked like indifference to the government's worsening situation was, in fact, distraction induced by emotional turmoil. Things fell apart for Trudeau in the period from 1974 to 1979 in all the major areas of his prime ministerial concerns.

At the beginning of the period Trudeau had reverted briefly to his philosopher-king grandiosities. Flushed with his regained majority and flattered by unrealistic punditry that talked of the Trudeau era running till the end of the century, he agreed to another fanciful experiment in rational planning. The so-called priorities exercise of 1974–75 was meant to define the government's strategy for decades ahead but managed mainly to fritter away the crucial first year of the Liberals' renewed mandate. His allegedly democratized cabinet committee system, now run by Michael Pitfield, who had been appointed clerk of the Privy Council, induced bureaucratic paralysis rather than political dynamism.

Having trounced the Conservatives at the polls in 1974 by mocking the unfeasibility of Robert Stanfield's proposal for a wage and price freeze, Trudeau found himself only a year later forced to adopt controls and restrictive monetarism under ever-growing inflationary pressures. He lost control of the Quebec agenda, first to Robert Bourassa, who defied federal bilingualism by declaring Quebec a unilingual French state, and then to René Lévesque, his sometime reformist ally, who had formed the separatist Parti Québécois in 1968 and whose election as premier in 1976 made a mockery of Trudeau's expressed certainty that separatism was dead.

To add to his difficulties, Trudeau was becoming increasingly isolated as leader. His combative personality and political troubles had driven important ministers from his cabinet, including the popular finance minister, John Turner. His old friend Gérard Pelletier had left Ottawa to become Canada's ambassador in Paris, charged with defending the federalist position against Quebec's claims for treatment as an independent nation by France. His political mentor, Jean Marchand, who was suffering from serious illnesses as well as battle fatigue, had resigned from the ministry of transport. Other loyal and experienced ministers, including Donald Macdonald, Charles Drury, and Mitchell Sharp, who all had valuable connections to the business community, were preparing to depart, exhausted by the exigencies of office. He had to rely more and more on the two strong ministers still with him, Marc Lalonde, who had run for office in 1972 and become his minister of health and welfare, and Allan MacEachen, the House leader, a hold-over from the Pearson era, who had a valuable command of House of Commons procedures.

Despite his proliferating problems, when Margaret Trudeau left her husband in March 1977, sympathy for Trudeau's dignified response to her shenanigans swelled in Liberal ranks. With the party again ahead in the polls, thanks to public concern about the Lévesque phenomenon,

Trudeau was urged to call an early election. He refused, saying he was just not in good enough emotional shape to cope with the rigours of a campaign. Most Liberals accepted his decision with good grace, but it soon became obvious that sympathy could not prevail indefinitely over self-interest. By the fall of 1978 the party was staring defeat, not re-election, in the face, as public support deteriorated once more in the light of petty government scandals and the country's continuing economic woes.

By this time, the Liberals held power in only one province, Prince Edward Island. The hegemony they had enjoyed in federal politics for over forty years was lost. In the west, where they had once been a dominant force, anger at them had become chronic, along with the belief that Liberals were obsessed with Quebec and totally incapable of responding to western needs. Liberals in the business community, the remnant of a once-strong wing of the party, were beset by complaints from their peers, who had come to loathe Trudeau and his ideas. For most businessmen in the late 1970s, the "can-do" Liberal Party of Louis St. Laurent and C.D. Howe had become the "can't-do-anything-right" party of Pierre Trudeau. And among the core of progressive Grits who turned up for riding meetings and kept the extra-parliamentary party machinery functioning between campaigns, there was general dismay at the extent to which Trudeau had come under the sway of the professional pols who had replaced the technocratic super-group of the 1968–72 period.

This new group was led by James Coutts, the Toronto management consultant Trudeau had installed as his principal secretary in 1975, and Senator Keith Davey, the man he had reluctantly but shrewdly appointed national chairman for the 1974 election campaign and had kept on as campaign chairman-in-waiting for the next election. For all their accumulated years of political experience and

loyal service to the Liberal Party, these backroom opera-
tors and their associates were seen as having become too
clever by half. Their expert jockeying for electoral
advantage was regarded as the key factor inducing the
leader to sacrifice Liberal principles to political survival,
even on issues close to his heart, such as abolishing the
death penalty. It was widely feared that one of Trudeau's
enduring political assets, his reputation for stubborn
integrity, had been tarnished beyond restoration.

Because of these problems, Trudeau and his close advisers decided not to call a general election campaign in
1978, the year it would normally have fallen due, but to
hold by-elections instead for fifteen parliamentary vacan-
cies that had to be filled. To their dismay, the result of
these by-elections in October of 1978 was a near rout: the
Liberals won only two of the fifteen seats. The government seemed to be doomed. The coming general election,
which by law would have to be called in 1979, was viewed
as a certain defeat, a Gritterdämmerung, as an old joke
making the rounds in Ottawa described it.[26]

In the face of this adversity, Trudeau's entourage rallied.
Coutts and Davey had put together a highly competent
political staff for Trudeau whose most important members
in the late 1970s were Tom Axworthy, a political scientist
from Winnipeg with academic expertise in the Liberal
Party's history, and Colin Kenny, an autocratic organizer
known as Colonel Klink, who was the best advance man
in the business. They also were dependent for advice on
two Torontonians they had worked with for years, Martin
Goldfarb, who had an astute command of polling techniques, and Jerry Grafstein, a Liberal lawyer and communications expert. Coutts and Davey knew from Goldfarb's
survey research that Trudeau remained the Liberal Par-

ty's major asset. They were not given to intellectualizing
– whatever socio-political theory they drew on was provided by Grafstein, who had founded and edited the
short-lived *Journal of Liberal Thought* in the 1960s, and by
Goldfarb, who had been trained as an anthropologist. But
they knew instinctively that something of the charismatic
appeal Trudeau had for the public in the late 1960s still
clung to him. That quality of "passionate will" that Max
Weber thought political leaders in democracies must possess in order to be effective was still there in Trudeau –
and still evoked a residual respect in Canadians. While
many voters hated his guts, just as many still admired his
intellectual strength, his moral commitment, and his federalist stance. In a television-dominated politics that emphasized leadership qualities over all other factors, his
electric persona might still win a campaign, especially
since he was pitted against the nervous and unconvincing
young Conservative leader, Joe Clark, who had replaced
Robert Stanfield in 1976.[27]

Even to optimists like Coutts and Davey, it was
unlikely that Trudeau could manage another majority victory with the Margaret factor, which they calculated had
worked for him in 1974, now working against him. Since
the Rolling Stones episode in 1977, Margaret Trudeau had
been jetting back and forth across the Atlantic, and up and
down the continent, trying out men, jobs, and hallucino-
gens in a rampage of publicity that seemed mainly aimed
at wreaking revenge on her husband for having kept her
well-shod and pregnant in his prime ministerial fortress.
When she was in Ottawa, she lived in a suite on the third
floor of 24 Sussex, quarrelling with her estranged husband
almost constantly over money and other matters, visiting
close friends to gossip about her exploits abroad, but
remaining out of sight during the official functions she
hated so much. Trudeau's office staff could always tell

from his distraught mood when she was home, and her international exploits were often reported in the Canadian media. When she was in New York or London or Paris, she stayed in expensive hotels or with her new-found friends and temporary lovers, spending freely the money she had earned as an actress in a couple of low-budget movies shot in Montreal and the south of France or in a brief stint as a freelance photographer for *People* magazine, which soon lost interest in her services when her contacts with world figures proved too ephemeral to get her and her camera into Buckingham Palace or Elizabeth Taylor's country house. Her behaviour had succeeded in disorienting Trudeau, who had been able throughout his adult life to distance himself from emotional uproar. Supervising the upbringing of his three young sons was not the problem, since he proved to have a natural talent as a parent. What was difficult was coping with their mother, who continued to alternate outrageous behaviour with poignant requests for understanding that neither her husband nor her friends knew how to meet. At one point, the couple attempted to negotiate a reconciliation. Trudeau agreed to quit politics and leave Ottawa by the end of 1978, but his wife ultimately backed out of their agreement, realizing she would not be able to live harmoniously with him whether he was in politics or not.

Even though for a few weeks, the possible reconciliation meant that Trudeau's political staff did not even know for sure whether "the boss," as they called him, would be fighting another campaign or not, they held fast to their game plan, setting up public appearances for Trudeau and bolstering his troubled ego as if they were his dressers and he an aging star who could still be coaxed on stage to deliver a masterful performance. "Only you can save the country," they told the Liberal leader, hoping to arouse him for one more confrontation with the forces of evil –

this time in the form of the Parti Québécois and its proposed referendum on Quebec independence, which was expected to take place within the next year.

They psyched him up to deliver a brilliant, two-hour attack on the Conservatives in the House of Commons that mocked Clark's weaknesses and implicitly reminded Canadians that Trudeau was still the country's strongest leader. They prepared him for television interviews with prying reporters in which he gave no quarter. (Question: "What about your marital difficulties, Mr. Trudeau?" Answer: "I'll tell you about my marital difficulties if you tell me about yours.") They arranged for him to fly to Europe to consult with heads of state and remind Canadians of his stature in international affairs. They helped him to mount two more constitutional conferences in the hope – which proved futile – of achieving his goal of patriating the British North America Act with a charter of rights.

But as Trudeau came to the bitter end of his majority mandate in March of 1979, their efforts appeared to have had little effect. Margaret Trudeau's latest money-making, publicity-garnering scheme had involved the writing of a memoir, *Beyond Reason*, whose publication in London and New York was infelicitously timed to coincide with the beginning of the campaign. The book launch was accompanied by a series of splashy interviews with American television personalities and magazine journalists in which, like some mad, bad child, she would embellish her stories about her adventures with the celebrated in order to attract more attention to herself while twisting a knife in her husband's pride. Her constant capering had by this time damaged Trudeau's reputation as a political leader as well as his dignity. "How can you trust a man whose judgement of people is so bad?" columnists and phone-in show hosts kept asking.[28]

Charles Mitchell/Canapress

The child as father of the man: Pierre Trudeau at sixty and at twelve, as prime minister and schoolboy, displaying facets of a complex personality – determination, sensitivity, and sartorial style.

Trudeau Family

In the bosom of his family: Pierre Trudeau at three with his sister, Suzette, and baby brother, Tip; at thirteen with his parents, siblings, and grandfather, Philip Elliott, on board the *Champlain*, the ship that carried them to Europe for a holiday in June 1933.

In the role of muscled savant: Pierre Trudeau at eighteen in a pose as Rodin's *Thinker*, and at twenty as a collège classique graduate.

Jean-Marie Gaul

Home... The two dwellings of Pierre Trudeau's early life – the first a modest row-house on Montreal's Rue Durocher, where he lived until the age of twelve, the second his mother's unpretentious establishment in Outremont, where he lived until he was forty.

Jean-Marie Gaul

... and school: The two institutions of Trudeau's early education –
his elementary school, Académie Querbes, and Jean-de-Brébeuf,
the Jesuit college where he excelled at logic and languages.

The inveterate traveller: Trudeau as an insouciant student in post-war Paris, an adventurer in the Middle East, and a fearless fact-finder with Jacques Hébert in Mao's China.

The dutiful son: Pierre Trudeau at thirty-two with his widowed mother Grace on his shoulders; at thirty-three with his family in Montreal (mother, sister Suzette Rouleau, brother Tip Trudeau, and Tip's wife, Andrée); and at forty with his whole family at a friend's wedding celebration in 1960.

The advocate of change: Pierre Trudeau in his thirties and forties acted as a polemicist for *Cité libre* and worked as a labour lawyer (here with union leader Gérard Picard) before joining the federal Liberal Party in 1965, "in a frantic hurry to change reality."

Soul-searching titles on books published at the time (*Must Canada Fail? Canada in Crisis!*) echoed the widespread belief that the Canadian experiment had gone irreparably wrong and that if there was a way out of the country's difficulties, Trudeau did not know it. His government was described everywhere as exhausted, scandal-ridden, unprincipled, and incompetent. His election slate was weak and likely to remain so, since several of the important candidates recruited to strengthen the Liberal team had backed out during the long run-up to the election's call or had been defeated in by-elections and refused to stand again. His relations with the media and with the intellectual community had remained abysmal. Labour leaders still reviled him for what they considered repressive and unfair wage and price controls that had been far more effective in holding back union demands than in restraining the escalation of prices.[29]

All Trudeau had going for him as he faced up to the election, which was finally called on March 26 for May 22, 1979, was the Quebec electoral strength that his colleague Marc Lalonde had held together for the last three years since taking over from Marchand the chore of Quebec lieutenant, the professionalism of his Toronto political advisers, and his own bravado. "I can lose but I never do," he told a group of reporters, in what they took to be a display of his arrogant pugnacity but was in fact the defiance of a courageous man who was going to the electorate almost certain that he would lose.[30]

These assets were not enough to re-elect Trudeau. All the Liberals managed, in a taxing campaign waged in front of the hostile media, was to snatch a narrow defeat from the jaws of political destruction. With Marc Lalonde's iron control of the Quebec party organization, the Toronto group's sophisticated mastery of the techniques of electoral manipulation, and Trudeau's residual appeal to the public imagination, the Liberals were able to enhance their solid base in Quebec and hold onto enough seats in English Canada to prevent the Tories from gaining a majority victory.[31]

The Trudeau who stood on the platform in the Château Laurier ballroom on the night of May 22, 1979, bravely promising to fight again another day, may have thought the worst was behind him. But there were further vicissitudes to come. Having been defeated politically, he was no longer diverted by the urgencies of power from confronting the full implications of the life crisis into which his still-unresolved marital troubles had led him.

CHAPTER 7

DEFEAT, HUMILIATION, AND RESIGNATION

In the next few months, while the Tories prepared to run their minority government as if it were a majority and the Liberals set up shop in the leader of the opposition's office, Pierre Trudeau said nothing about the cataclysmic effect on him of the twin defeats he had suffered at the hands of the electorate and his wife. The day after the election, newspapers throughout the world had carried a wire-service photo of his wife boogying the night away in Studio 54, a notorious celebrity hang-out in New York. It had been taken in the early hours of the morning of May 23, while Trudeau was absorbing the news of his election losses, and it showed Margaret, daffy smile fixed on her lovely face, arms waving, leg kicking, "wearin' my pink pedal pushers and my dancin' shoes ... I thought I could get over the cruel disappointment of it all ... if only I could *smile* and *dance*!" The picture was too perfectly symbolic of Trudeau's downfall to need elaboration, and the cutlines the newspaper deskmen wrote to run with it were mostly deadpan. Margaret Sinclair Trudeau had become a mythical figure in the Canadian landscape: the dingbat in the northern attic, the flower child run wild.[1]

Throughout this latest season of betrayal, Trudeau had continued his practice of remaining silent, keeping a dignified distance from his wife's shenanigans, maintaining steadfastly that his personal life was his own business. His political advisers had tried to keep him from reading her book and had been appalled to find him poring over newspaper excerpts from it in hotel rooms at night as he toured the country on the campaign trail. Once he was defeated, Margaret had come home to Ottawa again, ostensibly to pack up her belongings from the 24 Sussex Drive house and the prime minister's country residence at Harrington Lake and to comfort the three Trudeau children during the family's move to Stornoway, the house provided for the leader of the opposition. As usual, her presence provoked one domestic scene after another. When one old Liberal hand went to Sussex Drive for a consultation with Trudeau, he was confronted by a particularly embarrassing tableau. Margaret was holding an impromptu farewell party for the household staff, including the RCMP security officers, and was trying to induce a couple of the men to throw the former prime minister into the swimming pool as their contribution to the general hilarity. When Trudeau refused to be dunked, the Mounties resorted to force. For the onlookers, it was an unforgettable sight: the intellectual-statesman clinging grimly with both hands to a door jamb until the two beefy Mounties succeeded in breaking his hold and pitching him into the water fully clothed.[2]

Trudeau's political staff, now reduced to a palace guard, marvelled that he could absorb this kind of indignity in private and still occasionally display his old insouciance in public. When he made his official farewell call as prime minister on the governor general, he drove himself to Rideau Hall in a Mercedes convertible he had not been seen in since 1968; and after the formalities were over inside, he vaulted into the car and roared away in style just before Joe Clark and his new cabinet arrived to be sworn into office. In the same spirit, he attended the elaborate wedding of the daughter of the American ambassador, Thomas Enders, proposing champagne toasts to his deposed ministers at the reception and dancing suavely with all the bridesmaids, as though making sure, as Sandra Gwyn wrote in *Saturday Night*, that everybody in the room got the message: "You're going to be sorry when I'm gone."[3]

Apart from giving a single press conference in July, when he dealt with speculative questions about his future with the cocky assertion "My judgement, as of now, is that I am the best [possible leader of the Liberal Party]," he withdrew from the Ottawa scene to spend the summer engrossed in favourite pursuits as though trying to recapture the spirit of his pre-political life. He made an arduous canoe trip in the Northwest Territories, paddling all day for a week with men twenty or thirty years younger than himself. He grew a beard and was seen dating the glamorous classical guitarist Liona Boyd. He travelled to China with his friend the architect Arthur Erickson, not quite in the old wandering-with-a-rucksack style since he had appointments with officials in Beijing, but more in the spirit of an adventurous holiday rather than an official visit.[4]

Early in the autumn, after this long summer of escape and denial, reality hit on both the personal and political fronts. Margaret Trudeau, who had been quiet for the summer months, became the subject of controversy once more. Among the soft-porn short stories and photo layouts of male nudes that constituted its standard fare, the American magazine *Playgirl* published in its September issue an interview with her that set a new standard in indiscretion. Into an editor's tape recorder Margaret Trudeau had poured further memories and reflections that she had left out of her book: stories about the occasions when she had indulged in celebrity love-making (a sport apparently much like celebrity tennis but conducted on shifting playing grounds, such as the back of a Daimler or the men's washroom of a famous hotel); about the abortion she had undergone in her teens; about the way she was now buying her own caviar and refusing to sniff amyl nitrate like the perfect lady she wanted to become; about the pleasure she was taking in invading Trudeau's privacy by graphically describing their life together to strangers and intimates alike. Hard on the heels of these revelations a photograph was published, this time in another magazine, called *High Society*, in which Margaret was shown once again cavorting in a New York club, sitting with legs apart, nether parts unclad.[5]

While these outrages were being clucked over in political circles, preparations were accelerating for the opening of the first sessions of the thirty-first Parliament, which the newly elected prime minister, Charles Joseph Clark, had delayed for over four months while his fledgling cabinet prepared to govern. The Rt. Hon. Pierre Elliott Trudeau, MP, would have to face the House of Commons in the unaccustomed roles of leader of the official opposition and the nation's most famous cuckold. Not surprisingly, his appearances there were infrequent (newspapermen calculated he was in the Commons during October and early November only about a fifth of the time it was sitting) and his performance – apart from a powerful Leaders' Day speech scripted by Tom Axworthy – was widely described as lacklustre. Newspaper columnists and television analysts kept up a running series of commentaries to the effect that Trudeau would never again be prime minister and that the Liberal Party was in the process of withering away.[6]

The seriousness of this situation reverberated throughout Liberal ranks, adding fresh fuel to the party's discontent. After years of being treated as ignorant footsoldiers expected to mobilize at election time but acquiesce in between, Liberal militants, who had remained publicly steadfast though privately seething during the government's deterioration in the 1970s, were now insisting on their right to be heard inside and outside the party's formal machinery. In recent months, the party's national executive had been the forum for an acrimonious battle between English-Canadian Liberals, who wanted to be rid of Trudeau so they could rebuild the party under a leader more attuned to their concerns, and French-Canadian Trudeauites, who – though critical of his deadening impact on the extra-parliamentary party – were desperate to defend him against repudiation. At the national executive's quarterly meeting in July, it was only the procedural dexterity of Jean Marchand, now a senator and a Quebec representative on the national executive, that postponed a crucial decision that had become the focus of the anglophone campaign to oust Trudeau. The question involved the timing of the next biennial convention, at which the party constitution required an automatic secret ballot on whether to hold a leadership convention. Since this leadership review could be made to serve as an impersonal mechanism for forcing Trudeau out, most of the anglophones on the executive wanted to hold the convention as soon as possible. The French Canadians wanted to wait at least until the autumn of 1980, after the Quebec referendum had been decided. The vote was a close shave, with the francophones winning a reprieve until the next meeting in November. Anglophone dissidents had tears of rage in their eyes at being thwarted, but they maintained discipline and said nothing to the press.

No sooner was the review question contained temporarily than another brushfire broke out. The Grindstone Group, an informal collective of party reformers that included activists from the extra-parliamentary wing, former ministerial assistants, and a few caucus members, had been meeting for several years to talk about Liberalism's future. This ginger group decided that since the party leadership was unwilling, they would organize a policy conference to start the process of ideological renewal that they believed Liberals should undertake before they could select a new leader. They commissioned eight policy papers for discussion and invited some two hundred of the party's most energetic militants (both francophone and anglophone), including over two dozen MPs and former ministers, to a weekend thinkfest in Winnipeg "to broaden the party process by generating fresh forward looking ideas and initiatives that may serve to revitalize the Liberal Party." Conspicuous by their absence were the leader himself, his principal secretary, senior policy adviser, former campaign manager, and Quebec lieutenant.[7]

Their absence spoke volumes about the party's disaffection with its leadership. Having won the leader's job in the first place as an eloquent advocate of participatory democracy, Trudeau had fallen prey to oligarchy's iron law. The tight little clique in his office that party adherents resentfully described as the "PMO in-group" was a textbook illustration of Robert Michels's famous analysis of how a leader is isolated by his "camarilla" or palace guard of advisers. In the less-regimented atmosphere of defeat, Liberal activists expressed openly their poisonous hatred for the leader's staff for supposedly having given him advice they thought had run the Liberal Party into the ground. They were less open in expressing their anger at Trudeau's own behaviour, a feeling they voiced mainly in whispers in the corridors and coffee shops of the conference hotel.[8]

Although Trudeau had made some effort to attend party meetings across the country in the summer and early fall, his performances at these gatherings had been half-hearted. He balked at the pressure his staff put on him to sell himself to the "second-rate men of action," which was the way he described the people serving on the party's provincial executives. "They know who I am," he told James Coutts, who was still his principal secretary in opposition. For one important party gathering – a weekend meeting of British Columbia Liberals in Vancouver – he did not show up at all, having sent word that he was suffering with the flu, though he was spotted by photographers entering a New York nightclub with a date. Even without this mishap, it was virtually certain, despite the efforts of Trudeau's staff and his francophone allies, that the national executive would vote at its next meeting on November 24 on whether to hold the party convention in the spring with its automatic ballot on the leadership. Given the state of the party's morale, it was clear that the executive's decision would be yes and that Trudeau would have to suffer the humiliation of fighting to retain his leadership.[9]

As these problems swirled around him, Trudeau had become withdrawn and intermittently depressed. His insouciance had vanished along with the rose from his lapel. He looked and spoke as though he felt his age and his defeat fully for the first time. Coutts had tried valiantly to talk him out of this state of mind by telling him that if only the Liberals played their cards right, the Tory government could be defeated and he would be prime minister once more. He had responded to these pep talks listlessly, as though such promises were of diminishing interest. Finally, on the morning of November 21, just three days before the national executive meeting, Trudeau called his key staff members to his office at the unusually early hour of nine o'clock to tell them he intended to resign. He had written a letter to the party president, Senator Alasdair

Graham, advising the national executive to convoke a leadership convention to choose his successor.[10]

The announcement took the country by surprise, although the resignation was soon seen as having been inevitable. After all, the Trudeau era had lasted for eleven years and had really ended on May 22. Trudeau was yesterday's man. The features pages and the television news shows dragged out their standard photos and footage summing up the brilliant career in visual images. The editorialists and columnists paid him their last respects, though the general tone of their offerings was grudging. He was said to be leaving the public stage an enigma still, a prime minister whose great promise had never been fulfilled, the stubborn proponent of an impossible dream, a failed politician who would now fade away into the oblivion where grand old men abide.[11]

For Trudeau's camarilla these "obituaries," as they took to calling them, were galling. Tom Axworthy, who had been acting as chief policy adviser in the leader of the opposition's office, said afterwards, "I couldn't sleep the night he resigned. I kept pounding my pillow and saying to my wife, 'The son of a bitch. He shouldn't have done it. We could have got it back for him.'"

The sentiment Axworthy was expressing – fierce loyalty in the face of great odds – had permeated the opposition office since Trudeau's staff moved there after his fall from grace in May. They had left behind them in the Prime Minister's Office a sign that proclaimed, "We'll be back." James Coutts, who prided himself on his capacity to keep cool under pressure, had spent the summer and fall resolutely telling all comers, "We were defeated, not destroyed." What Coutts was not telling anybody outside his own small circle was that he had concocted a careful strategy for snatching the government back. Very few other people wanted to listen to his optimistic pronouncements, in any case, or to take part in his comeback schemes.[12]

Coutts had been in bad odour in the gossipy world of Canadian politics for two or three years. Having once been seen among the powerful and would-be powerful as a wit and a great little guy, a politician both acute and accommodating, he was now described as an arch-manipulator, a political operator without principle – and, what was worse, a man whose stratagems had not worked. *Le tout Ottawa* professed to be glad to see him and his boss out of power in the summer and fall of 1979, happy to know that they had got their comeuppance. Coutts bore with fortitude this abuse from people who had previously curried his favour, drawing comfort from precepts he had absorbed in the course of his long career. One of his favourites was a wry maxim Lester Pearson had been fond of quoting: "Be nice to the people you encounter on your way up the ladder of success. You're bound to run into them again on your way down."

Under the circumstances, Coutts had not expected to be commended for his performance as Trudeau's amanuensis on the campaign trail in 1979 – as he had been in 1974 – although in many ways, the services he rendered his leader during that bleak electoral season were more remarkable than anything he had done in a quarter-century of devotion to Liberalism that had begun when he was a teenager in a small Alberta town. His party loyalty had continued through his years as a law student, provincial campaign organizer, appointments secretary to Pearson, candidate for an MBA at the Harvard Business School, Toronto management consultant, and finally principal secretary to Pierre Trudeau. A small man with a sunny demeanour that concealed a calculating mind, Coutts had been acutely aware that the chances of a Liberal victory in the 1979 election were almost nil. But while all around him Liberals were talking of Armageddon, Coutts remained calm. In that horrendously difficult 1979 campaign, he had steered Trudeau through eight weeks of punishing performances on the hustings without losing his resolve or his determination to use every wile he and his colleagues could command to try to keep the Tories from a majority. (He had on one occasion lost his cool in public and had been seen with tears in his eyes, which he claimed were the result not of frustration but of having been moved by one of Trudeau's speeches.) Coutts knew that Canadians had trusted the Liberal Party for over forty years because of its historic managerial competence and that they mistrusted the Tories' shaky young leader. Coutts had a longterm agenda and the first item on it was to struggle to keep the party's losses to a minimum so they could live to win another day. Even though the Liberals won twenty-two fewer seats than the Tories on May 22, they lost twenty of them by less than a thousand votes and pulled 40 per cent of the total vote, as against 36 per cent for the Conservatives, 18 per cent for the NDP, and 5 per cent for Crédit social.[13]

That feat having been achieved, Coutts set about getting ready for the next election, which he was sure would come within the year. While nearly every other Grit in the country was in despair in the aftermath of the 1979 defeat, Coutts was hard at work. It was Coutts who had advised Trudeau to stay out of the limelight during the summer of '79 while Clark was enjoying his brief honeymoon with the press and public. It was Coutts who had insisted that the leader of the opposition's office operate as much like a PMO-in-exile as possible with weekly strategy meetings and extensive briefing notes for the leader. It was Coutts, with the expert help of Axworthy, who had proposed the make-up of the shadow cabinet and the caucus policy committees that were intended to energize the Liberal MPs in opposition. It was Coutts who "fought off the alligators" by trying to contain Trudeau's critics within the Liberal Party, calling up every procedural manoeuvre in the book to stall the national executive's deliberations, deciding to "smother with love" the reformers' policy meeting in Winnipeg by urging loyal caucus members to attend, turning aside questions about party feuds with bland assertions about democracy in the ranks and the need for participation and renewal. It was Coutts who maintained that Joe Clark and his Tories would defeat themselves.[14]

Coutts had held the newly elected Conservative prime minister in some disdain ever since their days as student politicians at the University of Alberta, Clark having played Tory leader of the opposition to Coutts's Liberal prime minister in a mock parliament. He had looked on while Clark dropped out of two law schools, worked as a not particularly distinguished assistant to Robert Stanfield, and then fetched up as an earnest backbencher in the House of Commons as the MP for Rocky Mountain. After Clark's fluke election as leader of the Progressive Conservative Party in 1976 when he was only thirty-six years old, Coutts did everything in his power as principal secretary to exploit his inexperience and the general scepticism about his leadership capacities. He saw to it that Clark was given a hard time in the House of Commons by the Liberal front bench. He persuaded Trudeau, when he was still prime minister, to hand out plum appointments to Conservative MPs who might have added to Clark's strengths as opposition leader. He encouraged and contributed to the endless stream of "Joe Who?" jokes with which members of the business and political élites entertained themselves in the late 1970s and that quickly found their way into the newspapers, helping form the public impression of the Tory leader. (Sample joke: Joe Clark is walking along a street in his Alberta home town of High River, with a duck under his arm. "What are you doing with that turkey?" a passer-by inquires. "That's not a turkey," Clark answers kindly. "It's a duck." "I wasn't talking to you, stupid," retorts the passer-by, "I was talking to the duck.")[15]

Even when Clark was ensconced as prime minister and observers spoke of conservatism holding sway in Canada for the rest of the century, Coutts buoyed himself and his cronies with the conviction that the Tory syndrome of governmental inexperience, internal conflict, and alienation from Quebec would trigger the self-destructive behaviour that had dogged every Conservative government since World War I. He downplayed the fact that Clark, under the shrewd campaign management of his friend Lowell Murray, had won the spring election by beating the Liberals at their own game of superb organization and masterful strategizing, preferring to blame the Liberals' defeat on their own loss of policy direction in the 1970s. This version of events implied that the Liberals were still the rightful governors of the country who had been temporarily displaced, an attitude that had persisted in the Liberal Party for decades and helped set the tone for the Ottawa press gallery's interpretation of the Clark government's performance as the Tories set about learning how to wield power in the summer and early fall of 1979 after sixteen years in opposition.[16]

From a caucus oversupplied with MPs from the west and undersupplied with members from Quebec, Clark had managed to put together a cabinet more progressive and more promising than Trudeau's last lengthy ministry. In the expectation that he could govern for two or three years with his substantial minority, Clark had proceeded with caution. He had given his ministers four months to prepare their legislative programs for presentation to the House of Commons. He had reconsidered his campaign threat to purge the senior ranks of the civil service on the grounds of its Liberal colouration. (He did fire Michael Pitfield, the clerk of the Privy Council, who was widely thought to hold his important job because he was Trudeau's close friend; but Clark kept in place the cabinet committee system that Pitfield had created and even adopted Pitfield's advice on how to correct its flaws.) This approach to government soon won over sceptical senior bureaucrats, who found Clark more effective as chairman of cabinet than Trudeau had been in the late 1970s. It was Clark's misfortune that outside official Ottawa, his earnest approach to his new job was interpreted as timidity rather than prudence.[17]

By the time Parliament had reconvened in October, Clark's persistent image as a "wimp" – an ugly Americanism the media were using to indicate he was a weak, limp leader – had been etched still more clearly on the public's mind by his difficulties in fulfilling his election promises. His campaign commitment to stimulate the economy by lowering taxes had come to grief at the hands of his own finance minister, John Crosbie, who had been quickly converted by officials in the Department of Finance to the tenets of fiscal conservatism. Another campaign promise – to move the Canadian embassy in Israel from Tel Aviv to Jerusalem – had foundered on the realities of Middle Eastern politics, in particular the threats of economic retaliation by the Arab oil states. His undertaking to privatize the Liberals' state oil company, Petro-Canada, had come up against the stubborn opposition of bureaucrats in the Energy Department, who were concerned about the need to offset the impact of yet another OPEC crisis that had blown up earlier in the year. Energy was also at the heart of an even more serious problem, Clark's inability to deliver quickly the co-operative federal-provincial relationships he had vowed would replace Trudeau's confrontational federalism. In federal-provincial exchanges over the summer and fall he proved unable to stand up to the scornful belligerence of the Conservative premier of energy-rich Alberta, Peter Lougheed. At the same time, his apparent readiness to yield to Lougheed's demands for increased oil prices angered William Davis, the Conservative premier of the industrial province of Ontario. The disharmonies of the Trudeau years had been replaced by disgruntlements of a different kind.[18]

Despite these difficulties, Clark and his close advisers believed his careful course was the right one and that he was safe in office, particularly after Trudeau resigned in late November. They were reckoning without the further machinations of James Coutts and the will to win of Pierre Trudeau.

CHAPTER 8

Restoration, Transformation, and Resurrection

James Coutts had been momentarily downcast by Pierre Trudeau's decision to resign in November 1979. He showed his upset visibly for a couple of days, smoking incessantly and talking distractedly at dinner with a friend the night after the announcement, scarcely even trying to put the best face on the situation. For Coutts and his close allies, Trudeau's departure would mean not just the end of the Trudeau era but the end – at least in the short term and perhaps even permanently – of their own political influence, given the widespread animosity their efforts on his behalf had aroused.[1]

But within a week Coutts had regained his jauntiness. At a party given to honour the government economist Sylvia Ostry, in Toronto on November 29, where the presence of the chief contenders for the Liberal succession, Donald Macdonald and John Turner, was adding an extra buzz to the festivities, Coutts moved smoothly among the guests, comforting his friends with his aphorisms, confounding his detractors with his wit. Half-way through the evening, Murray Frum, a real estate developer and shrewd observer of élite accommodation, asked a friend, "How come Coutts is in such a good mood? He must know something we don't."[2]

What Coutts knew was that some as yet unreleased polling data would prove what he had been telling Trudeau all fall. The "numbers" were there for the Liberals to win a sudden election, even if Trudeau was still their leader. Coutts also knew that there was a fighting chance the Tory government could be toppled in the vote of confidence that would occur routinely in the House of Commons during the budget debate the following month.[3]

December began auspiciously when the newspapers published a Gallup poll showing the Liberals had the support of 47 per cent of decided voters, against the Conservatives' 28 per cent and the NDP's 23 per cent, figures that confirmed the Goldfarb polls Coutts had commissioned himself. He kept his comforting calculations to himself, however, and told inquiring journalists that the Gallup results made no difference now that Trudeau has resigned. To close friends he said he needed to think about his own future and intended to fly to Florida for a few days to stay in the Palm Beach house of Paul Desmarais, the Montreal multimillionaire.

By the time he returned to Ottawa on December 9, Coutts was restored to his usual fine fettle. It was budget week in the capital and he was certain that a drama of some sort would unfold, though for all his determination, not even Coutts could know in advance how profoundly the events of the next ten days would shake up the Canadian political world.

The first surprise came on Monday morning, December 10, when John Turner, the former finance minister turned Bay Street lawyer, called a press conference in Toronto to announce that he would *not* seek the Liberal leadership, a prize many Liberal loyalists in both French and English Canada were certain was his for the taking. Political Ottawa was still mulling over this news the following evening when the House met to hear the details of the

Conservatives' "face-the-facts" budget. With the Commons galleries crowded with the curious, the finance minister, John Crosbie, began to read the government's austere economic measures, interspersing his text with partisan jibes in his practised Newfoundland lilt. Sitting in the gallery, Coutts could scarcely contain his delight. The budget's tax increases were so resolutely regressive, so tough on the little guy, so oriented to the affluent, it went beyond his fondest hopes.[4]

Not just Coutts but several other clear-headed Grits in the chamber – particularly Allan MacEachen, who was still the Liberal House leader, and Marc Lalonde, now the party's energy critic – knew immediately that the budget could be attacked with vigour as an affront to the ordinary voter. Their view was confirmed after Crosbie's speech was over, when Liberal MPs talked over the budget's provisions with officials and journalists in the Commons lobbies and at the post-budget office parties. The Tories' proposed 18-cent-per-gallon increase in the tax on gasoline may have been fiscally sound in its conception as a way to finance one election promise Clark was determined to keep, that of giving a tax credit for mortgage payments and property taxes. But this backhanded way of penalizing working people to subsidize middle-class home ownership was a huge political mistake. It was a signal that Tory times are hard times, tangible proof that although Clark might talk like a prairie progressive, his finance minister was Bay Street's navy-blue tool.[5]

The next morning at the weekly Liberal caucus, the Liberals' determination to take action firmed up as the party's MPs, guided by a persuasive speech given by Allan MacEachen, admonished one another not just to vote against the budget of this heartless government but to stand together to bring it down. By Wednesday evening at the annual Liberal Christmas party, alcohol and the exhilaration of the impending parliamentary battle created a kind of euphoria among the Liberal throng. For the first time in years the Liberals as a collective felt they could agree on what the party stood for. It was as though the traumas and confusions of the 1970s, when the party was seen as corrupt by outsiders and was riven by factionalism within, could be left behind. No matter how much personal success or power Liberals strove for and attained, most of them harboured the notion that they belonged to a reform party concerned with social equity, that they were indeed liberals. In one stroke the Tories had given them back a sense of purpose.

Thursday morning rumours began to circulate on Parliament Hill that Clark and his cabinet had failed to recognize how precarious was their hold on power. The Tories had agreed earlier, through their House leader, that the night of Thursday, December 13, would bring the traditional vote of confidence on the budget, but they had neglected to make sure that they could muster a majority of votes in the House to defend it. Several of their own members were away from the capital. Their sometime ally the Créditiste leader Fabien Roy, who had backed the Conservative minority in two confidence votes held earlier in the autumn, was upset by the government's insensitivity to the impact the new gas tax would have on Quebeckers, particularly on farmers and small-business owners in his own constituency in the Beauce. He let the Conservatives know through an intermediary that his caucus, which had shrunk to five (one member having defected to the Tories), would abstain from the vote unless the government made a commitment to use the new gas revenues for energy projects in Quebec. Clark, who thought he could squeeze the Créditistes into joining the Conservatives' diminutive Quebec contingent, rejected Roy's proposal outright. The prime minister's thinking, which was heavily influenced by advice from his election campaign chairman, Lowell Murray, was based on the belief that when the crucial vote came that evening, the Liberals would lose their nerve. Surely with the party leaderless, the Grits would not be able to persuade their full caucus to vote against the government in company with the New Democrats, who were eager to precipitate an election campaign before the Liberals had resolved their leadership imbroglio. Even if the Grits were cocky enough to engineer such a manoeuvre, the Tories believed they themselves would win the ensuing election. It would be like 1958 all over again, that glorious year when the previous Conservative prime minister, John Diefenbaker, had followed his minority win of 1957 with a huge majority victory by campaigning against the Liberals and their ineradicable arrogance.[6]

Clark's advisers had declined to conduct polls of their own since August, despite the opinion of their pollster, Allan Gregg, that their support was softening, and had dismissed the Gallup results of the previous week as an aberration. Refusing to postpone the vote of confidence at least until the following Monday by a procedural delay that would have brought their ranks back to full strength and broken down the tenuous solidarity in the Liberal caucus, the Clark Conservatives went stolidly into the House at eight o'clock on Thursday night prepared to meet their fate. When it was suggested afterwards to a prominent Liberal that the Tories' decision to honour their commitment to the vote was both brave and principled, he remarked, "That wasn't bravery. It was stupidity. Those klutzes can't even count."[7]

The Liberals, of course, could count. And they had pulled into the House of Commons that night every Liberal MP but one, including a member who had to come by ambulance from an Ottawa hospital. At 10:23 P.M. they got their reward. The government went down to defeat by a vote of 139 to 133, and Prime Minister Joe Clark rose to announce he would seek out the governor general forthwith and ask for a dissolution of Parliament. The first half of Coutts's game plan had been achieved: the election was on. The second half depended on the Liberal Party and its erstwhile leader responding as Coutts's reading of their respective characters led him to hope they would.[8]

Throughout this drama, Trudeau had maintained the distanced attitude towards politics and politicians he had adopted weeks before. During the Wednesday caucus he had agreed that the Tories deserved to be defeated on the budget, while at the same time reminding his colleagues that his opinion had no more relevance than anyone else's since he would not be Liberal leader in a sudden election in any case. Then, during the ensuing strategy session on that afternoon's Question Period, he had flatly refused to pose the leading questions about the budget that the Liberals' transport critic, Ed Lumley, had drafted in order to drive a wedge between Clark and the Créditistes. "I'm finished [as leader]," he explained. When his parliamentary assistant, Joyce Fairbairn, remonstrated, "Sir, you've been proven right [on their energy tax]," he cut her off curtly with the statement, "I'm out of it." At the caucus Christmas party that evening he had been visibly ill at ease; the mask he usually put on at such affairs – that of the seigneur among his people – was nowhere in evidence.[9]

Thursday's spellbinding events did not appear to alter his attitude. He went through the motions of voting the government down in the House apparently unmoved. When the Liberals caucused on Friday morning to discuss what should be done about the party leadership in view of the impending election campaign, Trudeau turned delphic. When the possibility of his return was raised, he said, "The sovereign would have to ask me three times on bended knee." Requesting that the caucus hold a secret ballot on the question, the ex-leader left the meeting precipitately and drove off to spend the weekend in Montreal, where he was in the midst of negotiating the purchase of a house. The message he left behind him was ambiguous. Some MPs interpreted his remarks to mean that Trudeau was unwilling to return to the fray. Others felt he was playing an elaborate game of tease, holding out his arm and saying, "Here, twist it and force me to return." Still others saw him as uncertain about what to do and needing persuasion one way or the other. Allan MacEachen belonged to the last group. As one of the few Pearsonian Liberals still on the public stage, MacEachen was a left-wing Catholic and saw himself very much as a liberal Liberal. He believed Trudeau's return was vital for the survival of the Liberal Party, and to this end he put to work the eloquence learned with the Gaelic he had heard in Cape Breton at his mother's knee. When the caucus broke into regional components to discuss the Trudeau question, he had little difficulty persuading his fellow Maritimers. But when the whole caucus reconvened later in the afternoon, he discovered it was a long way from unanimity.

The tiny western group was vehemently opposed, saying Trudeau's return would abort the leadership hopes of the Winnipeg MP Lloyd Axworthy and doom the party's candidates west of the Great Lakes to almost certain defeat. The Ontario caucus was split on the question. MPs who were supporting the still-unannounced bid for the leadership of Donald Macdonald, the other former finance minister practising law in Toronto, balked at the idea, while those who had supported John Turner's aborted candidacy now preferred to have Trudeau back in harness temporarily if this would increase their chances of getting Turner to reconsider and run at a later date. The Quebec caucus was solidly in favour of reinstating Trudeau. (The surprising exception was Marc Lalonde, who felt that Trudeau should be spared the ordeal of yet another election campaign, which he thought the Liberals would lose.) Jean Marchand urged his confrères to abstain from the vote in the national caucus lest its sixty-seven members be seen as using their majority to force Trudeau down the Liberal Party's throat. In the interest of national unity, he felt the decision should be left to the forty-seven MPs representing the anglophone provinces.

Facing these strong cross-currents, MacEachen stood up to deliver what his colleagues would later recall as the most brilliant speech of his career. Reminding the caucus members that just two days earlier, they had decided to do everything in their collective power to bring down the Conservative government, he called on them now to be consistent in their actions and true to their principles. MacEachen knew from talking to Martin Goldfarb that the Liberals had a twenty-point lead in the polls his firm had conducted. He knew, too, that no party's pre-election support had ever fallen by more than 10 per cent during the course of a campaign since the first use of modern polling techniques in the 1940s. Clearly, the party was assured of a majority victory. What it could not afford was to have its candidates' energies sapped by a bitterly divisive leadership race in the middle of an election campaign. The speech proved to be a turning point. Member after member rose to speak in support of MacEachen's position. By the end of the evening, the caucus agreed unanimously (but without holding a secret ballot, which would have allowed the doubters to manifest their dissent) that Trudeau be asked to return as leader forthwith. The sovereign had bent his knee a first time.

To persuade a caucus experiencing the catharsis of a highly charged collective experience was one thing. To achieve consensus within the extra-parliamentary party's angry executive would be quite another. When the national executive of the Liberal Party convened in an emergency meeting on the morning of Saturday, December 15, most of its anglophone members were infuriated by the caucus decision, which they felt had been manipulated by Coutts through MacEachen and had made Trudeau's return a virtual fait accompli. Knowing there was no way he could win unanimous support for Trudeau from this group even in a voice vote, MacEachen marshalled his arguments once more, relying on the francophone caucus chairman, Jacques Guilbault, to make the case for Quebec and trusting that some of his anglophone allies from the extra-parliamentary wing would see the light. Gordon Dryden, the party treasurer, reported that, yes, the party's finances could sustain an election on short notice. Some speakers then demanded that this time the party executive must participate in formulating the campaign platform, voicing their determination that the "PMO in-group" be restrained from dominating the leader. Finally, a motion was put to the meeting that Trudeau be asked to return as leader: twenty voted in favour, five were opposed, and six abstained. Afterwards, a francophone member of the executive sought out Lorna Marsden, the University of Toronto sociologist and a party policy activist for several years, who had previously supported the call for an early leadership review but now favoured Trudeau's return. He told her that he was relieved to discover she was not a racist after all. French-English wrangling in the executive that had gone on for many months was now set aside. The sovereign had bent his knee a second time.[10]

The party's chief power brokers then planned to gather at Stornoway on Sunday afternoon, when Trudeau returned to Ottawa, to tell him what had transpired over the previous forty-eight hours. Coutts and Axworthy arrived early to give their boss the results of a secret telephone poll that Goldfarb's firm had carried out in six key ridings on Friday and Saturday. It confirmed that the Liberals would win the election, doing as well with Trudeau in English Canada as they would with any other potential leader and far better in Quebec. Once this news had been discussed, the three men were joined by Torrance Wylie, the Liberal Party's official agent, Senators Alasdair Graham of Nova Scotia and Gil Molgat of Manitoba, representing the national executive, and Allan MacEachen and Jacques Guilbault, representing the anglophone and francophone sections of the caucus. Conflicting ideas and arguments were aired. Trudeau summarily rejected the suggestion that he would have to accept the conditions that the party executive might want to impose. Tom Axworthy pointed out that Trudeau's chance of affecting the referendum campaign would be enhanced if he were prime minister rather than simply a citizen, no matter how distinguished. The overall message was: the party needs you to win the election, Quebec needs you for the referendum, and the country needs you to hold it together. The sovereign had genuflected for the third time, but his subject still had to decide whether to accede to the request.

On Monday, December 17, Trudeau continued to ponder the imponderable. He telephoned his friend Gérard Pelletier, at the Canadian embassy in Paris, and his friend Jacques Hébert, in Montreal, for advice. He called Michael Pitfield, who was now lecturing at the Kennedy School of Government in Cambridge, Massachusetts, to inquire whether he would return to his former job as clerk of the Privy Council if Trudeau were to win the election. He went to lunch at the Château Laurier Grill with Gordon Robertson, his previous clerk of the Privy

Council and secretary to the cabinet for federal-provincial relations, who was retiring from the public service after thirty-five years. After Robertson finished lunch and departed, Trudeau joined Coutts, Axworthy, Davey, and MacEachen, who were eating together in one of the dining room's side alcoves. He had a series of "hypothetical" questions to put to these loyalists. Supposing he did return – and he was far from such a decision – what would the party do for policy? Axworthy assured him that his research staff would be able to pull together a platform in short order with the help of some selected party people. Trudeau did some other nitpicking, but his tone was such that even Coutts began to feel uneasy.

Coutts and his accomplices had trotted out every argument in their arsenal but the boss still would not budge. Coutts went back to his office and telephoned Ed Lumley, the caucus transport critic, who, as an ardent Turner supporter, had first thought the budget manoeuvre would be disastrous. Once the Tory government had been toppled, Lumley had come round to MacEachen's view: there would be blood on the floor if a leadership campaign were held now. He had phoned Turner, who agreed that Trudeau was the best man in the circumstances. MacEachen had urged Lumley on Sunday to tell Trudeau that party support for his resurrection now went well beyond his staff and the Liberal left wing. Now Coutts, who had done his best to isolate Trudeau from party dissenters, pressed Lumley to talk directly to the boss. Lumley asked Don Johnston, another MP from the party's so-called right wing, who was also Trudeau's Montreal lawyer, to accompany him to Stornoway, where they talked with the former prime minister for over an hour. Although Trudeau said he was touched that these anglophones would come to say "We need you," Lumley and Johnston reported back to Coutts at dinner that they could not tell which way he was leaning. Eventually, Coutts excused himself and went back to the leader of the opposition's office to ask Axworthy to draft two speeches for Trudeau to choose from at the press conference scheduled for the next day, one rejecting, the other accepting the party's request that he return from retirement.

On the morning of Tuesday, December 18, uncertainty still prevailed. When Coutts telephoned Stornoway first thing, Trudeau told him his answer was probably no. Coutts rushed to Rockcliffe in order to recite his arguments once more. In summing up, he challenged Trudeau head on. "What are you afraid of?" he asked and went on to spin his carefully considered argument. You have nothing to lose, he told Trudeau, other than a couple of months for the campaign. If we lose the election, you will be in exactly the same position you are in now. But if we win – and the numbers indicate we can win decisively – you will be able to achieve your political goals. You can battle Lévesque on the referendum and move immediately on the constitutional agenda as you proposed in the spring campaign. *Then* you can retire and the obituaries they write will be very different from the ones you saw in November.

It was an encounter operatic in its intensity. Coutts, an unlikely Mephistopheles in bow tie and suspenders, was offering Faustus a final chance to make his heroic dreams come true. At almost the last moment, Trudeau made up his mind. The two men drove downtown to the press conference together, with Coutts the only other person in the country who knew that Trudeau meant to reassume the Liberal leadership. The other chief perpetrator of the "keep Trudeau steady" scheme, Tom Axworthy, was anxiously watching the press conference on television from the leader of the opposition's office when Trudeau entered the National Press Building's conference room and prepared to read his declaration. Only when Axworthy saw Trudeau pull from his pocket the longer of the two texts he had written the night before did he know that Trudeau's decision was in the affirmative. The shorter statement was a graceful "Thanks, but no thanks" speech that would now never be delivered. Trudeau had resolved to fight again. There was a battle in the offing and he was ready to smite his enemies once more.

What went on in Pierre Trudeau's mind that December day at Stornoway? Was he persuaded by the wily Coutts? Or had he decided that he wanted another chance at the Liberal leadership as soon as the government's downfall became apparent and then managed the situation adroitly in order to create that opportunity? When asked such questions directly by reporters at the time he was characteristically opaque. Throughout his public career Trudeau was always at pains to suggest that he never actively sought power for himself, but that it was thrust upon him by the workings of fate or the demands of others or the necessity of defending his principles.

Years later, in talking about what had motivated him to withdraw his resignation and return to political life in 1979, he still spoke carefully, as if viewing his own actions from a great distance, implicitly rejecting the notion that he had been involved in a conspiracy to regain power and explicitly underlining the importance for him of his unfinished fight with René Lévesque, the premier of Quebec, for the hearts and minds of French Canadians. In a conversation in June 1985, he said of those events:

"When I resigned in November 1979, I saw an election coming, probably in the spring. I resigned because I wanted the Liberal Party to have time to choose a leader with a chance of winning that election. My resignation was sincere. It had something to do with my family, with the hope that once out of politics, things might . . . Well, the less said about that the better. What was of real importance was my recognition that I'd had my chance. From the time of my taking this decision [to resign] and the actual event, Clark brought down his budget.

"You could ask, 'Why did you vote against [the budget] if you didn't want an election?' It had become obvious that Clark couldn't hold his party or government together until the late spring, by which time the Liberals could be ready under a new leader to fight an election. In brief, the budget brought things to a head.

"At the same time, Lévesque had made it clear the referendum was at last going to be held. . . It was almost as though Lévesque was timing the referendum for when I was gone. . . Lévesque never posed the question until I was defeated [and had resigned]. . . Essentially, he hated my guts. He has said this to friends of mine. In essence, this influenced me.

"[I decided] if the party wanted me back I was ready to come back. In saying 'The sovereign will have to ask me three times on bended knee,' I was quoting an old Chinese legend about a mandarin being asked to return to his post and responding that he would only come if the emperor would ask him on his knees three times. I didn't want to come back unless I was asked three times, that is, unless I was absolutely certain that I was wanted. I counted that as having happened when I was asked by the caucus, the national executive, and my close colleagues, Coutts, MacEachen, Davey, and the rest. My friends were advising me against it. Lalonde, Marchand, Pelletier, Hébert told me not to run. 'You're going to be hurt very badly,' they said. They thought I would be badly beaten in the election. This was in the days just after Clark's government was defeated.

"By then I knew I was ahead in the polls – but not how much ahead, however. Things are written about polls that are not actually true. . . It was really the referendum that interested me. I felt I wasn't risking anything [in making the decision to come back]. The polls weren't relevant. The argument Coutts put to me was: 'What are you risking anyway? Just a couple of months of your life. You run and win. Or you run and lose and you're in the same place.' This was not literally true, but still I felt [my return as leader] was possible when you took into account this argument. I sensed the referendum would clear the air on separatism. But it would also force the Canadian people, and their leaders particularly, to do something on the constitution."[11]

These statements are as interesting for what they reveal about Trudeau's political motivations as for what they conceal about his personal responses. Fourteen years after entering the political arena, he was still fixated on the federalist–separatist struggle. For him, the possibility of plunging into it once more from a position of renewed strength overrode all other considerations, including the faint, and probably vain, hopes he still nurtured of reviving his marriage. At the age of sixty, he knew what he wanted from life, and when the moment came, he called on the courage he had painstakingly developed as a puny boy and shy young man and seized this last best chance that history was offering him.

The previous few months had been, according to Margaret Trudeau's later testimonial and the assertions of several of Trudeau's own close colleagues and friends, a time of severe testing for Pierre Trudeau. His political reversals along with the continuing deterioration of his marriage forced on him the kind of intense self-examination that most men experience sometime between thirty-five and forty-five but that he had managed to postpone until he was sixty. It was as though the inner turmoil that most people undergo in the middle of their lives, the suffering over and then acceptance of their losses and flaws, the recognition of their own mortality, their ordinariness, their humanity – the self-examination and suffering that Trudeau had resolutely escaped by remaining eternally youthful, rigorously rational, consistently a winner, as resolutely invincible as inherited wealth and outstanding intelligence could make him – had to be confronted by him now in a professional and personal crisis of truly heroic proportions. Circumstance was forcing him to examine his options, to deal with the disappointments of his marriage and his life's work, to review and evaluate his past (which aspects of it he could keep and which he had to say farewell to), and to consider what the possibilities were for his future. He had to find his way out of this transitional period in his life and to achieve what the social psychologists call "the good-enough solution."[12]

The tacticians on his staff, who were trying to hold him steady as opposition leader, saw him in this period as being in a state of suspended animation, unreliable, quixotic, distant, removed from their political concerns. His intimate friends saw him as undergoing a profound change, as turning inward once more after all the years of public grandstanding. "It was as though," as Jean Marchand described it, "his suffering over his losses was deepening him, making him into a far more mature human being. His pain was ennobling in a way that his victories had never been. His arrogance began to fall away."[13]

For the first time, Trudeau was able publicly to admit defeat and weakness. As he had put it to an interviewer from Le Devoir at the time of his resignation in November, "I came to the conclusion that I wasn't the man to rebuild the Liberal Party and to negotiate a new federalism over the next decade." For the first time he was compelled to consider the emotional needs of others before his own. His children's difficulties in dealing with their parents' separation became paramount to him that autumn, as they suffered taunts at school about their mother's behaviour and their father's ignominious position as a political loser. They seemed distraught as they bounced back and forth from Stornoway to Margaret's new house in New Edinburgh and as the hostility between their parents, which had long been played down in front of them, was now openly expressed. The family's troubles were compounded by the fact that Margaret Trudeau was taking heavy doses of mood-altering drugs as a prescribed therapy for her problems; at the same time, she was experiencing high anxiety about her financial situation since her husband refused to give her support money and her publishers had gone bankrupt without paying her the royalties she was owed for the book of revelations that had titillated the world's mass media eight months before.[14]

Earlier in the year, Trudeau had talked about the best treatment for Margaret Trudeau's erratic behaviour to various friends and acquaintances, including David Owen, who was a physician as well as the foreign minister in the British Labour government of James Callaghan, and Stuart Smith, the leader of the Liberal Party in Ontario, who had been a practising psychiatrist before entering politics. After his defeat, Trudeau had listened to representations from various friends who thought his treatment of Margaret was too harsh and unforgiving. His attitude towards her remained censorious. He did not appear to have come to grips with his own role in his marriage breakdown. Margaret was mentally disturbed, he kept saying, she needed treatment for her disorders, the lithium prescribed by a psychiatrist recommended by Stuart Smith would help her to shape up, to mother their three sons on a regular basis again and behave in ways he considered appropriate for his wife. The implication was that if only *she* would change, then their married life could be resumed.[15]

His decision on December 18 to re-enter politics put an end to such hopes almost as soon as he made it – as he suspected it would. A fortnight later, he came to a watershed moment in his marriage. The Trudeau family spent an awkward, unhappy Christmas at Stornoway, a holiday that Margaret found "horribly painful" since "there was not one single present for me under the tree." But it was not until New Year's that the catalytic event occurred. Trudeau had taken his sons to Montreal to see the spectacular house he had bought there in anticipation of his retirement, a coolly classical masterpiece in the Art Deco style. Margaret had spent the New Year's holiday in Montreal as well and had arranged to travel back to Ottawa with her husband and sons. The journey ended in an experience she described as follows:

"Pierre came into [my] house to help me put the boys to bed. As he was about to leave, I asked him for some money. I tried to sound reasonable. [Trudeau was notoriously close with his money and had quarrelled bitterly with Margaret over her extravagances for years.] 'Perhaps, Pierre, since you will be campaigning for the next couple of months and the boys will be living here, you might give me some sort of allowance for their keep?' was how I put it.

"Pierre reached casually into his pocket and took out his wallet. 'I don't think I've got much on me, Margaret. Will fifty dollars do?' His narrow eyes and slightly sneering laugh seemed to mock me. Something burst inside me. A three-hundred-thousand-dollar house [in Montreal] and all he was proposing was fifty dollars. It wasn't just mean, it was humiliating. He knew my debts. What did he think I was going to do?

"I don't remember much after that. I know I went for his eyes with my nails and had every intention of blinding him first and killing him afterward. I know that at that instant I hated him with a purer hate than I knew I possessed.

"Within seconds I found myself pinned down by his arms on the ground: Pierre is a brown belt in judo and had little trouble protecting himself. But I kept screaming, the sound coming from my mouth in bursts. The children awakened and stood, shocked, observing us.

"'Daddy, don't hurt Mummy,' Sacha kept pleading. Pierre shook me: 'Be quiet, Margaret, pull yourself together.'

"I kept yelling.

"In time the rage passed, but it was really Micha [the youngest Trudeau child, who was then four years old] who saved the day. As Pierre and I were sitting weakly in the bedroom, Micha called to Pierre to come to his room. They were gone half an hour, talking things over and Pierre always says that Micha put a lot of sense into him. Then he left."[16]

Trudeau apparently never again expected the marriage to work and shortly afterwards began a series of family counselling sessions in tandem with Margaret in order to discuss with a psychologist how to manage the upbringing of their sons. They were able to work out an arrangement for joint parenting and to stabilize their children's lives, a situation made much easier by Margaret's own decision to abandon the lithium treatment she felt had been forced on her and to put her own financial affairs in order by getting a job as an interviewer on a local television show.[17]

Trudeau began to take a different attitude not just to Margaret but to other people who were closely involved in his everyday life. When he turned up in his office prepared to carry out the first tasks of the 1980 campaign, his staff found him energetic, responsive, and unusually co-operative. Jerry Grafstein, the Toronto lawyer who was in charge of Liberal advertising (as he had been in the 1974 and 1979 campaigns), took Trudeau to an expensive haberdasher's to help him buy new clothes. His advisers had been disturbed by his sartorial vagaries over the previous year. In the 1979 campaign, he had insisted on constantly wearing a beige corduroy suit that made him "look like some kind of deep-thinking academic who didn't give a damn about his appearance." Over the summer he had resumed the adventurous-world-traveller look he had affected thirty-five years before by growing a beard that turned out to be almost white and made him look more like an aging prospector than a dashing graduate student. Then in the late fall he had adopted a different style altogether, that of a European boulevardier in a tight-waisted overcoat and a Borsalino hat. He seemed to be trying on costumes in order to redefine himself through his clothes.

Now, to Grafstein's amazement, Trudeau agreed to dress for political success, saying he would wear whatever Grafstein thought he should, his only caveat being that the Liberal Party would have to pay for the clothes. "At one point," Grafstein said afterwards in wonderment, "he actually seemed grateful for my advice on ties. He even remarked a little sadly that he hadn't had anybody care about how he looked since Margaret left him in 1977. He was an altogether different guy from the man I'd had to deal with the year before."[18]

Throughout the campaign that followed, Trudeau continued to behave like "an altogether different guy." To some observers, it seemed obvious that he had undergone the kind of personal transformation that psychologists call integration. It was as though in the crucible of the autumn and early winter, he had come to accept his limitations and his strengths, had decided what he could reasonably expect from the rest of his life and what kind of compromises he was prepared to make to achieve his goals. At the end of a painful period of near despair, he seemed to have come to an understanding of himself and others that he had never had before, to have gained an emotional maturity that matched his spiritual and intellectual development. He had become a whole man.[19]

This new attitude allowed him to submit to the election strategy devised by James Coutts and Keith Davey to keep the spotlight on Joe Clark's ineptitudes and off Trudeau's still-controversial style, a strategy they called "low-bridging the leader." Trudeau even agreed – though with reluctance – to his staff's plea that he keep silent on the constitution, the issue that he had insisted on stressing the previous May. They were basing their advice on the findings of Goldfarb's opinion polls that any mention of the national unity question reduced Trudeau's support in English Canada.[20]

Amazingly, Trudeau was also willing to listen to the economic advice of Herb Gray, a nationalist Liberal whom he had formerly banished from his cabinet to the backbenches. In the closing weeks of the 1980 campaign, he made vigorous speeches promising an industrial strategy and a more interventionist approach to the auto industry, to foreign investment, and, above all, to energy self-sufficiency. He resolutely held his temper in public, ignoring hecklers' taunts, and even gave in to his staff's demands that he appear at the traditional end-of-the-campaign party for the journalists travelling on his plane, who had taken to trading lines of poetry with him in an elaborate game devised to alleviate their boredom with what they saw as a "non-campaign." It was clear to most members of the media that the Liberals had mounted a shrewd and cynical exercise in image management, meant to manipulate the electorate's fears of Clark's perceived ineptitudes and to evoke memories of their own reputation for managerial competence without arousing any more latent public distrust of Trudeau than was absolutely necessary.

The strategy worked brilliantly, and on February 18, 1980, Trudeau found himself once more at the Château Laurier for an election-night celebration. This time the ballroom was thronged with cheering Grits celebrating their victory. This time their leader's face was luminous with pleasure as he delivered his thank-you speech. "Welcome to the 1980s!" he called out as an opening, and the line met with an atavistic roar of a kind that had not been heard since 1968. Twelve years of overblown hopes and wrenching disappointments were forgotten. Trudeau had climbed into the Canadian pantheon with John A. Macdonald and William Lyon Mackenzie King, the only other prime ministers who had managed to come back from electoral defeat.[21]

The speech was graceful, generous, and warm, and it ended with a quotation from "Stopping by Woods on a Snowy Evening," by the American poet Robert Frost:

> The woods are lovely, dark and deep,
> But I have promises to keep
> And miles to go before I sleep.

Most people in the Château ballroom thought he was referring to the campaign's implicit promise of new ideas for a new decade, of a regenerated Liberalism and a revitalized commitment to the role of the state. And they were partly right. But the promises uppermost in Trudeau's mind were the ones he had made to himself thirty years before when he decided that his mission in life was to save Quebec from its parochial nationalists and bring it into the modern world. At the age of sixty, he was facing the climactic years of a long struggle and he was determined, in a way he had never been before, to win the victory that really mattered to him.

PART II

TRUDEAU AND THE CONSTITUTION: THE MAGNIFICENT OBSESSION

CHAPTER 9

PICKING UP THE REINS OF POWER

Not long after he won his new majority, Pierre Trudeau spent an evening in the company of his old friend Madeleine Gobeil. As part of a general conversation devoted to catching up on each other's lives, she began to describe her job as a cultural affairs officer at UNESCO in Paris and finished by saying that she loved the power of it.

"Moi aussi," said Trudeau, happily. "J'adore ça. Chaque jour est comme le premier."[1]

For Gobeil the exchange was fraught with meaning. She and Trudeau had become closely involved in each other's lives in the mid-1950s when she was an undergraduate at the Université de Montréal. They had continued to see each other regularly after she became a lecturer in French literature at Carleton University in Ottawa and he went into academe himself and then into politics. Although they had never lived together, she had seen them as a couple, in the manner of Jean-Paul Sartre and Simone de Beauvoir, who were close friends of hers from her years as a graduate student in Paris. Trudeau's marriage in 1971 had taken her by surprise – though he had told her he was in love with Margaret Sinclair – and later that year, she had left Canada permanently for France. After completing a doctorate at the Sorbonne, she found engrossing work at UNESCO, where she eventually became a high-ranking official. For years after she left Canada she had refused to see Trudeau, telling people who sought to act as go-betweens that any encounter with him would be too painful for her to endure. Now that he was single once more and they were in the habit of meeting again as old friends in both Canada and France, she found him altered, as interesting and compelling as ever but more tranquil than the man she remembered. "There seemed to me to be something about him that was neither French nor English. Something transcendent, almost Oriental in its aspect. What was left unspoken was as important as what was said."[2]

One of the things that was said on this occasion – that the power to affect events and people brought with it a particular joy – summed up Trudeau's state of mind in the first few months after he was once more sworn in as prime minister, in March of 1980. He had returned to office as a man who, having absorbed and understood his losses, was ready to harness his talents in a renewed bid for the place of importance in history that he felt he had failed to achieve by the time he gave up the struggle in 1979. "What was of real importance [in my decision to resign then] was my recognition that I had had my chance," he remembered afterwards. But now fate was giving him another chance and he was ready to seize it. He was proving himself remarkable once more, displaying an unusual ability to evolve and learn. At a time in life when his contemporaries were settling into older age he was once again full of intellectual and physical vigour, committed to the federalist cause and to the nurturing of his children, who had become the centre of his emotional world.[3]

It wasn't that Trudeau was euphoric in early 1980. When his friend Jean Marchand carefully explained on television on election night that there was no gloating in the Trudeau camp, the anglophone Liberals who were

sitting with the newly re-elected prime minister watching
the screen in his living room at Stornoway were surprised
by Trudeau's emphatic agreement with Marchand's sentiments. Trudeau wasn't gloating and he wasn't overconfi-
dent. He had no intention of haring off for a holiday or
building a swimming pool or redecorating the official
residence at 24 Sussex Drive, post-election rewards he
had indulged in during the Margaret years. Instead, he
was determined to set to work. He was a re-empowered
leader with a vision of his country that he had been rumi-
nating on for decades and that he now intended to implement.[4]

He was also acutely conscious of the entrenched problems his government was facing. The anger at central
Canada that had been simmering for generations in the
west had been exacerbated by this most recent Liberal
victory, which had all but shut the four western provinces
out of federal power. The business community was sullen
in its disenchantment with Canadian politicians in general
and with Pierre Trudeau in particular. Disappointed by
the failure of Joe Clark's Tories to usher in a neo-
conservative era in Canada that would match the political
climate in the United Kingdom and in the United States,
Canadian businessmen were now concerned that the interventionist rhetoric of the Liberal campaign heralded a
leftward turn by the new government. Paradoxically, the
bitter hatred of big business for Trudeau did not translate
into enthusiasm from big labour. Trade union leaders still
disliked Trudeau intensely as a consequence of the Liberals' wage-and-price-control program in 1975 and the
Bank of Canada's tight money policy that had accompanied it. The Quebec élite was chronically antagonistic to
Trudeau personally. And as if this were not enough enmity for one prime minister to cope with, Trudeau was
also resented by the fourth estate, the political journalists

whose general dislike for him had deepened in the wake of his victory, which most of them saw as the result of his apparatchiks' manipulations of Parliament and the electorate. "This is unbelievable," the talking heads on the television networks had said to each other over and over again on election night. In addition to this unyielding domestic environment, Trudeau was facing a daunting international situation. Canada's vulnerable economy was experiencing a severe competitive squeeze as a result of the changes in global capitalism that were shaking even the United States, on whose prosperity the country was so dependent.[5]

Though the challenges facing him and his new government were familiar, Trudeau's own attitudes were very different. He had learned several important lessons from the paralysis of the late 1970s. This new term in office would be run as a "strategic prime ministership," to use a phrase coined by his adviser Tom Axworthy to indicate that it would be a regime focused on two or three top priorities. At the eleventh hour of his political life, Trudeau intended to apply rationalism more rigorously to governmental processes so he could subordinate peripheral policy issues to his own goals and control government expenditures at the same time. In everything he did, he intended to be mindful that this second chance would be his last. He had stated publicly that he would stay on as Liberal leader for only two or three years, until his agenda had been completed and a new direction for the Liberal Party established. His political life had been marked by fifteen years of theorizing followed by fifteen years of practice. Now he meant to achieve a new praxis in office, with every action related to the philosophy of government that he had developed in Montreal in the 1950s and early 1960s and had modified through his experience of power in Ottawa in the late 1960s and 1970s. "By the time

I returned to office in 1980, I had learned the lessons of politics," he said many years later. "I knew you could not exhaust yourself on every issue that came along. That if you hoped to accomplish those things that were of principal importance to you, you had to compromise. I had realized earlier in my political career that while the academic theoretician looks for the best of all possible solutions in the best of all possible worlds, the practical politician looks for the best achievable solution in the real world. I [was now] prepared more than ever to live with that . . . because there were things I wanted to achieve before my [final] retirement."[6]

To this end he began to show a new aptitude for managing men that grew out of his realization that he could no longer pretend to carry on *tout seul* à la Cyrano. He needed to animate, and to place strategically, the politicians and officials who had clustered around him in the 1970s. Within a few weeks of the 1980 election, Trudeau had in place a personal staff made up of people he knew to be like-minded and completely loyal to him – always prerequisites for any sort of good working relationship with Trudeau – and who had proven themselves to be unusually competent. He made James Coutts his principal secretary once more and elevated Tom Axworthy to the role of Coutts's deputy in charge of policy development. Michael Pitfield was called back to Ottawa from Harvard University in order to preside again over the government machinery as clerk of the Privy Council. Michael Kirby was summoned from Halifax, where he had been president of the Institute for Research on Public Policy, to become secretary to the cabinet for federal-provincial relations, a responsibility Trudeau had decided to keep for himself because Marc Lalonde, who had been Trudeau's previous minister in charge of constitutional issues, had insisted on taking charge of implementing the radical energy program he had persuaded the party to accept as part of its platform in the recent election. Trudeau named as his executive assistant Ted Johnson, a young Liberal lawyer from Ontario, reinstated Patrick Gossage as his press secretary and Joyce Fairbairn as his legislative assistant, and kept on Keith Davey, his perennial campaign chairman, as principal link with his communications experts in Toronto, Martin Goldfarb and Jerry Grafstein, the most important figures in what had become a permanent Liberal campaign organization. In addition, he appointed as Speaker of the Senate his old friend Jean Marchand, whom he still regarded as possessing an uncanny intuition for the vagaries of Quebec politics. His other old friend Gérard Pelletier was dispatched as Canadian ambassador to the United Nations in New York, where he would be close enough to the Canadian situation that he could confer frequently with Trudeau on domestic problems, yet at the same time remain in touch with international issues to which he would bring the same general worldview as Trudeau's.

Drawing on advice tendered by these loyalists of varied sensibilities, Trudeau assembled a workmanlike cabinet, assigning his ablest ministers to tackle the most pressing challenges his staff saw looming, particularly on the economic front. With Marc Lalonde ensconced in the vital energy portfolio, Allan MacEachen, now revered as a political wizard because of his role in engineering the Clark government's downfall, was handed the Department of Finance in order to wrestle with inflation and preside over tax reform. Any excesses of reformist zeal that MacEachen and Lalonde might display would presumably be balanced by the pro-business instincts of Don Johnston, who was made president of the Treasury Board and charged with reining in government spending. Herb Gray was given Industry, Trade and Commerce, apparently to implement Trudeau's campaign conversion to a comprehensive industrial strategy, and Ed Lumley was made minister of international trade to play midwife to the promised state trading corporation. Jean-Luc Pepin, whose commitment to a decentralized, binational federal state differed sharply from Trudeau's but who was widely respected in the journalistic and business communities for his acumen, was given the unwieldy Transport Department, an attempt to keep him fully occupied but at the same time a little removed from the Quebec situation. André Ouellet, a Quebec politician of the old style, was made minister of consumer and corporate affairs to bring about the long-delayed reform of competition policy. Roméo LeBlanc was returned to the fisheries portfolio in order to soothe the discontent of the Atlantic provinces, and Eugene Whelan was reconfirmed in Agriculture because of his cultivated rapport with the country's farmers. Lloyd Axworthy was appointed to the employment and immigration portfolio so he could bring his left-Liberal ideas and rare western-Liberal credentials to the task of rewriting Canada's labour-market policy.

Among the non-economic ministers, Jean Chrétien had pride of place as minister of state for social development, attorney general, and minister of justice. Monique Bégin was reinstated at Health and Welfare, Francis Fox was made secretary of state and minister of communications, James Fleming was promoted to minister to rethink the government's position on multiculturalism, and Gerald Regan was made labour minister for the entirely political reason that he was a former premier of Nova Scotia and had coattails in that province. John Roberts was appointed minister of science and technology and minister of the environment so he could apply his facility for policy-making at a time when acid rain was being discovered as the new American menace. Gilles Lamontagne was installed as minister of national defence with instructions to keep military issues quiescent and off the political agenda. Mark MacGuigan, a law professor from the University of Windsor, was rewarded for twelve years of earnest loyalty on the backbenches with the plum portfolio of external affairs, where he was expected to behave with sufficient docility to allow Trudeau's international ideas to prevail.

Trudeau and his closest advisers, Jim Coutts, Tom Axworthy, and Michael Pitfield, took equal care in the appointment of deputy ministers, trying to deploy the available senior bureaucrats to best effect so their strengths could balance the cabinet ministers' weaknesses. Many deputies were left in the departments where the Tories had assigned them so that stability could be maintained in special areas. Arthur Kroeger was kept on as deputy minister at Transport, Gaétan Lussier stayed at Agriculture, Paul Tellier at Indian Affairs and Northern Development, and Roger Tassé at Justice. John Manion continued as secretary at the Treasury Board, Gordon Osbaldeston as secretary in Economic Development, and Allan Gotlieb as under-secretary at External Affairs. Other deputies were moved to fill important gaps or to fulfil special missions. Ian Stewart was assigned to the Finance Department to replace the Tories' appointee, Grant Reuber, and to buttress MacEachen with his expertise in economic policy. Mickey Cohen was transferred to Energy, Mines and Resources to help Marc Lalonde become familiar with the energy business. Robert Johnstone was made deputy in ITC to keep an eye on Herb Gray's interventionism. Huguette Labelle was made deputy at Multiculturalism, the sole woman now holding senior official status, and Pierre Juneau was brought back to Communications to consolidate the government's cultural policies. And so it went. To each according to Trudeau's priorities, from each according to Trudeau's needs.

This careful marshalling of the political and bureaucratic talent available to him was part of an overall plan to enable Trudeau to devote his vital energies to what Lise Bissonnette described in an editorial in *Le Devoir* as "ses obsessions anciennes."[7]

CHAPTER 10

THE REFERENDUM I:
THE GENERALS MOBILIZE

Trudeau was not the only French Canadian obsessed with the Quebec/Canada situation in the winter of 1980. At this point in his life his "ancient obsessions" were also those of his society. For many people in Quebec, changing their collectivity's constitutional relationship with Canada had become a dominant concern, embodying a deep psychic need for symbolic acknowledgement of Quebec's distinctiveness and an urgent desire to reshape its geopolitical space. In gearing up for the coming referendum on sovereignty-association, it was as though the whole province were preparing for the climactic event in a tribal war, a battle of Homeric scope.

The referendum had been looming ever since the separatist Parti Québécois had come to power in 1976 with the promise that Quebeckers would be given a chance to vote directly on whether they wanted to continue to be part of Canada or would prefer to become politically sovereign as a separate state. It was to be the culmination of all of Quebec's post-war struggles, when French Canadians with conflicting views had attempted to liberate and modernize their society, to cause it to leap two centuries in two decades. The referendum was expected to provide the answer to the question that had held Canada in its grip for so long: what do Quebeckers really want?[1]

What the Quebeckers Trudeau castigated as national-ists wanted was more of what they had accomplished in the fifteen years since Trudeau had quit the provincial scene for Ottawa, a period when the Quebec *nation* – as the French-speaking collectivity was now referred to – had experienced a turmoil of cultural and social develop-ment of unprecedented creativity that had been spear-headed by the prolific legislation passed through the Assemblée nationale. For Quebec nationalists already run-ning what one academic book identified as the Quebec state-in-waiting, the word "province" simply served as a reminder that Quebec's constitutional status was out of sync with its political, economic, and psychological real-ity. The explosion of indigenous theatre, literature, music, television, and film production over the previous decade and a half had been largely financed by federal agencies devoted to cultural development that had taken on specifi-cally Québécois personalities: Radio-Canada, the Office national du film, and the Conseil des arts. Ironically, the political impact of this renaissance was a new self-confi-dence that left little place in the Quebec mindscape for a continued dependence on Ottawa's ministrations. Modern universities staffed by young professors who had qualified for their doctorates in Paris or Chicago were producing cadres able to run a modern political economy. A new breed of technocrats had constructed a modern govern-mental structure able to meet the social-policy needs of the general public and the business-support needs of the burgeoning capitalist class that had been taught entrepre-neurial principles in the province's faculties of Hautes études commerciales. What Quebec's opinion leaders seemed to want by the time Trudeau welcomed Canadians to the 1980s was sufficient autonomy for the Quebec state to continue developing, unconstrained by its political rela-tionship with the rest of Canada.[2]

What they did *not* want was the kind of continuous political tension that had marked the years since the Quiet Revolution began. Growing labour militancy and nationalist sentiment had made transnational business increasingly nervous about Quebec's stability. Anglo-Canadian capital was in retreat, with companies stealthily moving personnel and money out of the province. Each such incident of betrayal caused fresh outbursts of anglophobia, the most memorable being when Sun Life, a large insurance company with a landmark building in downtown Montreal, decided to move its head office to Toronto in 1978. Whatever their political alignment – federalist, neo-federalist, or separatist – Quebeckers hoped that the referendum would resolve a tense, uncertain situation that was no longer tolerable.

When Trudeau was sworn into office on March 4, 1980, just ten weeks before the referendum was scheduled to be held, on May 20, he had very little time to decide how to intervene in a situation that was outside his jurisdiction by the provisions of the Quebec government's referendum law. To the anglophones in his office it was obvious that in approaching the fight ahead, he saw himself as a kind of statesman-general in the mould of Napoleon. He wanted to act as master strategist for the federalist forces, though it was by no means clear how – or even whether – they could be effectively deployed. A quick survey of the field of battle brought with it the recognition that it was occupied by a separatist enemy in a position of commanding strength facing federalist allies in a state of disarray.

The opposing general, of course, was René Lévesque, the premier of Quebec, whose fear and loathing of Trudeau was now more or less openly expressed. The two men had met twenty-five years before in the cafeteria of the old Radio-Canada building in downtown Montreal and had entered into contention on sight, like two cocks strutting and crowing, daring each other to fight. Their animosity was not entirely predictable since they had many characteristics in common. They were both the sons of lawyers who had died prematurely, leaving them fatherless in their teens. Both had been educated in Jesuit classical colleges and had gone on to study law, although Lévesque had abandoned academe in 1944 without getting his degree in order to work in Europe as a French-language reporter for the U.S. Office of War Information. Both had returned home as internationalists after adventuring abroad, determined to transcend the claustrophobic society in which they had grown up. They had both engaged in the struggle for democratization in Quebec, Trudeau as a polemicist with a small élite as his reading public and as a lawyer with unions as his clients, and Lévesque as a television broadcaster with a devoted mass audience. Each of them had reluctantly chosen the Liberal Party as a vehicle for turning his ideas into action, Lévesque in 1960 at the provincial level and Trudeau in 1965 at the federal level, and had rapidly become a political star. They had even formed a wary alliance of sorts in the early 1960s when Lévesque was a minister in the Quebec government and Trudeau was a law professor. Their mutual friend Gérard Pelletier convened a series of meetings at his house where issues were discussed and advice was given to Lévesque by Jean Marchand and André Laurendeau as well as Trudeau, who argued vigorously against Lévesque's nationalism in private while praising him in print as the only leftist in the Lesage cabinet. But as the Quebec drama unfolded thereafter, Lévesque and Trudeau emerged as ideological opponents debating the uses and abuses of nationalism, and then evolved into political antagonists going their separate ways. The year Trudeau was elected leader of the federal Liberal Party, Lévesque was busy founding a separatist movement of his own, having stormed out of the provincial Liberal Party over the issue of sovereignty for Quebec.[3]

In Trudeau's first term as prime minister, when he was putting on the arrogance of power like a mask, Lévesque was struggling for a foothold in the Quebec political system as the leader of the newly constituted Parti Québécois. Trying to maintain his commitment to democracy and moderation in the face of the demands for a more radical and intolerant route to independence from many of his separatist supporters took a heavy toll, and the difficulties Lévesque experienced altered him greatly. He developed a persona that was more and more remote from the racy, super-confident foreign correspondent of his Radio-Canada days, a time when his interest in Quebec was peripheral to his involvement in world events. He was distanced too from the firebrand-cabinet-minister stance of his years in the Liberal government, when he engaged in fierce duels with Anglo business. A prophet who had forged a motley of dissenting factions into a dynamic progressive movement, he was now cast as the determined leader of a competent political party and the anguished champion of the French-Canadian "oppressed."[4]

As a public figure, Lévesque had always been Trudeau's opposite. Intuitive and emotionally expressive, he was a man whose life was chaotic, open, played out in public. A smoker, drinker, and womanizer of fabled charm and prodigious energy, his sins of commission only added to the immense popularity that had come to him early in his life because of his natural rhetorical gifts. His fame as a television journalist was based in part on a remarkable facility for making complex issues easily understandable, and when he applied these gifts to elucidating the separatist option, he made Quebec's future as an independent state sound both exciting and plausible.

In politics he was guided by his "nose," disdaining logical argument, official documents, and long-term planning in favour of emotionally charged discourse and spontaneous responses to situations as they arose. Speaking in school auditoriums in working-class districts to people packed so close together there never seemed to be enough air in the room, he was Chaplinesque, the little man personified, his ill-fitting suits like something a factory foreman would wear on a Sunday, strands of his long hair dragged across his balding head, smoke from his chain of cigarettes curling around his jug ears. Musicians appearing with him would warm up a crowd by getting people to sing the refrain "Gens du pays, c'est votre tour," from the song that had become an alternative anthem for the PQ. Lévesque would then come to the microphone and begin to speak, making sly, slangy jokes about Trudeau, his ministers, and their sell-out to the English, mocking Trudeau's background and his Parisian French, weaving these insults together with promises for Quebec's future, speaking, as he kept saying, "au fond de mon coeur," appearing to be not *above* the crowd but *of* it, not charismatic in the Weberian sense but empathetic with the audience, who would cheer and laugh and weep with him when he talked. His hopes were their hopes, his style an extension of their own. It was his attitudes as much as his ideas that set Lévesque apart from Trudeau with his paternalistic, grand-seigneurial manner and seductive rationalism.

A class gap between them became evident in the 1970s and was played on shrewdly by Lévesque. Although they were both offspring of the post–World War I French-Canadian bourgeoisie, Trudeau's life had been far more privileged. Dominique Lévesque, René's father, had barely made a living practising law in the English-dominated town of New Carlisle in the Gaspé and had left his widow ill provided for when he died at an early age. Even if his son had been endowed with an easy aptitude for scholarship – which he emphatically was not – there would not have been enough money for an extended education or time for the kind of contemplative life that had allowed Trudeau to formulate his political thought so definitively. Lévesque had gone to work at a radio station in his teens, had never stopped in the thirty years since, and had resolutely avoided turning into an élitist no matter how famous or powerful he became. The men even looked in late middle age as though they came from different social strata. Trudeau was athletic, soigné, more attractive than he had been as a young man. Lévesque looked haggard, fragile, and far older than Trudeau despite the fact that he was three years younger. His flaws and accessibility endeared him to many, especially to journalists in French and English Canada who identified with his racy language and manner, while Trudeau's perfections made them anxious or envious or both. It became a standard story line that Trudeau was the man of grey matter, Lévesque the man of heart, and the confrontation of their ideas and personalities took on a mythic aura. Each man represented a tradition rooted in Quebec history. Lévesque was seen to embody the defensive, mystical, nationalist tradition of Louis-Joseph Papineau, the Abbé Groulx, Louis-Alexandre Taschereau, and Maurice Duplessis, based on racial solidarity. Trudeau was presented as the inheritor of the expansive, pragmatic, federalist-constitutionalist tradition of Louis-Hippolyte Lafontaine, George-Étienne Cartier, Sir Wilfrid Laurier, Ernest Lapointe, and Louis St. Laurent, focused on the accommodation of the French Canadians to the finality of the Conquest and based on a more abstract concept of brotherhood beyond blood ties.

When Lévesque entered directly into Trudeau's orbit in his new role as premier of Quebec in 1976 and became a dominant participant in federal-provincial conferences in the late 1970s, it was small wonder that the ideological and political frictions that had festered for years between them soon solidified into a deep personal enmity. After a number of antagonistic exchanges in public and private – many of which the Quebec premier lost – Lévesque began to say intemperately that he hated Trudeau's guts. Trudeau was icy and controlled in response, attitudes that fuelled Lévesque's rage and shored up his contention that Trudeau was an anachronism, "a goddam snob from Outremont" who had sold out to the English.[5]

Whatever his difficulties with Trudeau on the national scene, Lévesque's own first years in office were extraordinarily successful. He had won power mainly by campaigning against the scandal-ridden Liberal regime of Robert Bourassa and by promising that good government rather than independence would be his first concern as premier. Bolstered by a talented cabinet, he quickly put into effect most of his party's reform agenda, passing anti-scab legislation, instituting legal aid, partially nationalizing the asbestos industry, laying down new rules for political party financing, and putting forward the PQ's own solution to the province's historic concern for linguistic security in the famous Bill 101, which was designed to make Quebec safe for francophones by enforcing French as the sole language of the workplace and the streetscape.

By the time Trudeau was defeated in 1979, Lévesque was poised to capitalize on his party's strategy of *étapisme*, a gradual approach to achieving Quebec's independence by stages that had been conceived by his minister of intergovernmental affairs, a former bureaucrat named Claude Morin who believed that only after the PQ had attained the respectability of government and shown it could deliver on its promises should its plans for separation be put to the electorate. Having proven their competence by providing effective government for nearly three years, the Péquistes had grown sufficiently in the public's esteem to move to the next stage in their gradualist plan by holding a referendum on what they called sovereignty-association, a form of political independence from Canada that would retain an economic relationship under a common currency. Their prospects were further enhanced by the fact that the new prime minister, Joe Clark, had promised that the federal government would stay clear of the sovereignty debate in Quebec, where he had virtually no political base.

At this juncture, Lévesque and his colleagues felt confident. They had well over a year left in their mandate, and the longer they waited to hold the referendum, the more likely it would be that Trudeau would retire from politics entirely and the federalist cause would lose its greatest champion. They argued among themselves throughout the summer and fall of 1979 over exactly what it was they wanted to negotiate with Canada and exactly how they would present their indépendantiste option to the Quebec electorate. By December 19, when they finally managed to phrase the crucial question to be used in the referendum vote the following spring, they had missed the flood tide. Joe Clark had been defeated in the Commons and Lévesque's nemesis was on his way back to the prime minister's office.[6]

Even with Trudeau in power in Ottawa once more, Lévesque had good reason to expect that his federalist opponents would rely on Claude Ryan, the leader of the Liberal Party in Quebec, to lead the referendum fight, especially since the Péquiste legislation intended to keep federal politicians out of the campaign had been heartily endorsed by Ryan himself.

For years, Claude Ryan had been a force to be reckoned with in Quebec, a man of unusual intellect and integrity. He had grown up in poverty, the second son of a woman of iron will and ardent faith who had been abandoned by her husband when her three children were very young. A Spartan, stubborn egoist with a pietist bent, Ryan had rejected the priesthood as his life's work and studied social work and industrial relations at the Université de Montréal instead. In his early twenties he took a job with Action catholique canadienne, the lay movement where so many of the early Citélibriste reformers had started out as social activists, and made an important first career out of his commitment to the organization, serving as its tireless national secretary for seventeen years. In 1962, seeking an even more influential voice in public affairs, he accepted an offer to write editorials for Le Devoir, Quebec's most respected newspaper, where he was to stay for sixteen years, fourteen of them as director, a job that in his case combined the functions of publisher and editor.

Under Ryan's predecessor, André Laurendeau, Le Devoir had steered its own constitutional course. It refused to endorse either the radical separatists who wanted Quebec to become an independent, socialist state, or the traditional nationalists who wanted more autonomy for a Catholic, capitalist Quebec, or the liberal federalists who wanted Quebec to participate as an equal partner in the Canadian federation. Instead, Laurendeau espoused an interventionist, reformist government that would keep Quebec within Canada but with enhanced powers greater than those of the English-speaking provinces.

Ryan took these ideas further, developing his own brand of neo-federalism based on the belief that the Canadian federal system was acceptable in principle but that

Quebec required a special status with significantly increased legislative power, so that the province's particular
cultural and social-welfare needs could be adequately met
through an activist use of its own provincial state. This
stance, offering a position midway between the extremes
of separatism and federalism, reaffirmed the long-
established influence of *Le Devoir* among the Quebec élite,
who found "special status" an attractive notion. It also
made Ryan into a powerful figure in the constitutional
debates that raged in the province in the 1960s and 1970s.
Politicians of every stripe sought his counsel and he was
widely described, not altogether jokingly, as "le pape de
St. Sacrement," in reference to the omniscient tone of his
editorial pronouncements and the tiny street in the old
city of Montreal where his newspaper was located.

Ryan's espousal of special status for Quebec would have
estranged him from Trudeau politically in any event. But
a personal antipathy had grown up between them as well.
Some of their mutual friends believed it was partly based
in Ryan's case on envy of the privileges that wealth had
brought Trudeau, especially his protracted, expensive
education and extensive travels abroad, advantages that
Ryan had never been able to afford. In the early 1950s,
Ryan had managed to spend two years in Rome living
frugally and studying Church history under the sponsorship of Action catholique, the only time in his life he was
able to read and think unburdened by the need to make a
living. Trudeau had passed through Rome on his way to
some exotic destination in Asia, looking rich and talking
radical. This was in the period immediately after he had
given up his job in the federal public service, when he was
looking for a social activist role so he could fulfil his now
clearly defined commitment to personalism. Although this
was a philosophy the two men shared, Trudeau's interpretation of it must have seemed to the impoverished Ryan

something of a dilettante's fantasy. After they had lunch together, they paced the streets of the Eternal City with Ryan attempting to convince Trudeau that he should follow the way of the Lord and give away his inherited wealth. Back home in Quebec, they engaged publicly and privately in serious intellectual discourse over the next dozen years. Although they had many ideas in common, having both been influenced by Cardinal Newman and Lord Acton, as well as Emmanuel Mounier, they never were at ease with each other, and Ryan frequently chided Trudeau editorially during the period when he was emerging as the dominant federalist thinker in Quebec. It was Ryan's contention that Trudeau's mastery of logic led him to serious errors of judgement. In order to demolish his opponents' arguments, Trudeau would present them in an overly simplistic way and, in so doing, would miss entirely essential elements in their thought to which he ought to have paid attention. In other words, Ryan believed Trudeau's rarefied education had skewed his common sense – an attribute that Ryan believed he himself possessed in abundance because of his own hard life.[7]

Trudeau's reciprocal grievance developed later, after he had joined the Liberal Party. It stemmed from Ryan's refusal to support him editorially when he was the only French-Canadian candidate in the leadership race in 1968. Ryan had spitefully backed Paul Hellyer, a Torontonian whose reputation had been made as the cabinet minister who championed the controversial integration of Canada's armed forces, whose command of French was minimal, and whose interest in the national unity question was peripheral. In the general election that followed, Ryan endorsed Robert Stanfield, the Conservative leader. After these betrayals, Trudeau and his allies, particularly Marc Lalonde, who had known Ryan well in his Action catholique days, regarded his pontifications as the unreliable projections of a man who believed his own views to be the will of God.

This mutual antipathy flared into an ugly incident in October 1970 when Trudeau – responding to pleas for help from both the premier of Quebec, Robert Bourassa, and the mayor of Montreal, Jean Drapeau – invoked an "apprehended insurrection" of terrorists as justification for declaring a state of national emergency and the suspension of civil rights under the War Measures Act. It became public knowledge that Trudeau and Marc Lalonde suspected Ryan was at the centre of a plot to set up a "Committee of Public Safety" to take power away from the Bourassa government during the emergency caused by the FLQ kidnappings. Ryan vehemently denied this allegation, with its echoes of revolutionary France and Third World coups d'état, and seized on it as an indication of the paranoid fear that gripped officials in Quebec City, Montreal, and Ottawa in this crisis.[8]

Eight months later Ryan had his revenge. In June 1971, after an intense, closed-door conference of first ministers at Victoria had produced a constitutional agreement that had been under negotiation for three years, Ryan used all the considerable authority of his newspaper to provide intellectual ammunition for the common front of labour unions, business groups, and nationalist organizations that spontaneously erupted to pressure Bourassa to rescind his original decision to sign the accord. In a series of editorials Ryan criticized not just the substance of the Victoria deal, which would "consolidate the central government's preponderance in Canadian affairs and reduce Quebec to the level of a province like the others," but the process. The twelve-day deadline for accepting or rejecting the Victoria charter without any possibility for alteration constituted an anti-democratic "ultimatum" that denied both the citizens and their representatives in the federal and provincial parliaments their proper role in debating and contributing to this proposed recasting of Canada's basic law. Ryan subsequently exulted in Bourassa's rejection of the Victoria agreement and then called for Trudeau's defeat in the federal election of 1972. Although he temporarily redeemed himself in the Trudeauites' eyes by supporting the Liberals in the 1974 federal election, he committed the ultimate outrage against federalism by endorsing Lévesque's Parti Québécois in the provincial election of November 1976.[9]

Just over a year later, Ryan did an apparent about-turn and declared himself a candidate to succeed Bourassa as leader of the Quebec Liberal Party. He was responding to the blandishments of a group of provincial Liberals who were desperate to find a "national figure" with sufficiently impressive credentials to revive a party that had been without a clear direction since Bourassa's resignation shortly after his electoral defeat. Next to Trudeau and Lévesque, Ryan was easily the best-known Quebecker in English Canada. He had been appointed co-chairman of Walter Gordon's nationalist Committee for an Independent Canada in 1970 and was a familiar figure to anglophones across the country as a compelling participant in many of the numerous conferences and television shows that were devoted to the Quebec crisis in the 1960s and 1970s. The Quebec Liberals saw in Ryan's pan-Canadian renown and austere integrity a way to redeem their party's reputation. With this deeply moral Catholic as leader, they reasoned, the telling charges of corruption made against them by the PQ would be erased.

Ryan's neo-federalism was particularly compelling for those provincial Liberals who had never been comfortable with Trudeau's doctrinaire rejection of special status or indeed with the federal Liberal Party itself. For at least fifty years, there had been tensions between the Liberals' federal and provincial wings that Trudeau's leadership had done little to alleviate. A carefully orchestrated campaign soon persuaded the party rank and file that Ryan had both the *je ne sais quoi* necessary to best Lévesque and the capacity to deal with Trudeau as an equal. He was easily elected leader in April 1978 at a convention that had the air of a cardinal's investiture.[10]

Having been hailed as the only man who could save the provincial Liberals from extinction, Ryan came to the leadership obligated to no one and promptly set about bending the party to his will. He proceeded to run it in the same autocratic way that he had directed *Le Devoir*, controlling every appointment, signing every cheque, and approving every detail. He withdrew from the Liberal power brokers their traditional backroom function as fundraisers. He froze out his rival for the leadership, Raymond Garneau, an economist and veteran member of the legislature, by refusing to make the small gestures of reconciliation that might have won his co-operation. He deliberately diminished other stalwarts in his caucus who had offered him their enthusiastic support because he thought they were insufficiently intelligent, chaste, or humble. He even forced Michel Robert, a respected lawyer and one of his chief bagmen in the leadership race, to resign from the chairmanship of the Pro-Canada Committee, an important Montreal group raising referendum campaign funds, ostensibly because Robert had dared to change the committee's name without seeking Ryan's prior approval.[11]

Despite these clumsy tactics, the risk the provincial Liberals had taken in recruiting Ryan appeared to be paying off publicly. The party won all seven of the provincial by-elections held after he assumed the leadership. And his capacity for clear analysis seemed custom-made for the task of poking holes in the Péquistes' panacea for an independent Quebec. He exposed the sloppy thinking in the government's White Paper on sovereignty-association when it was released on November 1, 1979, with an attack that was surprisingly effective given the PQ's popular appeal. The Péquiste document claimed that, while "sovereignty would reside entirely in the State of Quebec ... Canada can be preserved intact as an economic entity" since the two states would "remain in association, not only in a customs union or a common market but in a monetary union as well." Ryan scornfully dismissed the vagueness of these ideas, calling them a house of cards and claiming Quebec would never achieve equality with Canada in such an unlikely situation, where Quebec's say in the common institutions would be proportional to its economic strength. "I don't understand this lack of logic," he said. "Does it mean that we would have made all these changes to arrive again in a situation in which Quebec would find itself in a minority position in [a new] regime's very structures?" By the end of November, with Trudeau having withdrawn from the fray in the meantime, there was no question that Ryan had become the undisputed boss of the forces lined up against Lévesque.[12]

Even so, many French-Canadian federalists were uneasy about his capacities as a political strategist. Their fears were exacerbated in early January 1980 when Ryan made what seemed a decidedly imprudent move by publishing his own party's proposal for constitutional reform. For over a year, teams of provincial Liberals had been holding hearings throughout Quebec, consulting academic and legal experts, drafting and re-drafting papers in a startlingly ambitious project initiated by Ryan to produce a detailed blueprint for a reformed federation. Their efforts resulted in a party document called *A New Canadian Federation*, which was intended to serve as Ryan's platform in the referendum campaign and to provide a concrete and detailed alternative to both Trudeau's federalism and Lévesque's separatism. The Ryan Beige Paper, as it was quickly labelled because of the colour of its cover, was recognized by scholars as a substantial contribution to Canadian constitutional thinking in general and to the reworking of the neo-federalist position in particular. Whether it was good politics was less certain.[13]

The document could not help but provoke controversy. While it had the merit of not claiming special powers for Quebec, its proposed devolution of extensive powers to all the Canadian provinces gave federalists cause for concern about maintaining a balance between the federal and provincial governments. At the same time, it left the federal government with too much authority for true separatists to stomach and, as a result, offered the Péquistes an easy target and a welcome diversion of public interest from the equivalent flaws in their own White Paper.

The Beige Paper's publication caused another, more damaging distraction. Ryan insisted that his rank-and-file party members debate at the riding level and ratify in formal convention the minutiae of his constitutional proposals. This exercise had only the most tangential relevance to the forthcoming referendum and it diverted the provincial Liberals' energies during the crucial early weeks of 1980. As a result Ryan's caucus was woefully unprepared for the debate on the referendum question begun in the National Assembly in early March, when the PQ formally launched its campaign. The Liberals and their leader appeared petty in their carping about the specific meaning of sovereignty-association and their quibbling over the ambiguity of the referendum question. The contradictions inherent in the Péquiste position, which Ryan had so effectively itemized the previous fall, now seemed unimportant in the face of the Liberals' painful ineptitude at exploiting them.

Since the proceedings of this historic debate were tele-
cast across the province in prime time every night for
three weeks, Ryan's stiff-necked austerity revealed to
thousands of voters the incompatibility of this master of
the printed word with politics in the television age.
Rather than looking resolute and authoritative, Ryan
seemed old-fashioned and mean-spirited on the screen,
like a self-righteous monseigneur out of the repressive
Québécois past. It began to look as though his intellectual
and moral attributes would prove of little practical value
when it came to marshalling opposition forces for the
referendum campaign.

In contrast, the Péquistes' management of the legislative
debate on the referendum was a political work of art.
Brilliantly organized by the minister responsible for parliamentary affairs, Claude Charron, who programmed,
coached, and co-ordinated each deputy's speech down to
pauses for applause, the Péquiste debaters performed with
heightened eloquence. Lévesque himself made a stirring
appeal to the pride of the Québécois, displaying once
more his oratorical gifts, which the journalist Graham
Fraser described as a spontaneous capacity to let loose "a
torrent . . . an original mixture of joual, popular phrases,
freshly coined words, American and English expressions
that had been more or less gallicized . . . plaited [together]
with an incredible association of ideas." Lévesque's cabinet ministers and backbenchers followed him, producing
biting critiques of Canadian federalism, impassioned
speeches on the economic advantages of sovereignty, and
calls for solidarity from a nation now being offered the
chance to take its destiny into its own hands. Every evening, hour after hour, this proud rhetoric was beamed
from the government benches into the living rooms of

Quebeckers through their television sets. Long before it was over, the debate had turned into a smashing victory for the PQ, apparently confirming the validity of its approach to the referendum and the power of its hold over the electorate.[14]

At this stage, the Péquistes' campaign strategy seemed impeccable. They felt they could count on the one-fifth of the voters who were outright indépendantistes and another fifth who supported the more ambiguous concept of sovereignty-association. Since they had written off the 20 per cent of the Quebec electorate who were anglophones and another 20 per cent who were francophone but federalist, the outcome obviously would swing on the remaining fifth who were francophone but neo-federalist, people who wanted increased power for Quebec but still saw themselves as Canadians with a valid place in Confederation.

It was the need to attract this neo-federalist support that impelled René Lévesque and Claude Morin to fight off their more radical cabinet colleagues, who wanted to put a hard, clear question to the public, asking Quebeckers to say yes or no to immediate independence. The referendum question that had finally emerged from the cabinet was deliberately "soft" and far from clear. It asked only for a mandate to *negotiate* an agreement that would give Quebec political sovereignty yet maintain the safety of economic association with the rest of Canada. While supporters of independence and sovereignty-association would have to vote Oui for lack of an alternative, neo-federalists could vote Oui to strengthen Quebec's bargaining position since they would get to pass judgement on the eventual deal in a second referendum.[15]

Once the legislative debate was over in late March and attention began to switch to door-to-door campaigning, success for the Oui campaign seemed assured. All the Péquistes had to do was build on their endorsement by the major labour and community organizations, maintain the morale of their troops in the field, and keep up the momentum through triumphal sweeps by their popular premier around the province, and victory would surely ensue.[16]

For the Trudeauites, assessing the referendum situation from their Ottawa base, federalism was facing a cataclysm and Claude Ryan seemed unable to cope. Campaign organization was understandably not the forte of a former newspaper editor, but Ryan's failure to hold an organizational meeting of the Non campaign committee until March 27, after the legislative debate had ended, was a cause for grave concern. The professionals in his party who were trying to put together a referendum campaign machine had been thunderstruck to discover that their leader dismissed as irrelevant the modern political tools of polling and advertising. Ryan saw the campaign as a series of intellectual encounters between his vision of Quebec and an attentive, rational public, a version of the Action catholique meetings he had held in the 1950s for the faithful, who had turned up in small-town parish halls to hear the word from the most active lay Catholic of the day. He intended to travel the province doggedly in his rented plane (soon dubbed the "DC-Non") so he could address community meetings night after night, blithely disregarding the need to produce newsworthy items for the electronic media's early-evening deadlines. When these plans were reported to the Trudeauites in Ottawa they realized that Ryan would drag the Non campaign with him into political oblivion unless they came to the rescue.

Ryan had stubbornly maintained that the referendum was a battle among provincial politicians. But when a poll taken after the National Assembly debate showed that the

Non support had fallen behind that for the Oui, he became marginally more open to the idea of co-operation with the "federal cousins" although he still expected to remain in charge of the campaign. In truth, he could no longer control the situation. Whether Claude Ryan liked it or not, Pierre Trudeau was poised to enter the referendum battle.

Ever since his return to office, the question had been not whether but how Trudeau would use the powerful resources of the federal government to fight the referendum. By the very fact of his reappearance as prime minister, Trudeau had already broken the monopoly over the Non leadership that Ryan had worked painstakingly to achieve. Bolstered by a Quebec caucus of seventy-three newly victorious Liberal MPs from the province, Trudeau's re-election put back into the field an alternative to sovereignty-association that rivalled Ryan's. His unrepentant Quebec-must-stay-in-Canada-as-a-province-like-the-others federalism was easier to grasp than the complicated tangle of neo-federalist proposals that the Beige Paper had revealed.

The federal Liberals had accepted Ryan in 1978, *faute de mieux*, as the provincial Liberal leader. Marc Lalonde, taking into account the desperation of the federalist fight with the separatists at the time, had said, "Well, at least he's a guy you can do business with." Trudeau had proceeded to do just that, making very correct public appearances in Ryan's company during the run-up to the 1979 federal election. Ryan had responded by paying fulsome tribute to Trudeau on his "retirement" later that year in phrases that some observers thought showed as much relief at the fact that Trudeau had bowed out as they did respect for his accomplishments. But the Trudeauites had never quite forgotten Ryan's endorsement of their political enemies over the years and his trenchant editorials chastising Trudeau for his "arrogant intransigence" and "detestable tendency to judge from on high and afar problems that he does not understand." Now the mix of decentralization and dualism in Ryan's Beige Paper, along with the ineptitude of his political style, had confirmed how unreliable an ally he was in what they felt was the ultimate fight against separatism. While they were convinced their political moxie and federal muscle were needed to save the Non campaign from disaster, the Trudeauites were also aware that any overt attempt to brush Ryan aside would be divisive and counter-productive. He had to be persuaded to co-operate with them through an appeal to his intellectual vanity, his piety, and his patriotism. It was decided that only Trudeau could manage this manoeuvre.[17]

In an apparent gesture of solidarity, Trudeau invited Ryan, as chairman of the Non campaign, to lunch at 24 Sussex Drive on Good Friday, the holiest of Catholic holy days. Ryan accepted the invitation in order to explain to Trudeau why neo-federalism had to be the Non committee's official position. But Trudeau somehow turned the tables on his old critic in the course of their encounter by deftly addressing the question of doctrine. For the first time since the 1950s, Trudeau was treating Ryan as a comrade-in-arms and intellectual equal. The same Trudeau who had never deigned as prime minister to seek Ryan's advice in the years when nearly every other powerful political figure in the country had come to call on him at Le Devoir was now soft-spoken, flatteringly attentive to Ryan's views, and at the same time brilliant in his reasoning. Apparently dazzled by the ambiance of the prime ministerial residence and by Trudeau's new demeanour, the leader of the opposition in Quebec let himself be persuaded to drop the Beige Paper's tortuous neo-federalist position for the duration of the campaign. When he heard of this discussion, Claude Forget, the Liberal MNA who had been the principal author and organizer of the Beige Paper process, was astounded. The previous autumn he had been charged with publicly warning Trudeau, then the leader of the opposition in Ottawa, to keep his nose out of the referendum campaign. Now with one long lunch Trudeau had overturned all of Forget's hard work, neutralizing Ryan as an ideological pole in the debate while at the same time re-energizing him for the fight to come.[18]

Once this feat had been accomplished, the Trudeauites set about achieving co-operation at the organizational level with the Non committee, a tricky task given the volatility of the situation and the Quebec Liberals' suspicions that their federal confrères would try to sweep them aside. In anticipation of such resentment, Trudeau had given the formidable task of directing federal resources in the referendum to Jean Chrétien, his minister of justice and attorney general.

Chrétien was only forty-six years old in 1980 but his connections with Liberalism in Quebec went back so far he was like a walking history lesson, a one-man *son-et-lumière* show that illustrated decades of French-Canadian political and social development. He had been born during the Depression in Shawinigan, a pulp and paper town in the Saint-Maurice Valley, an area famous in Quebec for its lively politics and its great populist orators. The second-last child in a family of nineteen, he was a genetic Liberal whose ancestors had been closely connected with the nineteenth-century reform tradition of Sir Wilfrid Laurier and *les rouges*. His grandfather, François Chrétien, was the mayor of the village of Saint-Étienne-des-Grès for thirty years. His father, Wellie Chrétien, made his living working as a machinist in a Shawinigan paper mill, but his true vocation was politics and he was tireless in organizing and proselytizing on behalf of the Liberal Party.

Later in his life, Jean Chrétien could barely remember when he first decided to become a politician. He followed his father around Shawinigan when he was still in short pants, listening to him inveigh good-naturedly against the evils of Duplessis, who came from a nearby town. By the time Jean was eighteen and working in the mill for the summer, he was confident enough politically to jump on top of a table in the cafeteria and get in some oratorical licks at Duplessis himself. His parents were determined that their children would be well educated and they scraped together the money to send their sons away to school. Chrétien attended Duplessis's old classical college in Trois-Rivières, where he was a wayward student more notable for his high spirits than his marks. After achieving a baccalaureate, he went on to law school at Laval because of his father's conviction that the law was the best training ground for an aspiring politician. After all, the two French Canadians who had achieved the prime minister-ship were Liberal lawyers. Every *rouge* worthy of the name knew that.

When Jean Chrétien finished his studies and came back to Shawinigan to set up practice in the late 1950s, he devoted valuable time and prodigious energy to working for the Liberal Party as an organizer until he secured a nomination and was elected to Parliament himself in 1963 at the unusually young age of twenty-nine. His arrival in Ottawa coincided with Lester Pearson's first minority government, and people who met him then never forgot his eagerness to learn. He had rarely been out of Quebec before and could scarcely make himself understood in English, but he turned these handicaps into strengths by dint of great natural charm and relentless application. Doug Fisher, who was then an NDP MP and later a newspaper columnist, was showing Chrétien the Commons chamber soon after his arrival and told him that if he wanted to get off the backbenches and onto the front, he would have to work very hard.

"Don' worra, Dog," said Chrétien. "I do eet, Dog. I wanna work hard, Dog." Fisher didn't have the heart to tell him that "Dog" sounded suspiciously like a translation of *chien* and that maybe the old Dale Carnegie technique of sprinkling your conversation liberally with your listener's name was a shade obvious. He did have the prescience to see that Chrétien's ambition was more than just talk.[19]

Chrétien was unnervingly attentive to the opinions of anglophones in Ottawa in those days. He would sit silent in a meeting or at a dinner table, his deep blue eyes intent on his colleagues' faces as though he were trying to puzzle out not just what they were talking about but how their minds worked. He was engagingly direct in stating his purpose: he wanted to figure out the system and learn how to make the most of the chances it brought his way. And make the most of them he did, progressing in the eventful years from 1963 to 1968 from backbencher to parliamentary secretary to minister without portfolio and finally minister of national revenue. In the Liberal leadership race in 1968 he supported Mitchell Sharp, who had been his mentor when he was parliamentary secretary to the minister of finance, and when Sharp withdrew in favour of Trudeau, Chrétien went with him, bringing along his fervid loyalty and his deeply ingrained knowledge of the politics of the Quebec hinterland. He was minister of Indian affairs and northern development in the first Trudeau regime, then president of the Treasury Board, then minister of trade and commerce, and finally, in 1977, the first francophone minister of finance in Canadian history.

It was a job Chrétien had had his eye on for fifteen years, but his performance in it was mediocre at best. It was mainly Chrétien's disarming ease in talking to journalists about his own limitations, coupled with opposition members' concerns about appearing to be racist if they attacked too vehemently the first Quebecker in the job, that prevented him from being publicly excoriated. Privately, he was condemned as inept by none other than his predecessor in Finance, John Turner, then a Bay Street lawyer whose firm circulated to its clients a newsletter larded with scornful comments about the Trudeau government's economic failings. But Turner was in a minority. Instead of blaming Chrétien for the Liberals' inability to manage Canada's economic difficulties in the late 1970s, most members of the media and the business community kept on repeating their endless complaints that the mess in the economy was all Trudeau's fault.

Chrétien's difficulty in Finance was a matter of particular satisfaction to several of the intellectuals in René Lévesque's cabinet, men like Claude Morin and the minister of finance, Jacques Parizeau, who had always seen him as the lightweight in the federalist camp, an old-fashioned pol, all sentiment and artifice, a *vendu* born and bred. The separatists were wrong. Chrétien may have been old-fashioned, but he was also shrewd, with an intuitive understanding of how to read the public mood and a highly developed sense of how to get the most out of the government machine.[20]

From the day he came to Ottawa in 1963, Chrétien had used as a guide for his behaviour the old Quebec tradition of the paternalist populist who trusts his own instincts about what the people want and relies on competent bureaucrats for advice on how to give it to them. He had learned what he could from Mitchell Sharp, who had been a bureaucrat before becoming a cabinet minister and whose knowledge of the financial system in Canada, and the interchange between the business community and the bureaucracy, went back to the 1940s and the famous Liberal economic ministers C.D. Howe and Douglas Abbott. Although Chrétien was never interested in the minutiae of policy, he mastered the knack of first getting his officials to brief him on the essence of an issue, then making their ideas his own, and finally defending his department's interests in cabinet. He had also been adept at recruiting political aides and securing their fierce loyalty. He took on as executive assistants two young men who were both clever themselves and the offspring of establishment figures: first John Rae, the son of the diplomat Saul Rae, and then Eddie Goldenberg, whose father, the Montreal senator Carl Goldenberg, had been Trudeau's chief constitutional consultant in 1968 and was one of the most respected legal advisers on labour disputes in the country. Rae and Goldenberg understood both modern party politics and government, and Chrétien had learned to use their advice just as he was able to take direction from ambitious officials in the various portfolios he held. At the same time, he never forgot that he was a "working-class lawyer," according to his own description, just a "little guy from Shawinigan," who could empathize with the aspirations of all the other little guys from rural and small-town Quebec, who had prospered since the 1950s and were wary of the separatists and their rhetoric.

Trudeau himself had been scornful in the past of Chrétien's "p'tit gars" prose and populist poses. Once, early in their political careers, they sat side by side on a long plane journey from Ottawa to western Canada. Trudeau immersed himself in official papers without uttering a single word for several hours while Chrétien twisted in his seat and stared out the window in bored discomfort. As the plane was about to land, Chrétien, who had been made desperately nervous by Trudeau's silence, plucked up the courage to utter the pleasantry "It's raining outside." Trudeau looked up from his dossiers, considered the windowscape, glared at Chrétien, and responded, "If it's raining, it's got to be outside." Over time, Chrétien had been able to disarm Trudeau, along with almost everybody else he met. As a child who had been mildly disabled at birth (he was deaf in one ear and had a slight facial distortion that was disguised as a crooked smile) and who was the least academically adept offspring of a clever family, he had learned early on how to turn aside taunts. He always made some kind of self-disparaging joke before others could wound him with their superiority.

Despite his continuing doubts about Chrétien's intellectual prowess, Trudeau had come to value him for his loyalty, tenacity, and political acuteness. His recognition in 1980 that Chrétien would be the right man for the job of overseeing the federal presence in the referendum campaign was yet another sign of the new Trudeau. Years before, he had remarked to reporters that "the management of men – or of women, for that matter – is not my strong suit." In this regime he was determined to function as a leader who *could* manage men and women surpassingly well. All his new sensitivity and power of persuasion had to be called up to convince Chrétien to take on the Department of Justice. Justice and Public Works were the traditional Quebec ministries because they were so rich in patronage opportunities. Steeped in the folklore of *les rouges*, Chrétien regarded the Justice Department as tainted by its history and a definite step down from the economic portfolios he had held in the 1970s, a place where his resolute honesty might be questioned and where separatist jibes about his anachronistic attitudes might better find their mark. His own larger ambitions – he was already thinking hard about how to succeed Trudeau – had convinced him that External Affairs would be a better assignment for his image.[21]

With this in mind, he went to see Trudeau after thinking over the offer of the Justice job in order to object, saying (in French), "Pierre, why don't you do for me what a big brother would do for his little brother?"

"Okay, Jean," Trudeau replied, apparently without a scintilla of scorn for the unabashed sentimentality in Chrétien's approach, the sort of appeal that in former times might have called forth a wounding putdown. "If you take this job you're minister of justice, you're attorney general of Canada, you're minister of state for social development, you're in charge of the referendum and the constitution. I hope my little brother will not say that his big brother has no confidence in him."[22]

In effect, Trudeau was appealing to Chrétien's fealty and ambition at one and the same time by telling him he was needed. He left the impression – which sent Chrétien happily on his way to the front lines in the referendum battle – that he was the only man who could play this crucial role in the noble battle to rescue the Canadian dream.

CHAPTER 11

The Referendum II:
The Bloody Great Fight

Jean Chrétien was well aware that the task Trudeau had asked him to take on would call on every political trick he had ever learned and every resource at the federal government's command. To co-ordinate the federal initiative a crisis management team had been put together in the Federal-Provincial Relations Office – an arm of the PCO – so officials there could act as liaison with key sectors of the federal bureaucracy. Also located in the FPRO was the Canadian Unity Information Office, whose polling and advertising budget was inflated to cover the cost of beaming into Quebec in the last six weeks of the campaign television commercials costing millions of dollars and ostensibly intended to give information about federal government programs but really selling the idea of federalism.[1]

Chrétien was determined to use the forces available to him without alienating the personalities whose skills had to be harnessed in this complex operation. Not only would he have to contend with the powerful appeal of René Lévesque, he would need to manage carefully his relationship with Claude Ryan, who had already expressed resentment at his participation. Despite the Non committee's need for Ottawa's help, Chrétien was a "federal cousin" whom Ryan held in low regard. Chrétien thought this hostility stemmed from an incident two years before, when he had been approached to run for the leadership of the Quebec Liberal Party at the same time that Ryan was considering the job. Chrétien had gone to *Le Devoir* to discuss the situation and with honest intent had taken it on himself to tell Ryan that politics was not a trade for which he had a natural talent, a statement Ryan apparently found impertinent and infuriating. Now Ryan rejected out of hand Chrétien's offers of federal support in the form of either polling data or advertising dollars. Ryan also vetoed Chrétien's breezy suggestion for the campaign's slogan – "La séparation? Non, merci!" – in favour of his own, more intellectual play on the similar-sounding words for no (*non*) and name (*nom*) – "Mon Non est Québécois!"[2]

Chrétien realized he would have to take charge of the Non campaign without letting Ryan know he had lost control. With his alter ego Eddie Goldenberg co-ordinating his efforts in Ottawa, Chrétien proceeded to do just that, throwing his frenetic energies into the cause, ostensibly as Ryan's humble collaborator. Typically, he would go from a noontime strategy session at the FPRO to an afternoon meeting with a committee of Quebec MPs, who were monitoring the electoral mood in their own ridings, to an evening rally in some Quebec town where he would make a fiery speech about the virtues of federalism and his love for Canada. Since the Liberals held every seat in Quebec but one, they could use their MPs to blanket the entire province with propaganda that documented the benefits of federalism. Campaigning door to door, the MPs embodied the federalist message of pride in a bilingual Canada that the federal ad agencies were playing in the media. Their forays were co-ordinated for the most part by provincial Liberal organizers whose campaigning capacities had been honed in repeated and successful by-election encounters with the PQ.

In making their pitch to Quebeckers, the federal Liberals were also able to count on the support of the English-speaking provincial governments. For the first time in nearly a decade of intergovernmental strife, Ottawa was fighting a federal-provincial battle on only one front. After consultation with the FPRO, the anglophone premiers obligingly delivered a series of messages calculated to play on Quebeckers' nervousness about the costs of separation. Premier Peter Lougheed said that an independent Quebec would have to compete for Alberta oil with international customers. Premier Allan Blakeney predicted that an independent Quebec would be treated by Saskatchewan and the other anglophone provinces like a separate country. Premier William Davis announced that Ontario would never negotiate any form of economic association with an independent Quebec.[3]

Also drawn into the Non coalition were representatives of the plethora of anglophone citizens' committees that had formed and re-formed to fight the separatist threat ever since the PQ had come to power in 1976. The most prominent and effective group of anglophones active in the Non cause was the Positive Action Committee, whose co-chairmen were Storrs McCall, a professor of philosophy at McGill, and Alex Paterson, a Montreal lawyer who came from an English-speaking family that had prospered in Quebec for at least two hundred years.[4]

McCall and Paterson were sophisticated representatives of the class that had once dominated the province and was now grappling with the realization that English-speaking Quebeckers had become a beleaguered minority in the province. Tired of listening to relatives and friends fretting in their clubs and corporate offices about the gradual exodus of their tribe to Toronto and the impact on business of the separatists' anti-English language law, McCall and Paterson had taken it on themselves to organize anglophones as a pressure group first for the Bill 101 language-law debate in 1977 and then for the referendum campaign. By the spring of 1980 they were working full out for the No cause, driven on by the feeling that the collective life of English-speaking people in the province hung on the referendum. Accustomed to easy wins in federal and provincial elections for federalist candidates in anglophone areas where the Parti Québécois was anathema, they knew that this time it was the total number of votes in the province, not the number of riding victories, that would determine the outcome. Turning out every potential No voter became their obsessive goal. They thanked God daily that the federal government had weighed in to bring some direction to Ryan's faltering efforts. But they also believed that without the provincial party's organizational strength and without the preliminary work of committees like their own to sensitize and then mobilize different pockets of federalist opinion over the previous several years, the No campaign would have been lost no matter what magic Chrétien was able to bring to bear in the last eight desperate weeks of the referendum fight.

That he was magic in his way, they had to admit. The populist oratory of the "p'tit gars de Shawinigan" soon gave the Non campaign a grass-roots tone in telling contrast with the highly intellectualized messages of the Ryan team. Out on the hustings where he discreetly "joined" Claude Ryan on countless community hall stages, Chrétien hammered away at the ambiguity of the referendum question and the hidden meaning behind the vote. "I was amazed at Chrétien's political skills," said Alex Paterson, who knew Ryan well and admired him. "He was completely correct in his treatment of Claude as well as cool and competent in a way that the folksy stuff we knew about him had kept hidden."[5]

Night after night Chrétien asked Quebeckers to think about why the separatists needed a mandate.

> To do what? To make us lose our Canadian passport? To make us lose our Canadian citizenship? To make Pierre Trudeau the last French-Canadian prime minister of Canada? To make us lose the riches that have always belonged to us? A mandate to make [us] a little country in a world that is more and more interdependent?[6]

In this way Chrétien was managing, as the journalist Michel Vastel observed, to get Trudeau's vision of Canada applauded from one end of Quebec to the other. He appealed to his compatriots' ambitions by equating them with his own. "Who will be the ambassadors after independence? Who will be in the king-sized Cadillacs with the chauffeurs and the flags on the hood? It will not be you and it will not be me. It will not be the little people. It will be the bourgeois from the Grande Allée and Outremont." He mocked the rarefied language of the Péquiste intellectuals. They called a tank of gas "un reservoir d'essence," whereas Chrétien (and his listeners) spoke of "un tank de gaz." There were ironies here that Chrétien's slangy eloquence disguised. For one thing, charging the Péquistes with being too cerebral when he was acting as front man for the most intellectual prime minister in Canadian history was in itself an oddity. For another, the insults ignored the practical strengths the PQ intellectuals had displayed in the management of Quebec's affairs as well as their resolutely Spartan political style.[7]

Chrétien was the most gifted populist speaker deployed in the federalist cause. But there were twelve other francophone ministers in Trudeau's cabinet and most of them were also charged with delivering the federalist line. Every Tuesday morning in Ottawa Chrétien met a francophone cabinet committee to orchestrate their departments' efforts in the cause. For the duration of the campaign these ministers were told not to travel or speak anywhere outside Quebec without permission from Trudeau himself: their energies were to be devoted to the referendum. The health and welfare minister, Monique Bégin, had a bilingual flyer inserted with the monthly family allowance cheques that were sent out across the nation. "No thanks is easy to say" was innocuous enough as an anti-alcohol message for English Canada. For Quebec the *double entendre* had a more political message: "Non merci: ça se dit bien." Marc Lalonde, as Quebec leader in the caucus, instructed Léonce Mercier, the director of the Quebec wing of the federal party, to marshal all available resources to the cause. Jean Marchand, the government leader in the Senate, toured Quebec as a triumphant symbol of the Quebec federalists' power in Ottawa, showing his old unionist fire in delivering a message of pride and accomplishment.[8]

> *We* have fought and battled for official languages legislation, for regional expansion grants, for highrise office towers in Hull. *We* have proved it's possible for French Canadians to wield power in Ottawa. *We* have ended the feeling of inferiority that had dogged Quebeckers. Sure, everything is not resolved but you have to participate in Canadian politics to get results for Quebec.[9]

Using the debate on the speech from the throne in mid-April as their chance to get back at the Péquistes for their onslaught on federalism in the National Assembly the month before, federal ministers painted a gloomy picture of Quebec under sovereignty-association. André Ouellet, the minister of consumer and corporate affairs, predicted reduced quotas and subsidies for Quebec farmers as well as severe economic decline in Montreal if the Canadian government stopped spending its annual "$5 billion in wages, social assistance, subsidies, capital expenditures, guaranteed loans and contracts." Marc Lalonde, as minister of energy, maintained that "Quebec would immediately, and I insist immediately, have to pay $3.8 billion more a year for its oil," translating that as $400 more for each Quebec family to heat their homes, $450 more to drive their cars. Monique Bégin warned Quebeckers about the dubious future of social services such as the child tax credit, the pension supplement, and free ambulance services, which "could certainly not be paid in a separated Quebec without substantial tax increases or cutbacks in the programs of other departments." The message from Ottawa was forceful: voting "Oui" meant deprivation for Quebeckers, giving up the gains that had been made under the Trudeau government, giving up their hold on Canada.[10]

The debate put on the parliamentary record all the themes that were being hammered home by federalists in Quebec itself at service club lunches, in church halls, and during interviews given to small-town newspapers and radio stations. It also served to launch Pierre Trudeau's own intervention in the campaign and as such was part of a carefully devised broader strategy.

In company with Michael Pitfield, his cabinet secretary, who was a constitutional lawyer as well as an anglophone Quebecker, and Robert Rabinovitch, the deputy secretary to the cabinet, who was adept at strategizing, Trudeau had assessed the risks of being identified with failure if the Non side lost and the danger of undermining Ryan's position if he intervened too much. They decided he should make a limited number of major speeches "at the invitation of the Non committee," a device that provided an excuse for his intervention. The speeches were to be aimed at polarizing the shades-of-grey rivalry between Ryan's neo-federalists and Lévesque's proponents of sovereignty-association into a black-and-white contest between straight federalism and straight separation. Ever since the PQ's victory in 1976 Trudeau had been insisting that the referendum should be a once-and-for-all affair with a clear question and a clear decision. Several years later he was still proud of his pugnacity on this point. "I had made a speech at the Chamber of Commerce in Quebec City in 1977 calling for a referendum immediately, saying, 'We need a clear question on this issue and we need it soon and we need the answer to be durable. Let's get it out of our blood.' " Having already persuaded Ryan to bury his Beige Paper ideas for the duration, he intended to transform by his oratory the soft phrasing that Quebec voters would read on the referendum ballot into the hard question about independence that was already lurking at the back of their minds.[11]

First, he wanted to clear away the cobwebs about sovereignty-association, and for this purpose the throne-speech debate was the ideal forum. With his francophone ministers massed on the parliamentary benches around him to demonstrate to the Quebec television audience the reality of French power in Ottawa, he spoke eloquently about Canada, a fortunate nation in a world where misery was prevalent, a nation at the peak of human happiness but in danger of falling prey to divisive racial conflict, "the enemy within." Having established the importance of the national will to the survival of Canada, he attacked the ambiguity of the PQ's ideas. If the anglophone premiers had no interest in a common market with an independent Quebec, there could be no "association." If Lévesque wanted pure "sovereignty," the wording of the question would give him no mandate for that, even with a Oui majority. In any case, Trudeau himself had just been re-elected with seventy-three other MPs from Quebec's seventy-five ridings "to exercise sovereignty for the entire country." The overt message was that a Oui vote would only yield a stalemate. The subliminal message was: "French Canadians have never had it so good, and under a re-dedicated federalism it can be even better."[12]

Once this parliamentary performance re-established his importance as the arch-federalist in the great debate about Quebec's destiny, Trudeau put his energies into preparing for three public appearances in the province. They were to be three of the great speeches of his career. He was very conscious of the oratorical tradition in Quebec – a society where speech-making still mattered, a developed intellect was respected, and the man of the word had authority – and well aware that he occupied a particular place within it, that he was in the tradition of Wilfrid Laurier and Henri Bourassa. "I heard Bourassa speak when he was already old, during the conscription fight of the 1940s," he once said in a rare display of admiration for another man, "and he was marvellous still. He could stir the crowd not by demagoguery but by a display of his intellect and his imagination."[13]

Ever since his teens, when he had studied elocution and memorized reams of classical poetry and prose, Trudeau had striven to achieve that kind of emotive prowess. At sixty, he was at the peak of his powers. After delivering hundreds of speeches on election platforms, he knew how to play on the feelings and prejudices of a particular crowd while at the same time remaining supremely logical. His physical elegance was still remarkable. His voice, from which he had so meticulously expunged all traces of joual, was as supple as an actor's. His face, released from the unhappiness of the previous six years, was compelling in its strength. Lean, lightly tanned, clear-eyed, clad in expensive clothes, he looked above all like a man of the world, the kind of "guy who could go anywhere and meet anybody and talk so smart it would make you proud to be a *Canadien*," as a French-Canadian caller said in English on a radio phone-in show at the height of the referendum campaign. Bringing these formidable assets to bear, he chose his audiences and polished his speeches for the maximum effect.

On May 2 in Montreal, Quebec's financial capital, performing for a downtown audience of businessmen at a Chamber of Commerce luncheon, Trudeau used a mixture of relentless logic, open scorn, shameless fearmongering, and direct taunting of Lévesque. He attacked separatists as intellectuals and academics who showed contempt for Canada and ordinary Canadians, "knights of independence" who were lacking in courage and would lead Quebeckers into "the valley of humiliation." Suggesting that a Oui vote would not result in economic association with the rest of Canada, he evoked Fidel Castro and Jean-Claude Duvalier as examples. If Cuba or Haiti voted in a referendum to join Confederation, "should we, in the name of fair play, be bound to say, 'Of course, yes. The vote was unanimous, there is nothing we can say'?" Laughter and applause greeted his casuistic extension of his opponents' position to its logical absurdity. The effect of his style was to make Lévesque look naïve, marginal, perhaps even a little sinister, a man who might humiliate Quebec by turning it into a banana republic begging Anglo Canada for succour.[14]

On May 7 in the Old World capital city of the province, Trudeau appealed to his compatriots' pride in Quebec's past. He stood on a platform shoulder to shoulder with Claude Ryan and the two former Liberal premiers, Robert Bourassa and Jean Lesage, the father of the Quiet Revolution who was now suffering his final illness, and talked about the wonderful things that had been accomplished by French Canadians within Confederation. During thirty-six of the past hundred years there had been

French-Canadian prime ministers defending Quebec's interests in Ottawa. All this pride and power would be lost if the separatists won the referendum. He again mocked the Parti Québécois for not having the courage to pose a clear question on independence; perhaps Lévesque was not being honest about his long-term plans.

The effect of the onslaught of the federal Liberals had not been anticipated by the Lévesque government, and Trudeau's attacks began to rattle the confidence of the Péquiste troops, whose morale had already been seriously shaken by an error made early in the campaign by Lise Payette, one of the party's most popular and normally most perceptive MNAs. A former television host on Radio-Canada, Payette had dedicated herself to the cause of feminism as Lévesque's minister responsible for the status of women. At a rally early in the referendum campaign she had spoken of the need to rid school textbooks of sexism. After reading an excerpt from a Dick-and-Jane-style primer about a sweet little girl called Yvette who was docile and without ambition, she went on to say how she, like most Québécoises, had started out in life as an Yvette. Turning up the partisan heat, she added that Claude Ryan was the kind of man who wanted women to remain Yvettes – that is, dedicated to hearth and home – and, carried away by her rhetoric, she added, "Anyway, he's married to an Yvette." As a throw-away line, this final jibe was just so much campaign hyperbole until it caught the attention of Claude Ryan's successor at *Le Devoir*, Lise Bissonnette.[15]

In a devastating editorial Bissonnette turned the sexism charge back on Payette, pointing out that she was attacking Madeleine Ryan through her husband, an elementary violation of feminist decorum. In any case Madeleine Ryan was far from an Yvette, having been an activist citizen and leading volunteer in many education commissions, community committees, and Catholic movements since the 1950s. "Through her it is not Claude Ryan Lise Payette is insulting but all those women she is appointed to defend ... It is their own dignity, their own solidarity which she is burying along with the little progress towards respect they have made over the last years."[16]

It made no difference that Payette got up to apologize the very next day in the National Assembly. Having inadvertently provided a focus for the irritation and fear many women felt about independence, she dislodged their collective anger. Three weeks after Payette's gaffe, the Non committee attracted fifteen hundred women to a brunch in Quebec City's Château Frontenac. Just over a week later, ten thousand people, mostly women, crowded into the Montreal Forum to hear accomplished compatriots such as Thérèse Casgrain, Monique Bégin, Sheila Finestone, Solange Chaput-Rolland, and Jeanne Sauvé along with many others express the indignation that was rallying masses of Quebec women to protest what they perceived to be an élitist attack on their dignity. The sense of the Oui campaign's solidarity with the people of Quebec was shattered by this largely spontaneous protest movement, skilfully exploited by the Non campaign. It did not matter when Lysiane Gagnon, the principal columnist for La Presse, pointed out how negligible a role women actually played in the Quebec Liberal Party. The damage had been done.[17]

Within the PQ itself, Payette's error was seen as the kind of mistake to which Lévesque himself was prone when his passion overwhelmed his reason. His colleagues had long despaired of the qualities that accompanied the premier's spontaneity: a confidence in his intuition that disdained strategy, a nonchalance about careful planning and tactics, a preference for improvising as he proceeded, a proclivity for ambivalence and ambiguity in his messages.[18]

As the campaign wore on and the tide began to turn, Trudeau's sarcasm got under Lévesque's skin. With reporters obligingly passing on the prime minister's taunts and pressing for the premier's reactions, Lévesque's mood turned and his tone became embittered. He became ugly in his anger. He accused the federal Liberals of lying about the benefits they claimed Quebec would get from contracts to build the new American fighter plane, the F-18A. He dismissed the disappointing results of a Gallup poll, saying an organization based in Toronto would naturally have rigged the questions. He attacked his federalist antagonists as traitors. It was a mistake to slur those whom Quebeckers had elected only a few weeks before. It was an even greater mistake to tangle directly with Trudeau, but Lévesque seemed unable to help himself. He challenged the prime minister to a television debate, handing Trudeau the chance to point out sanctimoniously, in a press release that he wrote himself, that Lévesque was violating "the spirit and letter of his own referendum law" by inviting federal intervention and not debating with Claude Ryan, the Non committee leader. Therefore "my answer to him is an unequivocal 'Non, merci!' "[19]

Lévesque's worst mistake was yet to come. It involved a racial slur against Trudeau that not only was foolish, it went against Lévesque's own principles. This decent and dedicated democrat, who had always been revolted by the racist undertone in the rhetoric of hard-core indépendantistes, who had fought hard against their desire to squeeze every last anglophone out of Quebec, reverted in his frustration to the free-wheeling Gaspé boy who had flunked out of Laval and resented the arrogance of Trudeau, the legalistic Brébeuf snob and pious Citélibriste intellectual. Exhausted by the rigours of leading both the referendum campaign and the government, he blurted out an exasperated aside about his opponent – the one who was fighting

from his impregnable federal fortress, contrary to the
rules laid down by the referendum legislation – by ex-
horting a heckler in a senior citizens' home to remember
that Trudeau's other name was Elliott and this meant he
had "decided to follow the Anglo-Saxon part of his heritage." Lévesque's remark was made on May 8, just twelve
days before the vote and six days before Trudeau was
scheduled to give his last major speech of the campaign.[20]

This climactic speech was delivered to the largest Non
campaign audience yet, who were gathered in the Paul
Sauvé Arena in Montreal, a site normally identified with
the PQ's victory celebrations but on this occasion packed to
the rafters with federalist partisans who had turned out
for a final rally. The campaign's fervour was at its peak.
The province was mobilized into two armies who faced
each other with the intensity of zealots in a religious war:
the Oui and the Non. Old friends had turned against one
another. Families were divided. And the scene was set for
Trudeau to make the speech of his heroic fantasies.

It was a mixture of logic and high emotion. This was a
great occasion, Trudeau said, this referendum, rare in the
history of democracies, an occasion when a people could
decide their fate, an occasion that "our children and perhaps, if we are lucky, our grandchildren," will want to
know about. Where did you stand? they will ask. For the
Yes or the No? He then ran through the options, giving
those who leaned to the Yes all due respect but suggesting
that they were being misled into an impasse "by these
hucksters of sovereignty," that Lévesque was quite possibly deceiving himself as well as them, that he was being –
oh unkind cut! – illogical. And cowardly, don't forget
cowardly. If he and his colleagues had the courage to ask
the real question that was on their minds – *Do you want to
leave Canada?* – the answer would be *no!* One must say *no*
to ambiguity. *No* to trickery.

The crowd roared its approval. And then came the electric few minutes when Trudeau addressed the question Lévesque had raised about his name.

> And one must say *no* to contempt, because they have come to that. I was told that ... Mr. Lévesque was saying that part of my name was Elliott and, since Elliott was an English name, it was perfectly understandable that I was for the No side, because, really, you see, I was not as much of a Quebecker as those who are going to vote Yes. That, my dear friends, is what contempt is. It means saying that the Quebeckers on the No side are not as good Quebeckers as the others and perhaps they have a drop or two of foreign blood, while the people on the Yes side have pure blood in their veins ...
>
> Of course my name is Pierre *Elliott* Trudeau. Yes, Elliott was my mother's name. It was the name borne by the Elliotts who came to Canada more than two hundred years ago. It is the name of the Elliotts who more than one hundred years ago settled in Saint-Gabriel-de-Brandon where you can still see their graves in the cemetery. That is what the Elliotts are. *Mon nom est Québécois* but my name is a Canadian name also and that's the story of my name.

He then went on to ridicule Lévesque for his racism, pointing out that several of the PQ ministers had English names – Pierre-Marc Johnson, Louis O'Neill, Robert Burns – that the leader of Quebec's Inuit people was called Charlie Watt, that the chief of the Micmac Indians at the Restigouche was called Ron Maloney. Were these people, all of them French-speaking, not Quebeckers? At one point, he pointed to his face in an aside that did not appear in the text of his speech and said, "I ask you: is this the face of an exclusively European man?" an ambiguous question that alluded to what was much talked of in Quebec – the rumour that Trudeau must have had an Indian ancestor whose genes had produced the high cheekbones, the proud attitude, the hint of exoticism in his face. His romantic language and demeanour conjured up three centuries of Quebec history, the coureurs-de-bois, the wigwams, the struggles, the battles, the early deaths, the hard lives, the hopes and fears of a brave, beleaguered people. He may have been talking about the Elliotts in his background, but this was no effete snob from Outremont. This was Charlie Trudeau's smart boy up there emoting, a fighter, an activist, a patriot who had travelled the world and conquered it but had come home because Quebec was what mattered most to him, a man who contradicted parochial nationalism by his very being, showing in his person what a Quebecker could achieve in a larger Canada. Trudeau ended this part of his speech with a paragraph that invoked both patriotism and the progressive spirit of *les rouges*.

> My dear friends, Laurier said something nearly one hundred years ago . . . "My countrymen," he said, "are not only those in whose veins runs the blood of France. My countrymen are all those people – no matter what their race or language – whom the fortunes of war, the twists and turns of fate, or their own choice, have brought among us."

Passion and polarization were what Trudeau was bringing to the Non cause. But the fiery orator also managed to remain the cool rationalist in the heat of this fight for Quebec's allegiance. To passion and polarization he added a portentous promise.

> I know that I can make a most solemn commitment that following a No vote, we will immediately take action to renew the constitution and we will not stop until we

The full-fledged politician: Trudeau's first public triumph was as the justice minister who modernized divorce laws in 1967.

Moments of triumph: Trudeau's march to the apex of power was swift. First he won the Liberal leadership, next he won the country campaigning on charisma (here with Gérard Pelletier), and then he took his place gleefully in the prime minister's chair.

Days of glory: For Pierre Trudeau in his late forties, the joys of power were many as journalists, activists, and beautiful people (Jennifer Rae, a diplomat's daughter, and the entertainers Barbra Streisand, Yoko Ono, and John Lennon) flocked to his side.

Years of bliss: In his early fifties, Pierre Trudeau courted and married Margaret Sinclair, a liaison that developed rapidly from first date to secret wedding to campaign partnership but ended sadly in temperamental differences that tore the pair apart.

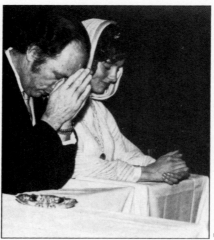

Canapress

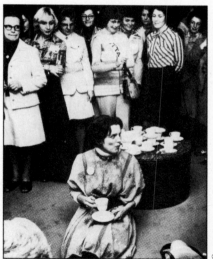

Canapress

Trials of single parenthood: In his late fifties, Pierre Trudeau looked after his children as Margaret Trudeau danced around the world.

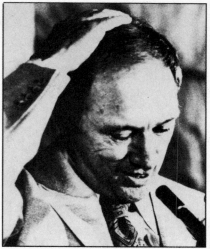

Doug Ball/Canapress

Trudeau in crisis: As he approached the age of sixty, Trudeau's personal and political problems converged, and he lost first an election and then his composure before deciding to resign in 1979.

Dave Buston/Canapress

Trudeau in triumph: But in 1980, after a series of astonishing events, Trudeau returned to office determined to resolve his magnificent obsession and bring the Canadian constitution home.

have done that. And I make a solemn declaration to all Canadians in the other provinces: we, the Quebec MPs, are laying ourselves on the line because we are telling Quebeckers to vote No and telling you in the other provinces that we will not agree to your interpreting a No vote as an indication that everything is fine and can remain as it was before. We want change and we are willing to lay our seats in the House on the line to have change.[21]

In the dying days of the campaign, when Quebeckers' attention was focused on the momentous decision they had to make about their collective future, Trudeau had sounded the chord of pan-Canadianism: Quebeckers needed a new contract with Canada, one that would guarantee their equal place in Confederation from coast to coast. It was an inspired performance, probably the crucial act that secured the soft neo-federalist vote, directing it away from the Oui and towards the Non.

The next day the Parti Québécois militants in the field were disoriented. What could they say to the public when Trudeau's promise had subverted their strategy and transformed the nature of their question? He had succeeded in turning gentle gradualism into an immediate, final decision and in redefining the meaning of sovereignty-association. If a Non vote now meant Oui to constitutional change, he had turned the referendum on its head, making the negotiation of a new federalism the patriotic option.[22]

Le vingt mai, the day Quebeckers voted Oui or Non to sovereignty-association, was one of those dates destined to enter the collective consciousness of contemporary French Canada just as le vingt-deux juin and le quinze novembre had done before it. The birth of the Quiet Revolution in June 1960 and the election of the Parti Québécois in November 1976 had been turning points in French Canada's electoral history, when ballots marked for a party candidate had produced profound changes in the province's political direction. But May 20 was different.

Quebeckers were being consulted directly about their political fate. In a society that the young intellectual Pierre Trudeau had castigated only thirty years earlier as undemocratic, politically immoral, and corrupted by its authoritarian troika of church, state, and big business, this exercise in democracy was a moving spectacle. A national liberation movement rooted in ethnicity and language was pursuing its goal of self-definition in an open, democratic exercise, relying solely on the spoken and written word. For the first time anywhere in Canada, a province's whole population was being asked to decide what kind of political framework it wanted. Although nothing in the Canadian constitution granted a province the prerogative of secession, anglophone Canada's acceptance of a spectator's role in this all-or-nothing drama implicitly condoned the Parti Québécois's claim that Quebec had the right to national self-determination.

By the time referendum day dawned, few Quebeckers doubted the stakes. A life-or-death struggle between rival visions of Quebec's historical destiny and of the Canadian federation was seemingly being forced to a climax. By the end of the campaign, thanks in good part to Trudeau's interventions, each side had everything riding on the outcome. Complex and cloudy though the PQ's question had been, Trudeau had managed to ensure that the simplicity of the answer – Oui or Non – forced Quebeckers into an extraordinary process of self-identification and decision. The referendum campaign had become a catalytic collective experience as Quebec was forced to do what a political system generally avoids: confront itself and act.

Trudeau and Ryan on one side and Lévesque on the other had forced the whole Quebec population to choose between apparently irreconcilable visions of their future. Titanic figures personified the Utopias that they themselves had constructed. All three belonged to the political generation that had risen to prominence two decades earlier with the Quiet Revolution. Each headed a powerful political formation, but they shared common beliefs in reform, state interventionism, and individual rights. Each knew the others intimately, but it was the intimacy of opponents who had been fighting an ideological civil war for twenty years on behalf of cherished panaceas. Once the polls closed and the media had broadcast the results, the three champions appeared before the cameras and microphones one after the other to give their responses to the people's decision: 60 per cent Non, 40 per cent Oui. Even among francophones, only 48 per cent had voted Oui.[23]

For René Lévesque it was a body blow. His whole political thrust as the PQ leader had been a process of compromise, reflecting his integrity as a democrat. He had believed in his compatriots' right to independence but had rejected the notion of a revolutionary liberation movement in favour of forming a political party that would play by the rules of the parliamentary federalism from which he wanted to liberate them.

The results seemed to prove once again that successful reformers make poor revolutionaries. Lévesque himself had demonstrated this old axiom several months earlier when he had addressed a joint meeting of the Toronto Canadian and Empire Clubs, those bastions of Anglo-Canadian capital from which he was trying to extricate his province. With his engaging, slightly self-deprecating wit, his candid, unpretentious style, and his colloquial, Americanized English, he had proudly recounted all the campaign promises his government had kept. Language law, labour law, electoral law: the list of reforms was long. But his record raised two troubling questions. Since the Quebec government had managed to implement its electoral program, had it not proven Trudeau's argument from the 1950s that Quebec had all the constitutional powers it needed to protect French culture and initiate new vistas of social justice? Moreover, if the achievement of linguistic security and a welfare state had increased job opportunities for francophones and decreased their sense of alienation, why would they want to support sovereignty-association and risk upsetting their improved situation?[24]

Abandoned by his colleagues on referendum night when the electorate gave its answer to *étapisme* – only Corinne Lévesque, his wife, and the courageous Lise Payette had come with him to the stage of the Paul Sauvé Arena to concede his loss – Lévesque acknowledged he would have to swallow the verdict and pointed out simply that the political ball was now in the federal government's court. In the audience, young Péquistes wept openly and hugged one another in their sorrow. "À la prochaine!" their champion said hoarsely before he left the stage, in a tone that was both sad and defiant: there would be a "next time." He was still premier of Quebec and he could regroup his forces for the next encounter. His chanting supporters were trying hard to believe that their leader was down but not out.

In contrast, Claude Ryan's response to the news of the results was dismayingly sour. His victory statement, which should have been a short, generous call for the healing of wounds among Quebeckers, was instead a twenty-five-minute-long, vengeful harangue. Impervious to the needs of the television networks and the attention span of the viewers, he went on and on, presenting himself, in the words of the journalist Doug Small, as "the Grim Reaper of Quebec's Catholic heritage." He showed no sympathy for his separatist adversaries who had battled so valiantly, and he demonstrated his own arrogance by a futile demand for a speedy election on the grounds that his provincial Liberals should negotiate on behalf of Quebec at the next constitutional conference. The speech revealed a political reality that his formal leadership of the Non committee had partly disguised: Ryan had been rendered powerless. He had been powerless to reject Jean Chrétien as the director of the federal forces and powerless to prevent Trudeau from seizing control of the Non campaign's agenda. Now he was powerless to dictate how either Lévesque or Trudeau would act in the referendum's aftermath. Although Ryan himself did not realize until later that he had been marginalized by this campaign, it was clear to many viewers on referendum night that the real power on the Non side, both moral and temporal, resided with Trudeau.[25]

"We are experiencing tonight the fullness of democracy, with all its joys and sorrows," Pierre Trudeau said when his turn finally came to address the public. Recognizing the extent to which his compatriots, even those on the Non side, had been torn apart by the battle in which many felt they had gone against their better selves, almost betraying their own people in its best interest, he found words of balm as if he himself had experienced this trauma from the inside, as though he empathized with all Quebeckers – which included people in his own cabinet who had been traumatized by the referendum fight that pitted them against their own friends and relatives.

"To my fellow Quebeckers who have been wounded by defeat," he said, "I wish to say simply that we have all lost a little in this referendum. If you take account of the broken friendships, the strained family relationships, the hurt pride, there is no one among us who has not suffered some wound which we must try to heal in the days and weeks to come."[26]

Trudeau's words of conciliation were followed by words of warning. "[Although] I am unable to rejoice without qualifications . . . those who fought with conviction [for the Oui] will have to bend before the majority verdict." Many of the Non supporters, who felt almost as devastated as the partisans of the Oui, were unclear about the implications of their victory. In truth, as Gérard Bergeron, the Laval political scientist, observed immediately afterwards, the Non vote did not resolve the fundamental question about the malfunctioning of Canadian federalism that even the prime minister had acknowledged as serious six days before, by making his commitment to change.[27]

The very next day, May 21, Trudeau revealed that he understood "the majority verdict" to mean another round of constitutional negotiations, but this time they would be entered into on his terms.

CHAPTER 12

THE RELUCTANT BRIDE

On May 21, 1980, the day after the referendum vote, Pierre Trudeau rose in the House of Commons to announce that he intended to move immediately to keep his promise to patriate and renew the British North America Act. Jean Chrétien was to be dispatched that very night to the provincial capitals to inform the premiers of his plans to break the country's constitutional impasse.

In the course of his speech, Trudeau remarked that he had been calling for constitutional renewal and a charter of rights for Canada for several years. In fact, his involvement with the issue went back to wartime Montreal, when his interest in the Canadian constitution was first piqued by a guest lecture given in 1943 at the Université de Montréal by F.R. Scott, the poet and professor of law at McGill. Scott was a romantic figure, an unusually tall man with an aquiline face and a strongly evocative speaking style, the radical offspring of an English-Canadian establishment family and a member of the Co-operative Commonwealth Federation who advocated socialism in open defiance of his superiors at McGill. As an anti-imperialist, Scott had supported strongly the defiant position against military conscription taken by most French Canadians in the early 1940s, a bold act that had caused some of his own colleagues and relatives to castigate him as a traitor to his class and country while the French-language press had lauded him as a rare ally.

It was in the wake of the conscription crisis that the Université de Montréal law students gathered to hear Scott talk about the role of the British North America Act in Canada's evolution from colony to nation and the need for its federal principle to be construed by lawmakers as an instrument for realizing both the aspirations of their compatriots and the dual culture of Canada. What he had to say – and the elegant way he said it – was electrifying to students accustomed to part-time lecturers who usually laboured at practising *la loi du bumper*, the small-time law open to French Canadians, and who gave courses that were "tediously mechanical – contracts and the like," as Pierre Trudeau remembered them. For the restless, twenty-three-year-old Trudeau, these petty concerns seemed intolerable in the midst of the dramas of the worst war in history, especially when he was asking himself basic questions about the meaning of democracy, the nature of liberty, and what made citizens obey the state – the kind of issues Scott was prepared to address. Charles Lussier, one of Trudeau's classmates, was so intrigued by Scott's views that he went on to study constitutionalism privately with him at McGill. Trudeau himself vividly remembered the courageous figure Scott cut as he delivered a lesson in constitutional theory that challenged his fellow English Canadians' war-heightened intolerance for such niceties as minority rights.[1]

But the idea of the prime importance of the constitution as a political society's basic law did not become an intellectual absolute for Trudeau until he began his postgraduate studies in 1944. It was at Harvard University, the intellectual capital of liberal America, that the young Trudeau definitively adopted the ideals and values that were emerging as the belief system of the élites in the newly victorious democratic states. This post-war positivism held that carefully crafted constitutions were a bulwark against the re-emergence of totalitarianism. From Merle Fainsod, the dean of American Sovietology, with whom he took Government 8a, a course on dictatorship and bureaucracy, Trudeau appropriated the idea that the unchecked domination of citizens' lives by all-powerful state machines stood among the worst of all political evils. At the same time he was indoctrinated into the virtues of constitutionalism by two equally authoritative professors. From Charles McIlwain, then ending his distinguished career as a passionate apostle of the subordination of governments to a higher law, he learned that the state must be limited by fundamental principles establishing and consecrating individual rights. He also enrolled in two courses with Carl Friedrich, a scholar of both totalitarianism and constitutionalism, who very soon put his constitutional theories into practice by returning to his native Germany to advise the American military governor, General Lucius Clay, on how to devise a lasting democratic constitution for what was to become the Federal Republic of Germany.[2]

In 1946–47, when Trudeau was studying at Sciences Pô in Paris, French politicians were battling over their latest constitutional confection, that of the Fourth Republic. French history was littered with constitutional debris marking the violent swings of fortune between revolutionaries and reactionaries. Once ensconced in power the winning faction promptly proceeded to rejig the constitution to buttress its own positions and weaken its enemies' chances. Over the past two centuries debates about the nation's fundamental law had become part of the perpetual struggle between left and right. In contrast, Trudeau's stint at the LSE in London the next year coincided with a less tempestuous kind of class war, the struggle to construct a modern welfare state. Though the ideological debate was heated, the Fabian vision of social justice was being implemented by the Attlee government in the context of a national consensus about the largely unwritten British constitution, which was made up of a body of laws and conventions that had evolved over several hundred years.

During these years spent studying abroad, Trudeau ingested a medley of notions drawn from Western political thought. From Locke he took on the idea of liberty as the *summum bonum*: each individual must be guaranteed liberty in order to realize his potential. From Rousseau he retained the democratic view that, in the ideal state, citizens enter a social contract in which they consent to obey laws that are the product of their own general will. In the actual political systems he studied, constitutions were simply the means necessary to achieve the desired end. They represented the basic prerequisite for achieving what really excited Trudeau's Quebec-centred imagination: a liberal democracy in which citizens participate through their elected representatives in making laws so they can enjoy the fruits of their individual liberty while protected, via the judicial system, from abuses of power.[3]

It was only by chance that Trudeau became directly involved with practical constitutional questions early in his career. When he fetched up at the Privy Council Office in 1949 to begin his first job in Ottawa, one of the tasks he was handed by his bureaucratic boss, Gordon Robertson, was an assignment to research the problems and possibilities inherent in trying to bring home the British North America Act from the British parliament at Westminster, where it was still lodged eighty-some years after the Fathers of Confederation had concocted it in order to make a political entity out of several of Britain's remaining North American colonies. The BNA Act of 1867, which created Canada, guaranteed certain powers to these colonies, making them provinces in a federated system and creating a powerful "dominion" government to be situated in the new capital city of Ottawa. Britain had *not* granted Canada the authority to control its own foreign relations or the right to change this constitutional document – which would have made it a fully sovereign nation – and for the next half-century, Canadian governments accepted their continuing quasi-colonial condition.

It was not until sixty thousand Canadian troops died on French soil in defence of the mother country in World War I without their own government having any say in their deployment that Ottawa moved to appropriate from Britain control over its own foreign relations. Even so, it took until 1931 for the Statute of Westminster to be passed by the British parliament, formally recognizing that its dominions – Australia, New Zealand, and South Africa as well as Canada – were sovereign and equal to Great Britain, "in no way subordinate one to another," as the Balfour report of 1926, on which the statute was based, had expressed it. At the time, Canada declined to assume responsibility for future adjustments to its own constitution. Dominion-provincial tensions were too acute for a consensus to emerge on how constitutional changes should be made, so the power to amend the BNA Act was left in British hands. By this time, the British wanted to be quit of their responsibility for Canada so their agreement to retain these powers was reluctant, more *noblesse oblige* than nostalgia for lost imperial splendours.

For the generation of English-Canadian intellectuals who made up the small federal public service in the late 1940s – the Ottawa men who had suffered various humiliations in war and peace under the command of autocratic British officers and the tutelage of disdainful Oxbridge scholars – bringing home the constitution was an important goal nevertheless, one of the last steps in the long effort to turn their country into a nation. The wiliest man in this sterling lot, Jack Pickersgill, was chief of staff in 1949 to the newly anointed Liberal prime minister, Louis St. Laurent. Pickersgill, who had been trained as a historian but found his true calling in government early in life, had been keen for many years on reaching a final resolution of the question of Canadian independence from Britain. He had failed to convince Mackenzie King, his former political master, of the sagacity of undertaking such an endeavour, but he did convince himself that his own fervour for patriation had resonance with St. Laurent. "Pick" believed that the new Liberal leader's prim, lawyerly façade disguised a flaming patriot who could be sold to the electorate as their deliverer from the last vestiges of colonialism. St. Laurent had given a Pickersgillian speech during the 1949 election campaign, which in effect promised the Canadianization of the BNA Act (a goal that was assumed to require provincial agreement to a formula for making future amendments); a bill of minority rights; and legislation that would make the Supreme Court of Canada, rather than the Judicial Committee of the British Privy Council, the final court of appeal in all Canadian law cases. The third of these promises was fulfilled within weeks of St. Laurent's resounding electoral victory, through an act that made the Canadian Supreme Court supreme in Canada. When the young Pierre Trudeau read about this triumph, he felt "heartened that St. Laurent was willing to tackle tough issues." He had no way of knowing that the two other constitutional goals St. Laurent had set would not be fulfilled for thirty years.[4]

The problem was the classic Canadian difficulty: the need to reach an agreement between the federal government in Ottawa and the far-flung provinces with their disparate needs, complaints, and fears. Canadian politicians had been struggling sporadically and unsuccessfully for a generation to find a solution to the problem of reaching an agreement on the amending formula. As a first step, the St. Laurent government decided to enact a resolution requesting that the Crown transfer to the Canadian parliament amending rights in purely federal fields of jurisdiction. For full amending power, it still felt that the approval of the provinces was needed. To this end, St. Laurent decided to convene a dominion-provincial conference in January 1950. The research Gordon Robertson assigned to his young assistant, Pierre Trudeau, formed part of the briefing papers prepared for this conference. Trudeau attended the meetings in what he later described as his "lowly role as a minor official" and began to learn some hard realities about the Canadian state.

For months, he had been working long hours to help Robertson develop a proposal for a constitutional amending power that would prove acceptable to the ten premiers of the day. But instead of following through with his advisers' carefully constructed proposal, St. Laurent dithered and conciliated at the conference, apparently afraid of incurring the rage of Maurice Duplessis, who was then approaching the height of his political career and had become hypersensitive to any federal proposal that might affect his power as premier of Quebec. Rather than use his prime ministerial authority and electoral popularity to impose his views, St. Laurent sought a consensus among the premiers – a consensus that was not forthcoming at this conference or the second one that followed later in the year.[5]

Trudeau's memory of these meetings was dominated by his impressions of Duplessis, whom he saw in action there for the first time. Nearly forty years later he could still recall his disgust, his sense of Duplessis as the tinpot dictator of a little people. Duplessis would throw out cigars and expect his advisers to scramble for them. Or he would crack vulgar jokes and then, preening himself, look around to make sure his delegation – whose members behaved throughout like a mindless claque – was laughing loudly enough. In the staid assembly of English-Canadian politicians and officials, the premier's style caused eyebrows to be raised and discreet whispers to be exchanged. Trudeau "felt ashamed as a French Canadian" by this display, a calculated reminder to the English that Duplessis was not a premier like the others, and definitely not interested in seeing the constitutional question resolved. Agreeing to bring home the BNA Act meant accepting its definition of federal and provincial powers as then understood, which would reduce Duplessis's leverage in his constant resistance to Ottawa's incursions. If there was nothing in patriation to fortify the position of Quebec, then why bother to be accommodating? "On the human level, I saw him as a despisable human being," Trudeau said afterwards. "I never forgot his behaviour there when I was assessing his attitudes in other areas."[6]

The only saving grace at these meetings for Trudeau was the contribution of Frank Scott, who was acting as the constitutional adviser to the CCF government of Saskatchewan. The Quebec delegation was craven, most of the English premiers parochial, the Ottawa men impotent. Only Scott had a vision of the role of the constitution in a federal state. Everybody else was concerned with political advantage.[7]

As a result of these meetings, the enthusiasm for patriation that had been generated in post-war Ottawa dribbled away. By the end of 1950, St. Laurent had fallen into one of his periodic depressions, and there were pressing international and economic matters demanding his attention.

His staff soon developed an easy excuse for his missed opportunity, reasoning that Canadians cared more about continental development and the burgeoning Cold War than about vestigial colonial ties in any case.[8]

By the time Trudeau quit the capital to return to Quebec in early 1952, he had absorbed the official view that St. Laurent's failure to reach an accord in 1950 was not a matter of great importance. The very mandarins who had sought "patriation" – his Oxford-trained mentor, Gordon Robertson, among them – had reached the sanguine conclusion that the British North America Act, like the loosely defined British constitution from which it derived, was flexible enough to accommodate almost any kind of modification that might be required. Besides, the British had shown they were altogether willing to oblige the Canadian government in making whatever amendments might be necessary in the future. In that way, changes could be effected incrementally without provoking major dominion-provincial brouhahas.[9]

In the next few years in Montreal, as he participated with his fellow intellectuals in discussions about the need to reform Quebec's polity, Trudeau became notorious for opposing the view, increasingly accepted there, that constitutional change was crucial to Quebec's political, economic, and social development. He remained fixed in the belief that addressing the thorny question of constitutional review was a potentially ugly diversion from more pressing social tasks. Whenever the idea was put forward that Quebec needed enhanced powers within the federal system, Trudeau obstinately defended the constitutional status quo, even though he had already acquired a reputation as a left-leaning radical on other issues.

In 1955 he developed this line more fully, wearing his economist's hat in a brief he prepared for a trade-union presentation to the Royal Commission of Inquiry on Constitutional Problems, generally known as the Tremblay commission. Duplessis had set up the commission in response to Quebec nationalist concerns about Ottawa's gradual intrusion through its newly developed social and cultural policies into areas of provincial jurisdiction. Trudeau's position was straightforward. He reasoned that the BNA Act as it stood gave Quebec all the constitutional powers it required. What was important was to use them effectively in order to meet the really pressing priority, the crying needs of the province's working class for a decent standard of living and adequate social services. For the Quebec proletariat – as he called the working people whose unions he was representing – transforming the British North America Act was far less urgent than adapting Canadian federalism so it could benefit from Keynesianism, the economic doctrine he had absorbed at Harvard and the LSE that promised stable growth for capitalist systems. "Démocratie d'abord!" was his watchword throughout the Duplessis years. Constitutional pipe-dreaming would only divert French Canadians from achieving real democracy and making Quebec a progressive and modern society that would free individual citizens from collectivist shackles.[10]

As the Quiet Revolution fired up Quebec's imagination in the early 1960s, the idea that Canadian federalism offered a healthy balance of centralized management and provincial autonomy took on an even greater importance in Trudeau's mind. Quebec activists of all political stripes were centring their demands for a new deal in Canada on the need to alter the constitution radically. But Trudeau remained a constitutional conservative. He still argued that Canada had a perfectly adequate constitution in the BNA Act. Although a constitution was the sine qua non for building a just society, the genius of Canadian federalism, he insisted, was to balance the dominion government's exercise of economic management functions with the provincial governments' capacity to determine social and cultural policies region by region, a capacity that Ottawa should not interfere with by poaching in areas outside its proper jurisdiction.[11]

The fire-breathing activists in Jean Lesage's government were not in the least impressed by this train of thought. Paul Gérin-Lajoie, the minister of youth, who was a constitutional authority, having written an important book on amending the BNA Act, maintained that Quebec had the right to sign treaties in areas of its constitutional jurisdiction, such as education or culture, and he was taking steps to negotiate agreements with France that were designed to give Quebec more constitutional leverage in its ongoing power struggle with Ottawa. Daniel Johnson, as leader of the Union Nationale, was attacking Lesage for his willingness to accept the Fulton-Favreau formula, a proposal for amending the constitution put together by Davie Fulton, Diefenbaker's minister of justice, and Guy Favreau, a Montreal lawyer who was to become Pearson's minister of justice. In Johnson's eyes, their formula did not redistribute powers radically enough in Quebec's favour. For him the choice was *égalité ou indépendance* – constitutional equality between Quebec and the rest of Canada or formal independence. When the Lesage government showed signs of responding seriously to these pressures, Jean Marchand intuitively sensed the danger to Canada's federal system and felt Trudeau should do something about it.[12]

By this time, Trudeau was teaching constitutional law at the Université de Montréal, as one of a handful of constitutional experts in the province. He had come to love the law for its logical clarity, its philosophical depth, its potential as an agent for political change; and his attachment had grown steadily as he took on civil rights cases himself and watched Frank Scott use the courts to defend hapless victims of the state. When Marchand urged him to address the issue of the constitution publicly he was ready to respond, both as a lawyer and as a polemicist. As bombs started to explode in Montreal mailboxes in the name of the clandestine Front de libération du Québec and as the Lesage government became increasingly aggressive in its demands for "special status" within Confederation, Trudeau developed his counter-attack against both the outright separatists and the provincial Liberals' neo-federalism, which he saw as tantamount to covert separatism.[13]

Constitutional change should follow, not precede, political change, he told *Maclean's* in 1964. New relationships of power were emerging between the central and regional governments, "and they must be given time to work themselves out before any attempt is made to translate them into the basic law of the country." In a brief prepared in the spring of 1965 for the Constitution Committee of the National Assembly, exactly a decade after his study for the Tremblay commission, Trudeau was still in defiant opposition to the now accepted wisdom in Quebec about the urgency of undertaking constitutional reform. He remained a defender of constitutional passivity, refusing to be swayed even by the moderate views of the neo-federalists in the provincial Liberal Party who, like the editorialists at *Le Devoir*, were proposing that Quebec be given a special status within Confederation. Although he did not deny that the British North America Act could be improved – especially by adding a bill of rights to limit government power and to "put the French and English languages on an equal basis before the law" – he felt the province needed constitutional stability, not a disruptive debate for which no consensus had yet developed. "To my mind," he wrote, "the constitution has very little to do with the state of economic, technical, and demographic inferiority in which the French Canadians of Quebec find themselves today. I am not in a frantic hurry to change the constitution, simply because I *am* in a frantic hurry to change reality."[14]

At that point, when he was making his decision to go into federal politics, it was not because of the Canadian constitution. "The reason I went to Ottawa was because Quebec was getting strong enough. I was afraid of the collapse of the federal power." He was taking his studies to their logical conclusion.[15]

When Trudeau and Pelletier wrote their apologia for joining the Liberal Party, they mentioned neither the need for constitutional change in general nor a bill of rights in particular. What they stressed was a belief in "a democracy centred on social progress, a federalism that can reconcile a strong central power with autonomous and progressive provinces, finally a politics that is open to the left." A few months later, when invited to address the founding convention of the federal Liberal Party's Quebec section, Trudeau again defended his do-nothing-for-now constitutional position, which had become decidedly unfashionable even among French-Canadian federalists. He maintained that attempts to achieve special status or new foreign policy powers for Quebec were unnecessary in a conjuncture where "demographic, social and economic forces are in the process of transferring to provincial governments an enormous addition in power, without having to change a single comma in the constitution."[16]

By this time, Trudeau was an MP and the prime minister's parliamentary secretary, with an office down the hall from Lester Pearson's. He could hardly have found a better audience for his constitutional ideas. As a former mandarin, Pearson shared Trudeau's reluctance to open up the political Pandora's box of constitutional change. But their mutually agreed-upon passive stance on the question could not last in the face of the heated demands being made in Quebec. A year or so after Trudeau took on the parliamentary secretary's job, the constitutional issue changed dramatically when John Robarts, the premier of Ontario, announced that since Ottawa was not going to act, he would convene a conference of premiers to discuss the future of Confederation. The federal government could not afford to let the provinces set the agenda in such an important matter, and Pearson was forced to respond in order to regain control. Because Trudeau's fluency in constitutional matters and his clear-cut ideas on Quebec had so impressed Pearson, he decided to appoint him minister of justice and put him in charge of the whole question.[17]

Even this late in the decade of the Quiet Revolution, Trudeau saw the constitutional question as only one facet of his general mandate in the Justice Department. In his mind, the more important task was to bring Canada's laws up to date. Governments should not waste time in endless debates on the distribution of powers, particularly since the anglophone premiers might catch the Quebec disease and start making jurisdictional demands of their own. If Ottawa had to get involved in constitutional change, it should do so incrementally, adding an amending formula one year and patriating the constitution another, for example. He remained what he called "a reluctant bride on the constitution – I didn't want to address it until Pearson asked me to take it on. I still thought tackling it would be opening up a can of worms."[18]

Given the temper of the times, this attitude could not be maintained even by as cool a strategist as Trudeau. Tremendous pressure had built up over political inequities in Quebec and the abysmal condition of French-language services outside Quebec. In the space of two tense weeks in the late fall of 1967 the sovereignist Société Saint-Jean-

Baptiste held an "Estates General" on the constitution, with two thousand delegates so worked up that they jeered moderate nationalists such as Claude Ryan; Premier John Robarts held his Confederation of Tomorrow conference, giving Daniel Johnson a platform for his equality-or-independence ultimatum; and André Laurendeau and Davidson Dunton released the first volume of the report of their Royal Commission on Bilingualism and Biculturalism, which called for French to be made the other official language of Canada's federal institutions and for all parents to have the right to have their children educated in either language wherever the population was sufficiently concentrated. The Bi and Bi report was greeted as too little, too late by Quebec radicals, and their emerging champion, René Lévesque, dismissed it as simply a device to lull an awakened Quebec.[19]

Canada had caught the French disease that Trudeau had seen in post-war Paris. The constitution had become the proxy issue for a power struggle, in this case between Quebec nationalism and Canadian federalism. The question was how Ottawa should respond to the separatist challenge. Even though Pearson as prime minister was formally in charge, he left it to Trudeau as justice minister to establish the federal government's course. The day after he was sworn in as minister of justice, Trudeau went to visit Carl Goldenberg, the constitutional expert and labour negotiator and his former colleague at the Université de Montréal, to ask him to become his special counsel on the question and to set up a task force to advise him on possible areas of reform. The group, which involved professors from law schools across the country (Ivan Head from the University of Alberta, Mark MacGuigan from the University of Windsor, Gerald LeDain from Osgoode Hall in Toronto, Barry Strayer from the University of Saskatchewan, and Gerard La Forest from the University of New Brunswick), also included several seasoned federal government officials with a special interest in constitutional issues (Allan Gotlieb from External Affairs, A.W. Johnson from the Treasury Board, and Jean Beetz and Michael Pitfield of the Privy Council Office). They set out to indulge Trudeau's penchant for starting with a *tabula rasa* by proceeding to review the federal government's stand on all constitutional issues, while the justice minister himself plunged immediately into a frenetic program of overall law reform. Before too long the task force came to a strategic conclusion. They would recommend that the federal government seize the constitutional initiative by endorsing the notion of entrenching a charter of rights in the BNA Act.[20]

Trudeau could easily fit the case for such a charter into his federalist logic. Reflecting a few years earlier on the dangers of ethnic nationalism in a multicultural state, he had speculated about whether separatism could be offset "by investing tremendous amounts of time, energy and money in nationalism *at the federal level*." His considered conclusion was in the negative: nationalism could not provide the salvation of a federal regime. Instead, only "cold, unemotional rationality can still save the [Canadian] ship of state." And what could be more rational than a bill of rights? After all, a bill of rights had been discussed in legal circles for decades. J.S. Woodsworth, the founder of the CCF, had called for one in the 1920s. Frank Scott, who had been mentor, friend, and ally to all those who fought civil rights fights in the 1950s, had long been pleading the case in the legal community. Even John Diefenbaker had made political moves in this direction when he was prime minister by having a bill of rights enacted by Parliament. (Significantly, the statute proved to carry little weight in the courts because it was secondary to the BNA Act.) Furthermore, the constitutional entrenchment of fundamental human rights would be popular among immigrant groups conscious of the value of equality rights as a legal guarantee against discrimination. Beyond these considerations, the biggest attraction of the idea for Trudeau the politician was its potential impact on the debate in Quebec. If the charter expanded French-language rights to include educational guarantees across the country, it would carry a powerful emotional message to the country's francophones, who believed their collective desire to live in a French-speaking culture was threatened. Such a guarantee of minority linguistic and educational rights, which Trudeau presented as a matter of pure logic for both Canadian founding groups, would be a powerful means of accomplishing one of his major goals, fighting neo-nationalists of all stripes.[21]

Having worked through this logic, he handed Carl Goldenberg the task of drafting a speech advocating a charter. Goldenberg's text, revised extensively by Trudeau himself, was the landmark speech he delivered to the annual meeting of the Canadian Bar Association on September 4, 1967. A constitutional declaration of rights, Trudeau told the nation's lawyers, would do away with old power conflicts between the two levels of government in Canada. Rather than haggling over which jurisdiction should have which powers, "the power of both the federal government and the provincial governments would be restrained in favour of the Canadian citizen who would, in consequence, be better protected in the exercise of his fundamental rights and freedoms." In this perspective, he said, "we will be testing – and, hopefully, establishing – the unity of Canada."[22]

Standing firmly in the pan-Canadian footprints of Henri Bourassa, Trudeau was claiming that with a charter of rights, the central government would be better able to defend French-Canadian cultural interests and at the same time become a national symbol around which *all* Canadians could rally. That this proposal signalled the opening of a political war-game to be played out under the cover of constitutional activism became evident the very next day at the infamous press conference Trudeau gave in order to answer questions about his speech. When the hostility to his federalist ideas expressed by Quebec reporters caused him to lose his temper and curse all advocates of special status for Quebec, the whole constitutional exercise changed. Until then Trudeau had been assembling ideas about the constitution and turning them into elegant intellectual arguments for the benefit of his peers. Now his theories were being disputed in public by reporters who were rude, imprecise in language and thought, instinctively nationalist, and dismissive of him as a federalist *vendu*. Trudeau may not have been familiar with Oscar Wilde's aphorism about journalists – "By giving us the opinions of the uneducated, they keep us in touch with the ignorance of the community" – but it was plainly a sentiment with which he concurred. The street fighter in him came to life. He was no puny pen-pusher or vague theorist. He was the kind of guy who slugged back. "You call me 'Toto' [a hated diminutive] once more and I'll punch you in the mouth," was the threat he had hurled at his classroom tormentors as a schoolboy. Now he was saying to his journalistic tormentors as an adult, "You question my ideas and integrity and I'll show you who has the real power and the real knowledge as far as the constitution is concerned." Under pressure he was adopting once more his old the-best-defence-is-offence stance.[23]

From that time forward Trudeau was committed to changing the BNA Act. The constitutional incrementalist had been transformed into a constitutional activist. Five months later, when he attended the constitutional conference called by Lester Pearson for February 1968, it was evident that he had revised his script on how to shore up federal power against the threat from Quebec nationalism. Under his aegis, a number of documents had been published that laid out the federal government's constitutional position in terms that elaborated his own views on individualism, functionalism, and a charter of rights. He was pleased that the struggle with the Quebec government was being presented in the media as a confrontation. The federal government was saying to French Canadians that Quebec was not the only government that could speak for them. "So if we can get this across, then the rest is a normal power struggle."[24]

Trudeau's televised exchanges with Daniel Johnson, the premier of Quebec, at this conference had a dramatic impact on his forthcoming leadership candidacy as the man with a plan for saving Canada. But it also marked the start of twelve long years of such conferences when his constitutional plans, which seemed to him so eminently sensible and so minimally disruptive of the status quo, would be rejected again and again by assorted premiers of Quebec sullenly resisting any change that did not at the same time give the province significantly increased jurisdiction at the expense of federal power.

When he settled into the prime minister's official residence in the summer of 1968, buoyed by the public approval that had produced his resounding election victory in June, Pierre Trudeau found that the upper hand in constitutional matters was his. Pressure from Quebec for a brand-new constitution had died down. Daniel Johnson's poor health had caused his threat of *égalité ou indépendance* to fade as fast as the overall fortunes of the Union Nationale he led. And the provincial Liberals, now the official opposition under Jean Lesage's leadership, had apparently drawn a lesson from Trudeau's political success. At their convention in October 1968 they endorsed the notion of federalism, avoiding even the mention of special status. In English Canada, the anglophone premiers were either uninterested in or suspicious of constitutional change.[25]

At this point the idea of altering the British North America Act could easily have died from inertia. But Pierre Trudeau was now determined that constitutional change should be part of his general drive to bring Canada up to date. As part of his three-part plan, he hastened implementation of the Bi and Bi commission's major recommendation, the Official Languages Act, which forced federal institutions (such as the courts) and Crown corporations (such as Air Canada) to provide services in French for francophones right across the country. At the same time, he was making sure that French Canadians were given priority in government appointments so that their second-class status in federal politics could be obliterated. Ottawa would become a bilingual capital and a locus equal to Quebec City for defending French-Canadian interests.

But Trudeau knew that laws could be unmade as well as made. As Henri Bourassa had argued decades before, parliamentary democracy did not give a minority complete security. Franco-Manitobans had learned this unhappy lesson when the Anglo-Saxon majority had run roughshod over their rights in the 1890s and deprived them of French-language schools. If French Canadians were to be secure as a founding people of Canada, the Confederation agreement would have to be renegotiated to include minority-language education rights and official bilingualism as basic principles inscribed in the constitution itself, so that the courts could defend citizens against parliamentary dominance. Trudeau now believed that this constitutional question had to be resolved through a charter of rights before the boil of separatism could be lanced. This was the third part of his Quebec strategy, though obviously it would take longer than the other two since it had to be negotiated with all the provinces.[26]

Many of the constitutional advisers Trudeau had recruited for the Justice Department task force were retained to staff the working committee needed to maintain the federal-provincial dialogue on constitutional change established by the February 1968 conference. Michael Pitfield took command of the committee as part of his job in the PCO, in an attempt to impose on its bureaucratic deliberations an overarching scheme for the reinvention of the Canadian constitution. Trudeau himself soon became enmeshed in these deliberations. First he took part in lengthy PCO seminars dominated by obscure discussions of the meaning of functionalism. Then he had to keep abreast of the bureaucratic negotiations of the Continuing Committee of Ministers on the Constitution, the intergovernmental group that had been set up after Pearson's February 1968 conference, and to preside at a series of first ministers' meetings on the subject. By early 1971, as these federal-provincial negotiations on abstruse matters lumbered into their fourth year, it was obvious they had become bogged down in their own complexity. A new politics of constitutionalism was being created that was mind-numbing for most English Canadians and a constant aggravation for Quebeckers.[27]

Even Trudeau, whose patience in this process had been publicly commended, started to become edgy, particularly since separatism was again a serious concern in the wake of the October Crisis. He pressed his bureaucrats to encourage their provincial counterparts to produce some results. A federal election would have to be called within the next two years, and he wanted something to show Canadian voters for his efforts to resolve Quebec's discontent. Could the premiers agree to leave aside the sticky problems raised by a redivision of powers and concentrate instead on such relatively easy issues as an amending formula, a bill of rights, and patriation?

In the placid atmosphere of Victoria, the federal and provincial first ministers convened in June 1971 ready to discuss such a limited package of change. They emerged from three days of negotiation with an agreement: a formula for amending the constitution and a modest charter guaranteeing some rights and entrenching the Supreme Court, whose judges would be appointed with provincial approval. Trudeau had achieved his goal: constitutional peace in our time. Or so it seemed until Robert Bourassa, the new Liberal premier of Quebec, returned home and was subjected to a barrage of nationalist protest. Savaged by Lévesque's emerging Parti Québécois and squeezed by a trade-union common front against the Victoria deal, Bourassa backed down, withdrawing his consent.[28]

Trudeau had originally expressed great satisfaction when Bourassa, a federalist, had defeated the Union Nationale in 1970. Now he turned disdainful. All the patient hours spent in long seminars with his officials as they debated the perfect constitution, all the laborious discussions his cabinet secretary, Gordon Robertson, had held on his behalf with the provincial delegations, all the prime energy he had personally put into this issue at the cost of other policies had been wasted, leaving nothing to show beyond a thriving cottage industry of constitutional bureaucrats in every provincial capital. The Victoria débâcle reinforced Trudeau's view that neo-federalists were all crypto-separatists. Bourassa's dithering – he constantly left the negotiations at Victoria to phone back to Quebec for advice – had confirmed what Trudeau had suspected from the premier's panicky behaviour during the October Crisis the year before: Bourassa had no guts.

What was worse, the premier proceeded to grow more nationalist as the months passed and the Parti Québécois steadily gained favour. He started talking about "profitable federalism" and "cultural sovereignty" for Quebec in a "Canadian common market," notions that flew in the face of Trudeau's view that federalism was far more than a common market and that Quebec City was far less than the national capital of an emerging French-Canadian state. More annoying still, Bourassa started courting support from the anglophone premiers in his campaign for full jurisdiction over all social policy matters, from pensions to family allowances, the issue over which he had aborted the Victoria deal. In Trudeau's eyes, Bourassa was as bad as his predecessors, confirming his original view that whatever label they might carry – Union Nationale or Liberal – neo-federalists were closet separatists whose appetite for power could never be appeased, whatever concessions Ottawa made.

This gulf between the Liberal leaders in Ottawa and Quebec City resulted in several years of guerrilla warfare between their governments. Marc Lalonde, whom Trudeau assigned to the crucial health and welfare portfolio as soon as he was elected to Parliament in 1972, sparred for over three years with Claude Castonguay, Bourassa's architect of a fully integrated and Quebec-designed social policy. Gérard Pelletier, to whom Trudeau had entrusted federal cultural policy, found himself under constant pressure from Jean-Paul L'Allier, Bourassa's minister of communications, over the two governments' respective jurisdictions in matters like cable television.

Given this sour atmosphere when Trudeau returned to power in 1974 with a new majority, he was expected to let the constitution languish. The public was tired of the subject. Canada's economic troubles were becoming serious, and arcane arguments over linguistic rights and amending formulas seemed irrelevant. Even Trudeau's closest allies in the constitutional wars thought the issue was dead. Instead Trudeau chose to gear up once more a process he knew was not fully subject to his control. Reflecting on the choice eleven years later, Trudeau remembered, "I really thought, after winning the election of '74, that we could do it [achieve constitutional patriation]. It was one last try at the consensual approach, but Bourassa, that damn fool, . . . sensed I was determined to patriate the constitution and he wouldn't be able to hold me to ransom any more." Since neither man would give way, their conflicts escalated.[29]

In a private meeting with Trudeau in early 1976 about plans for the Olympic Games, which were to be held in Canada later that year, Bourassa refused to agree to Trudeau's proposal that the Queen make a stopover at Quebec City en route to the opening ceremonies in Montreal. Trudeau was livid. Shortly afterwards he unleashed a two-hour-long diatribe against Bourassa in front of a convention of the Quebec wing of the federal Liberal Party. His tirade was vitriolic, an amazing mélange of street slang, Brébeuf snobbery, and Citélibriste invective. The premier's Bill 22, which made French the sole official language of Quebec, was a "political stupidity," and as Trudeau made clearly understood afterwards to reporters, the premier himself was also stupid as well as a weak-kneed coward, a man with so little sense of style he ate hot dogs for lunch.[30]

The attack was intemperate in its rhetorical style and its lack of substance. Being attacked as "un mangeur de hot dogs" was not quite as bad as being called a "pepsi," the old pejorative anglophone Quebeckers had applied to French Canadians. But it came close. Although Bourassa did come from a lower-middle-class background – his father was a municipal clerk – the premier had been just as well educated as Trudeau was himself, at Brébeuf, the Université de Montréal law school, Oxford, and Harvard. Furthermore, he had married into the shipbuilding Simard family of Sorel, who had amassed one of the largest fortunes in the province. To snob Bourassa was to sneer at the whole Quebec business and professional élite, an act that added to the list of Trudeau's enemies. He had already enraged the intelligentsia and the arts community with the War Measures Act; now he was alienating the bourgeoisie.

Trudeau's attack on his Liberal "cousin" enhanced the credibility of the Parti Québécois. In mocking Bourassa, who already had serious problems, he was helping to push Quebec from the frying pan of ambivalent neo-federalism into the fire of outright separatism. On November 15, 1976, the hot-dog-eater was turned out of office by René Lévesque.

Trudeau accepted the election results with good grace, pointing out that the glory of the democratic system was to allow a separatist party to come to power without violence. But Lévesque's victory heralded the failure of Trudeau's constitutional effort for the 1970s. Lévesque had promised there would be no movement towards his party's goal of sovereignty-association before a referendum had been held on the issue. In the interim he would take part in federal-provincial negotiations like a normal provincial government. But since his ideological position completely dismissed the present federal relationship as a farce, Lévesque also affirmed there was no way that he would be party to a constitutional bargain until "Quebec has received a guarantee that it will obtain all the powers it needs in order to ensure its development." With unanimity generally accepted as the prerequisite for any constitutional decision, Lévesque's very presence at first ministers' conferences spelled stalemate.[31]

In contrast to 1967, when Trudeau had confidently told the Canadian Bar Association that the time was ripe for a constitutional declaration of rights, a decade later the time was wrong for whatever Trudeau wanted to do. He could not prevent the Péquistes from waiting out his term of office to hold their referendum. Nor could he impose on the anglophone premiers any sense of urgency that the constitution should be patriated forthwith, since constitutional negotiations had come up against another serious problem: the newly orchestrated demands of the English-speaking premiers. The anglophone provinces had taken their cue from the example set by Quebec as Trudeau himself had warned they might. His attempts to revive interest in patriation in 1975 met with a solid common front of antagonistic provincial premiers demanding more powers from Ottawa.

This new obstacle did not persuade Trudeau to give up. On the contrary, he made yet another effort to achieve constitutional reform and contain Quebec separatism in the wake of the Péquiste victory in November 1976. He created the title of minister of state for federal-provincial relations for Marc Lalonde and gave him the task of commanding the war against the Péquistes while relaunching the constitutional negotiating process. Lalonde took control of all federal business affecting Quebec, using a special task force headed by the young civil servant Paul Tellier to monitor and co-ordinate federal responses to whatever moves the Parti Québécois might decide to make. The Canadian Unity Information Office was opened to produce counter-propaganda. A bill was introduced to allow the federal government to hold its own referendum should it feel the need.

As well as being super-minister for Quebec, Lalonde tried to box Quebec in through the federal-provincial negotiation process. Gordon Robertson, acting as his deputy, was kept busy discussing constitutional issues with his provincial counterparts. The high-profile Task Force on Canadian Unity, headed by the ebullient former cabinet minister Jean-Luc Pepin and the popular former premier of Ontario John Robarts, was set up to hold hearings, write a report, and above all revive the public interest in the federal position on the constitutional issue. In the meantime, Lalonde presided over the drafting of a new set of federal proposals for a completely revamped constitution, published as a document called *A Time for Action*. This ambitious set of concepts was translated into laborious legislative prose in Bill C-60, which proposed to amend the Canadian constitution in matters under federal jurisdiction by an act of Parliament in which the provincial premiers would have no say at all. Since these matters included a charter of rights and a "House of the Federation" to replace the existing Senate, Bill C-60 outraged many constitutional experts. Even Eugene Forsey, an old comrade-in-arms from the union movement in the 1950s whom Trudeau had elevated to the Senate, denounced the measure as a "nightmare for the ordinary citizen and a nightmare even for the lawyers" and dissociated himself from the Liberal Party.[32]

The initiative was in any case stillborn. Alberta challenged the constitutionality of Bill C-60 before the Supreme Court, and when Trudeau met his provincial counterparts for two more constitutional conferences, the federal government was on the defensive, struggling not to give up too much ground in the face of the provinces' counter-pressure. Trudeau was painfully aware of his dilemma. "I've almost given away the store," he complained as the November 1978 first ministers' conference broke up, having failed to negotiate a charter of rights and an amending formula in exchange for giving more powers to the provinces.[33]

When the first ministers reconvened in February 1979, they asked for still more. In his desperation to get a deal, Trudeau was willing to offer more from his store, including giving the provinces jurisdiction over family law. He was saved from betraying his own principles entirely by René Lévesque's refusal to agree to any deal and by the anglophone premiers' seemingly insatiable demands. The public opinion polls promised Trudeau would be soundly defeated in the upcoming federal election. The premiers were sure they would be able to extort still-further concessions from Joe Clark, whose "community of communities" view of federalism coincided with their own desire for a more decentralized system.

As it turned out, they were right in the short term but wrong in the long. In not coming to a constitutional settlement with Pierre Trudeau, the premiers left the Liberal leader on the ropes but not knocked out of the fight. Flanked by his loyalists, he stubbornly fought through the 1979 election campaign. When he realized he was going to lose on May 22, he insisted on being defeated on his own issue. Defying his pollsters and media advisers, who knew that there were no votes to be won by talking about the constitution, he gave a major speech on just that subject to a hopped-up crowd of Liberal partisans in Toronto in early May. If elected, he shouted at seventeen thousand cheering Grits packed to the rafters in Maple Leaf Gardens, he would meet "one more time to seek consent of the premiers to bring the constitution back with an amending formula. And failing that, we will bring it back and consult the Canadian people in a referendum. And that's the way we will do it!"[34]

The next day he gave a long lecture spelling out his proposed new plan of action on the constitutional problem to a group of business people in Montreal. There would be a joint resolution of the two Houses of Parliament, one last meeting with the premiers, patriation, and, after two more years of negotiation on an amending formula, some kind of referendum to break the deadlock and complete the constitution-making process. The following day, back in Toronto, he reiterated his position at length to a fidgeting crowd of entrepreneurs who could hardly have cared less about the bloody boring constitution. Trudeau was about to be defeated, in any case, and good riddance was what they were murmuring to one another. Along with most of the rest of English Canada, the businessmen felt that the constitution had become a bizarre obsession with Trudeau, a form of self-defeating madness that had done the country far more harm than good. Defiantly looking defeat in the eye, Pierre Elliott de Bergerac was fighting on, hope against hope, one man against the multitude, a politician caught up in a fight he could not win.[35]

For a dozen years he had engaged in a federal-provincial power struggle without making any headway. The frustrations this situation aroused were, by his own admission, what compelled him back to office in the winter of 1980 and what made him determined now in the late spring of that year to get what he wanted, come what may. Racist opponents of Quebec in English Canada had said early in his prime ministerial career that he was trying to ram French down their gullets. Now it was constitutional logic – not language – that he intended to force down the collective Canadian throat.

CHAPTER 13

TRUDEAU TAKES ON THE PREMIERS

In retrospect, the outcome of Pierre Trudeau's constitutional quest in the early 1980s seems foreordained. There he was, the resolute nation-builder, still intent on realizing his grand design for a patriated constitution and a charter entrenching civil and linguistic rights. Against him was ranged a band of parochial premiers with retrograde attachments to provincial autonomy and parliamentary sovereignty. The struggle was protracted and difficult, but the stronger, wiser man (no woman, of course, having had any direct say in the matter) prevailed, and Trudeau ultimately had his way with the BNA Act.

In reality nothing was predetermined. The political struggle that took place in Canada between May 1980 and April 1982, when Queen Elizabeth II came to Ottawa to sign over Canada's constitution at last to the government of her dominion, was chaotic and open-ended. It was conducted by a few men at the summit of the country's political class, who became in the process largely disconnected from the economic forces and social interests that normally dictated their actions as they schemed and bargained to secure their own, often diametrically opposed, political goals. It passed through several phases with the outcome determined very much by the coincidence of who was in power, by accidents of timing, by changes in public opinion, by the shifting dynamics of coalition-building and deal-making, and by the deployment of propaganda that alternately illuminated and obscured what was at stake. Fights broke out in areas difficult for any of the protagonists to manage: in the mother of parliaments at Westminster, whose denizens refused to be dictated to by their ex-colonials, and in the superior courts of Canada, whose judges declined to respect the politicians' deadlines. In the end, this two-year-long mêlée of personalities, issues, and interests culminated in a complex deal patched together by exhausted bureaucrats and politicians, a deal that produced partial victories and partial defeats for both the prime minister and the anglophone premiers while delivering a savage blow to the premier of Quebec, whose jurisdiction had been the original catalyst for constitutional reform.

Not even the Quebec referendum vote of May 1980 made constitutional reform inevitable. If anything, the victory of the Non forces was open to interpretation in English Canada as a sign that the country had weathered the crisis of separatism that had consumed its energies for twenty years. The defeat of sovereignty-association could easily have been taken as the last chapter of the 1970s, the decade of Trudeau's futile constitutional negotiations. Instead, the referendum signalled the opening of the next constitutional round because someone had decided that federal-provincial politics would not revert to futile ad-hoc-ery. That someone was, of course, Pierre Elliott Trudeau.

"Si je ne le fais pas, qui va le faire?" Trudeau had asked his old friend Jean Marchand in discussing his constitutional options in the wake of the referendum decision. To both men the answer was obvious. Trudeau was in a historically unique situation that made decisive action on Canada's seemingly intractable constitutional impasse possible, practicable, and mandatory. Of all the prime ministers who had tried to break the constitutional deadlock that had plagued the country for half a century, Trudeau was the only one who had ever faced the challenge empowered by a double mandate. He led a newly elected federal majority government fortified by seventy-four out of seventy-five Quebec seats, and he had just won a decisive rejection of the separatist option in the provincial referendum.[1]

"Had I won the election in 1979, I could have done it with a clear mandate because I had made speeches about the crucial importance of reaching a constitutional accord during that campaign. But even though I did not discuss it in 1980, I felt that once I'd won that election and then the referendum, it was clearly time," he said long afterwards while reflecting on his role in provoking one of the most turbulent periods in Canadian history. While it was true that only Trudeau could launch with such legitimacy a new round of negotiations to deal with Quebec's status in Confederation, it was also true that only he felt obliged to take on the task. Constitutional change was mandatory because Trudeau had not wavered from the position he had come to in 1967, namely that the survival of Canada depended on it.

"*The Globe and Mail* said editorially [in 1980], 'What's the rush?' " Trudeau remembered, his voice thin with incredulity. "That was after fifty-four years of trying and a referendum campaign that had wrenched the soul of Quebec. When people said [in such circumstances] that there was no hurry, I felt it would never be done. At the same time, I had a real sense that the country wouldn't last if the issue wasn't [resolved]. It would become a confederation of shopping centres."[2]

"A confederation of shopping centres" was Trudeau's scornful phrase for the view of Canada that he attributed to the Clark Conservatives, with their "community of communities" concept of Canada, and to the grasping provincial leaders who gleefully bought that idea because it aggrandized their own power at the expense of Ottawa's capacity to define and defend the national interest. He knew that the English-speaking premiers, who had been 100 per cent on his side when national survival was seen to be at stake during the referendum campaign, were turning back to their by now natural role as the opposing team, ready to play hardball in the regular federal-provincial contests that pitted Ottawa in an endless, uneven fight against ten always demanding provincial governments.

What had changed was more than just the political conjuncture. The timing was right, but so was the attitude of the chief protagonist. What set the Trudeau of 1980 apart from the Trudeau of the 1970s was the integration of various facets of himself into a fully mature, versatile political actor. Hard-headed, visionary, and now focused on a single goal, he was ready to push for his complex objective knowing that he could draw on not just the strength of his renewed political legitimacy but the strength of a reanimated personal will. "There is a theory that I was so damned obnoxious compared with Pearson or Mulroney, or it would have been done earlier. My answer is there had been a hell of a lot of nice guys since 1926 and the constitution was never patriated. Maybe it took a nasty guy," he said afterwards.[3]

Revived by his political successes in the early months of 1980, Trudeau's charismatic aura, which had faded during his long tenure in office, could now be used to develop the mass public support he needed to combat the provincial élites. "People said I was arrogant. I never was with nice people. Only with those who goaded me. But I was still spoiling for a fight. I still had something of the Cyrano temperament." Now he had a chance to play Cyrano again as the leader of a powerful federal government. He had decided that if he could not get agreement from the recalcitrant premiers, then he would go it alone and unilaterally take a resolution endorsing his constitutional plan across the Atlantic, direct to Westminster. "One premier – of Manitoba," he recalled afterwards, having already forgotten Sterling Lyon's name, "had said [earlier, when Trudeau had threatened a unilateral solution], 'If you go it alone, you'll destroy the country.' I said to him, 'If it's destroying the country to bring back the constitution, then the country doesn't deserve to live. After all this time – more than half a century – if the country breaks up because of patriating its constitution, then to hell with it.' ... I was determined this would be it, with or without anybody else. I was relishing the thought of going to Margaret Thatcher and saying, 'This is what the Canadian government wants.' "[4]

Trudeau's new constitutional strategy did not stem entirely from his experience of inconclusive constitutional negotiations in the 1970s. Joe Clark's failure to reach federal-provincial agreements during his short term in the prime minister's office had shown him that the country's political impasse was not due simply to the premiers' personal hostility to Pierre Trudeau or to their partisan sniping at the Liberal Party. It was the product of a situation in which the implicit rules of the contemporary federal-provincial game prevented the federal government from winning. The unwritten understanding that all decisions of first ministers had to be made unanimously had encouraged each premier to withhold consent from a proposed agreement in order to extract ever-greater concessions for his province. Trudeau had lost control of constitutional negotiations in the 1970s when he had allowed the premiers to put their own long lists of issues on the table. An ever-extending agenda with no fixed deadlines for decisions had removed any discipline from federal-provincial meetings.

Now Trudeau was poised to transform the dynamic. Unanimity would no longer be sought. The agenda would be under his control. And he would fix the deadlines. "I was saying, 'This country will never be strong while the premiers hold the trump cards.' They were always saying, 'You can't get the charter unless you give us such-and-such.' This had been true since Victoria in 1971. Quebec said it then. Saskatchewan said it in 1976, Alberta in 1979. They were asking for the moon because they felt I wanted the charter so badly, I would give them the moon. Even with the support of Ontario and New Brunswick in 1980 [I felt] that was going to happen all over again."[5]

However much Trudeau wanted to break free and take his constitutional reform package straight to the British parliament in May 1980, he knew he had to appear to negotiate in good faith with the premiers one more time. To get public support for an action the premiers would be sure to oppose, he had first to be seen to make a consensus-building attempt at gaining an agreement, at least among the anglophone premiers. This was why, scarcely twenty-four hours after sovereignty-association had been declared politically dead by the Quebec electorate, the prime minister announced his intention to "launch the constitutional renewal and never stop working at it until Canada finally has a new constitution." He was entering another round of consultations by sending his indefatigable minister of justice, Jean Chrétien, to visit the premiers. "Once he has reported to me," he went on with studied obscurity, "I will be able to consult with the leaders of other parties in Parliament, to communicate with all premiers and advise as to the best means of achieving the renewal of the constitution."[6]

What Jean Chrétien discovered in his frantic consultation with nine provincial premiers (René Lévesque having refused to see him in Quebec City) was unsettling if unsurprising. Complacency was setting in among some of the premiers almost as fast as rigor mortis. Unless Ottawa could get its new constitutional proposals signed and sealed before the snow flew again, the chances of garnering altruistic provincial co-operation to honour Trudeau's promise to the Quebec people were slim. To catch the premiers' attention, Trudeau knew he would have to create a sense of urgency. He also knew that engendering co-operation among them was going to prove far more difficult than getting his own team of advisers fired up for action.[7]

Because Trudeau had restored so many of his former colleagues to their old jobs as soon as he was returned to office in March 1980, he was expected to recall Gordon Robertson to manage the constitutional dossier for him in the 1980s. After providing Trudeau's first direct contact with constitutional issues as an official in the PCO in 1949, Robertson had moved on to become a deputy minister, commissioner of the Northwest Territories, clerk of the Privy Council from 1968 to 1974, and then, until he retired in 1979, the cabinet secretary for federal-provincial relations, a job that put him in charge of the bureaucratic side of the interminable constitutional negotiations of the 1970s. Trudeau acknowledged that he owed "an enormous amount to Gordon" but he also knew that this time, he could not afford the luxury of an old Ottawa man's super-cautious approach. "Let's just say," Trudeau explained several years later, "that in this last stage I felt one needed almost a putsch, a *coup de force*, and Gordon was too much of a gentleman for that. It was clearly going to be rough and Gordon Robertson wasn't the man: a mandarin, concerned with the common weal, afraid of irreparable damage to the fabric of society. So I made a different choice."[8]

The man he singled out was not an obvious contender for the job. Michael Kirby, a former professor of business administration, admitted he knew nothing about the constitution, having consciously avoided getting involved in that quagmire of issues he had previously felt to be beyond solution. What he did know about was practical deal-making, a field he had come to unexpectedly when Gerald Regan was elected premier of Nova Scotia in 1970 and asked him to join his staff. After spending three years managing Regan's office, Kirby had moved to Ottawa as an assistant principal secretary in the PMO, where he had proved himself capable, resilient, and shrewd. He had been rewarded for his energetic loyalty to Trudeau with the presidency of a federal think tank, the Institute for Research on Public Policy, whose head office he had moved to his home city of Halifax with the intention of commissioning ideas from the roster of policy-makers he had met during his years in government. "There are five hundred important people in this country," Kirby once boasted, "and I know every one of them on a first-name basis."[9]

A smart, brash, bloody-minded pragmatist, Kirby had kept in touch from Halifax with his former colleagues from the Trudeau PMO/PCO, particularly with Michael Pitfield, Trudeau's closest bureaucratic associate, who came to Halifax periodically to give lectures at Dalhousie University while the Liberals were in opposition and stayed with Kirby's family when he was in town. The two men had discussed several times in the bleak autumn of 1979 what they hoped Trudeau could accomplish if he were ever returned to power. Kirby was not surprised to get a call from Pitfield a few days after the 1980 election asking him to come back to the capital "to do the Gordon Robertson job." The prime minister had taken charge of federal-provincial relations directly, having already decided what his constitutional strategy would be and who would be the best man to implement it. "Kirby was a mathematician so he saw constitutional negotiations as a chess game," Trudeau recalled, explaining his choice. "I knew he had no feeling for the subject but that he would know what pieces to cover, which tactics were needed with the premiers, the other cabinet ministers, and so on. He was a very good EA on this subject."[10]

What Trudeau got in Kirby was an executive assistant who unabashedly called himself "Trudeau's son of a bitch." Colleagues in the FPRO reported that Kirby had no understanding of Quebec or of legal matters but that he was fearless in tackling his formidable task. Whereas Robertson had been trained to respect the due processes of cabinet government, Kirby's preference was to short-circuit them, setting up continually shifting short-term structures to manage the issue of the day or the hour. Robertson's code of behaviour had been learned within a close-knit mandarin caste for whom political advantage was less important than seemly behaviour. Kirby cared not a whit about proper procedure or how he treated other people. Today's friend might be tomorrow's enemy. Either was manipulable in the interests of achieving the prime minister's immediate goals. Qualities in Kirby that would have been seen as liabilities in normal times were now assets for Trudeau. He had gone through two distinct phases in his attitude to the constitution. In the fifties and sixties he had been concerned with intellectual issues, consorting with constitutional experts of the quality of Frank Scott, Carl Goldenberg, and Eugene Forsey. In the

seventies, he had engaged in a bureaucratic phase of negotiating, leaning on public servants of the Robertson persuasion. Now he agreed with Pitfield that he needed a
"deal-maker and a negotiation-closer, not a thinker and
discussant," to execute an extremely tough strategy,
someone to get results at the cost of politicizing the constitutional game and polarizing the participants, someone
who could be wound up like a clockwork freight train and
kept going regardless of the noise he created or the colli-
sions he caused. As Trudeau explained, "I didn't need
advice. At that point I knew exactly what I wanted."[11]

What Trudeau wanted was to write his theory of federalism into the Canadian constitution. In his view, Canada
was one country made up of many groups of people, of
which the French and the English were the most significant. Minority-language rights were to be provided for
anglophones and francophones where they were not a
majority of the population. The French minority in Ontario would get the same treatment as the English minority
in Quebec. French Canadians would be treated as equal
partners in Confederation but the province of Quebec, as
such, would have no special powers. Equal rights would
be guaranteed to individuals, not to a collectivity. For its
part the federal government did need more powers for
directing the economy as a whole because of the long-
term threat that growing international competition posed
for the increasingly vulnerable Canadian economy.[12]

This broad Trudeauesque doctrine and its accompanying strategy were extremely attractive to the senior and
middle-level bureaucrats who made up the constitutional
team in the FPRO when Kirby arrived there in the spring
of 1980. Some of them were veterans of the constitutional
wars of the 1970s. When they realized in 1979 that not

even a Conservative central government had the capacity
to reach a federal-provincial agreement with Conservative
premiers that conceded to Ottawa enough power to carry
out its constitutional mandate to manage the national economy, Trudeau's ideas took on a new validity. His views on
constitutionalized bilingualism might no longer stir hearts
in Moose Jaw or Come-By-Chance, but they made sense to
an Ottawa mandarinate that wanted a vision of federalism
to believe in and work towards. They were prepared to
form a new symbiosis with their political masters by taking
on Trudeau's sense of mission and contributing to the formulation of a new set of negotiating tactics designed to
beat the premiers at their own game.[13]

When Kirby told them that the dynamic of federal-
provincial relations was to be changed, virtually at a snap
of the prime minister's fingers, from an engrossment in
the pedestrian issues of fiscal transfers and joint social
programs to a struggle over the country's social contract,
they were intrigued. No longer would the federal government give way continuously to provincial demands. Now
it would demand power back from the provinces – power
to prohibit provincial protectionist barriers that impeded
interprovincial trade and constrained the mobility of labour. Items tentatively conceded by Ottawa in the constitutional negotiations of 1978 and 1979, such as power over
interprovincial and even international trade in natural resources, were to be withdrawn from the table. Another
presumption of earlier negotiations – that a consensus had
to be achieved on every issue – was to be discarded. This
time, if agreement could not be achieved, the federal government was going to act unilaterally by taking its constitutional proposal direct to London.[14]

These tough tactics were based on a number of assump-
tions. The "feds" – as the Ottawa combine of politicians
and public servants had come to be called during the

1970s – thought their determination would undermine the unity of the provincial opposition. They believed that Trudeau's unilateral option was a viable alternative. They expected that the provinces would accept the federal government's constitutional proposal – the so-called "people's package" of rights and freedoms, which included patriation, a preamble, an amending formula, and a charter – in return for some concessions by Ottawa to their demands, to be formulated in a "government's package." They hoped divide-and-rule tactics would gain individual provinces' acquiescence in exchange for acceptance of their special hobby-horses – Senate reform for British Columbia, more power over trade in raw materials for Saskatchewan, further jurisdiction over fish for Newfoundland, and so on. Should negotiations fail, the feds trusted that Trudeau's idealism on the charter and language rights would strengthen public support for Ottawa's position in response to what would be seen as self-interested resistance to change from the premiers.[15]

On June 9, 1980, when the ten provincial premiers came to Ottawa for a day to meet the prime minister for a brief start-up conference, they were given a glimpse of this strategy. And they were dismayed by what they saw. The changes Trudeau was proposing amounted to the feds' wresting control of the constitutional issue away from them entirely. Accustomed to dominating the process throughout the 1970s, the premiers were not ready to accept this reversal of roles. They rejected the federal government's attempt to thrust its constitutional "people's package" to the top of the agenda. They disliked the idea of the federal government increasing its powers in the name of strengthening the so-called "economic union." They pooh-poohed the feds' suggestion that September –

when Trudeau proposed to convene a full first ministers' constitutional conference – was a final deadline for an agreement. Most of all they thought the talk of a unilateral move by Trudeau to London was sheer bluff. In short, they were far from sharing – or even acknowledging – Trudeau's sense of urgency about the whole operation.[16]

All they would agree to was a revival of the Continuing Committee of Ministers on the Constitution, the old intergovernmental group of politicians and bureaucratic experts in the constitutional field, which had been inactive during the Clark interregnum. The CCMC's deliberations, the premiers assumed, would dissipate the crisis atmosphere Trudeau needed to force their acceptance of his agenda. For his part, Trudeau realized that if he wished to be seen publicly as newly co-operative and consensus-seeking, there was little he could do but concur with this arrangement, at least for the rest of the summer. Several of the veteran constitutional negotiators in the FPRO were hopeful that the CCMC's summer negotiations might even prove fruitful. Given the intensity of the prime minister's pressure on them and the interest of the officials in most provincial delegations in achieving some positive result, they thought it was possible that the September first ministers' conference might even come to an agreement on general constitutional reform. In this optimistic frame of mind, they worked full out to prepare new federal position papers for each of the four week-long CCMC negotiating meetings to be held in Montreal, Toronto, Vancouver, and Ottawa during July and August. Every Friday they would prepare a memorandum on developments in each of the twelve negotiating dossiers, and every Monday the prime minister would meet three or four of their number to discuss the moves that should be made next.

With his fingertips pressed together, Trudeau would sit back in his chair, eyes narrowed in concentration – "like Napoleon in his tent," as one FPRO type remembered the scene – listening to the weekly reports from his commanders in the field. Gradually, the FPRO's optimism dimmed. When officials suggested Trudeau make a concession in order to reach some compromise needed for a specific deal, he would refuse. Did he believe that appeasement could not lead to a lasting settlement? Did he hope to persist until provincial resistance broke up against the inflexibility of his concerted positions? Did provocative public statements he made at the Liberal Party's convention in Winnipeg in July and the emotional television advertising the federal government initiated to mobilize public support for the "people's package" during the summer indicate he was preparing for a confrontation, rather than a negotiation, with the premiers? None of them really knew.[17]

Whether Trudeau's strategy was simply to prove that the provinces were too obdurate to make a deal, even his minister of justice, Jean Chrétien, was unable to say. Since his post-referendum tour around the provincial capitals, Chrétien had been playing the taxing role of front man for the feds with his usual zest. He went out into the country repeatedly that summer to meet with his provincial counterparts, delivering Trudeau's message with lavish applications of homespun charm at late-night drinking and talking sessions "wit' da guys." Chrétien complained in private that it was far harder to talk to the boss about these matters than to his provincial negotiating opponents. Even he began to wonder whether his consultations were required only to show good faith on the federal side in order to justify, when agreement eventually proved impossible, a unilateral federal move to London.

This was certainly the inference the provincial premiers drew from news of a memorandum written for Trudeau by his clerk of the Privy Council, Michael Pitfield, which advised on the timing of a unilateral action should the summer's negotiations end in failure. The apparent confirmation that Trudeau was simply biding his time, unwilling to compromise, poisoned the atmosphere at the premiers' annual meeting in August just before the constitutional conference Trudeau had scheduled for early September.

When the premiers met the prime minister for a formal dinner hosted by the governor general on the eve of their conference, the ambiance was so fraught with bad feeling that the previous three months of dynamic federal-provincial negotiation at the ministerial and bureaucratic levels might just as well never have taken place. Recollecting the emotions at that event, Richard Hatfield, the veteran premier of New Brunswick, affirmed he "had never been at such an ugly official function" in his life. "Some premiers weren't speaking to other premiers. Trudeau was unbearably hostile." He was annoyed by the bad service and contemptuous about the food. When the conversation turned to business and Premiers Lyon of Manitoba and Lougheed of Alberta floated the idea that one of their number should co-chair the conference with the prime minister, Trudeau shot back sarcastically, "Like *deux nations*?" At one point Trudeau testily instructed the governor general to finish his dinner quickly and depart so Trudeau himself could get the hell out of there without breaking protocol. René Lévesque chortled that "the princeling" seemed out of sorts.[18]

Lévesque had reason for his glee. A few days earlier another federal document, this one prepared by David Cameron in the FPRO for Michael Kirby's signature, had been leaked to the Quebec minister of intergovernmental affairs, Claude Morin, by a separatist sympathizer working in Ottawa's Department of External Affairs. Morin realized that the acquisition of this highly professional analysis of both the federal and provincial positions was a "gift from the gods," a time bomb that could be tactically deployed against its authors since it showed how cynical the federal approach to the summer's constitutional negotiation process had been. The Péquistes had planned the explosion for that night, and Morin himself brought copies round to the premiers in their hotel suites.[19]

Just as Lévesque had hoped, once the premiers realized how manipulable they were seen to be by their federal opponents, their anger made constructive negotiations impossible. The first ministers' conference dragged painfully on through its appointed week of televised harangues and privately expressed hostilities. The very act of committing their strategic ideas to paper in the Kirby memo seemed like a massive Freudian slip on the Trudeauites' part. Security on the document had been as tight as the FPRO could manage, and at first officials there were appalled by the leak. But the public revelation of the federal strategy had an unexpected result. It furthered the Trudeauites' game plan. The premiers' usual antipathy towards Trudeau was stiffened by their anger at the offensive memo, which had demonstrated in hard prose the gulf separating the different participants. Peter Lougheed of Alberta felt the prime minister had approached the conference with "a very high degree of cockiness and determination." His neighbour, Allan Blakeney of Saskatchewan, felt the conference "was never intended to succeed." Motivated by these reactions, the premiers' intransigence, which was displayed on national television for all Canadians to see, made Trudeau's stance look more reasonable. The premiers thought they were calling Trudeau's bluff on his threat to patriate unilaterally. In truth, he was calling theirs. If they stubbornly refused to admit the country was in crisis, he would now move to create a crisis they could not ignore.[20]

It was obvious to Trudeau that "none of the premiers wanted the constitution to be patriated while I was prime minister except for Davis and Hatfield, and even they were late converts. They wanted it to be done after I was gone. They did everything they could in 1979 to stop it. This was true in '80, '81, and '82 . . . If they had been able to wait until after I had gone, they would have obtained an accord on their terms – certainly without a bill of rights and with a massive transfer of powers to the provinces. The Senate would have been as Lougheed and [William] Bennett [of British Columbia] wanted it. This would have happened because Turner or Mulroney [his successors as prime minister] would have done what they wanted . . . As it was, they only reached an agreement with me because they had to." And they only "had to" because Trudeau was determined to force them to a decision.

"The issue was power to the provinces or, in essence, to the people," Trudeau said, putting his own position as if it were *vox populi* incarnate. "In such a situation you are bargaining with opponents who think you need their agreement no matter what. I had started to consider doing it unilaterally in '78-'79. In 1980 I went ahead and took away their goddam chips." For all his pugnacity, he still had qualms. "It was not without doing violence to myself," he wrote the Laval political scientist Gérard Bergeron, who objected to this extraordinary action, "that I decided to deliver the knockout punch."

This was no time for flinching or theorizing. Trudeau's role, in his eyes, was to take a step no other federal politician had been tough enough even to contemplate.

"At the final cabinet meeting before the September 1980 first ministers' meetings," Trudeau recalled, "I told my colleagues, 'We're going to have a hell of a fight. The premiers will be against us. The British will be nervous. The media will be critical. The [anglophone] academics won't say anything, as usual. We could tear up the goddam country by this action but we're going to do it anyway.' "[21]

In other words, the premiers could yell and scream all they liked, but with his majority in both Houses of Parliament, Trudeau would arm himself with a resolution on the constitution from the House of Commons and the Senate and go straight to London to ask the mother of parliaments to adopt it.

With Trudeau going for broke in the face of provincial opposition, an important question loomed: how big a constitutional reform would he dare propose? Would he suggest changes solely in the area of federal jurisdiction or would he trespass into provincial bailiwicks? For the answer Trudeau turned to his caucus and his cabinet.

When the federal Liberal caucus met on September 17, right after the aborted first ministers' conference, it was in a hawkish mood, buoyed by the prospect of a fight on the popular issue of the charter. The Quebec caucus especially wanted to draw blood. They had been vilified by the Péquistes as traitors during the previous spring's referendum campaign, and their wounds were still throbbing. Here was an opportunity to get back at the separatists by righting the wrongs created by their infamous Bill 101, which, directly flouting Trudeau's official bilingualism, had made French the sole legally permitted language of the legislature, the courts, the workplace, commercial signs, and most schools in the province. The federal cabinet, meeting the next day, was equally determined. The ministers knew that the idea of a charter of rights was popular throughout the country, even in the western provinces, where the Liberals held only two seats. By displaying his courage and his unmatched command of constitutional logic in the face of the premiers' opposition, Trudeau had seduced his colleagues into a consensus. They now wanted to deal dramatically and decisively with an issue they had grown so weary of in the 1970s that many of them had vowed they never wanted to hear the word "constitution" again.[22]

"When I went to caucus and cabinet," Trudeau recollected, "I got enormous support on this. I also got the feeling that patriation was not enough. Language policy wasn't all that important to the rest of the country outside Quebec. That's where the charter came in. People like Lloyd Axworthy [his minister of employment and immigration and one of his two western MPs] said, 'We can only do it with the charter.' . . . The argument kept coming up that we wouldn't have the people with us without the charter. Hazen Argue [the Saskatchewan senator] said, 'If you're going do it, let's go first class.' In French that's 'Roulons en Cadillac.' If you're going to go, take a Cadillac. The whole package was more difficult intellectually but less so politically."[23]

His constitutional package was politically less difficult because its bitter core – the minority-language education rights that were to be imposed on Quebec for anglophones and on the other provinces where numbers warranted for francophones – was to be coated with layer upon layer of sweetener. The notion of an entrenched charter of rights and freedoms would appeal to the legal establishment and civil libertarians among the country's liberal-minded intellectual élite. It would also attract those groups – the ethnics, the feminists, the disabled, the homosexuals, the aged, and the native peoples – who saw themselves as minorities in Canadian society, needing protection against discrimination. The economic right of labour mobility across the country would be endorsed by the business community and enthusiastically received by the Progressive Conservative government in Ontario, whose cabinet believed that the balkanization of the Canadian economy into protectionist provinces had to be rolled back to achieve greater market efficiency. Furthermore, the simple act of patriation would in itself draw support from those harbouring residual anti-colonial feelings as a response to Trudeau's argument that Canada was shamed by being the only industrialized democracy without the sovereign power to amend its own constitution.

Finally, the inclusion of an amending formula in the joint resolution of Ottawa's two Houses of Parliament in Ottawa – once ratified by Westminster – would end the impasse that had prevented the Canadian political system from changing its own constitution without having recourse to the British parliament. With all these favourable aspects of the package diverting attention, the "constitutionalization" of the official languages law and the entrenchment of minority-language education rights would be camouflaged. While this canny move to outwit Lévesque and the separatists was well understood in Quebec, it was not perceived as deceptive in English Canada, where the idea of citizens' rights was so popular that it overrode other considerations. A Chevy version of constitutional reform would have proposed changes that only affected areas of federal jurisdiction. This constitutional package was indeed a Cadillac and a Day-Glo pink, gold-spangled one at that.

Still, the Cadillac model was, in Trudeau's understated phrase, "more difficult intellectually" because it would intervene massively in provincial areas of jurisdiction.

Because the charter's rights were to apply to the provinces, the federal government was proposing unilaterally to constrain the provincial governments' powers as well as its own and to endow the courts with greater authority in the system. Changes would eventually be imposed through court judgements on provincial legislation dealing with disadvantaged groups, such as the disabled and women. Quebec's historic sovereignty in educational matters would be violated by the entrenched guarantee of minority-language education rights, and every other province that was jealously guarding existing prerogatives and deliberately pressing for more would be provoked.

The amending formula with which the patriated constitution would be equipped was bound to create further animosity. Not only did it embrace the Victoria formula of 1971 – which gave Quebec and Ontario a veto in future amendments and therefore put the other eight provinces into a second-class category – it proposed a still-greater outrage, one that would probably antagonize even the unflappable premier of Ontario, William Davis. This was a provision that, in cases of continuing federal-provincial disagreement on future constitutional amendments, would allow the federal government to call a national referendum to break the impasse. Designed to perpetuate the power that Trudeau was now wielding in making his unilateral request to the British parliament, the right to call a referendum would give Ottawa a permanent means to achieve constitutional change by making direct appeals to the public over the heads of the provincial premiers. *All* premiers, with the possible exception of René Lévesque, were likely to be opposed, and vehemently, to such an insertion of popular sovereignty into what had become in the past ten years a kind of exclusive club that they completely dominated, a political practice that had come to be called executive federalism.[24]

These were the controversial ideas that Trudeau revealed to the nation on television on October 2: he would send a joint resolution of the House of Commons and the Senate to London, requesting the British government to enact his constitutional package as an amendment to the British North America Act. Trudeau was proposing an exercise in the strategic use of intransigence. First he would force the British to respond to the Canadian government's request. Then he would force the provinces to bow to the legality, if not the conventionality, of his fait accompli. Since there was considerable room to question the constitutional validity of this strategy, its tactical co-requisite was speed of execution. According to both the Pitfield and Kirby memorandums, the federal government had to meet a tight deadline. The resolution would have to be rushed through Parliament in the autumn so it could be sent to London by Christmas – well before the opposing premiers could bring their own political resources to bear against it.[25]

To the Trudeauites' chagrin, a clamour immediately arose for parliamentary hearings on the constitutional package. Politicians of all parties, including many Liberals, saw an institutionalized airing of the constitution's patriation as a possible platform for every sentimental piece of rhetoric about Canada they had been saving up for years. There was a certain irony in the fact that the Trudeauites were facing a delay because of the popularity of their plans. They gave way with ill grace. Hoping to limit debate, the government proceeded on October 23 to invoke closure and to refer its constitutional resolution to a joint committee of the Senate and the House of Commons. The Liberals wanted to keep the committee's hearings low-key, a minimal operation that would speed the package on its way. But the Conservative opposition lobbied hard to have them televised to expose the arrogance of the Trudeau initiative. At first the Liberals resisted the presence of television cameras. Once they acquiesced, they did their best to control the proceedings, right down to considering which of their partisans would present the best image to the nation.

As co-chairmen of the Special Joint Committee on the Constitution, they chose two mavericks to signal that the process was being run not by Trudeau puppets but by patriotic, independent-minded Liberals. Senator Harry Hays, a loquacious and old-fashioned bagman from Alberta, was appointed along with Serge Joyal, an intellectual MP from Montreal who had been so rebellious in the 1970s in the name of provincial rights that the Quebec caucus leader, Marc Lalonde, had tried to expel him. Given a choice between defending Quebec's rights against Ottawa and redefining the very notion of constitutional rights in all of Canada, Joyal grasped the opportunity to be a latter-day founding father, knowing that the act would have personal costs. (A friend in the Parti Québécois, then president of the National Assembly, phoned him in a fury once his appointment had been announced, swearing the two would never speak again.)[26]

The Hays-Joyal committee's mandate was severely limited. Denied a travel budget, it could not hold public hearings across the country. Deprived of a research capacity, it could not mount an expert challenge to the government's positions. Still, to the chairmen's surprise, their hearings turned out to be very popular with citizens' groups, who used them to lobby for improvements in the charter's definition and protection of civil rights. Public participation in the constitutional debate, which had been prevented till then by the first ministers' monopoly on the process, was being made possible. And the joint committee's televised proceedings turned the spotlight onto the rights included in the proposed charter. As delegation after delegation appeared before the cameras seeking to make the charter more comprehensive for women, the physically or mentally disabled, the criminally accused, the aboriginal peoples, and the aged, Trudeau's "people's package" developed a legitimacy it had not enjoyed before. By demonstrating the popularity of the charter, the joint committee process abetted the federal strategy in another way. It took the issue out from under the control of the provincial premiers.[27]

CHAPTER 14

THE PREMIERS TAKE ON TRUDEAU

As 1981 began – and the feverish Hays-Joyal committee hearings continued – the Trudeauites still believed that even though they had missed their self-imposed Christmas deadline for clearing the constitutional resolution through Parliament, their forceful strategy on patriation was working well. Their own parliamentary troops were happy warriors in the cause. The majority of the Canadian public was with them, according to the opinion polls. And the constitutional experts in the Federal-Provincial Relations Office were confident that the BNA Act could still be brought home from London in time for the Canada Day festivities on the first of July. Little did they realize that 1981 would be a roller-coaster year when the strained state of the Canadian federation would be revealed as never before and their own resolute confidence would be seriously shaken.

The continuing assumption of success that the Trudeau team was displaying was based on a series of misjudgements, the most important of them being an underestimation of the strength of the dissident premiers' opposition to their plans. Far from agreeing with the federal view that they had grown too powerful over the previous decade, the premiers from the Canadian hinterland saw themselves as victims of Trudeau's obsession with national unity, which they believed was a cover for his determination to enhance the federal government's position at their expense. The prime minister loomed so large in their collective imagination that when they got together at first ministers' conferences or regional summits, they tended to talk intently about his actions and motivations like boarders in a boys' school discussing ways of outwitting an overbearing headmaster.

The anglophone premier who was the most adept at deciphering Trudeau's stratagems at this stage in the federal-provincial wars was Peter Lougheed of Alberta, who had himself become a polished player of intergovernmental power games, largely in response to the challenge of dealing with Trudeau's Ottawa. Lougheed sometimes told a wry story about his first official meeting with the prime minister, shortly after he became premier in 1971. He had been invited to lunch at 24 Sussex and had asked Harold Millican, his oldest friend from Calgary, to drive him there. The two Albertans were suffering the nervous alienation from central Canada that most westerners of their generation had come to feel through unhappy political and business experience. When they arrived at the prime minister's gate twenty minutes before the appointed hour, Lougheed insisted that Millican drive him around the streets of nearby New Edinburgh for a while in case Trudeau was not yet ready to receive him.

"I bet he's involved in important state business," Lougheed speculated. "Maybe he's receiving a new ambassador or something like that." Millican finally persuaded Lougheed that, early or not, he should proceed inside. He gunned the engine of their rented car, roared up the semicircular drive in front of the prime minister's house, and came to a full stop in front of the canopied entrance. Lougheed got out of the car reluctantly and approached the imposing front door. When it swung open two people were in the foyer waiting to receive him. He handed his coat to one and shook hands with the other, a man who was dressed in striped pants and a morning coat, the kind of get-up Lougheed figured diplomats wore on their daily rounds. He turned to this distinguished personage and said with what he hoped was appropriate gravity, "How do you do, Mr. Ambassador?" Seconds later, he realized that the man who was holding his coat was Pierre Trudeau and "Mr. Ambassador" was the butler. The embarrassment of that moment was something Lougheed was able to laugh at heartily later on but never entirely forgot. In his mind, it was too perfectly indicative for comfort of the way Albertans had presented themselves in Ottawa in the past – as rubes from the periphery coming cap in hand to treat with the sophisticates at the centre.[1]

Such attitudes suited neither Lougheed's self-image nor the way he viewed his political constituency. He was an ambitious man from a proud Alberta family. His grandfather, Sir James Lougheed, had come from Ontario to Calgary in 1883 when it was still a tent town and had grown rich there from real estate speculation and other shrewd investments in companies such as Calgary Petroleum Products, which developed the original Turner Valley oil field and was ultimately taken over by Imperial Oil. He had been named to the Senate by one Conservative prime minister (Sir John A. Macdonald), served as government leader in the upper house under another (Sir Robert Borden), was a cabinet minister under a third (Arthur Meighen), and practised law in partnership with a fourth (R.B. Bennett). Sir James's great fortune was lost in the Depression by his heirs, but his grandsons, Donald and Peter Lougheed, were expected to live up to his standards and aspire to his kind of achievement. Don Lougheed became an engineer and later a vice-president of Imperial Oil. Peter Lougheed studied law at the University of Alberta, played some professional football for the Edmonton Eskimos, went to Harvard for an MBA, and then started work at the age of twenty-six as a lawyer for Mannix Construction, a Calgary firm with world-wide interests. After familiarizing himself with the workings of the international corporate world, Lougheed left Mannix to set up his own law firm in partnership with another Calgary lawyer, John Ballem.[2]

Within a short time, he decided to go into politics and quickly became leader of the moribund Alberta Conservative Party. By dint of formidable application, a flare for organization, an understanding of how to use the media, and the aid of a circle of like-minded friends who were a combination football huddle and cosy cabal, he managed to replace the Social Credit government that had been in office in Edmonton since 1935. Elected as the white-knight defender of Alberta's newly rich entrepreneurial class – the business and professional men who were thriving in the shadow of the transnational petroleum giants' post-war exploitation of the province's energy resources – Lougheed was determined to use the provincial state to increase the benefits Albertans derived from their burgeoning economy. It wasn't the dominance of the American petroleum corporations that troubled the new premier; the transnationals brought with them access to American markets, large dollops of investment capital, and the latest technology when they flew into Calgary to do deals or into Edmonton to lobby the government on resource policy. What did offend Lougheed was the attitude to Alberta of the federal government in Ottawa.[3]

"My experience in a complex way was quite typical of what happened to most westerners," Lougheed explained. "Our destiny was formed by outside forces – the railways, the pipelines, the banks, and, above all, the federal government – acting on matters of direct importance to us but without consultation. Not all of these forces were negative all of the time. But our overall feeling was that the west had not had a fair deal in the Canadian federation. I belong to a generation that came of age after the war with a lot of confidence about the possibilities out here. I didn't go into politics in order to oppose Pierre Trudeau. I went into politics because I thought we could get things done provincially in Alberta that would right old wrongs."[4]

The old wrongs that Lougheed set out to right were rooted in a history that his province shared with Saskatchewan and Manitoba as the last frontier of white settlement in North America. The political-economy framework for prairie development had been decided by Sir John A. Macdonald when he formulated his famous National Policy in 1879. Macdonald proposed to further industrial development in Quebec and Ontario by a three-pronged strategy of railroads, tariffs, and settlement. A transcontinental railroad would funnel immigrants westward and haul the staple goods they produced eastward to the markets of central Canada, where protective tariffs would permit Canadian entrepreneurs to expand their operations and encourage American firms to establish branch plants.[5]

Macdonald's National Policy succeeded to an extent. The old Dominion of Canada's nineteenth-century western territories became the newly settled, twentieth-century "west," with Alberta and Saskatchewan carved out of Manitoba and constituted as separate governments in 1905. But the prairie provinces' formal political autonomy barely disguised the fact that their one-crop economies were caught in an aggravating, many-faceted dependence. Wheat farmers in all three provinces were dependent on the vagaries of nature for their harvest, dependent on world market fluctuations for the price their staple crop fetched, dependent on eastern banks to finance their farms, dependent on the Canadian Pacific Railway to get their grain hauled to market.[6]

As their populations grew and their political experience developed, demands for reform grew louder on the prairies. But whatever concessions westerners were able to extract from Ottawa – Sir Wilfrid Laurier's Crow's Nest Pass Rate in 1897 guaranteeing the shipment of grain from the prairies to market for a fixed price per ton, R.B. Bennett's concession to the Alberta and Saskatchewan governments in 1930 of constitutional control over their natural resources, or John Diefenbaker's National Oil Policy making Ontario a guaranteed outlet for Alberta oil and gas in 1961 – did little to erase the sense of grievance that westerners imbibed with their cowboy coffee. Populist expressions of this alienation dominated prairie politics for half a century. In Alberta the Liberal Party, which had formed the province's first government in 1905, was swept off the local map by a series of political movements (the radical United Farmers of Alberta, the fundamentalist Social Credit, Peter Lougheed's own entrepreneurial Progressive Conservatives) whose electoral dominance was based on campaigning against the politicians of the federal government and the capitalists of central Canada.[7]

Once he attained office in 1971, Lougheed soon proved himself more sophisticated than any of his predecessors at the use of provincial nationalism. With an overwhelming majority in the legislature, he put together an impressive cabinet that included some of the brightest business and professional men in the province, people he had persuaded to run for office and who shared his desire to foster Alberta's development. To back them up with the kind of expert policy advice they needed, he determined to modernize the Alberta bureaucracy. One of his first acts was the establishment of a Federal and Intergovernmental

Affairs Department and the appointment as its deputy minister of Peter Meekison, a prominent Alberta political scientist and student of federalism. Meekison was charged with developing a coherent plan for intergovernmental relations, with the emphasis on coping better with Ottawa. Lougheed then proceeded to use provincial agencies such as the Alberta Petroleum Marketing Commission and the Energy Resources Conservation Board to jack up the prices paid by out-of-province customers for Alberta natural gas and oil and to foster a local petrochemical industry. He also took steps to enrich his provincial treasury at the expense of the private sector and the federal government by raising royalties and taxes on oil and gas in order to cream off more of the economic rents coming from the province's non-renewable resources.[8]

These bold initiatives in province-building began to bear fruit just in time for the world oil crisis of 1973, when the Arab-dominated cartel, the Organization of Petroleum Exporting Countries, managed to double and then redouble the price for crude oil on which the economies of the industrialized world – including that of central Canada – were dependent. The Lougheed government's first major conflict with Ottawa erupted in the immediate aftermath of this crisis. Without consulting Alberta, the federal Liberals concocted a scheme to keep domestic prices low. They decided to freeze the amount Canadians would pay for oil at a price far below the new world-market level. Then they imposed new taxes on Alberta production, including an export tax on oil shipped to the U.S., in order to help subsidize the expensive off-shore oil that eastern Canada was still importing.[9]

Lougheed and his cabinet colleagues were enraged. For them this was a blatant move by Ottawa to siphon off cash from the petroleum industry – in the form of a hidden transfer of forgone revenue from Alberta – in order to subsidize the consumers and industries of Ontario and Quebec. The Liberals' so-called "national" oil policy was not national at all. It was a gross violation of provincial resource rights as well as a clear indication of Ottawa's central-Canadian bias. The federal government would never have dared to set prices, control exports, or impose taxes on hydroelectric power, an important source of revenue in Ontario and Quebec. When Albertans (and other westerners) railed against "the east" or "central Canada," they usually meant the financial capitals, Toronto and Montreal, where for decades the money men had been reluctant to invest in the west. Ottawa was their capital, the capital of fat-cat Ontario and whiny Quebec, not the capital of the plucky, pioneering west.[10]

Stung by the treatment he and his cabinet had suffered in their dealings with federal ministers in the aftermath of the OPEC crisis, Lougheed began to view his government's relations with Ottawa in a different light. It wasn't enough to modernize his bureaucracy or enrich his treasury, to think positively and apply the methods he had learned at Harvard and at Mannix to the management of Alberta's new resource riches. The old-timers were right: the east wanted to keep the west down. With his entire province ready to take up cudgels with him against Ottawa, Lougheed set to work to rectify ancient injustices. And for a time in the mid-1970s, it seemed that most of Canada was rooting for Lougheed and his team in their fight with the feds.

In the context of the world-wide oil-shortage scare, Alberta had become a bonanza land, the most desirable place in the country to live. Albertans were described as blue-eyed sheiks and their territory as Tomorrow Country, the last best New West. "Everything here *is* brand-new," Ed McNally, a Calgary lawyer and rancher, told a journalist from Toronto at the time. "The people are fresh, the air is fresh, the buildings are fresh. In Alberta you get up and see a clear sky. In Ottawa and Toronto, you get up and look at dark buildings covered with pigeon shit ... We're cocky as hell in the present and very sure about the future."[11]

This billowing confidence with its underlying resentment of central Canada made Lougheed's political message attractive in other provincial capitals. Alberta, whose wealth as Canada's principal depository of oil and gas had suddenly quadrupled, was not the only province to see itself as the beneficiary of rising world commodity prices. Saskatchewan's economy was also booming, thanks to the development of heavy oil on the Alberta border, the continuing revenues coming in from its huge potash reserves, and the prospect that rich new uranium deposits would be opened up. Across the prairies as far east as Manitoba, wheat farmers were exulting in a steady run-up of world grain prices. The buoyant world commodity market also meant growing yields in British Columbia from its gas fields, coal deposits, and luxuriant forests.[12]

When Lougheed decided to build alliances so he would not be isolated in federal-provincial diplomacy, he found other western premiers eager to collaborate. They too were building up the state apparatus of their provinces and creating a new class of political professionals who were ready to match wits with their counterparts in Ottawa. What had been noisily evident in Quebec during the 1960s was occurring so unobtrusively a decade later in the hinterland that Ottawa was taken by surprise. As the 1970s wore on, the federal Liberals were confronted by the opposition of a phalanx of western premiers united – despite differences in party labels – by their common interests as leaders of staple-exporting economies. Under Lougheed's leadership, they were beginning to realize there was strength in solidarity and that it was worth supporting one another's individual policy demands against the federal government.[13]

Once Trudeau reopened his constitutional dossier in the mid-1970s, the western premiers began to suspect there was a hidden link between his agenda for patriating the BNA Act and his government's unslaked desire to cash in on the west's resource cornucopia. They reasoned that if Trudeau was trying to build up the federal capacity to fight Quebec separatism, the same political muscle could be used to diminish the western provinces' control over their economies. Their suspicions were confirmed when the federal government supported American petroleum producers and potash companies in two successful appeals to the Supreme Court, in which Saskatchewan's attempts to levy new taxes on the oil industry and to regulate the potash market were ruled unconstitutional. Obviously, Ottawa was determined to weaken provincial control over resources, a power they regarded as sacrosanct, enshrined as it was in the BNA Act. Peter Lougheed, for one, firmly believed that Trudeau's continued advocacy of the Victoria amending formula – which gave a veto only to Ontario and Quebec – heralded a possible constitutional amendment in a future energy crisis that would formally deprive the provinces of their paramountcy in the management of resources. He thought it would allow for a "subtle ganging up of provinces from the oil-poor regions against the [oil-rich] provinces, particularly Alberta."[14]

Fearing that Ottawa would try to portray Alberta as the Scrooge of Confederation, the province that was unwilling to share its bonanza with the less fortunate, Peter Lougheed decided to extend his coalition strategy to include the premiers from the Atlantic provinces, where resentment of central Canada was just as strong as in the west. The Maritimes and Newfoundland had traditionally been the poor cousins of Confederation, but recent developments had given them hope that they would soon be able to rise up and holler, "Poor no more!" Canada's declaration in 1976 of sovereignty over an area 200 miles off the country's coastline had raised expectations for a new era of prosperity based on a greatly expanded harvest from the sea. At the same time, the discovery of the huge Hibernia oil field on the continental shelf and the location of promising natural gas deposits off Sable Island had added to the economic prospects of Newfoundland and Nova Scotia. Even tiny Prince Edward Island could expect to benefit from the coming fish boom and from higher prices for its potato crop, while New Brunswick saw the possibility of pushing into the world potash market. If they could fend off perfidious Ottawa, the four Atlantic governments could command a greater share of the rents from these developments.[15]

"We worked hard at getting allies in the Atlantic region as well as the west," Lougheed remembered. "When John Buchanan [the Conservative premier of Nova Scotia] came to his first federal-provincial conference, for instance, I went over to his hotel and picked him up so we could go into the meeting together. I knew what it felt like to come up against the federal government for the first time. We did this kind of thing at the ministerial and official levels, too, and at the social-personal level with people's wives at the annual premiers' summer meetings and so on. It wasn't just Alberta's financial muscle on resources that made us strong against Ottawa. It was that we made friends we could count on so we had the numbers around the bargaining table at crucial times."[16]

In responding to western overtures, the Atlantic premiers were doing more than simply feeding their dreams of future prosperity. They were gaining immediate access to a new source of capital. Lougheed had set up the Alberta Heritage Savings Trust Fund to channel some of the province's petroleum revenues into a development bank whose capital could be used to diversify the economy before the economic downturn that could be expected once oil reserves had been exhausted. Lougheed was willing to divert some of the surplus capital accumulating at almost embarrassing speed in this Heritage Fund to make loans at advantageous rates to his fellow premiers in the poorer provinces. By these canny moves, he was able to create a hinterland coalition, with both ends of the country united against the central-Canadian block of Quebec and Ontario, where the Liberals' electoral strength was concentrated.[17]

The establishment of this alliance in the 1970s fulfilled Trudeau's old prophecy from the 1960s that opening up the constitutional "can of worms" in order to satisfy Quebec would invite a feeding frenzy on federal power by other provincial governments. In the course of a decade, the anglophone premiers had learned to "constitutionalize" intergovernmental politics, translating their policy fights with the federal government into constitutional demands so they could horn in on the Ottawa-Quebec feud over the division of powers. Anglophone politicians who formerly had spent very little time worrying about the BNA Act or where it was lodged and who had grown up "thinking the British connection was forever and a good thing," in Dalton Camp's evocative words, were now wholeheartedly involved in the constitutional game. The dynamic had changed from a dualist struggle between Quebec and Ottawa to a pan-Canadian grouping opposing Ottawa's attempt to hold onto its prerogatives. The premiers' objectives varied. Some wanted security from federal raids on their resource riches. Others thought stronger provincial representation in Ottawa could be achieved by reforming the Senate. A few sought more power over the appointment of Supreme Court judges.[18]

The result of this dramatic change in Canadian politics was clearly evident at the first ministers' constitutional conferences of 1978 and 1979. When the government of Quebec made its demands, the anglophone premiers from the hinterland were no longer willing to watch from the sidelines. They acted as an alliance in which each supported the others in asking for extended powers. Although increasingly concerned about his colleagues' attack on Ottawa, William Davis, the Progressive Conservative premier of Ontario, was loath to come to the defence of the federal Liberals. Instead, he developed a wait-and-see position, which the members of his entourage claimed was statesmanship. As a result, the pressure for total capitulation by the federal government became intense. Even when Trudeau made major concessions in his effort to negotiate a constitutional settlement, the premiers rejected his proffered deal in the hope of milking still more from his successor, Joe Clark.[19]

These gang-ups gave the premiers a lot of satisfaction at the time, but they represented a strategic mistake for which the provinces would later pay a huge price. Clark was of course unable to meet the premiers' demands in his short term in office, and when they faced the now steely-eyed Trudeau after his resurrection in 1980, they found themselves involved in a fight that made their quarrels with him in the 1970s look like play-school.

When Trudeau made his announcement of a unilateral *coup de force* in October 1980, the premiers recognized that the situation had been transformed. Within hours they were in touch with one another, trying to rally provincial opposition, with Peter Lougheed once again taking the lead. Not only was the Alberta premier outraged by Trudeau's plan to proceed alone with patriation, he was bracing himself for

what he rightly anticipated would be Ottawa's most concerted attempt yet to violate provincial resource rights –
the forthcoming National Energy Program.[20]

For the premiers, Trudeau's broadside amounted to a
declaration of war. They considered the content of his
constitutional package unbelievably retrograde. William
Bennett of British Columbia was upset that his pet project
of Senate reform had been dismissed. Allan Blakeney of
Saskatchewan was angry that his hope for Saskatchewan's
control over international trade in its resources was being
frustrated. Brian Peckford of Newfoundland was so furious about Ottawa's rejection of his demands for jurisdiction over the fishery and offshore resources that he
reaffirmed his view that René Lévesque's version of Confederation was preferable to Trudeau's. In addition to
their individual disappointments, all the premiers were
enraged by a new idea Trudeau had included in his patriation package. Not only was he validating the Victoria
amending formula – which made all provinces other than
Ontario and Quebec into second-class powers – he was
suggesting a procedure that would allow Ottawa to initiate a national referendum on any constitutional amendment it might propose in future. In effect, he was
threatening to reduce the premiers' power by going over
their heads to the public.[21]

And then there was the infamous Charter of Rights and
Freedoms. Not only did the charter go against the beliefs
of committed parliamentarians among the premiers both
on the social-democratic left (Blakeney of Saskatchewan)
and on the conservative right (Lyon of Manitoba), it also
contained clauses such as mobility rights that could undermine the provinces' capacity to protect their own labour
markets from their neighbours. Just as bad, its sections on
equality and legal rights would force provinces to change
hundreds of pieces of legislation as well as a myriad of

programs. If Trudeau was not actually proposing a revolution in the federal-provincial relationship, he was certainly threatening the status quo to a degree that the premiers could not tolerate.[22]

Determined to bring Trudeau's venture to a quick end, Sterling Lyon, as official chairman of premiers' gatherings for 1980, convened an emergency meeting in Toronto on October 14 in order to work out a strategy for concerted action. William Davis of Ontario and Richard Hatfield of New Brunswick were quickly ostracized from the group. They had astounded their colleagues by declaring their support for Trudeau's unilateral plans – Davis because he felt that the coherence of the federation was now at stake and Hatfield because he wanted his province committed to bilingualism in the constitution. John Buchanan of Nova Scotia and Allan Blakeney of Saskatchewan were surprisingly indecisive despite their grievances and decided to sit on the fence for the time being in case they could negotiate improvements in the federal proposals. The premiers present, from British Columbia, Alberta, Manitoba, Prince Edward Island, and Newfoundland, proceeded to develop a three-part anti-Trudeau campaign strategy. They would take his unilateral initiative to the provincial courts to test its legality. They would expand their alliance to include the separatist government of Quebec, which was making overtures to them. And they would move immediately to make the British parliament a third front in their battle against unilateralism.[23]

That they were able to contemplate a "London strategy" at this stage was mostly thanks to the political capacity that Quebec had already developed in the British capital. The anglophones were about to rely on the sagacity of the francophones in their appeal for justice to the former imperial centre.

CHAPTER 15

THE ROAD SHOW MOVES TO LONDON

That Pierre Elliott Trudeau had manoeuvred himself into a position in late 1980 where he was reliant on the goodwill of the British government to achieve his heart's desire was an irony that his separatist enemies in Quebec loved to play on, one of the piquant aspects of the fight they were engaged in to prevent him from patriating the BNA Act.

As a student at Harvard and the LSE, Trudeau had absorbed so much from the English – their nineteenth-century liberalism and twentieth-century Fabianism, their attitude to public service, their cult of cool self-containment – that to many of his compatriots he seemed to have *become* an English colonial, a man who had forsaken his French-Canadian identity in favour of the British traditions he had supposedly inherited from his Elliott ancestors. This charge always seemed patently absurd to English Canadians since in their eyes Trudeau's intellectual and personal style was so intensely French. Moreover, he had frequently displayed an ambivalent attitude towards the United Kingdom that enraged Canadian monarchists and sometimes roused the drones of Fleet Street.

Like so many French Canadians of his generation, he had scorned Canada's all-out involvement in World War II on the basis that it was a British imperial conflict. After the war he had learned to be wary of British condescension from his close contact with the English-Canadian political class in the generation immediately ahead of him, the Ottawa men who had been educated at Oxbridge and patronized in Whitehall and had never forgotten the lessons learned in either place. During Trudeau's time in office, the British had shown an ever-diminishing interest in Canada, reflecting the general view in the United Kingdom that their former colony was now little more than an appendage of the United States, a dull down-market region of America that their dutiful Queen was expected to nurture with ceremonial visits and pale rhetoric about the importance of Commonwealth ties. Although Trudeau had good relations with individual British politicians, particularly in the Wilson and Callaghan governments, he knew very well that the Foreign and Commonwealth Office had next to no competence in Canadian affairs and that British foreign ministers tended to drop in on Ottawa on their way to or from Washington out of languid courtesy to their NATO ally. In reaction he was always insouciant to the point of cheekiness when confronted with British pomp, no matter what the circumstance.

The irony of Trudeau's dependent position vis-à-vis the United Kingdom in the early 1980s was heightened by the fact that the British prime minister he needed to approach for aid in the patriation process was Margaret Thatcher, a politician who could scarcely have been farther from him on the ideological spectrum that bound the western democracies. Over the course of their relationship, he would appear in her eyes astoundingly, incorrigibly, maddeningly "wet." And for him, she would seem amazingly, intractably, blatantly retrograde, a woman who rejected most of the modernist ideas that informed his political sensibility.

None of these tensions were evident when Trudeau arrived at No. 10 Downing Street on June 25, 1980, to have lunch with Thatcher. The two prime ministers had engaged in multilateral discussions at the economic summit held earlier that month in Venice, so the main point of Trudeau's visit to London was to advise her of his constitutional plans. All was civil at the lunch. In the course of a general conversation elaborating on their summit discussions, Trudeau delivered his message about the political situation in Canada and his intentions with regard to the constitution. He told Thatcher he planned to conduct a last round of negotiations with the provincial premiers during the summer, but if an accord was not reached at the first ministers' conference scheduled for September, his government would formally request that the British parliament expedite passage of an amendment to the British North America Act. As expected, the British prime minister gave assurances of support, saying that while she knew nothing whatever about the Canadian constitution, she did know her duty and that was to accede with appropriate dispatch to the Canadian government's request. Trudeau emerged beaming into the sunlight outside No. 10 and informed the waiting journalists that he had received approval from Thatcher for his constitutional drive.[1]

The amiable nature of the occasion was pointed up by an exchange between Margaret Thatcher and Justin Trudeau, who had come with his father to Europe and was waiting for him in a limousine so they could go first to the London zoo and then to Buckingham Palace. The Iron Lady and the eight-year-old were photographed shaking hands amidst much prime ministerial joshing, with Trudeau trying to intervene to prevent the photo session from continuing. When the Canadians finally drove away, Justin grinned, stuck out his tongue, and waved from the limousine's back seat.[2]

Afterwards, when things went wrong, Mrs. T. would claim that Mr. T. had tricked her at the Downing Street lunch, and he would insist he had not. What neither of them knew that day was that patriation could not be achieved by a simple exchange between two Commonwealth parliamentary leaders. Other forces would intervene to play havoc with the idea that Pierre Trudeau's desires could be so quickly accommodated.

In London, the Palace would become concerned that it might be compromised if the government of Canada put unseemly pressure on the government of the U.K. and the monarch were caught in the crossfire, since Elizabeth II was Queen of both countries. Sundry lords and ladies of the second chamber would be roused from their torpor and the Tory backbenches would see a chance to shoulder the white man's burden once more in order to make sure that justice was done on behalf of the lesser breeds across the sea. The Labour opposition would nourish hopes of using Trudeau's initiative as a means of slowing down the privatization plans of Her Majesty's Government. And legal scholars, with or without expertise in Canada's constitutional politics, would find themselves unexpectedly in demand and, predictably, enjoying it.

In Canada, the English-speaking provincial premiers would search frantically for ways to break up the Trudeau-Thatcher axis. The British government's representative in Ottawa, a diplomat on the verge of retirement, would involve himself in the provinces' machinations to a degree that put him in danger of expulsion. "Red Indians," as the British called Canada's native people, would apply for government grants and don formal feathers in order to take their protest against the constitution's inequities to the streets of London. And the ardently republican separatist government of Quebec would coolly play the monarchist card and urge Her Majesty's Government to interfere actively in Canada's affairs by appealing to the British sense of fair play.

Quebec politicians had always been ambivalent about bringing home the BNA Act since a resolution of Canada's long-standing constitutional problems would mean the loss of a bargaining lever that they had been using to good effect for years. The Parti Québécois, in particular, had viewed the prospect of patriation not only as a victory for their arch-enemy, Trudeau, but as a major defeat for *étapisme*, their plan to achieve political sovereignty by stages. Since their long-term strategy was to outwit and outlast Trudeau, their immediate aim in 1980 and 1981 was to block his London plans. The PQ's minister of intergovernmental affairs, Claude Morin, hoped that if he could delay indefinitely the passage of any Canadian patriation bill that Thatcher might bring forward, Trudeau either would have to call an election on the issue or would be forced out of politics. To this end, he had appointed as director of Quebec House, the provincial office in London, Gilles Loiselle, a delegate general of consummate skill. Loiselle was the kind of Péquiste who liked to taunt Trudeau with being an "English snob" although he was no stranger to pretentiousness himself. A former journalist at Radio-Canada who had lived for years in Paris, Loiselle spoke excellent English and Parisian French and knew a good deal about food and wine and even more about human behaviour. During his colourful career, he had developed the view that politicians as well as armies march on their stomachs and that flattery is a powerful weapon in lobbying as well as in love.

Once ensconced in an elegant apartment rented by his government in Mayfair, he began to frequent Westminster and quickly picked up some home truths about British parliamentary practice. The political culture of the British Houses of Parliament was considerably more complex than Trudeau had implied when he told Canadian journalists that Thatcher had promised to put on a "three-line whip" – in other words, to exert maximum party discipline – in order to have the BNA Act amended in compliance with his request. The British prime minister could not in fact guarantee to deliver quick passage of any amendment to the BNA Act requested by the Canadian government, particularly one so loaded with constitutional freight as Trudeau's proposed package. To begin with, MPs on the government backbenches were far more numerous and much less docile than their Canadian counterparts. Far from being easy to discipline, they were likely to insist on exercising their historic rights to debate and obstruct, which had existed long before the development of cabinet government. Backbenchers were willing to push through legislation implementing policy formally adopted by the party in its election platform, but they did not feel bound by government positions taken on other issues. Furthermore, British parliamentarians of all parties believed they bore a special responsibility for matters constitutional. And once Trudeau's package was found to contain a complex charter of rights that was antithetical to the British common-law tradition, Loiselle found it was easy to pique their interest and rouse their ire.

He decided to make a long list of woo-able MPs and peers, starting with a group of sympathizers he had already identified as friends of Quebec. Scottish, Welsh, and Ulster MPs with an interest in devolution were obvious candidates. Then came the parliamentarians likely to be interested in tricky legal issues and those intrigued by native people's rights. Anyone with a family or business connection with Canada was noted. Having been assured a hefty budget, Loiselle hired one of the best chefs in London and set out to lunch, dine, or otherwise court with good food, fine drink, and lashings of Cartesian logic each of the two hundred and fifty parliamentarians who fitted into these categories.

His stop-Trudeau mission was made easier by Trudeau's own proclivity for gratuitous provocation. British parliamentarians of all persuasions were more than a little offended to hear from the Quebec government's London representative that Trudeau had dismissed the possibility that they might obstruct a Canadian government petition by saying belligerently, "They had better not try." And when informed by Loiselle that the Canadian prime minister had also said the British MPs "should hold their noses" and pass the BNA Act amendment forthwith, parliamentarians on both sides of the House of Commons were primed for persuasion.[3]

Trudeau's supposed disrespect for British custom was part of Loiselle's basic pitch, which he adapted to suit his listeners. He reminded Labourites that the Parti Québécois was a social-democratic government to whose support they ought to rally. He impressed on Conservatives their constitutional responsibility to see that fairness was observed in Britain's former colony. And he offered intellectual aid to MPs who might be more deeply interested in taking up Quebec's cause by slipping confidential information over their office transoms. One of Loiselle's plain brown envelopes paid off handsomely. It contained the Kirby memorandum that described Trudeau's overall constitutional strategy and landed on the desk of Kevin McNamara, MP.[4]

McNamara was the leading Labourite on the recently established House of Commons Foreign Affairs Committee. He had a natural desire to obstruct Margaret Thatcher and hoped that debating the Canadian constitution might help delay her far-reaching plans for privatizing the public corporations that the Labour Party had striven for decades to consolidate. But his concerns were more than partisan. As a former professor of law, he was also genuinely dismayed by the apparent contempt for the British parliament revealed in the Kirby strategy paper, which seemed to take for granted that the desired amendment to the BNA Act would be enacted automatically at Westminster "whenever so requested by the Parliament and Government of Canada."[5]

When Trudeau implicitly confirmed in his October public speech on unilateralism what the Kirby memo had heralded, McNamara decided to consult his committee chairman, Sir Anthony Kershaw, whom he regarded as "a good Tory of the old school who knew his duty and did it – not like the jumped-up *poujadistes* you get these days." Kershaw agreed that the question of the British parliament's responsibility for the Canadian constitution would make an appropriate subject for a formal study and that the Foreign Affairs Committee should hire experts and call for testimony from interested parties. The Kershaw committee's hearings in the late autumn brought the whole question of Canada's constitutional troubles to the attention of political London. They were augmented by a sideshow "informal committee" of the Commons conducted by Jonathan Aitken, a Tory MP and grand-nephew of Lord Beaverbrook, as well as a full-dress academic seminar held at All Souls, Oxford, and a conference at the Institute of Commonwealth Studies in Kensington.[6]

Having launched his London campaign to great effect, Gilles Loiselle had flown out to Winnipeg in the meantime to tell a meeting of the dissenting premiers about his lobbying techniques and their results. Duly impressed, the premiers decided to bolster Quebec's efforts by mobilizing their own agents general in London. With the Lougheed government once more in the vanguard, a task force was set up at Alberta House in Mount Street to coordinate provincial lobbying. The agents general decided to consult regularly in order to be sure not to aggravate the British by duplicating their efforts or mixing their signals. As representatives of an NDP government, Saskatchewan lobbyists were deployed to convince British Labourites that Trudeau's proposed charter would produce a constitution "so rigid you could never get a socialist government." Alberta representatives went after parliamentarians who had an interest in the energy business. Provincial premiers and their senior public servants flew over to do some discreet lobbying on their own with British ministers and mandarins. Lavish restaurant dinners were laid on for backbenchers who had proven particularly responsive to Loiselle's gastronomic blandishments. After a few weeks' experience in lobbying à la carte, one agent general devised a rule of thumb: the further left the MP, the greater his gourmandise and the bigger the restaurant bill. In his experience, the Trots went for the caviar and the quenelles, while the Tories made do with consommé and game.[7]

All this activity caught Her Majesty's Government by surprise and presented it with a dilemma. On the one hand, Margaret Thatcher and her cabinet felt they had no choice but to do their duty and support the Trudeau government. This was the thrust of their response to Trudeau's emissaries, Mark MacGuigan and John Roberts, who were dispatched to brief HMG in London almost immediately after Trudeau announced his unilateral plan in October. Thatcher was businesslike if reluctant. The prime minister knew she could not, in a phrase that Whitehall favoured, "look behind" the Canadian parliament's resolution and become involved in assessing the pros and cons of internal Canadian conflicts. On the other hand, she already recognized that having a few dozen members of the British parliament clamouring to speak on the Canadian constitutional question could seriously delay her legislative schedule for 1981. Besides, she felt she was acting against her own political interests in helping bring a bill of rights into existence when her party was opposed to the very idea of one for Britain. "How can you expect me to be enthusiastic about your charter when we are against one," was the gist of her message to the two Canadian ministers.[8]

It was clear that Thatcher had been the victim of poor briefing by the foreign office on these questions and had not realized the full implications of what Trudeau was asking her to do. Furthermore – or so she insisted subsequently – he had never mentioned that there would be a charter of rights in his constitutional package and, even worse, he had downplayed the strength of the provinces' opposition. This failure to be frank so annoyed Thatcher that just describing it to a sympathetic Canadian caused "steam to come out of her ears." "Have you any idea what your prime minister told me?" she asked Alberta's agent general, James McKibbon, at a cocktail party at the Carlton Club in London. "He wanted my assurance it would go through quickly, but he never mentioned a bill of rights." As for the provinces, he had indicated that "only one or two would object."[9]

When Trudeau failed in the late autumn of 1980 to respond to news stories planted by the British government to the effect that only a simple patriation plan could be assured easy passage in London, it was decided at Downing Street that a more direct message would have to be conveyed. Thatcher and Lord Carrington, her foreign secretary, then called on the services of Sir Francis Pym, one of their party's most experienced parliamentarians. Pym was sent to Ottawa, ostensibly in his role as minister of defence, to tell the Canadian prime minister in person what a "hell of a mess" his intransigence was creating in London. To Pym's happy surprise, he found Trudeau immensely likeable. During a pleasant lunch at 24 Sussex, Pym warned Trudeau that his constitutional resolution would not get through the British parliament unless the charter of rights were dropped. "I was perfectly reasonable. And I found that what he had to say in reply was perfectly reasonable, too," Sir Francis said afterwards. "It just wasn't very practical. He gave me to understand he was going to charge ahead anyway and that he expected the British House of Commons to comply with his wishes."[10]

Pym came back to London feeling a distinct unease. Mark MacGuigan and John Roberts had already been to see the Queen at Balmoral to reassure her that the monarchy's position would be unaffected by her Canadian prime minister's plans. The two ministers had found the monarch extraordinarily knowledgeable about and supportive of her Canadian government's initiative. But Pym still feared that if Trudeau continued on his collision course, not only would the Palace be involved but the NATO alliance might be too. Trudeau was popular with the U.K.'s European allies – with the exception of the French – and if his motivations were to be maligned in a public spat with the British government, "all hell might break out" on that front, too.[11]

The British Foreign and Commonwealth Office was woefully unprepared for this crisis. Having failed to warn HMG about possible problems with Trudeau in the first place, it found itself playing "piggy in the middle between the British government and the British parliament," as one of its officers explained. It was trying to untangle misunderstandings on both sides of the Atlantic without adequate information or accumulated expertise. The end of empire, along with the absorption of the Commonwealth Office into the Foreign Office in the 1960s, meant in effect that the British relationship with Canada was mostly left to the Palace, where the Queen kept herself supremely well informed on what was going on in her dominion; to the trade ministry, where matters of commerce were dealt with; and to the defence department, where NATO concerns were tended to.

"Few people in the FCO even knew that the U.K. still had *any* responsibility for the Canadian constitution," remembered Sir Derek Day, who was under-secretary responsible for North America at the time. "I certainly hadn't focused on it myself until we were presented with the sticky problems that arose in 1980 and 1981." The FCO's legal adviser, Sir John Freeland, had stumbled badly in briefing Nicholas Ridley, the cabinet minister delegated by Thatcher to appear before the Kershaw committee to explain her government's response to Trudeau's request. The "We cannot look behind the Canadian government's position" line that Freeland propounded did not wash as readily with the parliamentarians in Westminster as it had with the bureaucrats in Whitehall.

The FCO also felt itself to have been ill served by its high commission in Canada. Sir John Ford, the senior British diplomat in Ottawa, was by his own admission "not a Commonwealth chap," yet there was some suspicion in London that he had become too emotionally involved in Canada's federal-provincial disputes – that he "had gone native, so to speak." The Ottawa posting was to be Sir John Ford's last job before his retirement from a long diplomatic career during the course of which he had learned to defend British interests abroad with rather more vigour than was usually necessary with Commonwealth nations.[12]

Having arrived in Ottawa in 1978, when Trudeau was approaching his all-time political low, Ford had taken a shine to Joe Clark and the Conservatives, whose world-view was closer to his own. After Trudeau's restoration to the prime ministership in 1980, Ottawa became in Ford's view a paranoid place under the direction of a government that was more secretive and more leader-centred than that of any other democracy he had known in the previous thirty years. He was appalled by Trudeau's uni-lateral strategy, which he thought would break up Canada and cause incalculable trouble in London. He made a point of getting to know the dissident premiers by visiting their capitals, and he came to sympathize with their problems. In late 1980, he took to feeding them information to sup-port their London campaign. And as tensions between London and Ottawa worsened in early 1981, Ford became more and more indiscreet. He buttonholed federal MPs, warning them of the trouble brewing in Westminster, and made undiplomatic remarks in public places, most notably during the governor general's annual skating party at Rideau Hall. Unknown to anyone in the Trudeau govern-ment, he also leaked information about Thatcher's un-happiness with Trudeau to the Toronto *Globe and Mail*, whose publisher had become an ally of the high commis-sioner's in his attempts to stop Trudeau's patriation plans.[13]

At first, Ford's behaviour was tolerated in Ottawa with only minor protests being expressed in the Canadian House of Commons. Then Ford went too far. Flushed with the excitement of finding himself in the middle of a possible international crisis when all he had expected of Ottawa was a dull duty post, and completely sincere in his belief that Trudeau might be capable of declaring Canada a republic, he made a major diplomatic gaffe. He phoned Richard Hatfield, the premier of New Brunswick, who had publicly expressed his concern that the monarchy was being endangered, to tell him that Trudeau would have to be got rid of and fast. After Ford elaborated these views, Hatfield described them verbatim to his deputy minister, Barry Toole, who was sitting in his office throughout the call; then he telephoned Jean Wadds, the Canadian high commissioner in London, and Michael Kirby in Ottawa to inform them of Ford's machinations. The matter was reviewed by the secretary of state for external affairs, Mark MacGuigan, who took it very seriously indeed. He had already heard about Ford's lobbying from Ed Broadbent, who was sufficiently disturbed to raise the issue in Question Period. It soon became clear that the British high commissioner was suggesting that a cohort of Conservative, NDP, even Liberal MPs should be organized to defeat the Canadian government in the House of Commons. Not only was this conspiratorial intervention in a foreign country's politics a diplomatic outrage, Ford's scenario for a possible internal revolt against Trudeau was absurd.[14]

The under-secretary of state for external affairs, Allan Gotlieb, flew to London immediately to demand that the FCO recall its high commissioner. An agreement was reached with the British that Ford's retirement would be announced. He was summoned home for a scolding but was allowed to return to Canada to complete the last few months of his posting. After his retirement, he remembered with some bitterness that he was banished to a kind of Coventry in the wake of his indiscretions and shut off from official contact with the Canadian government. Even Michael Pitfield, Trudeau's principal secretary and an ardent anglophile, stood him up for lunch, and Trudeau himself later professed not even to remember his name. "Was that the chap who did conjuring tricks at children's parties?" he asked in response to a question about the incident. "I think he invited me with my sons to Earnscliffe [the official residence of the British high commissioner] a couple of times."[15]

In the midst of the brouhaha over Ford's behaviour, the Kershaw committee filed its report. It was a bombshell. Since the Canadian government had boycotted the committee's hearings on the grounds that there was only one legal position to take – its own – the expert submissions solicited by Kershaw's committee, in consultation with the dissident provincial agents general, had been heavily biased on the provincial side. No matter that international law had clearly established Canada as sovereign and legally equal to the U.K. in every respect except the amending of its constitution. No matter that this exercise in investigating the validity of the Canadian government's action turned the clock back half a century to the imperial era of British responsibility for its colonies before the Statute of Westminster. The Kershaw committee was of the opinion that the British parliament should not "accept *unconditionally* the constitutional validity of every request coming from the Canadian Parliament" if there was not substantial provincial agreement. The dissident premiers were delighted. There was no longer any doubt that the federal constitutional package would run into serious trouble if it came to London with a charter and without provincial consent.[16]

The Kershaw report was the first major blow to the Trudeauites' damn-the-torpedoes unilateral strategy on patriation. A string of others would soon follow.

CHAPTER 16

JOE CLARK AND THE COMMONS

The Ford and Kershaw uproars had barely subsided when Jean Chrétien introduced into the Commons in Ottawa a new version of the government's resolution on the constitution, containing several significant changes based on the recommendations of the Hays-Joyal committee. As a consequence of much backroom wheeling, corridor dealing, and on-camera wheedling, the committee's deliberations had led to a series of amendments that strengthened the charter's guarantees of individual freedoms.[1]

Until this point – mid-February 1981 – the Trudeauites had downplayed the importance of the opposition in their calculations of how long it would take to get their unilateral patriation plan approved by the Canadian parliament so it could be whisked away to London. Their main concern was fitting the unavoidable debate on their latest constitutional resolution into a parliamentary schedule that was already heavily laden with the recent budget's controversial National Energy Program. They knew they could count on Ed Broadbent, who had already given Trudeau his assurance of New Democratic support in exchange for certain concessions. As for Joe Clark, his difficulties as leader of the Progressive Conservatives were such that the Liberals believed he would not be able to do much during the coming debate but bluster.[2]

The way Clark had been handling his vicissitudes since losing power in 1980 – by doggedly doing his duty – was typical of his political and personal style. During his brief term as prime minister, Clark had been determined to govern as though he had a majority. Now as leader of the opposition he was determined to oppose as though he enjoyed his party's loyalty.

In many ways, Clark was the ur-middle-Canadian of his generation, a self-effacing though self-possessed man who had grown up secure in a small Alberta town as the son of the local newspaper editor. Despite an ungainly physique and a pedestrian manner, he had achieved considerable success in student politics at the University of Alberta and had become a party apparatchik without ever having worked at anything else. He had spent nearly a decade serving as an eager political assistant to provincial and federal Tory politicians ("the perfect guy to fetch the coffee" was the way his detractors described him) before he won a seat in the House of Commons in 1972 at the age of thirty-three. In the years since, he had turned into a conscientious parliamentarian, not notably talented as an orator but genuinely devoted to the public weal. On important equality issues – feminism, language rights, religious liberties – he had shown himself able to transcend the values of the party and the region that had produced him. On matters of party organization and the management of government resources, he had proven surprisingly adept. But the label "Joe Who," the nobody from nowhere, that was slapped on him when he unexpectedly won his party's leadership had stuck despite his accomplishments.[3]

Having lost power so maladroitly, he was now in danger of being remembered as the Accidental Man of Canadian politics: the young MP who became leader of his party by accident in 1976, beating out the two strong front-runners,

Brian Mulroney and Claude Wagner, by a fluke of the convention balloting process and by virtue of the bitter divisions within the Conservative Party that made him the least disliked contender; the opposition leader who won office by default in 1979 because Pierre Trudeau was briefly out of favour with the electorate; and the prime minister who lost power in 1980 by absent-mindedly blundering into the trap the Liberals had contrived.[4]

A decent man whose chief assets were persistence and honesty, Clark represented the progressive element of his party, the so-called Red Tories who remained hopeful that he would survive this demoralizing season in opposition and become prime minister once more. At the same time, his enemies were trying to dislodge him from the leadership by fomenting discontent in his caucus, playing on the unhappiness that was rife throughout the extra-parliamentary party, and exploiting the general disdain for him expressed by the national media who ragged him mercilessly no matter what he did.[5]

Since the death in 1891 of the Conservative Party's founding father, Sir John A. Macdonald, the history of the Tory caucus had been written in the blood of its leaders, who had been undermined at every turn by the party's bitter factionalism. Clark was as crippled as Robert Stanfield had been by the Diefenbaker loyalists who still supported the Chief's "One Canada" policy and who adamantly rejected the Stanfield position that the Conservatives should proclaim and promote French as Canada's other official language.[6]

To compound Clark's caucus problems, the party's burgeoning right wing was working actively against him in the hope that he would make such a poor showing in the leadership review at the party convention scheduled for late February that he would be forced to resign. Because so many rank-and-file Conservatives held Clark directly responsible for the party's defeat in 1980, they blamed him for their loss of patronage positions, which they had expected in reward for partisan efforts during the fallow years in opposition. Clark's difficulties in formulating policy positions that would satisfy differing regional interests were dramatically illustrated by the barely disguised contempt towards him displayed by the Conservative strongmen, Premiers Lougheed of Alberta and Davis of Ontario. The two were mutually antagonistic, but each was surrounded by partisans who believed their man would be a far better federal leader than young Clark. Each group thought "poor Joe" was "just too close" to the other premier's positions. Clark could never be enough of an Albertan to satisfy Lougheed's loyalists or enough of a centrist to satisfy Davis's cadre.[7]

All these rumblings of discontent in the Conservative Party were amplified by a number of influential journalists who were friends of Brian Mulroney, the Montreal lawyer who was eager to unseat Clark. A man of swaggering ambition, broad connections, and cultivated charm, Mulroney had taken his loss at the 1976 convention hard; and in its aftermath, his disappointment had led to excesses in his personal behaviour that were much gossiped about in Montreal. His expressions of rage often centred on Clark and his closest political adviser, Lowell Murray, who had known Mulroney ever since they had met as politically active students at St. Francis Xavier University in Antigonish, Nova Scotia, in the 1950s. They were both bright boys from Catholic families, Mulroney an electrician's son from Baie Comeau, Quebec, and Murray the son of a superintendent in a Cape Breton coal mine. Their friendship continued after university when they both stayed involved in Tory politics, Murray as an executive assistant in Ottawa, Mulroney as an organizer and proselytizer in Quebec. To the surprise of their mutual friends, Murray had chosen to support Clark instead of Mulroney at the leadership convention in 1976; when asked why, he had replied, "Brian, you're not ready to be leader of a political party. You've never run for office and you've never addressed the large questions about the country that any leader has to consider." This response seemed to Mulroney to be mealy-mouthed, a piece of altar-boy prissiness. "What Lowell forgets," Mulroney would say, eyes aflame, "is that I've had to work for a living all my life. I had to support my mother and my sisters after my dad died while those buggers" – and here his voice would change from its normal resonant baritone to a mocking squeak – "were 'considering the large questions.'"[8]

After the 1976 convention, Mulroney had been appointed president of the Iron Ore Company of Canada, a job that involved acting as front man for a U.S. iron and steel conglomerate that had hired him for his reputation as a lawyer who knew how to soft-talk union leaders and cajole Quebec politicians. As well as a handsome salary, Mulroney had a generous expense account from Iron Ore and plenty of time to conduct a campaign of insidious carping against Clark among his many friends in the media. He would drop by the Bar Maritime at the Ritz-Carlton in Montreal or the lounge of the National Press Club in Ottawa and pass on the latest malicious misrepresentations of Clark's physical and intellectual capacities that were making the rounds of the business community. For years Mulroney had scorned Clark's career as that of a "guy who doesn't know anything about the world outside the Conservative Party. I mean, he couldn't get a job in the private sector if he tried. You wouldn't see John Craig Eaton [the chairman of Eaton's] coming after him if he was defeated. In fact" – and this witticism would cause Mulroney to snort with pleasure – "Joe Who would be lucky to get work in Eaton's *basement*." In addition to denigrating Clark, Mulroney was given to expressing admiration for Pierre Trudeau. This was not only because of Trudeau's federalist stand, which Mulroney had been supporting wholeheartedly ever since he started playing the Anglo-Montrealer to the hilt as a resident of Westmount, member of the Mount Royal Club, and ardent recruit to the Anglo business establishment. It was also because of Trudeau's record as a winner. "You've got to hand it to old Trude," Mulroney would say. "He's really got style. You wouldn't catch *him* dragging his ass through years and years in opposition. He knows how to win, unlike some others I could name."[9]

The effect of all this antipathy might have caused a lesser man to buckle, but Clark stubbornly soldiered on as opposition leader in the conviction that the future success of the Progressive Conservatives – and his own survival as leader – depended on breaking the Liberals' monopoly on the national unity issue. Clark and Lowell Murray, whom he had appointed to the Senate in 1979 and whom he still relied on as his closest adviser, were determined to overcome their party's reputation as a collection of unilingual francophobic rednecks destined to be shut out of Quebec forever. They were unhappily aware that the only time in the twentieth century that the Conservatives had won significant support in the province was in 1958, when Maurice Duplessis had decided to back John Diefenbaker by supplying him with a slate of candidates for the federal election drawn from Union Nationale ranks. When this support collapsed after a single term, the Tory caucus members were enraged by what they saw as French Canada's perfidy. "The Chief was crazy to trust the frogs," they would say to one another, falling back on hoary prejudice. "Everybody knows they're yellow-bellies who wouldn't go to war. The priests still tell them how to think. The Grits still buy their votes. And there's nothing we can do about it."[10]

These were sentiments Murray and Clark deplored as morally offensive and politically destructive, since they perpetuated Quebec's historic alienation from the party that had hanged Louis Riel in 1885 and imposed conscription in 1917. They were educated men who by determined effort had made themselves fluent in French and knowledgeable about Quebec's contemporary reality. They shared Trudeau's belief in bilingualism as a policy that was necessary to make French Canadians feel at home outside Quebec. But they were also sympathetic to the neo-federalist view that Quebec needed more powers than the anglophone provinces. It was an article of faith with them that the concerns of the other regions could be harmonized with Quebec's hopes.

During his brief term as prime minister, Clark had gone to the trouble of holding cabinet meetings in Quebec City in order to familiarize his ministers – most of whom were unilingual and some of whom had never even set foot in the province's capital –with French Canada's fears and aspirations. "I hoped they would discover there was a natural coalition between Quebec and the [English-Canadian] hinterland and that once they got used to hearing [simultaneous translations of] ideas being expressed in French, they would find they had a lot more in common with Quebeckers than they thought." Clark's stance on national unity issues – including his insistence that the government of Canada should not intervene in the sovereignty-association debate – had been admired by many thoughtful Quebeckers. But as Clark himself joked, "We keep winning *Le Devoir* and losing elections," a reference to the fact that, despite his efforts at rapprochement, his party's electoral support in Quebec had actually fallen in the two general elections held under his leadership.[11]

Clark's position in the early 1980s on national unity issues was complicated by a speech he had made as prime minister, calling for more fiscal muscle for the central government – a doubly courageous act since it was delivered in Alberta, the most recalcitrantly anti-centralist of all anglophone provinces, and since it reversed his own long-standing advocacy of a decentralized Canada he called "a community of communities." The experience of actually governing had made Clark realize how inadequate were the powers still under Ottawa's control. And during the heat of the referendum campaign he had abandoned neutrality on sovereignty-association and supported the No side by appearing on public platforms alongside Jean Chrétien and Claude Ryan. As a result, he was in danger of appearing to be an opposition leader whose only stance on constitutional issues was rampant me-too-ism.[12]

Despite his many handicaps, Clark was determined to carve out an independent position on what was obviously Trudeau's top-priority issue for the 1980s. Once the referendum was over, he had self-consciously developed a constitutional strategy, drawing on the advice of Jake Epp, a Manitoba MP to whom he had assigned the shadow-cabinet role of constitutional critic; Richard Clippingdale, a Carleton University historian he had hired as a policy adviser; and Arthur Tremblay, a career civil servant he had recruited from the Quebec government and appointed to the Senate in 1979. They decided to hold a series of caucus meetings designed to develop expertise and promote a consensus among Conservative MPs on constitutional issues. Almost miraculously, these meetings had a positive effect on many of the Tories who still maintained that the constitution was irrelevant to their party's welfare.

"I know to the day and hour when the shift in attitude came," Clark remembered afterwards. "It was when a western MP said something like, 'What have these French Canadians ever done for Canada anyway?' and Arturo [Tremblay] answered gently that his people had been calling themselves Canadians for three hundred years and had done plenty for Canada. Suddenly, everybody realized Quebeckers had a common history with ours. That simple fact seemed to change the general view that the constitution was the Liberals' issue. It became our concern, a pan-Canadian concern. And by the time Trudeau announced his unilateral patriation plan there was a new sense in our caucus that he could be effectively opposed."[13]

Clark realized his party could not take an antagonistic position on the content of Trudeau's proposed constitutional package, in part because he agreed with some of it and in part because his pollster, Allan Gregg, had told him it was popular. Having decided to attack not the substance but the process of the Trudeau initiative, he proclaimed that it was unilateralism that was misguided and confrontational, riding roughshod as it did over the provinces' objections and violating the country's constitutional conventions. "Because a constitution is so basic to a country it must be the product of the broadest possible consensus. It cannot be arbitrarily imposed on this nation by any one individual or government. Nor can it be achieved through threat, ultimatum or artificial deadline. That kind of constitution making does not serve Canada," was how Clark phrased his party's position. In this way he hoped to show himself sympathetic to the provincial premiers without giving up on presenting the federal Conservatives as a *national* party adopting a position based on what was good for the country as a whole.[14]

Despite its coherence, Clark's constitutional strategy got off to a shaky start. His attack on Trudeau's unilateral initiative ran into immediate trouble when the premier of Ontario came out in favour of the federal government's position. Ontario was the country's richest, most industrialized, most populous province, and the Ontario Progressive Conservative Party, which had been in power for almost forty years, was widely recognized as the country's most powerful, most competent political machine. When Bill Davis gave his open support to Pierre Trudeau's constitutional plans and urged Ontario members of the federal PC caucus to do the same in direct opposition to their national leader, Clark was acutely embarrassed. Once again he appeared in the media as a blunderer caught off balance.[15]

His troubles continued when the government's constitutional resolution was referred to the Hays-Joyal committee. Hoping to rouse public ire at Liberal arrogance and delay the committee's proceedings, the Tories insisted on its hearings being televised, only to find that this move made Trudeau's initiative more, rather than less, popular. When even the Conservative members of the committee joined in the rush to propose amendments to strengthen the charter, the outrage Clark had expressed earlier at the unilateral process appeared to be no more than standard partisan hypocrisy.[16]

It was only when the amended charter was brought back to the House in mid-February that Clark found solid ground on which he could make a firm anti-unilateralism stand. By this time the political tide was starting to turn against Trudeau. On January 27, Premier Allan Blakeney of Saskatchewan had declared his opposition to the federal position. On January 30 the Kershaw report was published. On January 31 *The Globe and Mail* had published the information leaked to it by Sir John Ford, contradicting Trudeau's claim that Thatcher had promised rapid passage of his resolution.[17]

Then in early February, women's groups banded together and mounted a much-publicized constitutional conference of their own on Valentine's Day in Ottawa that
was tellingly critical of the Trudeau government's high-
handedness. They demanded further changes in the charter's phraseology out of concern that it fell short of guaranteeing sexual equality. Discontent was also being
expressed within the Liberals' ranks for the first time,
with Louis Duclos, MP for Montmorency-Orléans, declaring his opposition and four senators indicating their intention to deny Trudeau's project easy passage through the
upper house. In this same period the dissident premiers
escalated the legal battle they had mounted against the
feds by appealing to the Supreme Court of Canada an
unfavourable ruling they had received from the Manitoba
Court of Appeal. Now known as "the Gang of Eight,"
the premiers were becoming an increasingly important
element in a situation that was slipping out from under the
Trudeauites' control.[18]

Heartened by these signs of resistance and by a rise in
the Tories' rating in the opinion polls, Clark won majority
support for his leadership at his party's convention in late
February. By the time the House resumed debate on the
government's patriation resolution in early March, he had
convinced his caucus to take an unswervingly obstructionist stance. Claiming the Liberals' unilateral approach
to resolving the country's constitutional impasse was divisive, Clark's constitutional critic, Jake Epp, urged that
the BNA Act be patriated with an amending formula agree-
able to the provinces. He also moved an amendment to
delete the government's controversial referendum procedure from its proposal. Although moving an amendment
was a standard opposition procedure, the Conservatives
used this one to produce a Commons stalemate. By debat-

ing Epp's amendment relentlessly, they managed to tie down the House for a full month.

When the exasperated Trudeauites tried on March 19 to limit debate to four more days, still hoping that they could bring the constitution home in time for Canada Day, the Conservatives started filibustering. Raising points of privilege and points of order continually, they effectively paralysed Parliament for another two weeks. The uproar these procedural quibbles created – Ed Broadbent attacked the Tories vociferously because the impasse prevented the NDP from introducing its own amendments to strengthen both native people's and women's rights – tested Joe Clark's determination to hold his caucus together. It also put to the test the ability of the country's first woman Speaker to maintain order in the male preserve of Parliament.[19]

Jeanne Sauvé, the Liberal member for Ahuntsic and a former cabinet minister, had taken on the Speaker's role reluctantly. Her early unease in the job had been exacerbated by an unusually fractious House. Tories had accused her of being pro-Liberal, Liberals and NDPers had derided her inexperience, and she herself found "the constitutional debate the most excruciatingly stressful period of my public life." By the end of it, her meticulous rulings had gained her a reputation for fairness and quick-wittedness on both sides of the House.[20]

As March drew to a close, and Sauvé began to cut back the time allowed the opposition on points of procedure and privilege, Clark realized he would not be able to keep his troops at the barricades much longer. The charter continued to be popular and Tory MPs reported that their constituents were growing impatient with the party's obstructionist ploys. Then on March 31, relief arrived. Clark lost no time in quoting to the House the unanimous decision by the judges of the Supreme Court of Newfoundland, who declared that the federal government had "no authority to request an amendment that would directly alter provisions of the British North America Act affecting federal-provincial relations . . . without first obtaining provincial consent."[21]

The Gang of Eight was jubilant. John Whyte, a senior adviser to the Saskatchewan government, recalled that "the effect of this Newfoundland judgement on the political situation was electric." Even though it was not well formulated, the judgement put the legitimacy of Trudeau's unilateralism in question all the same.[22]

Joe Clark was jubilant too. His formerly dispirited and divided caucus had managed to hold up the majority Liberal government's plans long enough for the premiers' London and legal strategies to bear fruit. With the legitimacy of his package challenged by a provincial supreme court, Trudeau announced that if the Conservatives would agree to end the debate, he would ask the Supreme Court of Canada to rule on the constitutionality of his package before taking it to London. With that capitulation, Clark's brief period of constitutional glory was over. But the attitude towards Quebec and national unity that he had imposed on his caucus was to have a far-reaching effect on both the Conservative and Liberal parties.

After a few more days of debate and a few hours of frenzied negotiations among party leaders about the mechanics of taking the federal case to the Supreme Court, attention turned back to the premiers and their strategy of appealing to the judiciary for aid in their battle with Trudeau.

CHAPTER 17

To the Courts!

Kevin Peterson, the publisher of the *Calgary Herald* and one of the most perceptive political observers in the west, once remarked that Peter Lougheed would have been a lesser politician without the challenge of coping with Pierre Trudeau. It was Peterson's view that Lougheed, who had striven all his life to be a winner, watched Trudeau's moves as though he were the inspired quarterback of a superior football team and then set himself the task of spotting the federalist's game and learning how to block and best his plays. Nowhere was this tendency more evident than in the court strategy that Lougheed and the other dissident premiers devised and carried out in 1980 and 1981 in order to obstruct Trudeau's unilateralism on the constitution.

Trudeau had a different way of dealing with opponents because he lived by a different metaphor. His mythic hero was no hunk of a quarterback huddling with his padded teammates; it was Cyrano the swordsman fighting for his cause in open combat against incredible odds. First as a polemicist, then as a politician, he had viewed the world as a Manichean universe where the forces of good were pitted eternally against the forces of evil. As the champion of liberty and democracy, his instinct was to define his enemies narrowly, challenge them relentlessly, and win by devastating them outright, with little thought given to conciliation or compromise. His primary response – on public display during the parliamentary debate on his constitutional resolution – was to turn back any encroachment on his position with a fierce counter-attack on his antagonists' weak points. A related technique was to lean on his mandate: he insisted that, having been elected, he could and should do what he thought best until the next election. "If the voters don't like it, they can turn me out of office," was always the implication when he threw democracy in the face of his critics. Another response was the lawyer's ploy of suggesting that his challengers should examine the legality of their positions. If they didn't like what he was doing, they could take him to the courts.

Waiting for a federal election that might not be called for another four years – by which time Trudeau's constitutional package could be irreversibly entrenched in a patriated BNA Act – was not an attractive option for the dissident premiers, especially when they knew how popular his charter of rights had become. Hauling him up in front of the judiciary would be quicker and probably more effective. And so it was to the courts that they decided to repair when they realized just how aggressive Trudeau meant to be in order to have his way with the constitution.

Their court strategy involved a different risk from the nothing-ventured-nothing-gained derring-do of their London lobbying. By challenging the legal validity of Trudeau's initiative, they were making a shift from the political to the judicial arena, where their chances of success would depend not on the emotional resonance their arguments had with the public but on their lawyers' capacity to convince supposedly independent-minded judges of their logic. They could not rely on the politically charged position that leaving the provinces out of the constitution-making process was an unconscionable violation of Canadian political tradition. They had to prove in the courts that it was illegal. The risk was that if they lost their court cases, they would not have a political leg to stand on in crying foul to the public. But if they won, the pay-off would be dramatic and immediate. Trudeau would be put in an untenable position. As an expert on the constitution himself, he could hardly flout the judges' wisdom by persisting with his unilateral appeal to London. In any case, British parliamentarians would take a dim view of the Trudeau government's petition in such a situation and would be quite likely to turn it down.

In order to carry out this bold approach, the dissident premiers decided to try to make sure that their legal team could match the one put forward by the federal government. Several of them were lawyers and, in concert with their attorneys general, were closely in touch with the practice and personnel of Canada's complex judicial system. Because provincial governments are unable to bring a test case directly to the Supreme Court of Canada, the dissident premiers had to turn to their own provincial courts of appeal for declaratory judgements, which, while not legally binding on either the Canadian or the British government, would be politically useful. The lawyers' weighty factums, or briefs, would lend credibility to the premiers' political objections. The judges' decisions would probably have some impact on the internal and external politics of Trudeau's unilateral move. Even if these judgements found against the dissidents, there was an advantage to be gained, since such defeats would give the premiers the grounds to appeal the provincial courts' positions to the Supreme Court of Canada for a ruling that even the headstrong Trudeau would not be able to ignore. With the British Columbia attorney general, Garde Gardom, and his deputy, Richard Vogel, acting as general co-ordinators of strategy, advisory committees of senior politicians and civil servants were struck in several provinces and the best legal counsel was hired to help the premiers decide which courts should be chosen for their cases and how the questions referred to the courts for consideration should be worded.

Given the catalytic role of Quebec in constitutional change and the Lévesque government's determination to block Trudeau's scheme by every means available, it was natural for the premiers to endorse the decision of the Quebec cabinet to take a case to its appellate court, where the judiciary might well be sympathetic to the dissidents' collective notion of Confederation as a compact made by the constituent provinces. They also supported a reference to the Court of Appeal of the Supreme Court of Newfoundland because Brian Peckford, the premier of that province, believed that Trudeau's patriation plan would be found to violate the agreement on the strength of which Newfoundland had joined the Canadian federation in 1949. As a third choice, they settled on the Manitoba Court of Appeal, because they wanted a western province in the mix and, time being of the essence, Manitoba's statutes made a quick judgement possible.[1]

While the provinces were plotting their legal strategy, choosing the right courts, the right questions, and the right timing, Trudeau's constitutional team was preoccupied with its parliamentary game plan. They had expected to get the patriation resolution through Parliament and over to London before the provinces could cause trouble in the courts. But every delay Joe Clark engineered in the Commons left them more vulnerable to their opponents' legal stratagems.

The Trudeauites had been deterred by a point of principle from pre-empting their opponents by resorting to a court judgement themselves. Since the prime minister was presenting his quarrel with the provinces as a political, not a legal, dispute, his advisers believed that it would show weakness for the federal government to refer its case to the Supreme Court of Canada for vetting. There was serious concern in the federal Justice Department about the provinces' legal strategy. But over in the Langevin Block at the FPRO – where "Trudeau's son of a bitch," Michael Kirby, was still in charge of tactics – the courts were of minor concern.

It was both his strength and his weakness in managing Trudeau's constitutional plans that Kirby was not a lawyer. As he liked to put it, he "began with the premise that the constitution was a political document that lawyers made legal, not a legal document that politicians sold to the public." In his eyes, the feds were seeking to strike a political bargain with provincial politicians. To achieve this bargain, he would resort to whatever means were necessary. And as a non-lawyer, he shared the lay public's illusion about the other-worldly impartiality of the judicial system. Since he had no reason to doubt Trudeau's rigorous position – that the unilateral federal initiative might be politically controversial but it was constitutionally legal – he sat back unperturbed to await the courts' decisions on the dissident premiers' cases. "You don't understand anything [about the courts]," Barry Strayer of the Justice Department shouted at him in exasperation at one meeting when the question of the premiers' court strategy came up and Kirby brushed it aside as inconsequential. "There is judicial politics and legal strategy, too!"[2]

Kirby's naïveté in legal matters was confirmed to federal officials in early February 1981 when the Manitoba Court of Appeal handed down its judgement. "We won! We won! It was three to two!" Kirby exclaimed, brandishing the news that the Manitoba judgement was in the federal government's favour as he burst into a meeting of deputy ministers in the Langevin Block. "Really?" responded Ian Stewart, deputy minister of finance, drily. "Did they take out their goalie?"[3]

Stewart's sarcasm was directed at more than Kirby's sporting enthusiasm. The score may have been in Ottawa's favour on this first judgement, but coming at a time when leaked cables from the Canadian high commission in London indicated that the British were very uncomfortable about passing a Canadian constitutional bill that was *sub judice*, the Manitoba split decision was as much a political defeat for the Trudeau cause as it was a legal victory. This was especially true since one minority opinion by Justice J.P. O'Sullivan maintained that the Trudeau initiative was indeed unconstitutional because provincial governments were sovereign in their own fields. It followed, O'Sullivan reasoned, that Ottawa could not unilaterally propose constitutional changes that affected provincial supremacy. This was a position the provinces lost no time in communicating to British MPs or in using to bolster their case when it was next presented before the Supreme Court of Newfoundland.[4]

The joy Kirby had experienced in the Manitoba majority opinion, written by Chief Justice Samuel Freedman – that there was no certain convention requiring provincial agreement to amendments to the Canadian constitution and that there was no validity to the claimed "compact" theory of Confederation, which made the federal government a simple creature and a dependant of the contracting provinces – was short-lived. The feds had now been put on the defensive and this fact was privately acknowledged even by the prime minister. Trudeau had accepted the advice of Roger Tassé, the deputy attorney general of Canada, that if either Newfoundland or Quebec ruled against the federal government, he should bow to the judges (whatever the merit of their reasoning), call a halt to his political timetable, and refer his constitutional package to the Supreme Court for an authoritative assessment. Since the dissident provinces were already appealing the Manitoba ruling to the Supreme Court, prudence counselled letting the judges have their say before patriation was enacted in London.

With this sobering prospect in mind, the federal government marshalled its forces in St. John's in mid-February to argue its position before the Newfoundland Supreme Court. The federal case was presented by Clyde Wells, a Newfoundland lawyer and sometime provincial Liberal cabinet minister. According to Wells, the proposed charter of rights did not alter the federal balance of power or limit provincial powers any more than did the federal government's already existing – though long unused – capacity to disallow provincial laws. He disputed the relevance of the provinces' claim that past practice constituted a convention requiring provincial consent to any federal amendment that might affect provincial powers, saying that this was "a matter of political science and not one for the courts to decide." Despite the competence of Wells's presentation, the Newfoundland court came down on March 31 with a devastating, unanimous opinion upholding the provincial position. The proposed Charter of Rights and Freedoms *did* infringe upon the powers of the provinces to legislate in respect to the property and civil rights that were in their jurisdiction under the BNA Act. Furthermore, there *was* a constitutional convention that constitutional amendments affecting provincial powers needed prior provincial agreement.[5]

However much scholars might question the juridical and historical logic of the Newfoundland judges – and even the anti-Trudeau forces admitted it would be unlikely to hold up on appeal – the political reality was incontrovertible: with this judgement the provinces had succeeded in bringing the federal unilateral initiative to a complete halt. It forced Pierre Trudeau to negotiate a parliamentary cease-fire so that the Supreme Court of Canada could begin hearings on the federal proposal. By April, both the provinces' appeal on the Manitoba decision and the federal government's reference of its own parliamentary resolution were before the Supreme Court. That the Quebec Court of Appeal ruled on April 15 in Ottawa's favour by a tally of four judges to one turned out to be an event of mere historical interest. The dissident premiers had succeeded in their prime objective. The Trudeau Express had been halted. Until the Supreme Court justices had heard the two sides argue their cases, had withdrawn to their chambers in order to ruminate on the problem, and had brought down a final judgement, the protagonists would have to bide their time.[6]

The delay caused by having to take their constitutional resolution to the Supreme Court was bothersome for the Trudeauites. But they had good cause to believe that the high court would expeditiously rule in their favour on the unilateral initiative, which they themselves were convinced was perfectly within the law. Furthermore, in the chief justice of Canada, they were dealing with a man whose judgements Trudeau generally agreed with and respected. Bora Laskin had been his first and most admired appointment to the Supreme Court, a former professor of constitutional and labour law at the University of Toronto, a federalist, and a civil libertarian who was now acknowledged to be an adornment to the judiciary and the country.[7]

To plead Trudeau's case before Laskin and his fellow justices, the federal government had hired Michel Robert, the eloquent Montreal Liberal lawyer who had been *bâtonnier* of the Quebec bar, and John J. Robinette, the preeminent English-Canadian barrister who at the age of seventy-five had achieved an almost legendary stature in Canada's legal world. It was Robinette's considered opinion that the federal government had in its leader, Pierre Elliott Trudeau, the best mind he had ever encountered in a long career spent contending with superior minds, a view that was confirmed when Trudeau became intensely involved with Robinette in formulating the federal case. Robinette would outline his proposals and Trudeau would respond, in the mode of one distinguished authority consulting another. He adamantly rejected Robinette's advice to drop the charter from the federal package in order to increase the odds for a favourable judgement. But he agreed that Robinette could concede the point that the charter would indeed impinge on the provinces' powers. Together they decided that Robert would attack the theory that Confederation was a compact created by the provinces and Robinette would argue that, whatever might have been the *convention* concerning constitutional amendments in the past, conventions "are purely political" and so are not matters for judgement and enforcement by the court.[8]

These were the main ideas that Robinette put forward in his succinct and elegant style during the five days that the constitutional reference case was before the Supreme Court justices in late April and early May 1981. Apart from Michel Robert, his main ally was Roy McMurtry, the attorney general of Ontario, who decided to argue his own province's case rather than hire counsel. Robinette's main opponent – appearing on behalf of the province of

Manitoba but arguing for all the dissident premiers that unanimous consent by all the provinces was required for every element of the federal package – was a Winnipeg lawyer named Kerr Twaddle. Twaddle was so painstakingly detailed in his four-and-a-half-hour testimony that one of the judges, Justice Willard Estey, was overheard asking another, Justice Julien Chouinard, whether he agreed that it was "about time we asked this guy how much more he has to say."[9]

When the hearing was finally over, the Trudeauites expected that they would hear the court's learned judgement within a month. And then, by God, they could proceed to London. But May turned into June, Canada Day came and went, the long, hot Ottawa summer ground on, and still there was no word from on high. The Supreme Court had not delivered the quick judgement that the prime minister had expected when he capitulated to Joe Clark's demands. "Laskin let me down," Trudeau recalled years later. "My whole gamble was that he would hold the hearings as soon as the Quebec appeal came down, that we would have the answer in a month. I had reason to believe that since the case was so important he would give it all kinds of priorities. Instead it was unexpectedly slow."[10]

Laskin had turned out to be a judge who would not fit his judicial tasks to anyone's timetable, even that of the man to whom he owed his great prominence. "We are the umpire of the Canadian constitutional system – the only umpire," Bora Laskin had once said about his beloved court. During the seven years he had been chief justice, he had presided over the Supreme Court's transformation from a relatively minor factor to a central institution in Canada's political landscape by boldly asserting its importance as another branch of government. The Laskin court had already enforced the bilingual rights established in the

BNA Act over the unilingualism of the PQ government's Bill
101 and had determined the boundary line dividing federal from provincial powers in a number of public policy
fields, from wage and price controls to resource management. But in the constitutional challenge of 1981, Laskin
faced a question of unprecedented importance, and he
faced it while suffering constant pain from a serious illness. In the context of the provincial courts' inability to
agree on the meaning of Canada's constitutional law, he
and his eight fellow justices were being asked to declare
themselves on a matter so serious that the country's political process had been brought virtually to a standstill.[11]

The stakes were enormous, nothing less than the shape
and even integrity of the country. If the court supported
Ottawa's initiative, it would be sanctioning a charter of
rights that would overrule further aspects of Quebec's
language law, abolish a century of discrimination against
francophones seeking education rights in English Canada,
eliminate provincial obstacles to a national labour market,
and give the federal government further centralizing
power through the ability to initiate referendums on future constitutional amendments. Should the court rule for
the dissidents, Canada would be a confederation in which
the provinces had equal power with the federal government to change the constitution, and Ottawa's authority
would be seriously diminished. That the Supreme Court
itself could be among the chief beneficiaries of their decision made it all the more onerous.[12]

If Trudeau's package were to be accepted and to become part of Canada's new constitution, the Supreme
Court would have vastly expanded power to pass judgement on the validity of statutes, both federal and provincial, and therefore to make policies on moral and political
issues – abortion and the funding of separate schools were
two important examples – that would have a large impact

on Canadian society. In effect, the Supreme Court would become less a British-style forum for adjudication and more an American-style institution actively engaged in directing the course of social change. The fact that it took them five months to reach their decision was a measure of how difficult the task turned out to be.

Finally, in late September, it was announced that on the twenty-eighth of the month, the court's judgement would be made public with all nine justices in attendance, wearing their scarlet robes and, for the first time in the court's history, giving their ruling live before the television cameras.

When the day arrived, there was palpable excitement in the magnificent Cormier structure on Ottawa's Wellington Street where the Supreme Court is housed. People gathered in clusters outside the building at seven in the morning, law students jostling young mothers with preschoolers in order to be part of a historic moment. But when the moment arrived at mid-morning and Bora Laskin began to read the court's forty-five-page judgement, no one could understand what he was saying. The sound lines set up for the cameras were not working properly, so Laskin's words came across in incomprehensible bursts. Furthermore, the academic experts dutifully assembled to tell the audience what the judgement meant were not provided with advance texts, so they could not give their learned interpretations when the journalists put their questions. "What's your gut feeling, Professor? What's the bottom line here?" a talking head would say to a legal expert, who would gently explain that he did not know the answers because he had not heard the judgement, let alone read it. Then the cameras would switch to the court's lofty neo-classical lobby, where Jean Chrétien and Eugene Forsey, for the federal forces, and William Bennett and Joe Clark, on behalf of the provincial opposition, were claiming a resounding victory for their respective sides.

It was all very perplexing for the viewing public – and for reasons that went beyond technical difficulties, since supreme confusion appeared to reign among the august justices of the Supreme Court. Whatever the merits of the decision – once it had actually been distributed and read, it was described variously as a professional cop-out and a work of collective genius – it was undoubtedly convoluted. On one of the three questions the provincial governments had put forward, the court's answer was unanimous. Yes, the federal package did affect the rights and powers of the provinces. On the other two questions, opinion was divided.[13]

Four judges – Brian Dickson, Jean Beetz, Julien Chouinard, and Antonio Lamer – expressed the court's disharmony. On the one hand, they agreed with their colleagues Ronald Martland and Roland Ritchie that Canada had developed a constitutional *convention* requiring substantial provincial consent for constitutional amendments affecting their powers. Changing provincial powers without the provinces' assent was therefore "unconstitutional in the conventional sense." On the other hand, they agreed with the chief justice and two other colleagues, Willard Estey and William McIntyre, that there was no *legal* requirement, no formal compact with the force of law, that prevented the federal parliament from asking the United Kingdom to amend the British North America Act.[14]

To get out of this impasse, the judges as a collective had reached a peculiarly Canadian compromise. Since the fate of both Trudeau's unilateral initiative and the dissident premiers' opposition hung on the court's decision, each side was given a partial victory and a partial defeat. By a vote of six judges to three, the provinces won substantial agreement for their case that provincial approval for constitutional amendments was needed, though the court talked of "substantial" rather than "unanimous" consent. But their victory was a moral, not a legal, one. By a vote of seven judges to two, the federal government was given sanction for its claim that it was perfectly legal to take Trudeau's unilateral resolution, duly passed by Parliament, to London for enactment by Westminster. But the judges in their wisdom were of the opinion that unilateralism, while legal, would be improper, even politically illegitimate, if carried out against the will of the provinces.

Confusing and contradictory though the nine men's separate judicial opinions may have been, they were in combination a political master stroke, pushing both sides back towards the bargaining table while decisively changing the bargaining context. As Peter Russell argued, the Supreme Court judgement may have been questionable jurisprudence but it was "bold statescraft": the two sides were being given "half a loaf" each and urged into another round of negotiation. The federal government had received a legal green light but a political red light as an inducement to set aside unilateralism in favour of resuming negotiations once again. The dissident provinces had been given a political green light but a legal red light as an inducement to compromise on their intransigence.[15]

When he heard this judgement, half-way across the world in a hotel in Seoul, South Korea, Pierre Trudeau was quick to recognize what had happened. The prime minister had stopped off in Seoul on his way to Australia for a Commonwealth conference in Melbourne. Before he had left Ottawa the previous week he had made an agreement concerning the Supreme Court judgement with William Bennett, who had recently taken over the chairmanship of the provincial premiers' group.

True to form, Trudeau had told Bennett that the feds held the best cards and the premiers were on the defensive. If the Supreme Court gave him a clear victory, he would go to London as soon as Parliament had passed the government's resolution. If the provinces won a clear victory, he still intended to take his package to London. However big a hullabaloo there was in Westminster, he was convinced the British parliamentarians would ultimately have to hold their noses and accede to the Canadian government's request. Margaret Thatcher had assured him of her support in the past, and he intended while in Melbourne to get her to reconfirm her commitment. The real problem, he had conceded, was what would happen if the ruling were mixed. He needed to know if the premiers were serious about having a last try to achieve a negotiated deal. If all they wanted was another chance to kick Trudeau around, he wasn't interested. Bennett replied that he believed there was good faith among the premiers and hoped that a deal could be reached. But at the same time, Manitoba had reservations about Section 23 of the charter, on minority-language education rights. "Bill, I've got to have language," Trudeau said simply. "It's the essence of my existence." The two men parted with an understanding about the signals each would give the other if the ruling were split.[16]

Now in Korea, he conferred with Michael Pitfield, still his closest adviser on matters of strategy, and prepared to face the cameras wearing a white suit, a pink rose, and a stern expression. In a press conference held in the early hours of the morning, Korean time, to be viewed live by Canadians in the afternoon, he appeared exhausted and ill-tempered but at the same time brazen. At first he claimed complete victory, saying, "I see no alternative but to press on." Then he added, almost as an afterthought, a statement that actually gave the pre-arranged signal to Bennett: "We will all wish to consider the reaction of the provinces." Translated from constitutionalese – the language of jargon and nuance that had evolved over more than a decade of intergovernmental constitutional wrangling – this meant he was game to make one last attempt to forge a deal with the premiers.[17]

CHAPTER 18

From Last Judgement to Final Deal

The first week of November 1981, when the accord was struck that patriated the Canadian constitution at last, was probably the most important in Pierre Elliott Trudeau's prime ministership, a week that saw the climax of the great drama of his public life, when the symbiosis he had achieved with the conflicted society that had formed him was at its most intense. However large the cast of characters that gathered in Ottawa for the event (and hundreds of people were involved), however flamboyantly the bit players strutted on the stage (and at least a dozen of them claimed afterwards that *his* role had been crucial in reaching the final outcome), there was no question who was the star. It was Trudeau who physically and figuratively wielded the gavel that caused the proceedings to unfold.

The prime minister went into the negotiations with the provincial premiers that week in a heightened state of awareness. He was like some old Zen master, conscious of history's weight but living in the moment, focused on his purpose and convinced of its rectitude. To him, his unshakeable certainty wasn't arrogance; it was a reflection of the cause that had animated his life. He still believed that what he was after in trying to patriate the Canadian constitution was a more fully realized democracy where "the people" as an entity would assume responsibility for the nation's social contract and at the same time achieve greater individual liberty through his proposed Charter of Rights and Freedoms. For thirty years he had been fighting to free French Canadians from what he saw as the authoritarian control of the élites who dominated the Church, the state, and the economy. Now this struggle, extended to all Canadians, was focused on his need to best the provincial premiers, whom he viewed as small-minded, self-interested regional barons who had been challenging his political vision with increasing insolence for nearly a decade.

Because he had become such a canny politician, having survived so many ups and downs in popularity, he realized that conditions would never be more auspicious for him to achieve his heart's desire than they were in the autumn of 1981. He had been told often enough by his pollster, Martin Goldfarb, that the public's fascination with his strength was a Janus-headed beast. Canadians expected him to protect them from the perils of the nation's existence. But when things went wrong their anger at him flared. "Why can't he fix things?" earnest citizens would ask pollsters testing the electorate's mood. "If only he cared enough, he could make it all come right," they would say as they projected their collective angst. In the waning months of 1981 public discontent was smouldering in Canada, and the national media were eager to fan it into a burn-Trudeau conflagration. The economic downturn that was soon to engulf the country in the worst recession since the 1930s had already begun. The west was heaving with rage over the federal government's imposition of its National Energy Program. Reagan's Washington was threatening retaliation against the NEP and various other sins of the revived Trudeau government's commission. As for the patriation of the constitution, the voters – who had traditionally felt excluded from the feuding of

Quebec and the politics of passion: Trudeau, the French Canadian who said No to independence, and Lévesque, the Québécois who said Yes, engaged in a desperate battle that divided a generation.

Quebec and the politics of change: In the 1950s Quebec moved
from one kind of political confrontation, between the paternalism
of Camillien Houde and Maurice Duplessis (top left) and the feisty
unionism of Jean Marchand, to the Quiet Revolution of the 1960s,
when the Quebec provincialists Lesage, Lévesque, and Johnson
clashed with the Canadian federalists Pearson and Trudeau.

Quebec and the politics of revolution: As the 1960s sped on to the 1970s, there were bombs in the mailboxes, soldiers in the streets, and a dynamic new political force in the Parti Québécois.

Canapress

Fred Chartrand/Canapress

Bill Grimshaw/Canapress

The referendum and the politics of choice: As the 1980s dawned and the fight for Quebec's future status escalated, the firm federalists Trudeau and Chrétien joined forces with their sometime opponents, Ryan and Lesage, to best the sovereignty-associationist Lévesque in a campaign that enflamed Quebec.

Patriation and the politics of compromise: In determining
to bring home Canada's constitution, the Liberal Trudeau
formed some unlikely allies with Tories at home and abroad,
Prime Minister Margaret Thatcher of Great Britain and
Premier William Davis of Great Brampton.

Constitutionalism and the politics of frustration: After countless first ministers' conferences on the constitution, Trudeau made a deal with the provinces and persuaded all the premiers (save Quebec's) to line up with him to bring it home to Canada at last.

Royal assent and the politics of triumph: In April 1982, after years of determined effort, Pierre Trudeau realized his goal, and the constitution was patriated in the presence of Canada's Queen.

the politicians over this abstruse issue – were once again impatient. The polls showed they were still massively committed to Trudeau's "people's package" for patriating the BNA Act with an entrenched charter of rights and a formula specifying how future amendments to it would be made. They seemed to understand intuitively that he was seeking an expansion of citizens' rights that would appreciably improve their lives. But they wanted the wrangling with the premiers to stop and they wanted patriation now.[1]

These public concerns weighed heavily in Ottawa on Sunday, November 1, the day before the first ministers' conference on the constitution was to begin, as the provincial delegations gathered in hotel suites around the city in order to get ready for the confrontation to come. They were a nervous crowd, already divided into two camps and soon to fragment further. Ranged against Trudeau was the so-called Gang of Eight, made up of the four premiers from the western provinces, three more from the east, plus René Lévesque of Quebec. Lined up on Trudeau's side was an unlikely duo, the Progressive Conservative premiers of New Brunswick and Ontario, Richard Hatfield and William Davis. Only Davis and Hatfield had been at the Victoria conference in 1971, when Trudeau and the premiers of the day had made a constitutional agreement that failed in the meeting's aftermath because Quebec decided to reject the compromise. And only Davis and Hatfield still had the heart after an embittering decade of failed federal-provincial negotiations to see through Trudeau's peccadilloes to the vision of a more egalitarian and united Canada that had animated his constitutional efforts in the first place.

Richard Hatfield's fascination with questions of federal-provincial power-sharing pre-dated his election as pre-

mier of New Brunswick in 1970. He had formed an attachment to Canada beyond provincialism and a commitment to social justice beyond Toryism as a young
executive assistant in Diefenbaker's Ottawa in the 1950s.
Because he believed in the Canadian federation so ardently, Hatfield not only had embraced official bilingualism as an ideal but had put it into effect in New
Brunswick. The province's French-speaking Acadian
population had reciprocated by giving him their votes,
thereby helping secure his long-lasting hold on the legislature. Hatfield's progressivism was particularly remarkable considering that he was the offspring of one of the
old provincial élites who had been holding Canada together since Confederation, the very caste Trudeau had
gone into politics to unhorse. The bachelor son of a prosperous New Brunswick family – he was Heber Hatfield's
boy from the St. John River Valley – and a lawyer who
had been groomed for a political career since childhood,
Hatfield had many strengths (most of them hidden) and
several weaknesses (all of them obvious) to bring to Trudeau as an ally.

Even though he had been in power in New Brunswick
for over a decade, his fellow premiers generally dismissed
him as a political lightweight because of his erratic personal behaviour – his penchant for flying off for frequent
holidays in exotic climes (Morocco, Manhattan, and
Montreal), his interest in folk art and fashion, his habit of
drinking far into the night with journalists whose gossipy
company he loved, and his tendency to get carried away
by emotionalism, particularly when displaying his devotion to the monarchy. "I love the Queen and dislike the
English," he was given to explaining. "Not just because
she's such a marvellous, *marvellous* woman with a deep,
deep knowledge of Canada but because she represents in
her person the finest aspects of the parliamentary system

that defines and ennobles us all." When Hatfield had flown to London the previous winter to express these sentiments publicly in support of Trudeau's proposed patriation of the Canadian constitution, the British had responded with astonishment. "What in God's good name is *he* all about?" a Labourite from the Scottish Lowlands had asked a couple of Canadians during a discussion of the problems that patriation had brought to the MPs at Westminster. "I mean, one would have thought his kind had all gone down with the *Titanic* and were at peace on the ocean's floor."[2]

What his detractors failed to understand about Hatfield was that under the foppish façade was a politician both intelligent and intuitive. Because of his long experience in public life and his essential loneliness, Hatfield had the capacity to cast a cool eye on his fellow first ministers, whose macho culture was alien to his temperament and his interests. He was equally dismayed by the churlishness of the dissident premiers – whom he saw as willing to wreck the Canadian federation out of "pettiness, power-mongering, or personal pique" – and by the confrontational manner Trudeau had adopted in response.[3]

Hatfield acted as his own intergovernmental affairs minister and prided himself on consulting with federal officials frequently so that he could understand the niceties of constitutional issues. But during the coming days of hard negotiating, he intended to stay out of the federal team's strategizing because he wanted to remain flexible and to be able to talk to people on all sides. In essence he hoped to help bring about patriation by floating free and conciliating surreptitiously. It was his view, in any case, that Bill Davis was the premier who could best cope with the vagaries of Pierre Trudeau.

. . .

Though he never would admit it, the chief reason that Trudeau was still able to contemplate going straight to London with his patriation package in the fall of 1981 was the support that had been given to his constitutional quest over the previous year by the premier of Canada's most powerful and populous province. Davis had first come out openly in support of Trudeau's constitution only the year before, but this latest expression of solidarity between Ottawa and Ontario had deep roots. Despite numerous confrontations between Queen's Park and Ottawa on the partisan political level, the federal interest had generally been Ontario's from the time of the country's first prime minister, Sir John A. Macdonald, who had seen the new Canadian federation's welfare as an extension of Upper Canada's. A century later Ontario had grown used to dealing with Ottawa on almost equal terms. By the early 1980s, the federal Liberal regime, which had held power for so long in Ottawa, and the Ontario Tory regime, which had lasted so long at Queen's Park, looked to many Canadians from the periphery like two facets of Big Government, Inc.[4]

The Ottawa-Toronto axis had been strengthened by the connections Davis's associates had made with Trudeau's constitutional team over the previous eighteen months. The federal minister of justice, Jean Chrétien, had been getting along famously with Ontario's attorney general, Roy McMurtry, since the summer of the CCMC negotiations, which had been co-chaired by Chrétien and Roy Romanow, the attorney general of Saskatchewan. This trio had made a point of cultivating their closeness, meeting regularly, telephoning often, and calling one another Big Roy, Little Roy, and P'tit Jean. Even more important, Trudeau's cabinet secretary for federal-provincial relations, Michael Kirby, had developed a rapport with Hugh Segal, the premier's associate cabinet secretary. ("Almost as soon as we met, Hughie became one of my best friends," was the way Kirby described a relationship that was institutionalized later when he and Segal formed a CTV network team of political commentators in company with Gerald Caplan of the NDP, who sliced through their bipartisan bonhomie with his sharp-edged, social democrat's wit.) At Segal's urging, the Davis government had moved one of its own bureaucrats into Kirby's Federal-Provincial Relations Office to enable an even closer liaison and had made sure that Ontario's officials in London worked in tandem with Jean Wadds, the Canadian high commissioner there, to help offset the dissident provinces' lobbying by quietly impressing on the Brits that the Commonwealth's longest-lived Conservative regime was backing Trudeau.[5]

However much rapport developed between the Ontario and Ottawa constitutional teams, the men who led them remained strikingly different in personality and style. Bill Davis was a provincial in the basic sense that he was rooted in the heartland that had produced him. A genetic Conservative, born into a solidly bourgeois Ontario family that had made its money on his mother's side in the manufacture of shoes, he had grown up in a rambling house in the leafy town of Brampton. His education was as solid and parochial as his home life. He had studied at the University of Toronto in its great days when the campus was alive with the ideas of Marshall McLuhan, C.B. Macpherson, Donald Creighton, Caesar Wright, Bora Laskin, S.D. Clark, and Northrop Frye. But Davis had majored in football with a minor in campus politics and had plodded through the study of law in order to please his father, a Brampton Crown attorney and pillar of the United Church. Grenville Davis had propelled his son into provincial politics when he was still a tongue-tied, plump young lawyer living with his wife and children across the

street from his parents' house. He all but inherited a safe
seat from one of his father's friends and was rapidly promoted from the backbenches into the education minister's
chair at a time when universities and community colleges
were proliferating in the province to accommodate the
needs of the baby-boom generation. Young Davis thrived
in that burgeoning portfolio and in 1971, when he became
the fourth Progressive Conservative premier to hold
office consecutively in Ontario, he was as antagonistic to
the federal Liberals as any provincial leader. But as the
1970s wore on and his experience in high office deepened,
Davis came to realize that the problems inflicted on Canada's political economy by federal-provincial confrontations were building towards a crisis that could seriously
threaten Ontario's long-term interests.[6]

The province's industrial prospects were constrained
by the barriers to interprovincial trade that had sprung up
as the hinterland provinces learned how to fashion separate and competitive economic strategies at Ontario's expense. Particularly dismaying was the realization that
resource autonomy for Alberta in the context of rising
energy prices could hobble Ontario's entrepreneurs and
burden its consumers with high energy costs. With an
interest in the Canadian "economic union" almost as big
as Ottawa's, the Ontario Tories came to the same position
as the Trudeau Liberals on energy policy in 1973 when the
first OPEC crisis inflated the world price of oil – a decision
that Alberta's Peter Lougheed regarded as "a deliberate
kick in the balls."[7]

Although Davis and Lougheed had got on well enough
when they became premiers within months of each other
in 1971, attending football games and visiting each other's
houses in the easy company of their wives, the historic
conflict between the hinterland and the centre over who
would profit from resource rents soon drove them apart.

Davis had hoped that the constitutional negotiations of 1978 and 1979 would help resolve this knotty interprovincial problem as well as his worries about political instability in Quebec, since the prospect of its separation from Canada imperilled Ontario's most important provincial market. His frustration when those conferences failed had been so extreme that he came to a parting of the ways with his fellow premiers, even though most of them were Progressive Conservatives and felt entitled to his partisan support.[8]

Once the newly installed prime minister, Joe Clark, showed himself too weak to withstand Alberta's demands in 1979, Ontario broke with Tory Ottawa, too. Davis, who was proud of being known as the Man from Bland, the amiable, pipe-puffing, self-effacing premier of the smuggest province in the federation, a man who had always been a conciliator, suddenly became a nonconformist in the premiers' club. And in the dispiriting election campaign Clark conducted against the reincarnated Pierre Trudeau in the winter of 1980, Davis made sure that his electoral organization, the experienced and efficient Big Blue Machine, offered only perfunctory help. The alternative to Clark was the big red machine of the federalist Liberals, and to Davis, as the defiant centralist, the alternative looked pretty good.

By this time it was obvious to Davis and his key advisers – Hugh Segal, Roy McMurtry, Tom Wells, his minister of intergovernmental affairs, and Eddie Goodman, a wily Toronto lawyer who was one of his closest cronies – that constitutionalism as it had evolved in the 1970s was doomed to fail. They were convinced that only bold action by the federal government could save Canada, and when Trudeau announced his unilateral constitutional package on October 2, 1980, it was clear to them that they should support it. (They also expected Hatfield to line up on Trudeau's side since he was connected to the Big Blue Machine through his friendship with its guru, the writer and advertising expert Dalton Camp.)

Although the Davis group believed that Trudeau's constitutional patriation plan was Canada's last chance to sustain a central government with enough power to manage the country, none of them really warmed to its chief proponent. Trudeau was too cerebral, too self-contained, and too sarcastic to inspire their affection. But as professional pols, they admired his longevity and as Canadians, his federalist ferocity. To them it was obvious that only Trudeau, as the incarnation of French power in Ottawa, could pull off patriation. Only he was tough enough in heart and mind to break out of the futile constitutionalism the country was enmeshed in and set it back on course. "We all knew he was a great man," one of them explained afterwards. "You couldn't be in a room with him and hear him argue his brief without understanding that. A great man. And so diamond-hard, he glittered. Sometimes it was easier to be an enemy of almost anybody else than to be an ally of Pierre Trudeau's."[9]

To the Ontarians' relief, their polling had confirmed that making common cause with Trudeau was good politics as well as good statesmanship. The charter of rights was enormously popular in multicultural, urban Ontario, as was the National Energy Program with its promise of affordable gas. What was not so popular was Trudeau's stand on language rights, but the Davis team had found a way around that. As Red Tories, Davis & Co. found the anti-French feeling that was rampant among the older Conservatives in their party's ranks a matter of embarrassment. They personally believed in a bilingual Canada and in sending their offspring to be "immersed" in the bilingual schools their own Ministry of Education had brought into being. But their party had been sustained in office for nearly forty years by voters in rural Ontario who emphatically did not. Having been made aware of this problem, Trudeau agreed, despite the anger of many Liberals, not to press Davis to accept the application to Ontario of Section 133 of the BNA Act. This was the clause that declared Quebec's legislature and courts bilingual and that Richard Hatfield wanted extended to New Brunswick. Avoiding official bilingualism in Ontario, despite the province's large francophone population, was politically necessary in Davis's eyes not only to protect himself against a redneck Tory revolt on language. He also needed to sustain some overt partisan tension so he would not be seen as too close to the Trudeau team. These calculations paid off handsomely in April 1981, when his party won re-election with a clear majority.[10]

As a politician at the peak of an outstandingly successful political career, the Ontario premier had every cause to be pleased with himself on the afternoon of November 1, 1981, as he switched off the football game he had been watching in his suite at the Four Seasons Hotel and prepared to drive out to 24 Sussex for a meeting with the prime minister. Davis was feeling so good, in fact, that when Trudeau greeted him wearing jeans, clogs, and his customary cool, and ushered him out to his glassed-in back porch for a two-hour strategy session, Davis scarcely batted an eye. "Bill's usual behaviour in Trudeau's presence was best described as 'watchful,'" said one of his associates afterwards. "Their encounters almost always made him nervous. But he would never show the nervousness or the anger and competitiveness that sometimes went with it, the way [Peter] Lougheed often did. When those emotions churned up Bill would suppress them. His motto was 'Steady as she goes.'"[11]

And steady Davis stayed as he and Trudeau elaborated their joint strategy for conducting the first ministers' meetings over the next three days, with Hugh Segal and Michael Kirby taking notes and occasionally adding to the discussion. In essence, the federalists' objective was to achieve what the Supreme Court had called "substantial" support for their constitutional position by breaking up the Gang of Eight. They could expect continuing enmity from Lougheed, Lévesque, Peckford, and Lyon. But now that Trudeau had agreed to give negotiation one last chance, the other anglophone dissidents were sending signals that they were looking for a way out of the impasse.

Davis was apprehensive that Trudeau's pugnacity might scupper this possibility. He had witnessed far too many federal-provincial meetings when Trudeau's intellectual testiness had torpedoed the possibility of agreement. Roy McMurtry had voiced these concerns the previous week to Jean Chrétien, who agreed with the Ontarians' fears. "Da boss he sure like to argue," said Chrétien. "And he win a lotta arguments. But I'm scared he lose da war." The two attorneys general decided that their task – and Davis's – in the coming negotiations was to restrain Trudeau's response to the dissident premiers' belligerence and to keep the lines of communication open with the more amenable among them. The slogan for the week was not "Divide and conquer" but "Conciliate and prevail."[12]

The Ontario delegation began to execute this game plan during the conference's opening meeting on the morning of Monday, November 2. One by one, the members of the Gang of Eight, wary of showing flexibility, trotted out their stale hostilities to Trudeau's patriation plan. Bill Davis, ignoring the bellicose atmosphere, made the first of two scripted gestures of conciliation. He signalled to the western provinces his acceptance of Alberta's proposed amending formula by declaring that Ontario was willing to give up its historic veto power over future constitutional amendments. The next day, he made his second gesture, proposing a simple trade-off: all the provinces should accept the charter of rights in return for federal agreement to the Alberta amending formula. To his surprise and alarm, Trudeau openly sneered at this idea as though it were emanating not from his sturdy ally, the squire from the Ontario fatlands, but from the bandits in the Gang of Eight.

By this time the gang, if not exactly a crumbling coalition, was riddled with unease. The seven anglophone premiers had differences of opinion among themselves about how unyielding they ought to be in their dealings with the feds. But their main problem was growing uncertainty over the intentions of Quebec. Ontario government people had been telling members of their delegations all autumn long that they were being naïve in trusting the Quebeckers. There was no deal that Trudeau would accept that Lévesque could ever sign. In the flat atmosphere of the November negotiations these doubts began to surface in the Anglos' minds. If Robert Bourassa's decision in 1971 to abort the Victoria agreement had drawn on the advice of Claude Morin, who was then Quebec's deputy minister for intergovernmental affairs, what chance was there that René Lévesque and Morin, who was now Quebec's minister for intergovernmental affairs, could accept a deal in which Trudeau's strong charter of rights would prevail over their key accomplishment of legislating unilingualism for Quebec?

On their part, the Quebec delegation had come to Ottawa already doubtful about their allies' willingness to sustain their opposition to Trudeau. For almost two years, the mercurial Lévesque and his phlegmatic strategist, Morin, had been living in a pressure-cooker. First they had experienced the relief of Trudeau's apparent retirement from politics. Next they had suffered the shock of his triumphant return to office. And then they had en-

dured the humiliation of allowing him to seize the referendum from them when he was riding high from his federal election victory. The seemingly definitive loss of the
fight for sovereignty-association in May 1980 had been
devastating to all Péquistes. "There was political suicide
in the air," Claude Charron, the party's House leader,
remembered. Serious talk was heard about entering into a
coalition with Claude Ryan to provide a united front of
indépendantistes and neo-federalists against the Trudeau
federalists or even acceding to Ryan's repeated demands
for an immediate election that the Péquistes would almost
certainly lose. These options were soon rejected once
Claude Morin decided to try to put together a coalition
with the anglophone premiers as part of a long-term
scheme for political recovery. In addition to his own long
experience in federal-provincial relations, he could draw
on the expertise of an intergovernmental affairs team that
was probably stronger than any in the country and included experts such as Louis Bernard, the secretary to the
executive council, and the deputy premier, Jacques-Yvan
Morin, who had been engaged with constitutional problems for decades. When "the princeling," as Lévesque
called Trudeau, announced in October 1980 that he would
not play the premiers' games any more and intended to
force Nanny Thatcher to give Canada the constitution he
wanted, Claude Morin's team was ready with a plan.[13]

They had already let it be known that, having lost their
fight for sovereignty-association, they were once again
seeking the same kind of greater provincial autonomy that
was the goal of the other dissident provinces. These
claims were substantiated when Morin's team produced a
blueprint for a decentralized federalism so cleverly contrived that it catered to each unhappy province's specific
demands and harmonized them all with Quebec's historic
need for self-determination. To prove their good faith, the

Péquistes then let the anglophones in on their London lobbying and agreed to synchronize their court strategy, manoeuvres that re-established Quebec as a central player in the pan-Canadian games and laid the foundations for an unprecedented provincial counter-attack against the federal government. Morin pulled off another coup in February 1981, when, as a result of several silky diplomatic meetings held in Montreal's Ritz-Carlton Hotel, the governments of Saskatchewan and Nova Scotia succumbed to his blandishments and joined the six original dissidents – British Columbia, Alberta, Manitoba, Quebec, Prince Edward Island, and Newfoundland, whose mutual loyalty had been generated by Peter Lougheed – to form the Gang of Eight.

Acknowledging that this support might prove a mixed blessing, Morin's cabinet colleague Claude Charron wrote later, "[We were] forced ... to seduce, quite provisionally and by anti-Trudeauism, the eminent politicians of Halifax and Regina, for whom making a pact with us or the Devil amounted to much the same thing." The Péquistes recognized that Blakeney in particular, as the lone social democrat among the anglophone premiers, had as many reasons to support Trudeau's initiative as to oppose it. An entrenched charter of rights had been part of his party's constitutional policy for decades. The NDP's federal leader, Ed Broadbent, was unequivocally on Trudeau's side. The Saskatchewan factum to the Supreme Court had argued that only "*a measure* of provincial agreement" was needed for constitutional amendments, and Blakeney himself had made it clear that he felt unanimity among first ministers was no longer a workable basis for federal-provincial diplomacy and that it was probably impossible for the PQ government to agree to any kind of constitutional settlement given the state of Quebec's politics. Because he wanted patriation over and done with, he did not even fault Trudeau for his unilateralism – although he felt the Supreme Court's blessing for such audacious action should have been sought by the federal government early on.[14]

Blakeney's problem was that the extra provincial power over resource policy that Ed Broadbent had negotiated with Trudeau as the price for the federal NDP's support was of no value to Saskatchewan, which had successfully used its income tax power to recoup what it had lost in the adverse Supreme Court decisions of the 1970s. Blakeney had academic and professional credentials that gave him a degree of ease with Trudeau that the other premiers had cause to envy. He had studied law as a Rhodes Scholar at Oxford and had been taking part in innovative governmental projects as a senior civil servant and cabinet minister in Saskatchewan since the early 1950s, when Tommy Douglas was running the first and most successful socialist government in North America. But he also had the old CCF-NDP distrust of Trudeau, who was thought of in his circles as a turncoat, a social democrat gone wrong. In addition, Blakeney was chronically cautious. Despite numerous attempts to lure him into the federalist camp during the previous year, he had continued to fuss and fume and dither. In the end, Blakeney joined the Gang of Eight, swayed by caution (grass-roots hostility to Trudeau among his electorate was visceral in the wake of the National Energy Program), political reservations (he did not like the idea of a non-elected Senate retaining a veto over future constitutional amendments), personal convictions (he disagreed with the federal NDP's support for a charter, fearing it would subordinate the people's will, as expressed by elected politicians, to the reactionary whims of judges recruited from the wealthy legal profession), and territorial solidarity (he did not want to make an open break with his provincial neighbours, Alberta and Manitoba). "The Trojan Horse, Blakeney with his wheat salesman's smile, had just joined us," Claude Charron observed. " 'Last in, first out,' I said to Roy Romanow, his minister."[15]

Despite Charron's reservations, the PQ's successful attempt at strengthening the opposition to Trudeau by putting together the Gang of Eight was viewed with widespread approval in Quebec, particularly among neo-federalists, whose rage at Trudeau's unilateralism exceeded that of the PQ. In their eyes, their trust in Trudeau, as displayed in their support of the Non side in the referendum, had been betrayed. They had assumed his promise of a renewed federalism through a patriated constitution meant greater powers for Quebec. Instead, the proposed charter of rights threatened their province's unilingualism, and his unilateral plans, if carried out successfully, would dash forever Quebec's hopes for levering further powers out of Ottawa in return for its eventual agreement to patriation. Even active federal Liberals in Quebec were dispirited by the prospect of a constitution they knew would diminish Quebec's autonomy. Prominent intellectuals, notably Léon Dion of the Université Laval and Michel Roy, publisher of Le Devoir, began to call for a united front, and perhaps even a new referendum, to mobilize Quebec opinion against Trudeau.[16]

Angriest of all those federalists and neo-federalists who had worked to pull off the Non victory was the Quebec Liberal leader, Claude Ryan. Ryan had already told Trudeau in private, and had stated emphatically in public, that his unilateralism was unacceptable. By imposing a strictly federalist constitutional proposal without consulting Ryan and without making any concessions to neo-federalism, Trudeau had put the provincial Liberals in an untenable position. "Trudeau's screwed me," Ryan kept repeating to his intimates in bitter and impotent exasperation as the constitutional drama unfolded. Ryan felt even worse when, running on the slogan "Faut rester fort," Lévesque triggered an election for April 1981 and trounced the Liberals so decisively that Ryan's resignation as leader became only a matter of time.[17]

In the immediate aftermath of the election, Lévesque made one of the impulsive blunders that were the despair of his advisers. The main point of the post-referendum, pan-Canadian strategy that Morin had put together for the Péquistes was to stop Trudeau's unilateral move on patriation and thereby sustain constitutionalism – the federal-provincial power game that had been rolling along for a decade and had proven so useful to the separatists in their resistance to Ottawa's authority. But while the Péquistes were busy with their election campaign, the anglophone premiers had put together an "alternative accord" to Trudeau's constitutional package and had managed to pressure Lévesque into coming to Ottawa to sign it only three days after his victory. Still exhausted by his electoral endeavours, Lévesque agreed at a late-night session of the premiers to accept a version of Lougheed's amending formula. It allowed any province to "opt out" of any future constitutional amendment that would give the federal government powers in a field where the provinces enjoyed formal jurisdiction. A province that did opt out would get "fiscal compensation" from Ottawa to pay for its own program in that field.

On the surface this proposal seemed reasonable enough. If Ottawa sought a constitutional amendment to make it legal for the federal parliament to legislate a nation-wide day-care program, for instance, and Quebec or any other province preferred to institute its own program, this would be sanctioned with federal reimbursement for the costs. Although "opting out with financial compensation" sounded like an important achievement, it had an implicit problem for Quebec that Lévesque underestimated. Accepting Alberta's amending formula, which was based on the principle that all provinces are equal, was tantamount to giving up the province's long-standing claim to a veto over all constitutional amendments as well as its basic demand for an entirely new division of powers before the BNA Act could be patriated. These drastic concessions, made by Lévesque apparently without a clear understanding of their implications, were roundly condemned in Quebec as an abandonment of the province's long quest for special status. Lévesque had made a tactical mistake from which he expected, characteristically, that he could eventually back off, since Trudeau was adamantly refusing further negotiations with the provinces and the gang's alternative accord would in all likelihood quickly be forgotten. But once Trudeau had been forced by the Supreme Court decision of September 1981 to meet the premiers again, Lévesque's error turned out to be more than tactical.[18]

By the time the first ministers reconvened in Ottawa in November, he and his colleague Morin knew that they were in an almost impossible position. The best they could hope to achieve at the conference would be its failure, an outcome possible only if they could sabotage any putative agreements between the federalists and the dissidents by maintaining the anti-Trudeau solidarity of the Gang of Eight. They realized that the gang's collective animus against Trudeau had already been undermined by his willingness to hold another conference. All of the anglophone dissidents were now edgy, and some of them – notably Bennett of British Columbia and Blakeney of Saskatchewan – were not only willing but eager to make a deal with Ottawa out of fear of the alternative: that Trudeau would carry out his threat to proceed to London, where they suspected Thatcher would ultimately have to give him his way. These tensions became increasingly obvious during the first two days of the conference as the provincial delegations responded warily to the self-possession of Trudeau and his team.

With his basic strategy firmly in mind – "to break the group of eight, to entice a couple [or more] of them away" – Trudeau held himself aloof at the Monday and Tuesday meetings, wielding his gavel, preaching the need for compromise, but dismissing his opponents' propositions as illogical, unacceptable, or both, and refusing to reveal in what way, if any, he might be willing to make concessions. By Wednesday morning it looked to almost everyone present as though the conference would break down in yet another impasse. As the premiers recycled their ideas yet again, Trudeau finally intervened with vigour. Suggesting that these meetings were not going anywhere, he brought up once more the idea of holding a national referendum in two years' time if no agreement could be reached with the provinces. This would let the people of Canada assert their sovereignty and decide between his constitutional package and that of the Gang of Eight. Trudeau knew that the very mention of a referendum was a red flag to the anglophones, not just because opinion in English Canada was overwhelmingly on his side but because a federally generated referendum might set a precedent that would forever undermine their legislative authority. The feds would be horning in on provincial territory, beating the premiers on their own ground. Trudeau also knew that Quebec's élites were very much in favour of a referendum. When the anglophone premiers at the table bridled at his suggestion, Trudeau – the unmatchable bilingual, bicultural man – turned to Lévesque and pounced. "You're the great democrat," he taunted his opponent in French. "You're the great believer in referendums. *You* can't be opposed to one . . . Or are you afraid to take me on?"[19]

Even before Trudeau issued this challenge Lévesque was acting jittery. He had been out of sorts since leaving, earlier that morning, the suite in the Château Laurier where the Gang of Eight had been gathering daily for breakfast to co-ordinate their strategy. At such gatherings, there was almost always a certain tension between the intellectual Péquistes, who were witty, nervy, and bold in their opposition to Trudeau, and the pragmatic anglophones, who spoke of "doing business" with him. Daniel Latouche, a professor and an adviser to the Quebec premier, referred to the gang's seven other members as "a bunch of Kiwanis presidents," a view that Lévesque largely shared though he had developed a strong rapport with Peter Lougheed, whom he regarded as "the only guy with real guts." On this particular morning the Péquistes' normal, barely disguised disdain for the gang was heightened when Allan Blakeney, the man they regarded as the prissiest of the lot, decided to play the earnest, honest broker. Blakeney brought forward an elaborate new proposal, on which his officials had obviously been working for some time, that included an amending formula without either a veto for Quebec or an opting-out provision. Lévesque rejected the proposal out of hand, angered by Blakeney's cavalier disregard for Quebec's position and upset at this indication that the Gang of Eight was falling apart. He hated this kind of nitpicking discussion anyway. It called on the kind of lawyerly skills that he had never developed. In fact, he hated the whole constitutional exercise. "I couldn't have cared less," he said afterwards when the game was lost. "Basically I was not interested in constitutional change and as a democrat, never did respect the Canadian constitution. It wasn't coherent. It was a goddam sacred cow."[20]

There was more to Lévesque's bad mood that morning than his distrust of his allies and his dislike of constitutionalism. Worn down by the strains of twenty years spent holding together the indépendantiste dream, he was already beginning to slip into his long decline. He seemed minuscule, old, exhausted. You could sense the million cigarettes, the perpetual late nights, the endless glasses of gin, the furry tongue, the early-morning fuzz in the once so agile brain. In his extreme fatigue that autumn, he had taken to obsessing about his nemesis, Trudeau, calling him "the Sonofabitch" as though this were his given name and making wild statements such as "I know for a fact that the Sonofabitch has his bags packed and will be moving into his big house in Montreal soon. He'll be out of there [Ottawa] by Christmas. We'll be rid of him." Lévesque had become a fading star, a kind of Piaf of the political stage, still lovable, still croaking out the old songs, but diminished now and sad.[21]

Sitting at the conference table on the morning of November 4, almost certain that the Saskatchewan proposal, with its easy dismissal of Quebec's particular needs, represented the emerging consensus among the anglophone premiers, Lévesque felt isolated and vulnerable. But once Trudeau issued his referendum challenge, a comforting thought swam into his consciousness. He figured he could win such a referendum in Quebec in view of the widespread outrage at Trudeau's unilateralism and thereby wipe out the shame of losing the referendum on sovereignty-association the year before. Summoning up his old bravado, he surprised both his enemy and his allies by responding to the federalist's dare with a simple "Okay. I'd like to fight the charter."[22]

As soon as he heard these words, Trudeau knew he had scored. The Gang of Eight was about to crack. Sensing the unease among the anglophone premiers – most of whom had experienced considerable difficulty in following the fast, colloquial French of the Trudeau–Lévesque exchange – Trudeau immediately adjourned the session for lunch. Heading straight for the waiting microphones, he announced deadpan the launching of "a new Quebec-Canada alliance." Once the reporters started to question him about the meaning of such an alliance, he could scarcely contain his glee. "The cat is among the pigeons," he said enigmatically, eyes gleaming, before turning away from the journalists' clamour. Lévesque took his place immediately, confirming what Trudeau had said by announcing that a referendum would be "an honourable way out" for Quebec.[23]

At first the Péquiste delegation felt triumphant. When they phoned Quebec City to tell their confrères the news, there was cheering at the other end of the line. It took them a couple of hours to realize that in rising to Trudeau's challenge, their champion had impaled himself on Trudeau's sword. By embracing – without prior consultation – a proposal the anglophone premiers were sure to loathe, Lévesque had broken the cardinal Gang of Eight rule that his own adviser Claude Morin had insisted on: that the dissidents should never change position without advance consultation.

When the conference resumed after the lunch break and Lévesque read the rules that the federal team was proposing for the referendum, he cried foul. But it was too late. By joining up with Trudeau, if only for an interlude, he had confirmed the anglophones' nagging fear. The ambiguities of his position had always added an element of uncertainty to the gang's alliance. Was Lévesque in it just to sabotage the process? Was there any deal that as a separatist he could possibly sign? Now they had seen with their own eyes – even if they hadn't quite been able to follow with their own ears – how blood ran thicker than promises. Trudeau and Lévesque were members of the same post-war generation of French Canadians, the brilliant generation who had gone abroad to expand their thinking and then had come home "to change the place," in Gérard Pelletier's phrase, the generation whose members were always more interested in one another than they were in anybody or anything else. Looking at these two was like looking into a mirror and seeing Quebec's two fractured images at one glance: *notre miroir à deux faces*, as Gérard Bergeron has called them. Now, as the Anglos perceived the situation, the two francophones had formed an axis that could exclude them from the deal-making, leaving them, rather than Quebec, out in the constitutional cold.

By hastily accepting Trudeau's referendum idea, Lévesque had liberated his sometime allies to make their own compromise with the federalist devil. The emotional solidarity of the gang was broken. Officials and politicians from the anglophone delegations immediately began meeting in small groups with the federalists in the hope of putting together a compromise proposal that would "fly." Their task was eased by the fact that they had been talking to one another at meetings much like these for months – in some cases, years – eating countless dinners together, killing bottles of Scotch, trading sports scores, dubious jokes, family stories. They knew one another's lingo. They had lived one another's lives. They made up a special subculture: the constitutionalists of the political élite. Now, at a moment of collective crisis, they were catapulted towards a solution in a kind of spontaneous release. As Lévesque was to remark bitterly afterwards, "Every one of them hated the goddam Sonofabitch. For their own particular reasons. But none of them had a vision of politics that couldn't be turned by a couple of cocktails. In the end they patched [a deal] together. And Quebec was once again left in the corner."[24]

Later on, many people were to claim credit for the solution that transpired. The most successful of those who did so were the old soft-shoe team of Big Roy, Little Roy, and P'tit Jean. McMurtry, Romanow, and Chrétien were hailed in the media for turning a conversation held in a little-used kitchen in the convention centre into the "kitchen accord" that was finally accepted as the ultimate deal. In essence, it was a modified version of the swap Bill Davis had proposed on Tuesday. Alberta would be allowed its amending formula with its opting-out component but without fiscal compensation. The Trudeau charter would include its minority-language education rights, but its sway would be limited by a "notwithstanding clause," proposed by Bennett earlier in the proceedings, that would allow provincial legislatures to override its provisions.

This proposal was bandied about from delegation to delegation, with the Saskatchewan suite at the Château Laurier serving as the site for an informal round of clause-trading that involved officials from all delegations except Quebec's. By early evening, the strongman of the Gang of Eight, Peter Lougheed, was satisfied that things were moving his way and went back to his suite at the Skyline Hotel, after telling his deputy minister, Peter Meekison, to let him know first thing in the morning what had been achieved.

While all this activity was under way downtown, Trudeau was ensconced at 24 Sussex with his key ministers and his key advisers: Jean Chrétien, Marc Lalonde, John Roberts, Mark MacGuigan, André Ouellet, Donald Johnston, Allan MacEachen, and Lloyd Axworthy from his cabinet, along with Michael Pitfield, Michael Kirby, Fred Gibson, and Tom Axworthy from the PMO/PCO and Roger Tassé of the Department of Justice. Stubbornly, Trudeau was still half hoping that a deal would not be reached. In agreeing to hold the conference at all he believed he had shown himself willing "to have one more political try.

But I was certain it would fail. And I was certain I was going to London all the same," he remembered, his defiance bubbling up six years after the deal was done.[25]

As late as nine o'clock, Trudeau was still reluctant to compromise, still insisting to his colleagues that he must have a referendum, that this was the way to let "the people" exercise their sovereignty. With clear indications from Michael Kirby, who had been dealing downtown through his buddy, Hugh Segal, with the group in the Saskatchewan suite, that most of the provincial delegations could live with some variant of the Davis package, Trudeau's own lieutenants lost patience with the boss. Neither Jean Chrétien, his chief constitutional negotiator, nor Marc Lalonde, his strongest minister and Quebec lieutenant, could stomach the idea of institutionalizing a referendum in the constitution. Having lived through the trauma of the campaign over sovereignty-association, they rejected the referendum idea outright as too divisive and dangerous for the country's good. It was a powerful argument that Trudeau had to consider seriously, especially since it was backed up by pressure from his two provincial allies.

Richard Hatfield had consistently supported Trudeau's constitutional positions, but earlier on Wednesday, when the prime minister was resisting any compromise with the premiers' positions, Hatfield objected. "He was vocal [on the need to compromise]," Trudeau reported, indicating this pressure was an important consideration but not the decisive one. The key naysayer was the premier of Ontario. In a long phone conversation at ten o'clock Davis conveyed a quiet ultimatum. He would not be able to continue his support if Pierre didn't agree to the deal that was being worked out. Without either Ontario or New Brunswick behind him, Trudeau would be turned back by the British parliamentarians if he persisted in going unilaterally to London. They would lean on the Supreme Court's position that Trudeau's package, while legal in a strict sense, was unconstitutional because it did not have "substantial" provincial support. Wined and dined, buttonholed and hobnobbed for months by the Gang of Eight's London representatives – the dissident premiers had even sent representatives to lobby at the Conservatives' annual conference in Blackpool earlier in the autumn – zealous backbenchers at Westminster would block the amendment to the BNA Act that Ottawa was proposing. Earlier that fall Lord Carrington had told Mark MacGuigan that, in his view, HMG could not control the House on the Canadian question and that the amendment would not pass. When MacGuigan passed on this devastating intelligence, Trudeau had appeared quite shaken.[26]

With all this in mind late in the evening of November 4, Trudeau realized Davis's dictum meant giving up the idea of the referendum. It meant accepting the override and so limiting the reach of the charter. It meant accepting opting out for the provinces, which could lead to something he had repeatedly castigated as "checkerboard federalism." But it also meant patriation – at last! – and a charter of rights that was better than none, in fact better than most of those already in place around the world. Davis's self-containment, his resolute calm, his consistent support had built an obligation that Trudeau could not ignore. "I realized then I might have to compromise," Trudeau recalled. "Davis told me if I didn't accept the deal, he and Hatfield would not go with me to London. I would have to stand alone. He said a referendum was unfair, that it would be issued only by the federal government and only we could ask the question. So I had to drop it. To my everlasting regret."[27]

In his maturity, Trudeau was able to set aside his Cyrano fantasy of climbing all alone to the mountain-top and to consider the bargain coolly and with intelligence. "I took what I could get," he said later. He was ready to accept the "good-enough solution" on the constitution as he had been willing to accept it in his personal life. He sent his ministers home satisfied with the compromise and went off to bed so he would be sure to have his wits about him for the finale in the morning.[28]

Across the river in Hull, at the Terrasses de la Chaudière, whence the Quebec delegation had decamped for the night, René Lévesque was drinking alone in his room, although rumours would later circulate that he had gone to Montreal. Elsewhere in the hotel, Claude Morin's officials, who knew very well that something was afoot on the Ontario side of the river, decided not to trouble their minister with further advice that they were convinced he would reject. It was probably better at that point for him to stay out of the deal-making, to let himself be abandoned, to end up the loner, to adopt the familiar Quebec stance of the betrayed during what would soon be called "the night of the long knives" rather than to keep working to stave off the inevitable disintegration of a gang gone soft.[29]

Early the next morning, Meekison briefed Lougheed, Kirby briefed Davis, and Mel Smith of the British Columbia premier's office briefed Bennett on the latest version of the original Davis proposal. And so it went around the circuit, with bureaucrats telling politicians what had been accomplished. At the premiers' regular Château Laurier breakfast, when Lévesque shuffled in late and bleary-eyed, he was shown the new deal. He was furious but subdued, remaining unresponsive when Lougheed took him aside and tried to offer his embarrassed explanations. An hour later, at the opening of the day's conference meeting, Brian Peckford presented the provinces' new consensus. Trudeau put up a brief fight, partly out of old conviction but largely to make a show, or so his aides surmised. He said he could accept the Peckford package in principle but insisted on three changes. The charter's protection of minority-language education rights must be exempt from any override by provincial parliaments. There must be a "sunset clause" of five years on any use of the notwithstanding clause. And finally, the question of aboriginal rights, which had been left aside in the commotion, must be put on the agenda for the next first ministers' conference on the constitution.

To general relief, the anglophone premiers agreed. A deal was struck while Lévesque sullenly rejected Trudeau's peace overtures and tears welled in Claude Morin's eyes. The accord spelled devastation for the Péquistes' hopes: an amending formula with neither a veto for Quebec nor financial compensation for opting out, and a charter with minority-language education rights (which would consolidate the English fact in Montreal) taking precedence over their much-prized Bill 101 (whose mission was to make the whole of Quebec overwhelmingly French).[30]

After thirty years of fierce resistance by six Quebec premiers – Duplessis, Lesage, Johnson, his successor, Jean-Jacques Bertrand, Bourassa, and now Lévesque – the British North America Act would be patriated without a single additional power for Quebec. It was a deal inferior to the one Bourassa could have signed after Victoria in 1971. Trudeau had won. "Il m'a fourré [He fucked me]," Lévesque sobbed on the government plane that took his delegation back to Quebec City. "Trudeau m'a fourré," he repeated to his minister of social affairs, Pierre-Marc Johnson, when he came to offer his sympathies.[31]

Lévesque was right. Whatever cowardice had been involved on the part of his former allies when they neglected to let him know they were concocting a final deal, it was

Trudeau who had bested him with his superior strategic sense, his greater staying power, his fierce will. As the telejournalist Denise Bombardier observed afterwards, "If Trudeau had become a separatist in the Sixties, Quebec would be independent by now." But it was Lévesque who had embraced indépendantisme. And it was Lévesque the separatist who was vanquished and Trudeau the federalist who had triumphed.[32]

Back in the convention centre in Ottawa, the victor made a couple of wry jokes, pounded his gavel one last time, and threw it down on the table. At this climactic moment of his political life, in the midst of the general jubilation, Trudeau seemed curiously restrained. It was almost as though he knew that trouble was coming on this and other fronts. That his constitutional victory, though hardly pyrrhic, was far from conclusive. And that the fight for the federalist vision of Canada would continue in the years to come.

END OF VOLUME 1

AFTERWORD

While the events described in *The Magnificent Obsession* were preoccupying the Trudeauites, many other major issues crucial to the survival of the Canadian state were demanding attention: issues of resource-sharing, of income equity, of regional development, and of national affirmation. In response, Trudeau and his team of governors took bold initiatives on a number of fronts such as energy policy, tax reform, industrial reorganization, and international relations only to find themselves pushed back by the forces of globalization, the antagonism of the private sector, the obstinate resistance of regional centres, and the power of the United States.

Volume 2 of *Trudeau and Our Times* describes some of these initiatives and their fate: the National Energy Program and its confrontation with Reaganite America, the attempt at sweeping tax reform and the revolt of the taxpayers against it, the battle over western freight rates, the attempt to reorganize the Atlantic fishery. It also follows Trudeau's further constitutional efforts and the discord they continued to cause between Ottawa and Quebec. It analyses the factors that led the Trudeau government to retreat from policies designed to build a "just society" and to lay the groundwork, inadvertently, for the rise of the right, the decline of liberalism, and the beginning of the neo-conservative era in Canada. And it assesses the role played by Trudeau the statesman on the world stage as the Cold War came to an end. In sum *The Fateful Delusion* concerns itself with the impact of Trudeau and the Trudeauites on the nation's political economy at a watershed period in its history, when inexorable pressures from within and without threw into high relief the dilemmas of governance in the fragile realm called Canada.

APPENDIX

THE 1980 CABINET AND DEPUTY MINISTERS

Ministry (Ministry of State)	Minister	Deputy/Secretary
Agriculture	Eugene Whelan	Gaétan Lussier
Communications	Francis Fox	Pierre Juneau
Consumer and Corporate Affairs and Postmaster General	André Ouellet	George Post
Economic Development	Horace (Bud) Olson	Gordon Osbaldeston
Employment and Immigration	Lloyd Axworthy	J.D. Love
Energy, Mines and Resources	Marc Lalonde	Marshall Cohen
(Mines)	Judy Erola	
Environment	John Roberts	Blair Seaborn
External Affairs	Mark MacGuigan	Allan Gotlieb

Finance (Finance)	Allan MacEachen Pierre Bussières	Ian Stewart
Fisheries and Oceans	Roméo Leblanc	Donald Tansley
Health and Welfare	Monique Bégin	P.A. McDougall
Indian Affairs and Northern Development	John Munro	Paul Tellier
Industry, Trade and Commerce (Small Business) (Trade)	Herbert Gray Charles Lapointe Edward Lumley	Robert Johnstone
Justice and Attorney General	Jean Chrétien	Roger Tassé
Labour	Gerald Regan	Thomas Eberlee
National Defence	Gilles Lamontagne	C.R. Nixon
National Revenue	William Rompkey	J.P. Connell
Privy Council	Yvon Pinard	
Public Works	Paul Cosgrove	J.A.H. Mackay
Regional Economic Expansion	Pierre De Bané	R.C. Montreuil
Secretary of State (Multiculturalism)	Francis Fox James Fleming	Huguette Labelle
Senate Leader	Raymond Perrault	

Science and Technology	John Roberts	L.D. Hudon
Social Development	Jean Chrétien	Bruce Rawson
Solicitor General	Robert Kaplan	P.A. Bissonnette
Supply and Services	Jean-Jacques Blais	Guy D'Avignon
Transport (Canadian Wheat Board)	Jean-Luc Pepin Hazen Argue	Arthur Kroeger
Treasury Board	Donald Johnston	John Manion
Veterans Affairs	Daniel Macdonald	W.B. Brittain

NOTES

CHAPTER 1

The Miraculous Year

1. On 1979 as a critical election: John Meisel predicted it "would in the long run be seen as a systems-altering election in the sense that the Canadian polity would develop quite differently after a Liberal than after a Conservative victory." The 1984 election was to prove him right. Meisel, "The Larger Context," p. 54.
2. Authors' interview with Thomas Axworthy, Feb. 20, 1980.
3. Results of the 1979 election in terms of seats in the House of Commons were: Progressive Conservatives, 136; Liberals, 114; NDP, 26; Social Credit, 6.
4. From "Desiderata" by Max Elormann, a lawyer from Terre Haute, Indiana, whose work was widely used on posters distributed by counter-culture street vendors in the 1960s and 1970s. Robert Sheppard, " 'Still a Beautiful World,' Trudeau Tells Faithful," *Globe and Mail* (May 23, 1979), p. 9.
5. "Miraculous year": After the poem "Annus Mirabilis," written by John Dryden in 1667, celebrating the English victories in 1665 against the Dutch and the subsequent fire of London, which rid the city of the great plague that had been devastating its citizenry.
6. On Trudeau's support: In 1979, the Liberals won 40 per cent of the popular vote as against the Conservatives' 36 per cent in the country as a whole; in Quebec the disparity was much greater, 62 per cent to 14 per cent.

7. Trudeau biography: Radwanski, *Trudeau*.
   Trudeau quotation: Conversation with the authors, Dec. 11, 1986.
8. De Gaulle, *Le fil de l'épée*.
9. Trudeau as magician: R. Gwyn, *Northern Magus*.
   Trudeau as solitary outlaw: Powe, *Solitary Outlaw*.
   Trudeau as Machiavelli: Ignatieff, "Longest Shadow."
   Trudeau as dove with falcon's claws: Vastel, *Trudeau le Québécois*.

CHAPTER 2

The Formative Decades

1. On the identity crisis: Erikson, *Identity, Youth and Crisis*, pp. 15-19; and Singer, *Boundaries of the Soul*, p. 210.
   Trudeau quote: Fremon, "Margaret Trudeau," p. 104.
   On Margaret's activities in this period: Margaret Trudeau, *Beyond Reason*. The ghost-writer was Caroline Moorehead of the London *Observer*.
2. Biographical information on the Trudeau family comes from the authors' interviews with, among others, Greta Chambers, Jean de Grandpré, Jean Le Moyne, Jean Marchand, Jeanne and Maurice Sauvé, Peter Scott, and Charles Taylor; and from conversations with Pierre Trudeau in 1985 and 1986. Also, interviews about the Trudeau and Elliott families conducted by Catherine Breslin in 1969, for her article "The Other Trudeaus": Allan Elliott; Conrad Joron, a business associate of Charlie Trudeau; his second cousin, Isidore Trudeau; his niece, Germaine Tremblay; various neighbours of the Trudeau grandparents in Saint-Rémi; and contemporaries of the young Pierre. Information was also drawn from chs. 3 and 4 of Radwanski's *Trudeau*, which were based on eight hours of interviews with Pierre Trudeau and conversations with his sister, Suzette Rouleau.
3. For a detailed description of the rise of early French-Canadian nationalism and the role Groulx played in it:

Wade, *French Canadians, Volume Two*, ch. XIII; and Trofimenkoff, *Dream of Nation*, pp. 218–32.

4. For information about Outremont in the 1920s and 1930s:
   Rumilly, *Histoire d'Outremont*, p. 469: "A citizen of Outremont,
   J.-C.E. Trudeau established the Automobile Owners' Association, which drew on the ideas of both cooperatives and private enterprise and which was to assure his fortune."

   Sociological information about the Académie Querbes
   and Rue Durocher from interviews by Jean-Marie Gaul
   with Outremont residents or contemporaries of Trudeau:
   Outremont health inspector Donat Ducharme; architect
   Marc Harvey; an archivist from the religious community of
   Saint-Viateur, Fr. Robert Hémond; a municipal worker for
   the city of Outremont, Guy Lalande; an Outremont con-
   tractor, Maurice Raymond.

   Extensive architectural commentary and photographs of
   the new preparatory school: "Inauguration de l'Académie
   Querbes à Outremont demain," *La Presse* (Oct. 21, 1916),
   p. 17.

5. On Charlie Trudeau's temperament: A contemporary
   remarked, "He was full of spit and damn good fun." Breslin, "The Other Trudeaus," p. 80.

6. Confidential interview.

7. On Charlie Trudeau's behaviour: Authors' interview with
   Edith Iglauer, drawing on unpublished interviews conduc-
   ted by her in 1968 and 1969 for her admirable study of
   Pierre Trudeau, "Prime Minister/Premier Ministre."

8. On Charlie Trudeau's involvement in Quebec politics: Robert McKenzie and Lotta Dempsey, "Pierre Trudeau: 'I
   Became Accustomed Very Young to Rowing Against the
   Current,'" *Toronto Star* (Apr. 8, 1968). Raymond Choquette,
   an accountant who worked for Charlie Trudeau, is quoted
   as having told the *Star*'s reporters that the colourful mayor
   of Montreal, Camillien Houde, would drive up to the Trudeau service station and say, "J'ai besoin d'oxygène," as a
   euphemism for needing money, and Choquette would be
   dispatched by the senior Trudeau to fetch $100 from the
   safe.

The story about the Liberal machine was told by Trudeau after the 1974 election at a party for the Liberal national campaign committee. See Christina McCall, "The Big Red Machine Is the Daveymobile," *Globe and Mail* (July 7, 1975), p. 7.

On Duplessis and Charlie Trudeau: Black, *Duplessis*, p. 559, n. 9.

9. Trudeau quote: Authors' interview with Edith Iglauer, Dec. 7, 1988.

10. On the kind of man who evolves outside the normal patterns of growth: For centuries philosophers and poets have tried to identify the various "ages of man" in both complex and simple formulations. In modern times, some psychologists have put forward the theory that just as there are set stages of growth through which children pass, adults also experience set developmental stages during the course of their lives as they confront a number of identifiable challenges in interaction with society. Beginning in 1969, an interdisciplinary team of social scientists and depth psychologists at Yale University, led by Daniel Levinson and inspired by the theories of Sigmund Freud and Erik Erikson, as well as Carl Jung, conducted extensive empirical research into patterns of male development. Their many provocative findings caused the group to formulate the thesis that there is a clearly identifiable sequence of stages in the evolution of a normal individual's life cycle during which standard emotional as well as physical developments take place. These overlapping stages, following childhood and adolescence, were identified as: the early adult transition (17–22), early adulthood (23–35), the Age 30 transition, middle adulthood (40–65), the mid-life crisis (40–45), the Age 50 transition, the later adulthood transition (60–65), and later adulthood (60 to death). It was their further observation that if the issues appropriate to a particular stage are not dealt with satisfactorily, the man will have to cope with aspects of them later if he is to mature successfully and live a fully realized or "individuated" life, to use the Jungian term. According to these insights, Pierre Tru-

deau's development differed from the usual pattern in significant ways that will be discussed later in this chapter. Levinson et al. published their work in *The Seasons of a Man's Life*.

11. Sauvé quote: Authors' interview with Maurice Sauvé, Nov. 27, 1986.

12. On Grace Trudeau's remarks: Radwanski, *Trudeau*, p. 55.
    On the Trudeaus' McCulloch Avenue house: Margaret Trudeau, *Beyond Reason*, pp. 68–69.
    Trudeau quote: Radwanski, *Trudeau*, p. 56.

13. On anger and grief: Kübler-Ross makes the point that the anger of the grief-stricken is sometimes greater after the death of an "ambivalent figure" in the mourner's life. *On Death and Dying*, pp. 44, 243.

14. Profile of Trudeau: Iglauer, "Prime Minister/Premier Ministre."
    Lussier quote: Authors' interview with Edith Iglauer, Dec. 7, 1988.
    For a discussion of human defence mechanisms: Vaillant, *Adaptation to Life*, p. 83.
    For a description of the idea of the "shadow" in Jungian psychology: Singer, *Boundaries of the Soul*, pp. 215–27.

15. Confidential interview.

16. On Taylor Statten camp: Authors' interview with Ramsay Cook, Mar. 20, 1981.

17. Tip Trudeau quote: Authors' interview with Edith Iglauer, Dec. 7, 1988.
    On intellectualization as an adaptive mechanism: Vaillant, *Adaptation to Life*, p. 385.

18. For an analysis of normal development in the early adult transition: Levinson et al., *Seasons of a Man's Life*, pp. 56–57.
    In many ways there was a striking parallel between Trudeau's behaviour in the late 1930s and that of Max Weber, the famous sociologist, who had grown up in Germany half a century before. In his brilliant introduction to *From Max Weber: Essays in Sociology*, C. Wright Mills points out the central importance to Weber's troubled adult life of the contrast between his parents. Weber's father was a right-

wing Junker whose chauvinism his son tried to emulate as a
university student by getting into duels and downing vast
quantities of beer; his mother was a liberal humanist, an
intellectually sophisticated woman with whom he sustained
an enduring emotional and intellectual intimacy. For
Weber, the conflict between father and mother was unre-
solvable; it haunted his inner and outer life in the form of
recurring depressions. As Mills put it, the "two [conflict-
ing] models of identification and their associated values,
rooted in mother and father, never disappeared from Weber's inner life." Trudeau was to spend years of his life dealing with the same kind of conflicts, and eventually he
transcended them.

19. Trudeau quote: Authors' conversation with Pierre Trudeau,
    Dec. 11, 1986.
20. On the COTC incident: Charles Lussier (as told to Bill
    Trent), "I Remember Pierre," *Toronto Star* (Oct. 12, 1982),
    p. F-1.
21. On the effect of the conscription crisis on the English in
    Quebec, see Djwa, *Politics of the Imagination*, pp. 200–205.

    On "Finie la flèche du conquérant, vive le drapeau de la
    liberté!" Trudeau's language was nationalist and radical:
    "There is currently a government which wants to invoke
    conscription and a people who will never accept it . . . If
    we are not a democracy, we should start a revolution with-
    out delay . . . They are asking our people to commit suicide.
    Citizens of Quebec, don't stand around blubbering. Long
    live the flag [*drapeau*] of liberty!" Other speakers reported
    in the paper were Michel Chartrand and D'Iberville For-
    tier. *Le Devoir* (Nov. 26, 1942).

    Trudeau's justification for his non-involvement in World
    War II was expressed in Toronto during the 1968 leadership
    race. Jack Cahill, "Trudeau Tells Why He Wasn't in War,"
    Toronto Star (Mar. 30, 1968), p. 1.
22. Trudeau quote: Radwanski, *Trudeau*, p. 35.
23. Rostand, *Cyrano de Bergerac*, pp. 93–94.
24. On adult development: Levinson et al. maintain that the com-
    ponents central to adult men's lives are occupation, marriage,

family, friendship, ethnicity and religion, and leisure. With most men, the first two – occupation and marriage – are of prime importance in their twenties and thirties. Trudeau postponed dealing with both until he was deep into middle age. Instead, he conducted in his twenties and thirties the search for meaning and enduring values that most people address in their forties or even fifties. In brief, he reversed the normal pattern. Levinson et al., *Seasons of a Man's Life*, p. 43.

On the life dream: Levinson describes the formulation of such a dream as being the novice adult's first task. The dream has the quality of a vision, an imagined possibility that generates excitement and vitality, though it may be poorly articulated and only tenuously connected to reality. Levinson et al., *Seasons of a Man's Life*, pp. 91–96.

25. De Grandpré quote: Authors' interview with Jean de Grandpré, Jan. 30, 1987.

26. On the denial of death: The Pulitzer Prize–winning American cultural anthropologist Ernest Becker's contribution to depth psychology was to develop the notion that the repression of the universal fear of death provides humans with a vital source of their psychic energy. Of particular relevance to Trudeau's psychology are Becker's observations that the "denial of death" is stronger for the child of the well-to-do since "his parents' powerful triumph over death automatically becomes his"; that the one who has had a premature experience with death "will be most morbidly fixated on the anxiety [this creates]"; and that the will to live a heroic life is a natural reflexive response to "the terror of death." Becker, *Denial of Death*, pp. 11, 14–15, 23.

27. On Trudeau's image as a young man: Authors' interview with Alison Ignatieff, Jan. 22, 1982, citing Gaby Léger.

On Trudeau's sarcasm to his fiancée, Thérèse Gouin: S. Fraser, "The Private Trudeau," p. 2.

28. By prolonging his education, Trudeau largely escaped the tasks that most young men contend with in this period – deciding on an occupation, establishing mentor relationships within it, forming a bond with a significant woman, and starting a family. In this he was ahead of his time: such delayed develop-

ment has become more normal in the late twentieth century. See Levinson et al., *Seasons of a Man's Life*, p. 91.

29. Vidal quote: Vidal, *At Home*, p. vii.

    On Parkin: Adele Freedman, "Parkin, a 'White Knight' of the Modern Movement," *Globe and Mail* (Nov. 26, 1988), p. C13.

30. Details of Trudeau's courses and professors are from a letter to the authors from the Office of the Dean, Harvard University Graduate School of Arts and Sciences, Aug. 11, 1989. We are indebted to Professor Peter Russell for Louis Hartz's impressions of Trudeau's enthusiastic response to liberalism when he was a fellow graduate student at Harvard.

31. On Trudeau's classes in Paris: Letter to the authors from the Fondation nationale des sciences politiques, Jan. 30, 1989.

32. On Laski and Clement Attlee: Herbert A. Deane, "Harold J. Laski," in David Sills, ed., *International Encyclopedia of the Social Sciences*, vol. 9 (New York: Macmillan, The Free Press, 1968), pp. 30–31.

    On Trudeau's studies at the LSE: Letter from the Academic Registrar, London School of Economics and Political Science, Oct. 4, 1988.

    On Trudeau's leftward turn at the LSE: Jeffrey Simpson, "Card-Carrying Canadian Is a British Institution," *Globe and Mail* (July 20, 1981), p. 7. "In their student days, [Robert] McKenzie was a partisan of the Cooperative Commonwealth Federation . . . but remembers Pierre Trudeau being even further to the political left, slightly disdainful of the plodding reformism of the CCF."

33. Trudeau quote: Authors' conversation with Pierre Trudeau, Dec. 11, 1986.

CHAPTER 3

Searching for a Cause

1. By this double-think, Duplessis had accomplished the feat of becoming a continentalist nationalist, a precursor of the

attitude that the Parti Québécois was to adopt in the 1970s and 1980s.

2. The Union Nationale's proportion of the popular vote and of seats rose from 36 and 53 per cent in 1944 to 51 and 89 per cent in 1948, then continued at 52 and 74 per cent in 1952 and 52 and 77 per cent in 1956.

3. Trudeau, "Epilogue," in his *Asbestos Strike*, p. 329.

4. In describing the breadth of Duplessis's support, Conrad Black writes, "The Union Nationale . . . was a bourgeois party of local entrepreneurs, a workers' party, a farmers' party, informally allied to much of big business and most of the clergy, subtly directed, powerfully financed, well organized, a remarkable fusion of ideology and expediency. The Union Nationale came to incarnate traditional Quebec. And Maurice Duplessis embodied the Union Nationale" (p. 299). See also Quinn, *Union Nationale*, p. 61: The UN "had the unofficial, but nevertheless effective support of all the various Catholic Action and patriotic organizations across the province: the Catholic trade unions, the farmers' organizations, the cooperatives and the credit unions, the youth organizations, the associations of French-Canadian businessmen and merchants."

5. Information on Trudeau in the PCO, 1949–51: Gzowski, "Portrait," p. 29; authors' interview with Gordon Robertson, Nov. 27, 1986; and conversation with Pierre Trudeau, June 6, 1985.

   "Les grecs": the reference by these intellectuals, steeped in a classical education, was to their superiority in the face of the Romans' (or English Canadians') greater power.

6. Pickersgill on Trudeau: Authors' interview, Nov. 30, 1986.

   "Trained donkeys" quote: Trudeau, "Some Obstacles to Democracy in Quebec," in *Federalism and the French Canadians*, p. 120.

7. Trudeau quote about personalism: "Frost over Canada," television interview by David Frost, broadcast by CTV, Feb. 23, 1982.

8. On the Church in Quebec: Pelletier, *Years of Impatience*, p. 49.

9. The quotation is taken from *Convergence*, the English-language edition of Le Moyne's collection of essays, translated in 1966. The French edition was published in 1961 and won the Governor General's Award the following year. Additional information and interpretation were provided by Jean Le Moyne, in an interview on Nov. 26, 1986. A deeply religious man, Le Moyne experienced Quebec's stultifying conservatism as a painful restriction on his own development as a writer and as a human being. Denise Bombardier, the television broadcaster and author, graphically documented the Church's sexual repression of women in her autobiographical novel, *L'enfance à l'eau bénite*.

10. A "remarkably large number of French historians and other influential figures were personalists . . . after the war." Hellman, *Emmanuel Mounier*, p. 10. Hellman's book includes brief references to the involvement of Trudeau and Pelletier with Mounier and his ideas: pp. 282, 323, 328. To describe personalism as left-wing is not to say it was Marxist. To use the French distinction, it was *marxisant*; much of its analysis borrowed socialist concepts though it rejected Marxism as atheistic.

11. On his guilt over wealth: Trudeau had written an anguished letter from Harvard to an ex-schoolmate, Pierre Vadeboncoeur, saying he thought he should divest himself of his money, as a monk would. See Charney, "Growing Up Private."

12. In January 1954 the trade unions made common cause with the Alliance of Catholic School Teachers of Montreal, staging a mass meeting in Quebec City to protest against Bill 19, which let the Quebec Labour Relations Board decertify a union if any of its officers were judged to adhere to communist doctrine, "communist" being undefined, and Bill 20, which let the board decertify any union some of whose members go out on strike in any public service. Bill 20 was made retroactive to 1944 and sheltered from judicial review any cases then before the courts. Wiseman and Scott, "March on Quebec."
For material on the 1950s reformers, see Gérard Berger-

on's chapter "Les transformations socio-économiques entre 1945 et 1960" in Bergeron and Pelletier, *L'État du Québec en devenir*; Djwa, *Politics of the Imagination*, ch. 19; Lévesque, *Memoirs*, ch. 23; Pelletier, *Years of Impatience*.

13. On Georges-Émile Lapalme: Whitaker, *Government Party*, pp. 269–306.

14. For a description of the post-war cultural flowering in Quebec: Bourassa, *Surrealism and Quebec Literature*; Monière, *Le développement des idéologies au Québec*; and Trofimenkoff, *Dream of Nation*, ch. 18.

15. Pelletier first discussed the possibility of a personalist review with several friends who had been colleagues in the JEC. They were Guy Cormier, Reginald Boisvert, Pauline Lamy, Jean-Paul Geoffroy, Renée Desmarais, Pierre Juneau, Fernande Martin, and Alec Leduc, Pelletier's wife. Of this group, Cormier, Boisvert, Geoffroy, Juneau, and Pelletier served on the editorial board of *Cité libre* in its first year. They were joined by Maurice Blain, Charles Lussier, Pierre Vadeboncoeur, Roger Rolland, and Pierre Trudeau. See Pelletier, *Years of Impatience*, pp. 99–130, and *Cité libre*, vol. I, nos. 1–4.

Though dated June, the first issue actually came out on July 14, leading the Citélibristes to celebrate its anniversary thereafter on Bastille Day in a tacit acknowledgement of their strong intellectual connection with French culture.

16. Authors' interview with Jeanne Sauvé, Nov. 27, 1986. See also Woods, *Her Excellency Jeanne Sauvé*, ch. 3.

17. Authors' interview with Maurice Sauvé, Nov. 26, 1986.

Hubert Guindon, the Montreal sociologist, had the same revulsion. "Even in boarding school . . . I was fighting Catholic Action, which I thought was a sort of fifth column: a hierarchy of holier people." Guindon, *Quebec Society*, p. xviii.

Although she was a friend and colleague of several of the Citélibristes, Jeanne Benoit did not become part of the magazine's editorial board at its inception. She had left Montreal to work and study in Europe in 1948 shortly after her marriage to Maurice Sauvé.

18. The Jécistes' suspicion of the Jesuits was enhanced by that order's sponsorship of the Association catholique de la jeunesse canadienne-française, a rival student movement that was élitist, nationalist, and conservative. They themselves were supported by the Dominicans, the Oblate Fathers, and the Fathers of the Holy Cross, orders more concerned with ministering to ordinary people and less preoccupied with power.

19. On Pelletier's friendship with Trudeau: Pelletier, *Years of Impatience*, p. 20; and authors' interview with Madeleine Gobeil, Dec. 23, 1988.

20. Authors' interview with Gordon Robertson, Nov. 26, 1986. Robertson was Trudeau's superior in the PCO from 1949 to 1951; he was clerk of the Privy Council and secretary to the cabinet from 1963 to 1975.

21. Authors' interview with Jean Le Moyne, Nov. 26, 1986.

22. Gérard Pelletier quoted in Iglauer, "Prime Minister/Premier Ministre."

   In *Duplessis*, Conrad Black refers to the Quebec premier's attitudes towards communism frequently. See pp. 300, 301, 307, 350, 384.

23. Trudeau had applied in vain to the law faculty of the Université de Montréal for a teaching job when he first came back from Ottawa in 1952. Later attempts to join the faculty there were foiled as well, and his reformer friends laid the blame on Duplessis himself, who was said to threaten to cut grants to institutions that appointed opponents to his regime; on Marcel Faribault, a distinguished conservative law professor; and on Archbishop Léger, who was the university's chancellor at the time and was seen as complying with Duplessis's bullying. See Peacock, *Journey to Power*, p. 135, and Pelletier, *Years of Impatience*, p. 33. Trudeau's critics said that he could have found academic work at Laval in Lévesque's social science faculty if he had really wanted to be a professor, or at Queen's University, not far from Montreal in Kingston, Ontario.

   "By the virulence, number and coherence of its attacks on Duplessis, *Cité libre* was perceived as the principal spokesman of the opposition during the 1950s." Carrier, "L'idéologie politique," p. 427. Eighty-eight issues of the magazine were published between June 1950 and July 1966: twice a year through 1954, four times in 1955, once in 1956, thrice in 1957, four times in 1958, and once in 1959. A "nouvelle série" began in January 1960 and the magazine was published regularly ten times a year until 1966.

The collective position of the Citélibristes was based on four explicitly formulated theoretical premises that derived logically from the editorial board's mix of personalist Catholicism and left-wing anti-clericalism. First came the *person*. In opposition to traditional Catholics, the Citélibristes gave prime importance to the needs of the individual French Canadian rather than the collectivity of French Canadians. From this it followed that *liberty*, not racial survival, was the necessary condition to be fostered, since it is only in an environment of maximum freedom that individuals can achieve their full self-realization. *Social justice* is required for all members of the community to enjoy the same material and intellectual conditions needed to develop their human potential. Finally, *democracy* is the political regime that ensures the individual can take action and participate in the exercise of power. Carrier, "L'idéologie politique," p. 427.

On the role of *Cité libre*: Bélanger, *Ruptures et constantes*, p. 70.

24. Pelletier, *Years of Impatience*, p. 118.
25. Black, *Duplessis*, pp. 559, 730.
26. Alec Pelletier, quoted in S. Fraser, "The Private Trudeau."
27. After he became prime minister, Trudeau's activities in this period took on mythic qualities in the memory of his loyal friends. The publisher Jacques Hébert, who had gone adventuring in China with Trudeau in 1960, painted him as living at the vortex of the reform movement's whirlwind. "Whenever a committee was formed for the defence of an imperilled civil liberty, for the release of an obscure citizen who had been illegally imprisoned, or against the proliferation of nuclear weapons, every time Pierre Trudeau was

there; always he was the most effective member of the committee." Hébert, "Prefatory Note," in Trudeau, *Approaches to Politics*, p. 21.

28. On *La grève de l'amiante*: Djwa, *Politics of the Imagination*, pp. 318–21.

   Trudeau's articles in *Vrai* were published later in *Approaches to Politics*.

   Trudeau's prize was won for "Some Obstacles to Democracy in Quebec," *Canadian Journal of Economics and Political Science* (Aug. 1958), later reprinted in *Federalism and the French Canadians*.

29. On Trudeau's escapism: Casgrain, *Woman in a Man's World*, p. 139; and authors' interview with Charles Taylor, Jan. 28, 1990.

30. Authors' interviews with Jean Marchand, June 1978 and Apr. 10, 1985.

31. On the *puer* as a psychological type: Von Franz, *Puer Aeternus*, pp. 1–2.

   On Grace Trudeau's holidays: Casgrain, *Woman in a Man's World*, p. 139.

32. Authors' interview with Bernard Ostry, Apr. 8, 1981.

33. Authors' confidential interview.

34. On the *puer aeternus* and women: Von Franz, *Puer Aeternus*, pp. 1–2.

35. On Trudeau and homosexuality: Authors' conversation with Pierre Trudeau, Dec. 11, 1986; and authors' interview with Madeleine Gobeil, Oct. 5, 1975.

36. On the *puer* and commitment: "Generally, great difficulty is experienced [by the *puer aeternus*] in adaptation to the social situation. In some cases, there is a kind of asocial individualism: being something special one has no need to adapt for that would be impossible for such a hidden genius . . . In addition, an arrogant attitude arises towards other people due to both an inferiority complex and false feelings of superiority. Such people usually have great difficulty in finding the right kind of job [as well as the right woman] . . . for whatever they find is never quite right or quite what

they wanted . . . There is always a 'but' which prevents marriage or any kind of commitment . . .

"There is always the fantasy that sometime in the future the real thing will come about . . . Accompanying this neurosis is often, to a smaller or greater extent, a savior or Messiah complex, with the secret thought that one day one will be able to save the world." Von Franz, *Puer Aeternus*, p. 2.

37. Sharp, *Secret Raven*, p. 82. Also Jung and von Franz, *Man and His Symbols*, p. 16.

38. Cook, *Maple Leaf Forever*, p. 41.

CHAPTER 4

Federalism Forever

1. For a description of the drama of Duplessis's death see Black, *Duplessis*, pp. 682–85.

2. The Liberals received just 4 per cent more of the popular vote and only five more seats than the Union Nationale. A shift of ninety-five votes in the five ridings where the Liberal majority was smallest would have prevented their victory. Trudeau, "L'élection du 22 juin 1960," p. 4, n. 1.

   Trudeau's writings: Trudeau, "De l'inconvénient d'être catholique," pp. 20–21; "Note sur le parti cléricaliste," p. 23; and "Les progrès d'illusion," pp. 1–2.

3. Trudeau to Edith Iglauer, quoted in "Prime Minister/Premier Ministre."

4. On Trudeau as late riser: Authors' interview with Carl Goldenberg, Dec. 12, 1986.

   On his Cuba caper: Don Newlands on CBC Radio *Morningside*, Mar. 2, 1984.

   On comments from Sardinia: Authors' interview with Ramsay Cook, Mar. 20, 1981.

   On stealing students' blondes: Authors' interview with François Lebrun, June 4, 1985.

5. For the authoritative description of the politics of the Quiet Revolution: McRoberts, *Quebec*, pp. 132–62.

On the role of key bureaucrats: Thomson, *Jean Lesage*, p. 199.

On reform of the labour code: Boivin, "Labour Relations in Quebec," p. 438; and Tremblay, "L'évolution du syndicalisme."

On interest-group participation: Clinton Archibald, "Corporatist Tendencies in Quebec."

On electoral reform: "The legislation was among the most *avant garde* in the field of party financing in the Western world." Thomson, *Jean Lesage*, p. 174.

On Quebec's fledgling language policy: Coleman, "Class Bases of Language Policy."

6. On Hydro-Quebec: Desbarats, *René*, ch. 5; and Gaudet, "Forces Underlying the Evolution."

On the secularization of the education system: Milner, "Quebec Educational Reform."

7. Authors' interview with Charles Taylor, Jan. 21, 1990.

8. On Trudeau in early middle age: In his early forties, Trudeau seemed to have reached the stage of development most men achieve by their early thirties, the stage of settling down. See Levinson et al., *Seasons of a Man's Life*, pp. 139–43.

On Frank Scott as dean of McGill Law School: Djwa, *Politics of the Imagination*, ch. 21, "Committing Deanery," pp. 359–70.

9. Trudeau's most developed political-economy analysis of the Quebec élites' "theoretical nationalism" is his longest published work: the introductory chapter, "The Province of Quebec at the Time of the Strike," in his *Asbestos Strike*, pp. 1–67.

10. Trudeau was already aware of the work being done by the sociologist John Porter that documented WASP networks of élite control and was ultimately published as *The Vertical Mosaic*.

The thesis of the new middle class was first elaborated by Hubert Guindon in his "Social Unrest, Social Class and Quebec's Bureaucratic Revolution," in *Quebec Society*, pp. 27–37. Guindon emphasized the political and economic élites' success in channelling working-class mobilization in the interest of the middle class. More recent treatments include A. Gagnon, "The Evolution of Political Forces in Quebec"; Renaud, "New Middle Class in Search of Social Hegemony"; Pinard and Hamilton, "The Class Bases of the Quebec Independence Movement"; McRoberts, *Quebec*, pp. 90 ff. For an extensive analysis of the class basis of Quebec nationalism: Coleman, *Independence Movement in Quebec*.

11. McWhinney, *Quebec and the Constitution*, chs. 3 and 4.

12. For Trudeau's attacks on the new Quebec nationalism: Trudeau, "L'aliénation nationaliste"; "The Practice and Theory of Federalism"; "Les séparatistes: des contre-révolutionnaires"; and "La nouvelle trahison des clercs." The "treason of the intellectuals" was a literary reference to Julien Benda, the French writer whose 1927 polemic, *La trahison des clercs*, was a radical denunciation of his nation's "clerisy," the intellectuals he felt should "defend eternal values" but who "have betrayed this role" by fashionable, sentimental, and intuitive thinking. A defiant nonconformist, an avowed bachelor, and a rigorous rationalist, Benda had no fear of controversy and may have served as something of a role model for Trudeau as a writer taking unpopular positions that provoked the wrath of Quebec's new clerisy, the nationalist intelligentsia. J.P. Beaumarchais, Daniel Couty, and Alain Rey, *Dictionnaire des littératures de langue française A-F* (Paris: Bordas, 1984), p. 233.

For his more detached writings on the virtues of federalism: "Federalism, Nationalism and Reason" and "Quebec and the Constitutional Problem."

13. The intellectual base for Trudeau's attack on nationalism had been provided by the Franco-Saskatchewan brothers Albert and Raymond Breton. See Breton and Breton, "Le séparatisme"; and A. Breton, "Economics of Nationalism."

14. At the meeting, Trudeau read only part of "Federalism, Nationalism and Reason." Having delivered the bulk of his argument, he startled the assembled academics by suddenly stopping in scholarly flight and announcing ingenuously, "I'm sorry, but this is as far as I have come in my analysis."

Recalling the incident some twenty years later, Peter Russell, the constitutional expert, remembered thinking, "If this guy has the guts to admit in front of all these professors that he's not got his paper finished, he probably does have what it takes to be a politician." (Authors' interview, Sept. 30, 1987.) Trudeau eventually finished the paper. It was published in P.A. Crepeau and C.B. Macpherson, eds., *The Future of Canadian Federalism* (Toronto: University of Toronto Press, 1965), and reprinted in *Federalism and the French Canadians*.

15. On Trudeau's dogmatic anti-nationalism, André Laurendeau expressed to Gérard Pelletier his concerns as follows: "In politics, I am apprehensive about a highly intelligent man whose logic is unswerving. I am afraid that Pierre's anti-nationalism may have become a dogma for him." Pelletier, *Years of Impatience*, p. 97.

On Duplessis's relations with the federal government and the Catholic church in Quebec: Black, *Duplessis*, pp. 411–46, 497–549.

On nationalism's impact on social mobilization in the Quiet Revolution: Louis Balthazar, "La dynamique du nationalisme québécois," in Bergeron and Pelletier, eds., *L'État du Québec en devenir*, pp. 37–58.

16. For a description of the Liberals' policy-making process in the years between 1958 and 1963, and the roles of Kent and Gordon, see Kent, *Public Purpose*, pp. 45–133.

17. Authors' interview with Marc Lalonde, Apr. 11, 1979.

18. As well as being quoted in many stories about the Quiet Revolution in daily newspapers, Trudeau was the subject of a long profile by Peter Gzowski, "Portrait of an Intellectual in Action," and was asked in 1964 to audition for the role of co-host of the Sunday-evening CBC-TV show *This Hour Has Seven Days*. See Koch, *Inside This Hour*, p. 45.

19. Besides Trudeau and Lalonde, the committee officially consisted of Albert Breton, Raymond Breton, Claude Bruneau, Yvon Gauthier, and Maurice Pinard. Versions of their manifesto appeared in the *Montreal Star* and *La Presse* as well as in "Manifeste pour une politique fonctionnelle," *Cité libre* (May

1964), pp. 11–17, and "An Appeal for Realism in Politics," *The Canadian Forum* (May 1964), pp. 29–33. Michael Pitfield was closely connected with the committee and translated the manifesto into English but did not add his name to the list of signers because of his status as a public servant.

20. On jumping into the mêlée again: Trudeau to Patrick Watson, quoted in Koch, *Inside This Hour*, p. 45.

    Charles Taylor's view of Trudeau: Authors' interview, Jan. 28, 1990.

21. Authors' interviews with Peter Scott, Nov. 18, 1988, and Nov. 29, 1989.

    When Trudeau was working on his introduction to *The Asbestos Strike* in Paris he went off to the Labour Party's annual conference in Margate, armed with a letter of introduction from Frank Scott, to whom he later reported that the "Left in every country (including Canada) seems to be going through an 'agonizing reappraisal.' Something for us to discuss, when we get this book out of the way." Djwa, *Politics of the Imagination*, p. 322.

22. Casgrain, *Woman in a Man's World*, p. 139.

23. On Quebec lieutenants: English, "The 'French Lieutenant' in Ottawa."

24. For Marchand's attraction to the Liberal Party: Authors' interview with Jean Marchand, June 6, 1978.

25. Trudeau, "Pearson ou l'abdication de l'esprit," pp. 7, 10.

26. See Gordon, *Political Memoir*, pp. 219–33.

27. Authors' conversation with Pierre Trudeau, Dec. 11, 1986.

    Trudeau and Pelletier, "Pelletier et Trudeau s'expliquent," pp. 3, 5.

28. Authors' interview with Jean Marchand, June 6, 1978.

CHAPTER 5
_____

Coming to Charisma

1. On the governing élite: Granatstein, *Ottawa Men*; McCall-Newman, *Grits*, pp. 177–238.

2. On Canada's role in Vietnam: Eayrs, *Indochina: Roots of Complicity*; Levant, *Quiet Complicity*; Ross, *In the Interests of Peace*; Taylor, *Snow Job*.

3. For Walter Gordon's views of Canadian-American economic relations: Denis Smith, *Gentle Patriot*; Gordon, *Political Memoir*.

   The University League for Social Reform, which brought together young central-Canadian academics from different disciplines, explored the new economic nationalism in *Nationalism in Canada* (1966), edited by Peter Russell, and then turned its attention to Canada's external affairs, in *An Independent Foreign Policy for Canada?* (1968), edited by Stephen Clarkson.

4. Peter Desbarats quote from the late 1960s: Confirmed in a letter to the authors, May 17, 1990.

   On *Seven Days*: Koch, *Inside This Hour*; and S. Stewart, *Here's Looking at Us*.

5. On Canada in the 1960s: Granatstein, *Canada 1957-1967*.

6. For a discussion of a society's "alienation potential": Schiffer, *Charisma*, p. 8. The notion that societies become a fertile field for charismatic leaders is examined from another point of view by William Sargent in *Battle for the Mind*.

7. On Trudeau's first term as MP: Authors' interview with Jean Marchand, June 6, 1978. See also Pelletier, *Years of Choice*, pp. 214–28.

8. On Quebec and the Canada Pension Plan dispute: Granatstein, *Canada 1957-1967*, p. 26.

9. For a more detailed account of Trudeau's involvement in the fight against Quebec's campaign for an independent foreign policy: Clarkson, "Vive le Québec libre!" pp. 55–69.

10. On Trudeau's ambitions: Authors' interviews with Jean Marchand, June 6, 1978; and Madeleine Gobeil, Oct. 5, 1975.

    For the liberation of the *puer* by work: Von Franz, *Puer Aeternus*, p. 5.

11. One of the first members of the Ottawa press gallery to recognize Trudeau's political strength was the veteran CBC

journalist Norman DePoe, who hosted a profile of him on
CBC-TV's *Newsmagazine*, May 16, 1967. Thoughtful pieces
were written about him by Anthony Westell in the *Toronto
Star*, Richard Gwyn in *Time* magazine, Harry Crowe and
Douglas Fisher in the *Toronto Telegram*, and Peter Newman in
the *Toronto Star*.

For the bureaucrats' and cabinet ministers' views of Trudeau: Authors' interviews with A.W. Johnson, May 1979;
and with Allan Gotlieb, Apr. 1974.

12. For a discussion of the relationship between the emergence
of key figures and the nature of their times: Boschette,
Sartre and Les Temps Modernes.

Weber's idea of charisma – borrowed from Rudolf Sohm,
a German church historian, and meaning in Greek "the gift
of grace" – was far more complex; it was rooted in his philosophy of history, which sprang from nineteenth-century
positivism. Weber saw charisma as a historic force that was
intended to correct humankind's tendency to excessive
rationalization and to the development in governments of
rigid bureaucracies made up of self-serving, self-perpetua-
ting élites. For him, charismatic leaders were both a cyclical phenomenon and a necessary agent of change in a
democracy. He saw the religious prophet as the prototype
of the political charismatic, a man with a special quality
that gives him an almost magical capacity to gather follow-
ers and evoke their personal assent to his actions. In Weber's scheme of things, the charismatic leader takes upon
himself responsibility for announcing a break in the established order and declares himself in significant respects to
be in explicit opposition to that order. He is not just intellectually engaged with his ideas, as a lawmaker or teacher
might be, but emotionally committed to them. At the same
time he appears selfless in that he is unlikely to benefit in
any monetary sense by their realization. It is society's good,
not his own, that he seeks to further. Weber, *From Max
Weber*, pp. 245–52.

13. For de Gaulle's foreign policy schemes: Grosser, *Affaires extérieures*, pp. 209–11.

14. Some such act obviously had been anticipated since an advance man for de Gaulle had made sure a microphone was in place beforehand, and de Gaulle himself had been observed practising his lines as he gesticulated into the wind from the bridge of the *Colbert*. Clarkson, "Vive le Québec libre!" pp. 58–59.

15. For Minister of External Affairs Paul Martin's more conciliatory response: Martin, *Very Public Life*, vol. II, p. 595.

16. *Une connerie* is slang for "vulva." It was as though Trudeau had said special status was a "cunt-ism." Some bilingual reporters explained to their anglophone confrères that it was not quite as bad as it sounded when translated literally but meant something closer to "a load of crap," an interesting indication of cross-cultural sexism.

17. Apart from Marc Lalonde and Michael Pitfield, Trudeau's early supporters were Jean-Pierre Goyer, Fernand Cadieux, Ed Rubin, Jim Davey, Gordon Gibson, and Donald Macdonald: Peacock, *Journey to Power*, p. 167.

18. "President Charles de Gaulle's News Conference," p. 615.

19. On the state in the bedrooms of the nation: "Unlocking the Locked Step of Law and Morality," *Globe and Mail* (Dec. 12, 1967), p. 6.

20. On the concept of Fortuna and the statesman: Machiavelli, *The Prince*, p. 147.

    On Pearson's support: Authors' interviews with Marc Lalonde, Apr. 11, 1979; Maryon Pearson, Mary Macdonald, Sheila Zimmerman, Claude Frenette, and Maurice Sauvé, Apr. 1968; and Walter Gordon, Aug. 1977. See also Pearson, *Mike*, vol. III, pp. 325–26.

21. *Canadian Annual Review: 1968*, p. 71.

22. On Trudeau at the Montreal convention: Peacock, *Journey to Power*, p. 199.

23. Roy, *Le choix d'un pays*, p. 163, cited in Brunelle, *Les trois colombes*, p. 272.

24. Bernard Dubé, "Trudeau – Pratfall and All," *Montreal Gazette* (Apr. 9, 1968), p. 19.

25. On the attributes of charisma: Weber, *Sociology of Religion*,

pp. xxxiii and 46–51; Schiffer, *Charisma*, pp. 24–53; and Sennett, *Authority*, p. 22.

26. Saywell, "Introduction," in Trudeau, *Federalism and the French Canadians*, p. vii. Saywell and Cook had joined their colleague William Kilbourn as members of the Toronto Committee for Trudeau set up by Ethel Teitelbaum. Peter Newman, "Opinion-makers Pick *Their* Man, Pierre Trudeau," *Toronto Star* (Jan. 13, 1968), p. 7.

    McLuhan, "The Story of the Man in the Mask."

27. Authors' interview with Jean de Grandpré, Jan. 30, 1987.

28. Trudeau led on all four ballots, the final result being: Pierre Trudeau, 1,203; Robert Winters, 954; John Turner, 195; Joe Green, 29. "How Voting Went Ballot by Ballot," *Toronto Star* (Apr. 8, 1968), p. 12.

    For one expression of scepticism about Trudeau's charisma: P.A. Dufil, "Trudeau 20 Years On: Time to Reconsider the Legends," *Globe and Mail* (June 24, 1988), p. A7.

29. On Frank Scott's interest in the notion of a "just society": Djwa, *Politics of the Imagination*, p. 183.

CHAPTER 6

Power Inflates, Hubris Destroys

1. On the 1968 election results: The Liberals won 155 seats to the Progressive Conservatives' 72, with 22 NDP seats and 15 others, mostly Social Credit. They did well in Ontario (64 seats) and Quebec (56 seats), made a surprisingly strong showing in the west (27 seats to the Tories' 25), but were outclassed in the Atlantic provinces (with only 7 seats to the Tories' 25) because of the "favourite son" impact of the Conservatives' leader, Robert Stanfield, a former premier of Nova Scotia.

2. Westell, *Paradox*, pp. 24–47.

3. On the promotion of Jews to positions of importance in the early Trudeau years: Allan Gotlieb was made deputy minis-

ter of communications; Bernard Ostry was appointed to the CRTC and then as an assistant under-secretary of state; Sylvia Ostry was made a director of the Economic Council and then chief statistician; Simon Reisman was named secretary of the Treasury Board and later deputy minister in Finance; David Golden was made president of Telesat Canada; Bora Laskin was appointed to the Supreme Court; Herb Gray became a minister without portfolio; and Barnett Danson became parliamentary secretary to the prime minister. David Croll, a dynamic politician who had served in the Ontario cabinet of Mitch Hepburn in the 1930s and been elected repeatedly to the federal parliament after World War II, had, by contrast, been denied a cabinet position because he was Jewish by prime ministers King and St. Laurent; the latter resolved this embarrassment by elevating Croll to the Senate in 1955. Louis Rasminsky, who was made governor of the Bank of Canada in 1961, and David Golden, who served as a deputy minister from 1954 to 1964, were forerunners of the Trudeau appointments. Zolf, *Just Watch Me*, pp. 61–81.

4. Quote from Suzette Rouleau: Breslin, "The Other Trudeaus," p. 87.

On Trudeau's female companions and supporters in the late 1960s: They included Joyce Fairbairn, a judge's daughter from Alberta; Jennifer Rae, daughter of ambassador Saul Rae; Alison Gordon, the daughter of John King Gordon, former diplomat and professor; Gwen Clarke, a cabinet minister's daughter from P.E.I.; and of course, Margaret Sinclair, daughter of the former cabinet minister James Sinclair.

5. For power's effect on leaders: "The archetype of the wise man, also called the 'mana personality,' tends to be projected upon human beings who set themselves up as leaders, secular or spiritual. This may have disastrous results, as when religious sects or political movements are led by charlatans or madmen. Alternatively, the subject may identify himself with the archetype, believing that he himself has superior wisdom. Analysts and priests, as well as politicians,

sometimes succumb to this danger, referred to by Jung as 'inflation.' " Jung, *Essential Jung*, p. 122.

Other psychoanalysts speak of political leaders assuming "the arrogance of power, the feeling that the rules are made for other people, not for oneself . . . There is a terrific seduction of the spirit that takes hold when you are surrounded by admiring throngs, when the red carpet is laid out for you. Unless you are aware of the blinding effect the adulation can have, your judgment can be impaired so that you begin to feel that you are immune to normal limits and penalties." Dr. Judd Marmor, as quoted in Daniel Goleman, "Sex, Power, Failure: Patterns Emerge," *New York Times* (May 19, 1987), p. 17.

6. "Nobodies": "When they get home, when they get out of Parliament, when they are 50 yards from Parliament Hill, they are no longer hon. members – they are just nobodies, Mr. Speaker." Canada, House of Commons, *Debates* (July 25, 1969), p. 11635.

Clement Attlee was angry when Harold Laski, the chairman of the Labour Party's National Executive Committee, made radical pronouncements as if he were speaking for the government. Asserting the primacy of parliamentary sovereignty over party democracy, he told the LSE professor that he had "no right whatever to speak on behalf of the Government." As quoted from Kingsley Martin, *Harold Laski* (London, 1953), p. 182, by McKenzie, *British Political Parties*, p. 333, n. 2.

7. The report of the foreign policy review, called *Foreign Policy for Canadians*, contained six booklets titled "Europe," "International Development," "United Nations," "Latin America," "Pacific," and "Foreign Policy for Canadians." The sole reference to the Canadian-American relationship was six hundred words in the sixth booklet on the prospective American impact on Canada's economy in the 1970s.

For the arrogance of the Trudeauites: W. Stewart, *Shrug: Trudeau in Power*.

8. Denis Smith, *Bleeding Hearts, Bleeding Country*; and Haggart and Golden, *Rumours of War*.

9. Trudeau quote: Shain, "Settling Up Sober," p. 29.

   For further evidence of Trudeau's political inflation and its impact on the 1972 federal election: P. Newman, "Reflections on a Fall from Grace."

   Election results in 1972: Liberals, 109 seats (39 per cent of the vote); Progressive Conservatives, 107 seats (35 per cent); New Democratic Party, 31 seats (18 per cent); Social Credit, 15 seats (8 per cent); and others, 2 seats (1 per cent).

10. On the remarkable interviews Margaret Trudeau gave: Fremon, "Margaret Trudeau"; S. Cameron, "Maggie: Happy at Last." Also see the autobiographies by Margaret Trudeau, *Beyond Reason* and *Consequences*, both books ghost-written by Caroline Moorehead.

    Margaret Trudeau quote: *Beyond Reason*, p. 112.

11. Kathleen Sinclair quote: "So Much in Love . . . Can't Take Eyes Off Each Other," *Ottawa Citizen* (Mar. 6, 1971), p. 39.

    Marshall McLuhan quote: Unpublished interview with Peter Newman, Mar. 15, 1971.

12. The date was arranged by Trudeau's office, which contacted her mother to arrange the rendezvous, and its events caused Margaret to write, "I decided that I wanted this man for myself." *Beyond Reason*, pp. 16, 44.

13. On Margaret's certainty: When Trudeau remarked, after hearing her account of her previous sexual adventures, that he was sure she would leave him one day, Margaret protested. " 'Never, never,' I replied passionately, furious that he could think of such a thing." *Beyond Reason*, p. 56.

    Grace Trudeau died in 1973.

14. On Margaret Trudeau's outpourings about freedom, etc.: The best description of her 1960s outlook is in Dan Turner, "Margaret: Mystical, Motherly – Her Own Woman," *Toronto Star* (June 23, 1973), p. 56.

    Margaret Trudeau quote: *Consequences*, p. 38.

15. Margaret Trudeau quote: *Beyond Reason*, p. 21.

    Trudeau quote: Authors' interview with Maurice Sauvé, Nov. 27, 1986.

16. Confidential interview.

17. Trudeau quote: *Beyond Reason*, p. 166.
18. Margaret Trudeau quote: *Beyond Reason*, p. 53.
19. Margaret on Pierre as playboy: *Beyond Reason*, p. 133.
20. Margaret's "Mother Earth" quote: Paterson and McEwan, "Margaret Trudeau's Struggle for Identity," p. 91.
    Margaret on the physical attraction between herself and Pierre: *Beyond Reason*, p. 133.
21. On Margaret Trudeau's role in the 1974 campaign: Callwood, "Margaret's First Hurrah."
22. On the Liberal campaign in 1974: Clarkson, "Pierre Trudeau and the Liberal Party"; and C. Newman, "Politicizing Pierre."
    On Margaret's political ambitions: *Beyond Reason*, p. 175.
23. Quotes from Margaret Trudeau on 1974 election: *Beyond Reason*, p. 175.
24. Margaret Trudeau on taking responsibility: *Consequences*, p. 192.
25. Japan incident: *Beyond Reason*, p. 212.
    "Not to kiss but to sniff me": *Beyond Reason*, p. 239.
26. On the by-election results: The popular vote showed how badly the Liberals had fared. They received 31 per cent, compared with 49 per cent for the Progressive Conservatives and 16 per cent for the NDP.
27. Weber quote: *From Max Weber*, p. 38.
28. On Margaret Trudeau's book promotion tour: *Consequences*, pp. 85–102.
29. Simeon, ed., *Must Canada Fail?*; and Carty and Ward, eds., *Entering the Eighties*.
30. For the Liberals' organization, strategy, and tactics in the campaign: Clarkson, "The Defeat of the Government."
31. The Liberals raised the number of Quebec seats to 67 (from the 60 gained in 1974), held steady in the Maritimes with 12 seats (compared with 13 in 1974), but fell to 32 in Ontario (from 55) and 3 in the west (from 13). Over a dozen cabinet ministers lost their seats including Iona Campagnolo (Minister of Sport) and Leonard Marchand (Environment) in B.C.; Jack Horner (Industry, Trade and Commerce) in Alberta; and Otto Lang (Transport), who ran third in Sas-

katoon East. Ontario's losers were Tony Abbott (Revenue); Bud Cullen (Employment and Immigration); Norman Cafik (Multiculturalism); Barney Danson (Defence); Hugh Faulkner (Indian Affairs); Alastair Gillespie (Energy); Martin O'Connell (Labour); John Reid (Federal-Provincial); and John Roberts (Secretary of State). Daniel MacDonald (Veterans' Affairs) lost in P.E.I. The Liberal loss in popular vote was less marked: falling from 42 per cent to 40 per cent, it was still greater than that of the winning Conservatives, whose vote rose only from 35 to 36 per cent but was more effectively distributed outside Quebec.

CHAPTER 7

Defeat, Humiliation, and Resignation

1. Margaret Trudeau quote: Fremon, "Margaret Trudeau," p. 116.
2. Mountie incident: Confidential interview.
3. On the palace guard: Trudeau's staff when he became leader of the opposition was cut to twenty-five from a prime ministerial staff of eighty-five. The operative personnel were James Coutts (principal secretary), Cécile Viau (personal secretary), Joyce Fairbairn (parliamentary liaison), Tom Axworthy (policy adviser), Jim Moore and André Burelle (English and French speech-writers), and Patrick Gossage and Suzanne Perry (press secretaries). Andrew Szende, "Whither Trudeau's Top Aides?" *Toronto Star* (July 16, 1979), p. A4. See also David Humphreys, "The Changing of the Guard," *Globe and Mail* (June 11, 1979), p. 7.

   Trudeau quote: S. Gwyn, "Inside the Tory Takeover,"
4. Trudeau quote: "Trudeau reste à son poste: 'Je suis encore le meilleur,' " *Le Devoir* (July 20, 1979), p. 1; and Andrew Szende and David Blaikie, "Pierre Won't Step Down: 'I'm the Best,' " *Toronto Star* (July 20, 1979), pp. A1–2.

On the canoe trip: Jean Pelletier, "Through White Water with Trudeau," *Sunday Star* (Oct. 28, 1979), p. D5.

5. On Margaret Trudeau's further revelations: *Consequences*, pp. 37, 99; and Fremon, "Margaret Trudeau."

   On the *High Society* photo: O'Hara, "Bedtime Story."

6. Commentators on Trudeau's gloomy situation: "Pierre Trudeau will never again be prime minister. He has no real political future. He is an opposition leader on sufferance, occupying the post only until some Liberal with better long-term prospects replaces him." Richard Gwyn, "Will Trudeau Ever Be the PM Again? I Think Not," *Toronto Star* (July 21, 1979), p. B5.

7. Grindstone conference details: Letter of invitation to the conference, authors' files.

   For two days and nights at this Winnipeg conference, Grits in workshops, Grits in plenaries, and Grits in coffee shops let off steam in an orgy of collective criticism. They talked of their party's irrelevance ("People are smarter now [in the west]: you could fool them with Jimmy Gardiner's machine but not with Otto Lang's"), policy incoherence ("Our position is about as attractive as a bucket of warm spit"), exhaustion ("We've used up our intellectual capital"), arrogance ("Cabinet has no respect for the value of other opinions"), and confusion ("Some of the people wanting to bell the cats [in the party establishment] are former cats themselves"). Remarks by Hu Harries, Tony Merchant, John Reid, Michel Rochon, and Gary Wilson. Authors' notes.

8. For the concept of camarilla: Michels, *Political Parties*, pp. 24, 104: "There arises in the leaders a tendency to isolate themselves, to form a sort of cartel, and to surround themselves, as it were, with a wall, within which they will admit those only who are of their own way of thinking."

9. On Trudeau's response to party complaints: Authors' conversation with Pierre Trudeau, July 21, 1979; and authors' interview with James Coutts, Dec. 19, 1985.

10. On Trudeau's 1979 resignation: Interview with Tom Axworthy, Nov. 4, 1984; and Davey, *Rainmaker*, p. 258.

11. On Trudeau's "obituaries": Confronted with the challenge of appraising the political work of the man who had led the country for eleven years, the media's editorialists responded with cliché, confusion, and the admission that they could not tell for sure what his passage in office had meant. For Walter Stewart he had proved a failure: "No politician promised so much and delivered so little . . . The Just Society proved to be a slogan, nothing more . . . Regional disparities are wider than ever . . . Parliament was not reformed, it was ignored . . . Unemployment doubled, inflation soared, government spending quadrupled, the federal deficit increased fourteen-fold . . . He also had an appetite for power, but not a feeling for politics . . . He could control images, but not reality": *Winnipeg Free Press* (Nov. 22, 1979), p. 7. For others he remained an enigma eleven years after becoming prime minister: *Vancouver Sun* (Nov. 21, 1979), p. A1.

12. Axworthy and Coutts quotes: "In September four or five of us in the leader's office formed a group," Tom Axworthy said later. "We decided we would (a) work to bring the government down and (b) try to keep Trudeau steady since we believed he could win again." This was the hard core of the Trudeau loyalists who connected through Keith Davey with Martin Goldfarb and Jerry Grafstein in Toronto. Authors' interviews with Tom Axworthy, Nov. 4, 1984, and July 22, 1990; and with James Coutts, Dec. 19, 1985.

13. For a fuller account of Coutts's career in the 1970s: McCall-Newman, *Grits*, pp. 135–74.

14. Coutts's strategy: Authors' interviews with Tom Axworthy, Nov. 4, 1984; and with James Coutts, Dec. 19, 1985.

15. On Liberal appointments of Tories: The Conservatives' only big-name MP from Quebec, Claude Wagner, was lured to the Senate; Gordon Fairweather, a stalwart MP from New Brunswick, was appointed commissioner of human rights; Jack Horner, a leading Conservative from Alberta, was enticed into crossing the floor with the promise of a seat in the Liberal cabinet.

16. On the Conservatives lasting until the end of the twentieth century: Authors' interview with Sylvia Ostry, Sept. 26, 1979.

On the "Tory syndrome": Perlin, *Tory Syndrome*,
pp. 190–201.

On the 1979 Tory campaign: Courtney, "Campaign
Strategy and Electoral Victory."

On the Liberals' arrogance developing from the party's
excessive tenure in office: Meisel, "Howe, Hubris, and '72."

17. On Pitfield's dismissal: Clark only fired one other senior
bureaucrat, the deputy minister of finance, William Hood,
because of a policy disagreement. Otherwise he conformed
to the Canadian practice of sustaining the political neutrality of the federal civil service. Bourgault and Dion, "Governments Come and Go," p. 15.

18. On Clark and the Canadian embassy in Israel: Adelman,
"Clark and the Canadian Embassy in Israel," gives a careful dissection of the various forces leading Clark to make
and unmake the damaging decision.

CHAPTER 8

Restoration, Transformation, and Resurrection

1. On Coutts and Trudeau's resignation: Authors' interview
with James Coutts, Nov. 23, 1979.

2. On the leadership candidates: "Turner, Macdonald Close to
Touching Off 'A Battle of Eagles,'" *Globe and Mail* (Dec. 1,
1979), p. 11.

Frum quote: Authors' notes.

3. On polling data: Authors' interview with Martin Goldfarb,
Mar. 8, 1980; and Gallup Poll report, "Tory Popularity
Plunges," *Toronto Star* (Dec. 3, 1979). In answer to the question "Is Pierre Trudeau a good leader of the Liberals?" 65
per cent of those queried said yes, 28 per cent said no.

4. On Turner's reasons for not running and Coutts's reactions
to the budget: Authors' interviews with Keith Davey, Mar.
10, 1980; and Tom Axworthy, Feb. 20, 1980.

5. For a description of the thinking in the Finance Department

and the debate within the Clark cabinet over this measure: Simpson, *Discipline of Power*, pp. 227–31.

6. On Fabien Roy's reaction: Roy had telephoned René Lévesque for tactical guidance, but the Quebec premier could not return his call and Claude Morin was in Africa, leaving Roy to take his policy cue from the PQ's finance minister, Jacques Parizeau, who had already denounced Crosbie's gas tax as an incursion into Quebec's jurisdiction. Authors' conversation on Mar. 2, 1990, with Daniel Latouche, a policy adviser in the premier's office at the time.

7. On Liberal reaction to Tory head count: Authors' interview with Tom Axworthy, Feb. 20, 1980.

8. The one Liberal absentee from the budget vote was Serge Joyal, who insisted on honouring his "pair" with the Conservative Alvin Hamilton.

9. On Trudeau's refusal to ask leading questions: Ultimately it was Allan MacEachen who asked the prime minister whether he would "be writing to the leader of the Social Credit group before the votes, giving him special reasons why that group should support the budget and, if so, would he make available copies of his correspondence to the rest of us, which might assist us in considering this extraordinary document?" Canada, House of Commons, *Debates* (Dec. 12, 1979), p. 2275.

10. On the national executive meeting: Authors' interviews with Gordon Dryden, Mar. 3, 1980; and with Lorna Marsden, Mar. 3, 1980.

11. Trudeau quotes: Authors' conversation with Pierre Trudeau, June 6, 1985.

12. The "good-enough solution" is what adult development theorists suggest men can hope to achieve in late middle age – the compromise, accepted with good grace, between their original dream and the reality imposed by their circumstances. Levinson et al., *Seasons of a Man's Life*, pp. 217–20.

13. Marchand quote: Authors' interview with Jean Marchand, Apr. 10, 1985.

14. Trudeau quote: Trudeau, "J'ai réfléchi . . . et j'ai compris . . . ," *Le Devoir* (Nov. 26, 1979), p. 5.

On Margaret Trudeau's financial and neurological worries: *Consequences*, pp. 130, 150.

15. On Trudeau's consultation with David Owen: Authors' interview with David Owen, Nov. 23, 1987. On consultation with Stuart Smith: *Consequences*, pp. 148–49.

16. Margaret Trudeau, *Consequences*, pp. 133–34.

17. On Margaret's subsequent actions: *Consequences*, pp. 185–86; on Trudeau family counselling: *Consequences*, p. 175.

18. Grafstein quotes: Authors' interview, Feb. 26, 1980. The haberdasher was Harry Rosen.

19. For an important view of integration and the role spirituality plays in its achievement: Jung, *Essential Jung*, pp. 229–97.

20. On the election strategy: Trudeau was himself leery – as he had been back in the heyday of Trudeaumania – of making campaign promises that he might have difficulty keeping, so he willingly complied with Coutts's suppression of most of the policies that had been frenetically negotiated by a "platform committee" of Liberal Party activists and caucus members, hastily convened over the Christmas break.

21. The results of the 1980 election were: 146 Liberals (44 per cent of the vote), 103 Progressive Conservatives (33 per cent), and 32 New Democrats (20 per cent). It was Trudeau's largest majority since 1968 and his greatest victory ever in Quebec, where he received 68 per cent of the vote and – after a quick by-election in Frontenac riding, where a Créditiste candidate had died in mid-campaign – 74 of the 75 seats.

CHAPTER 9

Picking Up the Reins of Power

1. Trudeau quote: Authors' interview with Madeleine Gobeil, Apr. 8, 1985.

2. Gobeil quote: Authors' interview, Apr. 8, 1985.

3. Trudeau quote: Conversation with the authors, June 6, 1985. On Trudeau's remarkable capacity to evolve: The social

psychologist Daniel Levinson points out that a capacity for continuing evolution in one's creative products and personal life is part of the unusual pattern of development that marks men who possess genius or aspire to heroism. He cites the case of the British philosopher Bertrand Russell, who found through his passionate friendship with Lady Ottoline Morrell a release from emotional sterility and a capacity for renewal of his creativity that continued into old age. It is tempting to draw a parallel between the Russell-Morrell duo and the Trudeau-Sinclair marriage, though the latter was more a trigger for further change than a relationship through which he could grow. Levinson et al., *Seasons of a Man's Life*, pp. 30–32.

4. On Trudeau's reactions on election night: Authors' interview with Keith Davey, Mar. 10, 1980.

On the decision not to redecorate 24 Sussex: The prime ministerial residence had been redecorated in 1979 by Maureen McTeer, the wife of Joe Clark. Margaret Trudeau described McTeer's efforts as a deliberate attempt "to bring that house down to middle class," to replace Margaret's own elegant style with "all that was mediocre . . . I mean there ought to be a Minister of Taste, or something, to make sure these things don't happen." These remarks led the journalist Roy MacGregor to suggest that Margaret herself should be appointed minister of taste since there was "published photographic proof that [she] can not possibly get caught with her pants down" – an ironic reminder of the photograph of Margaret taken in a New York nightclub in 1979 that showed her legs apart, without underwear. MacGregor, "Maggie, the 'T' That Dares to be Known by Taste Alone."

5. On western anger at the Liberals: In 1980 the Liberals elected only two members west of the Ontario border, and these were in urban Manitoba: Lloyd Axworthy in Winnipeg–Fort Garry and Robert Bockstael in St. Boniface. By 1980 the Liberals had become the west's third party, receiving 27 per cent of the vote in the western provinces to the NDP's 29 and the Conservatives' 43. In the individual prov-

inces the Liberals got 22 per cent of the vote in British
Columbia, 22 per cent in Alberta, 24 per cent in Saskatchewan, 28 per cent in Manitoba, and 37 per cent in the territories. For an analysis of the decline of Liberalism in
western Canada: David Smith, *Regional Decline of a National
Party*.

On the uncertain state of the economy: The second volume of *Trudeau and Our Times* will explore in detail the
political-economy context of the last Trudeau ministry.

6. On the "strategic prime ministership": Axworthy, "Of
Secretaries to Princes."

On the new Trudeau government's objectives: Authors'
interviews with Tom Axworthy, May 18 and July 11, 1984,
and Jan. 23, 1986; and Michael Pitfield, Dec. 9, 1989, and
Jan. 13, 1990.

Trudeau quote: Conversation with the authors, June 6,
1985.

7. Bissonnette quote: "Dans de vieilles artères," *Le Devoir*
(Mar. 4, 1980), p. 10.

CHAPTER 10

The Referendum I: The Generals Mobilize

1. This account and analysis of the referendum on sovereignty-
association is based on several dozen interviews and conver-
sations conducted between 1980 and 1990 with many
observers and activists, including Warren Allmand, Pierre
Bastien, Louise Beaudoin, Monique Bégin, Pauline Ber-
geron, Louis Bernard, Yves Bérubé, Lise Bissonnette,
Denise Bombardier, Bernard Bonin, Rémi Bujold, Pierre
Bussières, Greta Chambers, Jean Chrétien, Dennis Dawson,
Pierre Deniger, Alain Dubuc, Louis Duclos, André Dufour,
Patricia Dumas, Claude Forget, Yves Fortier, Francis Fox,
Graham Fraser, Joan Fraser, Richard French, Lysiane Gag-
non, Jean Garon, Gérald Godin, Eddie Goldenberg, Céline
Hervieux-Payette, Pierre-Marc Johnson, Don Johnston,

Serge Joyal, Jean-Paul L'Allier, Marc Lalonde, Daniel
Latouche, François Lebrun, Paule Leduc, Claude Lemelin,
Gérard D. Lévesque, René Lévesque, Storrs McCall, Eric
Maldoff, Jean-Claude Malépart, Jean Marchand, Alain
Marcoux, Paul Martin, Jr., Claude Morin, Michel Nadeau,
Robert Normand, Jean Paré, Alex Paterson, John Payne,
Norman Plante, Jean Riley, James Robb, Claude Roquet,
Jean-K. Samson, Roger Tassé, Charles Taylor, Paul Tellier,
Pierre Trudeau, and Gérard Veilleux. Among those asked
for interviews only Claude Ryan refused his collaboration, a
lacuna filled by the extensive treatment of his first years in
partisan politics by MacDonald, *From Bourassa to Bourassa*,
chs. 7–16. In addition we are indebted to Bergeron, *Notre
miroir à deux faces*; G. Fraser, *PQ: René Lévesque and the Parti
Québécois in Power*, chs. 12–14; McWhinney, *Canada and the
Constitution*, ch. 3; Payette, *Le pouvoir? Connais pas!*; Sheppard and Valpy, *National Deal*, ch. 2.

2. Bergeron and Pelletier, eds., *L'État du Québec en devenir*,
   offers a weighty collection of essays on the process of
   Quebec's evolution into a "state." The most authoritative
   and most accessible analysis of the socio-economic forces
   and political consequences of the Quiet Revolution is found
   in the third edition of McRoberts, *Quebec*, chs. 5 and 6.

3. On Lévesque's early life: G. Fraser, *PQ*, pp. 14–18; Desbarats, *René*; and Lévesque, *Memoirs*, pp. 49–97.

   On Trudeau's first meeting with Lévesque, the best published account is Pelletier's *Years of Impatience*, pp. 25–26.

   On Trudeau's praise for Lévesque: Trudeau, "L'homme
   de gauche et les élections provinciales."

4. The electoral progress of the Parti Québécois was impressive. From a standing start of 23 per cent of the vote in the
   election of April 1970 (for 7 seats), Péquiste momentum had
   built to 30 per cent (though only 6 seats) to reach 41 per
   cent in 1976, for their majority of 71 seats. *Canadian Annual
   Review: 1970*, p. 22; *Canadian Annual Review: 1973*, p. 78; and
   Canadian Annual Review: 1976, p. 121.

5. On Lévesque's dislike of Trudeau: Authors' interviews with
   René Lévesque, Oct. 21, 1981, and Dec. 12, 1986.

6. The debate on the referendum question had a long history in the Parti Québécois. Lévesque had consistently managed to water down the party activists' preference for unilaterally declaring independence and then negotiating an association with Canada. Although Morin did not coin the term *étapisme*, it was identified so closely with his political strategy that he was generally considered its author. G. Fraser, *PQ*, pp. 170–71, 191.

7. On Ryan's responses to Trudeau: Macdonald, *From Bourassa to Bourassa*, pp. 183–84, 193; and G. Fraser, *PQ*, p. 143.

8. For more complete accounts of the Trudeauites' response to the October Crisis see: Haggart and Golden, *Rumours of War*; McCall-Newman, *Grits*, pp. 181–86; Pelletier, *October Crisis*; Rotstein, ed., *Power Corrupted*; Denis Smith, *Bleeding Hearts, Bleeding Country*; Vallières, *Assassination of Pierre Laporte*.

9. Ryan's editorials in *Le Devoir* on the ultimatum: "L'inacceptable échéance du 28 juin" (June 18, 1971); on the substance: "Le dilemme de M. Bourassa" (June 22, 1971); on the process: "La réforme fiscale et la réforme constitutionnelle: deux méthodes différentes" (June 23, 1971); on the outcome: "Le 'non' d'un gouvernement et d'un peuple" (June 25, 1971).

10. On the historical relationship between the federal Liberal Party and the provincial Liberal Party in Quebec: Rayside, "Federalism and the Party System: Provincial and Federal Liberals in the Province of Quebec"; Wearing, *L-Shaped Party*, pp. 96–108; and Whitaker, *Government Party*, pp. 269–306.

11. On Ryan's extreme reaction to Michel Robert: Authors' interview with Alex Paterson, Dec. 9, 1986; MacDonald, *From Bourassa to Bourassa*, pp. 104–9. People close to Ryan speculated that, because he feared the Pro-Canada Committee might fall under the influence of the now nearly moribund Union Nationale, he demanded Robert's resignation in order to achieve complete control of the Non campaign.

12. Parti Québécois White Paper on sovereignty-association: Quebec, *Quebec-Canada: A New Deal*, pp. 51, 53.

On the drafting of the document: G. Fraser, *PQ*, pp. 195–99.

Ryan quote: "Ryan Calls PQ's Position Paper on Sovereignty a 'House of Cards,'" *Globe and Mail* (Nov. 3, 1979), p. 11.

13. The Beige Paper: Gordon Robertson hailed it as "the most important single document for future constitutional discussions." "Our Other National Sport."

14. On the National Assembly debate: G. Fraser, *PQ*, pp. 218–19; Bergeron, *Notre miroir*, pp. 220–1.

15. Exploiting their social science expertise, the Péquistes had commissioned extensive survey research to determine what phrasing elicited the best response from the public. As Claude Morin told Professor J. Stefan Dupré of the University of Toronto, they chose the wording that did best in the polls. The referendum question read as follows:

"The government of Quebec has made public its proposal to negotiate a new agreement with the rest of Canada based on the equality of nations;

"This agreement would enable Quebec to acquire the exclusive power to make its own laws, levy its taxes and establish relations abroad – in other words, sovereignty – and, at the same time to maintain with Canada an economic association including a common currency;

"No change in political status resulting from these negotiations will be effected without approval by the people through another referendum;

"ON THESE TERMS DO YOU GIVE THE GOVERNMENT OF QUEBEC THE MANDATE TO NEGOTIATE THE PROPOSED AGREEMENT BETWEEN QUEBEC AND CANADA? ____ Yes ____ No."

16. On the labour organizations' support: The Fédération des travailleurs du Québec came out for the Oui on March 15; the Confédération des syndicats nationaux followed on April 11; and even the federal body, the Canadian Labour Congress, added its stamp of approval on May 5 by endorsing the principle of Quebec's right to self-determination.

Throughout this period, Lévesque would turn up in a community to receive carefully organized *regroupements*, or delegations, of doctors, accountants, and other citizens who declared, apparently spontaneously, their faith in sovereignty-association. Afterwards Lévesque would reward them with scrolls that commemorated the happy event.

17. Ryan quotes: MacDonald, *From Bourassa to Bourassa*, p. 192.

18. On Forget's reaction to Trudeau's lunch with Ryan: Authors' interview with Claude Forget, Jan. 27, 1987.

19. Chrétien quotes: Authors' interview with Doug Fisher, Nov. 23, 1979.

20. On Chrétien's difficulties in Finance and the way that Jacques Parizeau, the PQ minister of finance, bested him in the spring of 1978: McCall-Newman, *Grits*, pp. 235–36.

21. Trudeau's remark on management was made in a revealing statement to reporters in his office after a cabinet shuffle on Jan. 28, 1972. *Canadian Annual Review: 1972*, p. 4.

On Trudeau's doubts about Chrétien: As late as November 1976, Charles ("Bud") Drury, who had been president of the Treasury Board before Chrétien got the job, told one of the authors in an interview that Trudeau was worried about Chrétien's ability to handle economic portfolios. Authors' interview with Bud Drury, Nov. 26, 1976.

22. On the little brother/big brother exchange: Chrétien, *Straight from the Heart*, p. 125.

CHAPTER 11

The Referendum II: The Bloody Great Fight

1. On Chrétien's FPRO crisis management team: Claude Lemelin came from the FPRO itself; Paul Tellier, deputy minister in Indian Affairs and Northern Development, was available with his anti-separatist expertise from the late 1970s; Robert Rabinovitch attended on behalf of the Privy

Council Office. Gérard Veilleux and Tommy Shoyama added the Finance Department's perspective, George Anderson that of External Affairs. Michel Robert provided partisan-cum-legal input.

On the Canadian Unity Information Office's budget: MacDonald, *From Bourassa to Bourassa*, p. 177.

2. On the Ryan–Chrétien exchange: Chrétien, *Straight from the Heart*, p. 122.

Ryan's objection to Chrétien's prominence in the Liberals' referendum planning had already been voiced at a meeting of the Non committee in the autumn of 1979, when the federal party was still in opposition.

3. On the other provinces' responses to Quebec: Sheppard and Valpy, *National Deal*, p. 33.

4. In addition to the Positive Action Committee, there were several other anti-separatist citizens' groups, including Rally Canada, Decision Canada, the Quebec-Canada Committee (which had 200,000 members, many of them francophones), and the Council for Canadian Unity, which acted as an umbrella organization, drawing in political parties such as the Union Nationale and the Créditistes as well as citizens' groups.

5. Paterson quotes: Authors' interview with A.K. Paterson, Dec. 9, 1986.

6. Chrétien quotes: G. Fraser, *PQ*, p. 229.

7. Vastel observation: "La réforme en question," *Le Devoir* (June 2, 1980), p. 1.

On the extraordinarily powerful role of intellectuals in the PQ and their impact on its constitutional radicalism: Pinard and Hamilton, "Le référendum québécois."

8. Joining the federal cabinet ministers were such francophone senior deputy ministers as Pierre Juneau from the Communications Department and Roger Tassé from Justice.

9. The thrust of his campaign oratory was recalled by Marchand in an interview with the authors on Apr. 10, 1985.

10. On the throne-speech debate: Canada, House of Commons, *Debates*: Ouellet (Apr. 16, 1980), p. 75; Lalonde (Apr. 16, 1980), p. 81; Bégin (Apr. 17, 1980), p. 110.

11. On Chamber of Commerce speech: Authors' conversation with Pierre Trudeau, June 6, 1985.

    In his actual speech he stated, "The choice must be definitive and final. If the referendum is lost, it should not be reopened for fifteen years." William Johnson, "PM Dares Levesque to Risk All," *Globe and Mail* (Jan. 29, 1977), p. 1.

    On the ambiguity of the referendum question: Professor Louis Balthazar of Laval University, speaking at the University of British Columbia before Trudeau became involved in the campaign, said that "the result of the referendum won't be 'yes' or 'no' but either 'yes but' or 'no but.' " Balthazar, "Quebec at the Hour of Choice," in Carty and Ward, eds., *Entering the Eighties*, p. 60.

12. Trudeau in throne-speech debate: Canada, House of Commons, *Debates* (Apr. 15, 1980), pp. 31–37.

13. Trudeau on Henri Bourassa: Authors' conversation with Pierre Trudeau, June 6, 1985.

14. Trudeau, "Translation of the Transcript . . . May 2, 1980," pp. 4, 10.

15. The school primer described the "Dick" figure, Guy, as a boy who "practises sports, swimming, gymnastics, tennis, boxing and diving. His ambition is to become champion and bring back many trophies." By contrast, "Yvette, his little sister, is cheerful and well-behaved, always trying to please her parents. Yesterday at dinner she cut the bread, poured the water in the teapot, brought the sugar bowl, butter dish and milk jug . . . Cheerfully she dried the dishes and swept the carpet." Payette, *Le pouvoir? Connais pas!*, p. 79.

16. Bissonnette quotes: "Dire non à ce courage-là," *Le Devoir* (Mar. 11, 1980), p. 8.

17. On women in the Liberal Party: "Once more women are being labelled, used, even manipulated," wrote Lysiane Gagnon on April 10. "After having spent years in the Liberal Party doing the most humble and necessary chores – knocking on doors, marking lists, phoning, sticking on stamps, working the polls – they had the politically genial idea to exploit Madame Payette's gaffe at the very moment when the party, still traumatized by the dreadful perfor-

mance of its leaders at the parliamentary debate, was short of ideas ... They will soon return to the shade where political party women stay, always ready to serve. The day after this great success at the Forum, the 'Quebec committee for the No' revealed to the press its executive committee: 13 men and 2 women at the end of the table. As usual." L. Gagnon, "Ni Lisette, ni Yvette," reprinted in her *Chroniques politiques*, pp. 16, 19.

18. Daniel Latouche, "La désinvolture chronique du Parti Québécois: autopsie d'une crise," *Le Devoir* (Dec. 4, 1981), p. 11.

19. On Trudeau's response to Lévesque: MacDonald, *From Bourassa to Bourassa*, p. 221.

20. Lévesque quote: Julia Turner, "Revived Levesque Aims Pitch at Crucial Francophone Voters," *Globe and Mail* (May 12, 1980), p. 15.

21. Trudeau, "Transcript of a Speech ... May 14, 1980," pp. 1, 10–11.

22. On the impact of Trudeau's speech: Authors' interview with Alain Marcoux, Mar. 20, 1986.

Jean Chrétien felt the Péquiste strategy was based on an internal contradiction. "In retrospect, the referendum was the biggest mistake made by the Parti Québécois. Until then its strategy had been extremely effective for Quebec and highly dangerous for Canada. It was described to me by Claude Morin ... 'We'll sever the links one by one, a little concession here and a little concession here and a little concession there ... and eventually there will be nothing left.' ... But the referendum focused the issue, even though the question was fuzzy. The people had to make a choice, and the separatists lost." Chrétien, *Straight from the Heart*, p. 151.

23. On referendum leaders: Sheppard and Valpy, *National Deal*, p. 36.

On the francophone vote: Since some neo-federalists, such as the former Quebec Liberal cabinet minister Jean-Paul L'Allier and the political scientist Léon Dion, had supported the Oui cause in order to strengthen Quebec's bargaining position within the federal system, this figure exaggerated the actual support expressed that night for independence. See Maurice Pinard, "Les francophones et le référendum: 52% contre 48%," *Le Devoir* (July 25, 1980), p. 9; and Daniel Latouche, "Après son échec du 20 mai, le PQ doit cesser de juger le peuple avec mépris," *Le Devoir* (June 4, 1980), p. 1.

24. Lévesque's Empire Club speech: Authors' notes, Jan. 24, 1980.

25. Ryan as Grim Reaper: Doug Small on "We the People: the Constitutional Dilemma," Global Television Network, Feb. 9, 1981.

    On Ryan's call for an election: MacDonald, *From Bourassa to Bourassa*, p. 238.

26. Trudeau's magnanimity was of a piece with the generosity of his response to the Parti Québécois election of Nov. 15, 1976, when he had acknowledged the democratic will of the voters and paid tribute to the intelligence and dedication of his opponents. G. Fraser, *PQ*, p. 79.

27. Trudeau on the referendum vote: "Statement by the Prime Minister," p. 1.

    Gérard Bergeron, "Une si mauvaise question . . . " *Le Devoir* (May 24, 1980), p. 14.

CHAPTER 12

The Reluctant Bride

1. Scott lecture: Djwa, *Politics of the Imagination*, p. 236.
    Trudeau quotes: Conversation with the authors, Dec. 11, 1986.

2. On the ideology shared by post-war western élites: Fussell, *Wartime*, ch. 12.

    McIlwain espoused "the mediaeval principle that there are some individual rights that even a people's government can never touch." Cited from *Constitutionalism and the Changing World: Collected Papers* (Cambridge: Cambridge University Press, 1939), p. 263, by Peter Bachrach, "Charles H. McIlwain," in David Sills, ed., *International Encyclopedia of the Social Sciences*, vol. 9 (New York: Macmillan, The Free Press, 1968), p. 512.

On Carl Friedrich: *The Annual Obituary, 1984* (Chicago: St. James' Press, 1985), p. 473.

3. The best formulation in print of Trudeau's political-theory ideas is his *Approaches to Politics*.

4. Trudeau on St. Laurent: Conversation with the authors, Dec. 11, 1986.

5. Descriptions of these conferences and the constitutional issues at stake are to be found in Harrison, *Canada in World Affairs*, pp. 177–78; Pickersgill, *My Years with Louis St. Laurent*, pp. 111–21; and Thomson, *Louis St. Laurent*, pp. 277–300. Further details were provided to the authors in interviews with Jack Pickersgill and Gordon Robertson and conversations with Pierre Trudeau.

6. On Duplessis: Authors' conversation with Pierre Trudeau, Dec. 11, 1986.

7. Djwa, *Politics of the Imagination*, pp. 265–66.

8. On post-1950 lack of interest in the constitution: Authors' interview with Jack Pickersgill, Nov. 30, 1986.

9. "Patriation," an apt word to describe the transfer of constitutional sovereignty from Britain to Canada, did not come into common usage until the 1970s.

10. On Trudeau's early views on the constitution: Authors' conversation with Pierre Trudeau, Dec. 11, 1986.

Trudeau's brief: *Mémoire*, pp. 11, 32–42. Trudeau acknowledged the contribution that both Frank Scott and Eugene Forsey had made to the argument in his brief.

11. Trudeau as a constitutional conservative in the 1950s: Trudeau, "Politique fonctionnelle – II"; "De libro, tributo . . . et quibusdam aliis."

Trudeau as a strict federalist defending local autonomy in areas of provincial jurisdiction: Trudeau, "Les octrois fédéraux."

12. Gérin-Lajoie, *Constitutional Amendment in Canada*.

Johnson, *Égalité ou indépendance*.

13. On Trudeau and the law: Djwa, *Politics of the Imagination*, p. 336.
14. *Maclean's* quote: Trudeau, "We Need a Bill of Rights."
    "Frantic hurry": Trudeau, "Quebec and the Constitutional Problem," in his *Federalism and the French Canadians*, p. 44. The italics are his.
15. Trudeau quotes: Conversation with the authors, Dec. 11, 1986.
16. On joining the Liberal Party: Trudeau and Pelletier, "Pelletier et Trudeau s'expliquent."
    Trudeau, "In Defence of Federalism," p. 112.
17. On Pearson's response to Robarts: Authors' conversation with Pierre Trudeau, June 6, 1985.
18. Trudeau's memory of these attitudes was expressed to the authors on Dec. 11, 1986.
19. On the concatenation of the three significant events: André Laurendeau reflected wrily in his diary that, as a nationalist after the war, he had defended federalism against the centralizers as had Trudeau, so it was "not illogical" that he was defending it now against the separatists. Laurendeau, *Journal*, p. 380.
    On Lévesque's response: *Canadian Annual Review: 1967*, p. 93.
20. Authors' interview with Carl Goldenberg, Dec. 12, 1986.
21. Trudeau, "Federalism, Nationalism, and Reason," in his *Federalism and the French Canadians*, pp. 193, 202–3. The italics are his.
22. Trudeau quotes: "A Constitutional Declaration of Rights," *Federalism and the French Canadians*, pp. 57 and 54.
    William Mathie explains – and attacks – the nation-building intent of Trudeau's bill of rights in "Political Community and the Canadian Experience," p. 11. Peter Russell explains the charter's national-unity rationale in "Political Purposes of the Canadian Charter," pp. 33–36.
23. In the parliamentary debate on the establishment of the provinces of Alberta and Saskatchewan, Henri Bourassa had expounded his view that the British North America Act of

1867 constituted a compact guaranteeing the rights of the French language. This compact was subsequently respected in the 1870 act establishing the province of Manitoba's constitution but had been violated by the anglophone Manitoba majority in 1890, which abolished the use of French in the legislature. "And if we wish ourselves to remain faithful to [the BNA Act's] principle, we should follow their example and provide that the French and English tongues will be for ever, and on an equal footing, official in Alberta and Saskatchewan, two provinces cut out, as was Manitoba, from those vast territories which are the property of the whole Canadian people. What I claim, is the carrying out of the same principle which was applied in connection with the establishment of the Dominion itself. It is the principle which Sir John Macdonald advocated when he proclaimed that there were no longer in Canada victors and vanquished, but two allies whose rights, equal by virtue of the constitution, are not measured by the numbers and riches of the various groups." Canada, House of Commons, *Debates* (July 5, 1905), pp. 8847–52, cited in Levitt, *Henri Bourassa*, p. 122.

24. The documents produced by Ottawa for the conference unmistakably bore the Trudeau stamp. Pearson, *Federalism for the Future*, spoke in the Trudeauesque language of functionalism, mentioning the rights of the individual, the dangers of separatism, the flexibility of federalism, and the crucial need to give protection for linguistic rights in the constitution. A second document, *A Canadian Charter of Human Rights*, was printed more appropriately over Trudeau's name as it reiterated the themes of his pre-political writings.

Trudeau quotes: Interview with Peter Newman, *Montreal Star* (Feb. 2, 1968), as cited in *Canadian Annual Review: 1968*, p. 71.

25. On the suspicions of the anglophone premiers: The day before the February 1968 conference opened, British Columbia's premier of the day, W.A.C. Bennett, had grudgingly given his deputy minister permission to attend with him, after admonishing him to be cautious: don't say anything at

the meetings and watch yourself in the coffee breaks, since that was when Ottawa men would attempt to sway his views and persuade him constitutional change was important. Authors' interview with Mel Smith, May 28, 1986.

26. Henri Bourassa's analysis is from *Les écoles du nord-ouest* (Montreal, 1905), as cited in Levitt, *Henri Bourassa*, pp. 115–18.

27. Functionalism, whether expounded in Trudeau's first *Cité libre* manifesto in 1950 ("Politique fonctionelle") or in his last such call to action in 1964 ("Manifeste pour une politique fonctionnelle"), was also a way to attack the nationalist claim that Quebec should exercise certain powers because they were needed to defend French Canadians' ethnic character. In the PCO discussions initiated by Michael Pitfield, it was decided that foreign and military policy were best suited to the central government, since their effectiveness depended on their being made for the whole country as a single entity. Education and social policy, by contrast, should be determined locally, since the individual provinces could best develop different programs suited to and desired by their own populations.

28. Between the first ministers' conference of February 1968 and the Victoria conference of June 1971, the Continuing Committee of Ministers on the Constitution met eighteen times and seven first ministers' conferences were held. Along the way Trudeau had agreed, at the insistence of Quebec, to add the division of powers to the overloaded agenda. Authors' interview with Mel Smith, May 28, 1986.

   On Quebec's constitutional objectives and strategy for negotiating with Ottawa during the early Trudeau years: Morin, *Quebec Versus Ottawa*, ch. 8.

   On the Victoria charter: *Canadian Annual Review: 1971*, pp. 50–59.

29. Authors' conversation with Pierre Trudeau, June 6, 1985.

30. On Bourassa, Trudeau, and the Queen's visit: R. Gwyn, *Northern Magus*, p. 266. On Oct. 20, 1964, the Queen's previous visit to Quebec City had been marred by police beatings and arrests of some separatist demonstrators, and the incident had

been turned by the media into folklore, an outrage celebrated as "le samedi de la matraque" (Truncheon Saturday).
 On Trudeau's subsequent attack on Bourassa: Michel Roy,
"En attendant la réplique de Bourassa," *Le Devoir* (Mar. 8,
1976), p. 4; "Le discours de M. Trudeau," *La Presse* (Mar. 8,
1976), p. A6; Bergeron, *Notre miroir*, p. 149.

31. *Canadian Annual Review: 1978*, p. 68.
32. On the Pepin-Robarts task force: Authors' interview with
Jean-Luc Pepin, Nov. 28, 1986.
 Forsey quotes: *Canadian Annual Review: 1978*, p. 445.
33. Trudeau quotes: R. Gwyn, *Northern Magus*, p. 169.
 Details of conferences: *Canadian Annual Review: 1978*,
pp. 59–69.
34. Trudeau, "Prime Minister's Remarks at Maple Leaf
Gardens," p. 7.
35. Trudeau, "Prime Minister's Remarks at Sheraton Mount-
Royal Hotel," pp. 16–19; and "Prime Minister's Remarks at
Confederation Luncheon," pp. 9–26.

CHAPTER 13

Trudeau Takes On the Premiers

1. Trudeau's question to Marchand: Authors' interview with
Jean Marchand, Apr. 10, 1985.
2. Trudeau on the constitution: Authors' conversation with
Pierre Trudeau, June 6, 1985.
3. Trudeau as "nasty guy": Authors' conversation with Pierre
Trudeau, June 6, 1985.
4. Trudeau quote: Authors' conversation with Pierre Trudeau,
June 6, 1985.
5. Trudeau on the provinces and the constitution: Authors'
conversation with Pierre Trudeau, June 6, 1985.
6. Canada, House of Commons, *Debates* (May 21, 1980),
pp. 1263–64.
7. On Chrétien's trip to consult the premiers: Authors' interview with Michael Kirby, Nov. 26, 1986. Jean Chrétien, in

Straight from the Heart, put a diplomatic gloss on these findings, saying "the mood among the premiers was good" (p. 166).

8. On Gordon Robertson: Authors' conversation with Pierre Trudeau, Dec. 11, 1986.

9. Kirby quote: Confidential interview.

10. On Kirby: Authors' conversation with Pierre Trudeau, Dec. 11, 1986.

11. Authors' conversation with Pierre Trudeau, Dec. 11, 1986.

12. On the constitution increasing federal government powers: Hudon, "Quebec, the Economy and the Constitution," p. 138.

13. On the civil service and the constitution: Sheppard and Valpy, *National Deal*, p. 73.

At Justice the chief players were Roger Tassé, the deputy minister, who acted as chief legal adviser on the substance of the constitutional issues, and Barry Strayer, a senior legal adviser who was to draft and re-draft the innumerable proposals and counter-proposals during the negotiations. In the FPRO, the team Kirby assembled included Fred Gibson, an experienced government lawyer seconded from Justice; Reeves Haggan, whom Pitfield had recruited to the FPRO and who worked up the federal positions on the Supreme Court; David Cameron, most recently the research director for the Pepin-Robarts task force; Gérard Veilleux, who came from Finance to take charge of the economic dossiers involving the division of powers; Claude Lemelin, a former journalist from *Le Devoir*; Jim Hurley, a political science professor; and Linda Geller-Schwartz, another policy analyst recruited from the Pepin-Robarts task force. Others called on when particular expertise was needed included Ron Watts, the principal of Queen's University and an authority on federal systems who acted as consultant on the Senate. The small staff at the Canadian Unity Information Office was run by the former diplomat Hershell Ezrin, who reported both to the minister of justice and to James Fleming, the minister of multiculturalism, who chaired the cabinet committee on political communications. Ezrin was actually available to the FPRO to supervise polling and mount advertising campaigns.

14. On the powers under negotiation during the summer of 1980: Milne, *New Canadian Constitution*, pp. 47–53; Romanow, Whyte, and Leeson, *Canada . . . Notwithstanding*, pp. 64–76.

15. On federal constitutional strategy: Milne, *New Canadian Constitution*, pp. 52–66.

16. On Trudeau's veiled threat to act unilaterally: He told the House of Commons on the day after the June 9 meeting that he was "convinced that if we fail to reach substantial agreement in September we will be courting disaster for Canada. In that event, the federal government would have to give very serious consideration to its options and recommend to Parliament a plan of action which would allow us to fulfil our responsibilities to the people of Canada." Canada, House of Commons, *Debates* (June 10, 1980), p. 1936.

17. Napoleon quote: Confidential interview.

18. "Deux nations": Sheppard and Valpy, *National Deal*, p. 3.
    Hatfield comment: Authors' interview, May 3, 1986.
    "Princeling": McMurtry, "Search for a Constitutional Accord," p. 43.

19. On the leaked federal document: Sheppard and Valpy, *National Deal*, p. 54; and authors' interview with Richard Hatfield, May 3, 1986.

20. On the premiers' attitudes: Jeffrey Simpson, "The Constitution: Vital Elements to End the Hang-up Were Missing," *Globe and Mail* (Sept. 16, 1980), p. 7.
    Lougheed and Blakeney quotes: Cohen, Smith, and Warwick, *Vision and the Game*, p. 22.

21. Trudeau quotes: Authors' conversation with Pierre Trudeau, Dec. 11, 1986.
    "Knockout punch": Letter from Trudeau to Gérard Bergeron, in Bergeron's *Notre miroir*, p. 96.

22. On cabinet position: Milne, *New Canadian Constitution*, p. 77.
    There were four dissident ministers – Jean-Luc Pepin, co-author of the 1979 task force report on Canadian unity, which had endorsed a version of special status for Quebec;

Jean-Jacques Blais, representing North Bay, who feared an English backlash against francophone rights; Charles Lapointe, who objected to the charter's proposed interference with Quebec's linguistic policy; and Ray Perrault, the B.C. senator, who did not relish the thought of a new and more intense round of federal-provincial confrontations.

On Bill 101: McRoberts, *Quebec*, pp. 275–82; *Canadian Annual Review: 1977*, pp. 85–87.

23. Trudeau quotes: Authors' conversation with Pierre Trudeau, June 6, 1985.

24. On constitutional referendum: Sheppard and Valpy, *National Deal*, pp. 74–75.

25. The federal strategy is best laid out in the Kirby memorandum, "Report to Cabinet," pp. 43–50.

26. Joyal incident: Authors' interview with Serge Joyal, June 4, 1985.

27. On citizen participation: Svend Robinson, an NDP member of the joint committee, recalled "the dignity and strength of the disabled community as they sat, day in and day out, and literally shamed the Committee and the government into moving [an amendment in their favour]." Howard Leeson, from the Saskatchewan delegation, contrasted the citizen participation that the joint committee engendered with the rest of the constitutional process in which only "the very elite level of the politicians were involved." Cohen, Smith, and Warwick, *Vision and the Game*, pp. 34–35.

CHAPTER 14

The Premiers Take On Trudeau

1. Authors' interview with Peter Lougheed, June 4, 1986.

2. On Sir James Lougheed's connection with the oil industry: Shaffer, *Canada's Oil*, pp. 61–62.

On Peter Lougheed's early life: Hustak, *Peter Lougheed*, ch. 3; and Wood, *Lougheed Legacy*, chs. 1–3.

3. On Lougheed's response to American capital: It was widely

shared by his electorate, in part because Alberta had the largest proportion of American settlers of all the Canadian provinces. "Americans and American ideas played an influential role in Alberta that was unparalleled in Canada." Wiseman, "The Pattern of Prairie Politics," pp. 311–15.

On the role played by U.S. firms in formulating Alberta's petroleum policy: The Social Credit governments had relied on companies from Texas and Oklahoma for advice on how to regulate the oil and gas industry as it developed from the 1940s. Richards and Pratt, *Prairie Capitalism*, ch. 4.

On the absence of anti-American nationalism in Alberta: Doern and Toner, *Politics of Energy*, ch. 5; and J. Laxer, *Oil and Gas*, ch. 6.

4. Authors' interview with Peter Lougheed, June 4, 1986.

5. On the National Policy: Brown, "The Nationalism of the National Policy"; Craven and Traves, "The Class Politics of the National Policy"; Dales, *Protective Tariff*; G. Laxer, "The Political Economy of Aborted Development"; and Phillips, "The National Policy Revisited."

6. On the impact of the National Policy on the western economy: Berkowitz, "Forms of State Economy"; Fowke, *National Policy*.

7. Constitutional control over resources was negotiated by the King government but came into effect after Bennett became prime minister: La Forest, *Natural Resources*, p. 42.

On Alberta's Liberal Party: Thomas, *Liberal Party in Alberta*, ch. 2.

On the politics of one-party dominance: Lipset, "Democracy in Alberta"; Finkel, *Social Credit Phenomenon*; Laycock, *Populism and Democratic Thought*, ch. 5; Long and Quo, "Alberta: One Party Dominance"; and Macpherson, *Democracy in Alberta*.

8. On province-building in Alberta, with the growing clash between Lougheed's economic provincialism and the transnationals: Pratt, "The State and Province-Building."

On FIGA and Alberta's governmental structure: Authors'

interviews with Wayne V. Clifford, Sept. 29, 1981; A.F. ("Chip") Collins, June 3, 1986; Lou Hyndman, Sept. 29, 1981, and June 4, 1986; Merv Leitch, Sept. 30, 1981, and June 2, 1986; Helmut Mach, Sept. 30, 1986; Peter Meekison, Sept. 29, 1981, and June 4, 1986; and R.J. (Randy) Palivoda, Sept. 30, 1981.

9. On the Liberals' new national oil policy: Doern and Toner, *Politics of Energy*, ch. 3; Doern and Phidd, *Canadian Public Policy*, ch. 16; Ilkenberry, "The Irony of State Strength"; Jenkins, "Reexamining the 'Obsolescing Bargain' "; and Toner and Bregha, "The Political Economy of Energy."

10. On Albertans' reaction to the Liberals' oil policy: Authors' interviews with Don Getty, Feb. 13, 1975; Lou Hyndman, Sept. 29, 1981, and June 4, 1986; Merv Leitch, Sept. 30, 1981, and June 2, 1986; and Peter Lougheed, June 4, 1986.

11. C. Newman, "The New Power in the New West," p. 23.

One indicator of Alberta's popularity was the almost tenfold increase of the population flow into the province. From an average of 3,800 per year from 1971/72 to 1973/74, immigration jumped to 34,000 per year until 1981/82. Source: Statistics Canada.

12. On the 1970s boom for staple exports: Donner, *Financing the Future*, pp. 83–84; and Letourneau, *Inflation*, pp. 70–76.

13. On province-building in the 1970s: Cairns, "Governments and Societies"; Chandler and Chandler, *Public Policy and Provincial Politics*, chs. 2–4; and Milne, *Tug of War*.

As early as 1973 when the federal Liberals convened a Western Economic Opportunities Conference, Lougheed made sure that the west gave the patronizing Pierre Elliott Trudeau a strong message. When the prime minister flew west to find out what the denizens of the distant provinces were complaining about, he was faced by a determined common front. *Canadian Annual Review: 1973*, pp. 44–50.

At that stage Lougheed was the only Conservative among the western premiers. The three others were New Democrats (Dave Barrett of British Columbia, Allan Blakeney of Saskatchewan, and Ed Schreyer of Manitoba).

14. On Saskatchewan's constitutional concerns in the 1970s: Romanow, Whyte, and Leeson, *Canada . . . Notwithstanding*, pp. 15–16 and 24–28.

    Lougheed quote: Cohen, Smith, and Warwick, *Vision and the Game*, p. 18.

15. On the Atlantic fishery's expansion in the 1970s: Pross and McCorquodale, *Economic Resurgence and the Constitutional Agenda*, ch. 2. Fish prices rose 360 per cent from 1971 to 1981: Wilkinson, "Canada's Resource Industries," p. 68.

16. Authors' interview with Peter Lougheed, June 4, 1986.

17. The loans made by Alberta to the poorer provinces were at the same rate as the best-rated corporate borrower, Ontario Hydro. Starting at a modest $47-million loan to Newfoundland in 1976/77, the loans accelerated to an average of $372 million a year, totalling $1.86 billion by March 1982. Source: Alberta Heritage Savings Trust Fund, *Annual Report* 1976/77 to 1983/84.

    Bill Davis's constitutional strategists waxed somewhat paranoid about Lougheed's use of his financial muscle; but in the one hinterland province that did not join the anti-Ottawa coalition, the premier and his deputy both denied that Alberta had tried to exploit its loans to influence New Brunswick's constitutional position. It is nevertheless a curious coincidence that no sooner was the constitutional spat settled than the Heritage Fund's Canada Investment Division stopped making loans. Authors' interviews with Richard Hatfield, May 3, 1986; Hugh Segal, Jan. 7, 1986; and Barry Toole, June 11, 1990. We are also indebted to Allan A. Warrack for sharing with us his paper "The Alberta Heritage Fund: A Force for Canadian Unity," presented at the University of Edinburgh, Apr. 1985.

18. On the provinces' constitutional objectives in the 1970s: *Canadian Annual Review: 1978*, pp. 59–69.

    Camp quote: "We're Free at Last . . . Eh?" *Toronto Sun* (Apr. 16, 1982), p. 11.

19. On Clark's constitutional stance, or lack of: McWhinney, *Canada and the Constitution*, p. 13.

20. On the National Energy Program: Alberta's struggle with Ottawa for control of the country's petroleum rents will be described extensively in *Trudeau and Our Times*, vol. 2.

21. On the premiers' reaction: Romanow, Whyte, and Leeson, *Canada . . . Notwithstanding*, p. 108.

22. Reflecting on his *coup de force* in retirement, Trudeau recalled that he had considered including a redistribution of powers that would enhance the federal government's authority at the expense of the provinces but had decided against it, lest such an act provoke a *real* revolution. Authors' conversation with Pierre Trudeau, Dec. 11, 1986.

23. On the premiers' Oct. 14, 1980, meeting: Authors' interview with Peter Lougheed, June 4, 1986.

CHAPTER 15

The Road Show Moves to London

1. Subsequent controversy over what transpired at the June 1980 luncheon has never been fully laid to rest. Prime Minister Trudeau was accused of misleading the press when he claimed Thatcher's unqualified support would include using a "three-line whip." He subsequently made a guarded admission that he might not have been entirely "candid." But long after the event, Trudeau insisted he would only have used such an expression as "three-line whip" if Thatcher had used it, since it was not part of the Canadian political vocabulary. To the further accusation of misleading his British counterpart about the full extent of his constitutional package and the likelihood of provincial opposition, he claimed he had raised both possibilities and that she had continued throughout the period to be fully co-operative. He remained convinced that his three greatest supporters in London were the "three women: the Queen, Jean Wadds [the Canadian high commissioner], and Mrs. Thatcher." Authors' interviews with David Halton, Apr. 23

and 24, 1990; Andrew Szende, Apr. 23, 1990; and James McKibbon, Apr. 22, 1986; and their conversation with Pierre Trudeau, Dec. 11, 1986.

2. On Justin Trudeau: "Iron Lady Melts for Young Justin," *Toronto Star* (June 26, 1980), p. 1.

3. Trudeau on the British parliament and the constitution: Sheppard and Valpy, *National Deal*, p. 201.

4. Sheppard and Valpy, *National Deal*, pp. 188–89.

5. "Report to Cabinet," p. 50.

6. McNamara quotes: Authors' interview with Kevin Mc-Namara, Apr. 23, 1986.

7. Authors' interview with Kevin McNamara, Apr. 23, 1986.

8. Authors' interviews with John Roberts, June 14, 1990; and Mark MacGuigan, July 12, 1990.

9. Confidential interview. Thatcher quote: Authors' interview with James McKibbon, Apr. 22, 1986.

10. On the planted stories: Jane Armstrong and Ron Lowman, "Keep Patriation Simple or Risk Delay, U.K. Says," *Toronto Star* (Nov. 1, 1980), pp. A1, A14.

    On the Pym-Trudeau visit: Authors' interview with Sir Francis Pym, Apr. 22, 1986.

11. On the Queen at Balmoral: Roberts and MacGuigan found Her Majesty better informed on both the substance and the politics of Canada's constitutional case than any of the British politicians or bureaucrats. Authors' interviews with John Roberts, June 14, 1990; and Mark MacGuigan, July 12, 1990.

12. "Gone native": Confidential interview.

13. *The Globe and Mail* respected Ford's request for confidentiality by publishing the information under a London dateline so it could not be traced to his Ottawa office. Authors' interview with Geoff Stevens, May 28, 1990.

    The *Globe*'s publisher, Roy Megarry, was so exercised over Trudeau's unilateralism that he went to London himself to inveigh publicly against "the duplicity, the deceitfulness, the treachery" of the "tyrant" Trudeau's "sneaking, conniving manoeuvre." Leslie Plommer, "PM's Style an Issue, Publisher Says," *Globe and Mail* (Feb. 4, 1981), p. 9.

14. Hatfield-Ford conversation: Authors' interviews with Rich-

ard Hatfield, May 5, 1986; Michael Kirby, Feb. 26, 1986; Barry Toole, June 12, 1990; and Mark MacGuigan, July 12, 1990.

15. Trudeau quote: Authors' conversation with Pierre Elliott Trudeau, Dec. 11, 1986.

16. On the legal relationship between Canada and Britain: McWhinney, *Canada and the Constitution*, pp. 66–68.

 The Kershaw report: Great Britain, *British North America Acts*, p. 1. Italics in original.

CHAPTER 16

Joe Clark and the Commons

1. The Hays-Joyal joint committee, the first to have all its hearings televised, met for 267 hours on 56 days. Sheppard and Valpy, *National Deal*, p. 137.

2. On Broadbent's support: Ed Broadbent requested that changes be made to strengthen the charter of rights and demanded the affirmation of provincial ownership of natural resources and further control over their management in order to satisfy the NDP government in Saskatchewan. Sheppard and Valpy, *National Deal*, p. 114; and Steed, *Ed Broadbent*, pp. 242–53.

3. On Joe Clark's political difficulties: Authors' interviews with Lowell Murray, May 23, 1984, and June 11, 12, and 14, 1985; and with Joe Clark, Nov. 26, 1986.

 Clark's sobriquet was bestowed the day after his selection as party leader by a dumbfounded *Toronto Star*, whose banner headline read "Joe Who?" *Toronto Star* (Feb. 23, 1976). Surprise was no less great in Tory ranks, where he had been "thought no more likely to become the Tory leader (or prime minister!) than a Swiss Guard to become Pope." Camp, *Points of Departure*, p. 28.

 A carefully documented account of Clark's nine months in office is provided in Simpson, *Discipline of Power*.

4. On the 1976 Conservative leadership convention: Clark was

the favoured second choice of the majority of voting delegates. Krause and Leduc, "Voting Behaviour and Electoral Strategies."

Clark's partisans claimed that the conventional picture of him as having stumbled into the 1980 election by allowing a vote of confidence in the House when he did not have the numbers on his side was wrong. According to them, he was not able to make an accommodation with Fabien Roy because John Crosbie, his minister of finance, threatened that if he did so, Crosbie would quit his post. "If you want to listen to Roy [on the question of the budget's excise tax on gasoline], you can make *him* your minister of finance," Crosbie is said to have told Clark. Authors' interview with Lowell Murray, May 23, 1984.

5. On the media's delight in Clark's blunders: One typical story involving the leader of the opposition's references to Margaret Thatcher was printed in the *Globe and Mail* on Feb. 9, 1981. "Speaking on the CBC program As It Happens last week, Mr. Clark referred to Britain's Iron Lady once as Mr. Thatcher and a second time as Mrs. Trudeau. With host Barbara Frum guffawing in the background, Mr. Clark paused every time thereafter he had occasion to refer to the British PM by name."

6. On factionalism in the Conservative Party: Perlin, *Tory Syndrome*.

On Robert Stanfield's leadership and ideas: Stevens, *Stanfield*.

7. On Lougheed's and Davis's antagonism to each other and to Clark: Authors' interviews with Hugh Segal, Jan. 7, 1986; Kevin Peterson, June 15, 1986; Eddie Goldenberg, Feb. 1986; and Peter Lougheed, June 4, 1986. See also Hoy, *Bill Davis*, pp. 147–48; Goodman, *Life of the Party*, pp. 217–19; Nurgitz and Segal, *No Small Measure*, pp. 17–20; and Speirs, *Out of the Blue*, p. 12.

8. Mulroney quotes: Authors' interview with Brian Mulroney, Apr. 18, 1978.

9. On Brian Mulroney's activities in the early 1980s: Authors' interviews with William Bennett, June 6, 1985; Denise

Bombardier, June 2, 1985; Joan Fraser, June 5, 1985; Lysiane Gagnon, June 2, 1985. Also Martin, Gregg, and Perlin, *Contenders*, ch. 3; MacDonald, *Mulroney*, ch. 8; Murphy, Chodos, and Auf der Maur, *Brian Mulroney*, chs. 6, 7.

Mulroney quotes and attitudes: Authors' interviews with Brian Mulroney, Apr. 18, 1978, and Apr. 10, 1979.

10. On Duplessis, Diefenbaker, and Quebec: Black, *Duplessis*; and authors' interview with Alvin Hamilton, Apr. 29, 1979.

11. Clark quotes: Authors' interview, Nov. 26, 1986.

On the ups and downs of Tory support in Quebec: Under Diefenbaker, the Conservative vote went from 31 per cent of the vote (for 9 seats) in 1957 to 50 per cent and 50 seats in 1958, then fell back to 30 per cent (for 14 seats) in 1962, 20 per cent (for 8 seats) in 1963, and 21 per cent (and 8 seats) in 1965. Stanfield held this share of the vote at 21 per cent but lost seats, winning only 4 in 1968, 2 in 1972, and 3 in 1974. In 1979 and 1980 Clark garnered only 13 per cent of the vote, and his Quebec caucus fell to 2 MPs and then one, the indestructible Roch LaSalle.

12. Clark's election speech on federalism: "We must face the fact that the federal government is not as able [as it used to be] to manage the national economy, to help overcome regional disparities, and to conduct major national policies." Simpson, *Discipline of Power*, p. 240.

13. Clark quotes: Authors' interview, Nov. 26, 1986.

For an account of his efforts to achieve a distinct position on constitutional issues: Sheppard and Valpy, *National Deal*, pp. 78–109.

14. Clark quotes: "Leaders' Comments on Patriation Plan," *Globe and Mail* (Oct. 3, 1980), p. 11; and Canada, House of Commons, *Debates* (Oct. 2, 1980), pp. 3292–93. In taking this stand, Clark also hoped to exploit Trudeau's personal unpopularity by saying, "[Trudeau] defends this package . . . as being an end to colonial status. Then he uses that very colonial status he deplores to seek approval of his personal package of amendments. Madame Speaker, the Prime Minister is the last of the great colonials. He doesn't trust Canada to approve his amendments so he wants to try to

sneak them past Westminster before he changes the rules."

15. On Ontario's support for unilateralism: Hoy, *Bill Davis*, p. 356; Romanow, Whyte, and Leeson, *Canada . . . Notwithstanding*, pp. 107–8; Sheppard and Valpy, *National Deal*, pp. 99–100.

16. On Tory amendments: Conservative committee member Jake Epp proposed several amendments, including measures providing protection for the disabled and property-owners and increased access to information. Nurgitz and Segal, *No Small Measure*, p. 65.

17. On the Ford leak to the *Globe*: "British deny Trudeau's Assertions of Blanket Approval on Patriation," *Globe and Mail* (Jan. 31, 1981); and authors' interview with Geoff Stevens, May 28, 1990.

18. On the Ad Hoc Committee of Canadian Women on the Constitution: Kome, "Anatomy of a Lobby."

19. On the Tory filibuster: between Mar. 24, 1981, and Apr. 8, 1981, Conservative MPs made more than 120 interventions on 60 points of order and privilege. Robert Sheppard, "Tories Strike Deal in BNA Debate," *Globe and Mail* (Apr. 9, 1981), p. 2.

20. On Jeanne Sauvé and the constitutional debate: Authors' interview with Jeanne Sauvé, Nov. 27, 1986; Woods, *Her Excellency Jeanne Sauvé*, pp. 150–80. Also John Gray, "Tory Weapons Are Dirty Words to Grits," *Globe and Mail* (Apr. 4, 1981), p. 11: "At the centre of it all, apparently calm and good-humored is Mrs. Sauvé, whose grasp of her job only a few months ago was hesitant, uncertain and clearly uncomfortable." Sauvé also earned deep respect from many of her colleagues in the House (but lasting enmity from others) for her effective clean-up of the House's scandalously lax procedures and extravagant perks, from which both staff and MPs had quietly profited for years: Cameron, *Ottawa Inside Out*, pp. 105–8.

21. Clark's quote of the Newfoundland court judgements: Cohen, Smith, and Warwick, *Vision and the Game*, p. 41.

22. Whyte quote: Cohen, Smith, and Warwick, *Vision and the Game*, p. 40.

CHAPTER 17

To the Courts!

1. On the provinces' court strategy: Authors' interview with Richard Vogel, Sept. 10, 1986. Also Romanow, Whyte, and Leeson, *Canada . . . Notwithstanding*, ch. 6.

2. On Kirby's view of the legal side of constitutional bargaining: Authors' interview, Feb. 26, 1986.

   Trudeau's opposition to making a reference to the Supreme Court on what he considered to be a political battle rather than a legal dispute was expressed to the House of Commons on Oct. 15, 1980: "I think it is wrong to get the courts to make decisions, not on conflicts of law which are derived from the constitution, but on conflicting views of Canada." Canada, House of Commons, *Debates* (Oct. 15, 1980), p. 3680.

3. On Kirby and the Manitoba court's decision: Confidential interview.

4. On the Manitoba court's judgement: Sheppard and Valpy, *National Deal*, p. 232; and McWhinney, *Canada and the Constitution*, pp. 74–76.

5. On Wells's presentation: Barbara Yaffe, "Provinces' Appeal Called Speculative, Political," *Globe and Mail* (Feb. 12, 1981), p. 8.

   On the Newfoundland decision: McWhinney, *Canada and the Constitution*, pp. 77–78.

6. On the poor reasoning of the Newfoundland court: John Whyte felt there was "no reason to suspect that it would be sustained" on an appeal. Cohen, Smith, and Warwick, *Vision and the Game*, p. 40.

7. Laskin was also the first Jew ever to be named to the highest court. Trudeau appointed six other Supreme Court justices during his years as prime minister, including the first woman justice, Bertha Wilson, in 1982.

8. On Robinette and Trudeau: Authors' interview with John J. Robinette, June 19, 1990.

   On Robinette's line of argument: John Hay, "Final Justice, Seen to be Done," *Maclean's* (May 11, 1981), pp. 21–22; and Batten, *Robinette*, pp. 234–35.

9. Estey quote: Robert Sheppard, " 'Forget U.K. View,' Manitoba Lawyer Says," *Globe and Mail* (Apr. 29, 1981), pp. 1–2.

10. Trudeau quote: Authors' conversation with Pierre Trudeau. Dec. 11, 1986.

11. Laskin quote: From a 1978 speech, cited by Sheppard and Valpy, *National Deal*, p. 224.

   During its early decades the court had been, in Laskin's own words, a "captive court" existing completely in the shadow of London's Judicial Committee of the Privy Council. Even after appeals to London had been abolished in 1949, the Canadian court remained diffident and deferential to British precedent. In Peter Russell's judgement, it was "a thoroughly second-rate institution." It was only in 1975 that it was given the power to be in charge of its own agenda. Russell, *Judiciary in Canada*, pp. 336–37.

   On the maturation of the Laskin court in the late 1970s: David Lancashire, "The Last Word – Legally," *Globe and Mail* (June 6, 1981), p. 7; and Russell, *Judiciary in Canada*, pp. 356–56.

12. Milne, *New Canadian Constitution*, p. 107.

13. Description of the Supreme Court's day of judgement: Authors' notes. Mike Duffy eventually brought the CBC's talking heads a summary of the judgement, which he had made by listening in the lobby to the public address system. Conversation with Peter Russell, July 11, 1990.

14. "The Constitution: Day of Decision"; and McWhinney, *Canada and the Constitution*, pp. 81–83.

15. "Half a loaf": Russell, *Judiciary in Canada*, p. 355; and Russell, "The Supreme Court Decision."

16. On the Trudeau-Bennett meeting: Authors' interviews with James Matkin, May 30, 1986; and Norman Spector, May 27, 1986. We are grateful to James G. Matkin for allowing us to see his unpublished paper "The Negotiation of the Charter of Rights: The Provincial Perspective."

17. "Trudeau Responds from Seoul," in "The Constitution: Day of Decision," p. D7.

CHAPTER 18

From Last Judgement to Final Deal

1. On Goldfarb's reports to Trudeau: Authors' interviews with Martin Goldfarb, Oct. 1977, Apr. 1979, and Nov. 12, 1984; and *Goldfarb Report* for 1980 and 1981.
2. Hatfield on the Queen: Authors' interview, May 3, 1986.
   British MP's quote: Authors' confidential interview, Apr. 1986.
3. Hatfield quote: Authors' interview, May 3, 1986.
4. Ontario's size and wealth: With a population of 8.6 million in 1981 and a gross domestic product of $132 billion, Ontario was 134 per cent larger and 162 per cent more prosperous than Quebec. Source: Statistics Canada.
   From Oliver Mowat through Howard Ferguson and Mitch Hepburn to John Robarts, there had often been serious tensions between Queen's Park and Ottawa, but the latter's protectionist National Policy had always benefitted Ontario as the most industrialized of all the provinces.
5. Kirby quote: Authors' interview, Feb. 26, 1986.
6. On Davis's family background: Hoy, *Bill Davis*, pp. 11–23.
7. Lougheed quote: Authors' interview with Harold Millican, Oct. 3, 1975.
8. Davis's constitutional views: McMurtry, "Search for a Constitutional Accord," p. 40.
9. "Great man" quote: Confidential interview.
10. On Ontario's commitment to a strengthened Canadian economic union: Hudon, "Quebec, the Economy and the Constitution," p. 141; Sheppard and Valpy, *National Deal*, p. 106.
    On Davis's problem with bilingualism: Authors' interview with Roy McMurtry, July 13, 1990.
11. On the impact of Trudeau on Davis: Authors' interview with Roy McMurtry, Apr. 25, 1986.
12. Chrétien quote: Authors' interview with Roy McMurtry, Apr. 25, 1986.
13. Claude Charron on political suicide: *The Champions, Part III:*

The Final Battle [film], directed by Donald Brittain (Montreal: National Film Board, 1986).

On Claude Morin's strategy for post-referendum recovery: Sheppard and Valpy, *National Deal*, p. 33; Morin, *Lendemains piégés*, chs. 1–10.

On the possibility of a Parti Québécois–Liberal Party common front: Léon Dion, "Faute de consensus, le Québec ne sera pas entendu: le rendez-vous constitutionnel de septembre," *Le Devoir* (June 30, 1980), p. 13.

14. Charron, *Désobéir!*, p. 46.

On Saskatchewan factum: Romanow, Whyte, and Leeson, *Canada . . . Notwithstanding*, p. 179.

On Blakeney's views: Authors' interview with Allan Blakeney, June 5, 1986.

15. Charron, *Désobéir!*, p. 46.

16. On the neo-federalist response to Trudeau: Léon Dion, "Pour sortir de l'impasse constitutionnelle," *Le Devoir* (Sept. 24, 1980), p. 1; Michel Roy, "Pourquoi pas des élections, M. Trudeau?" *Le Devoir* (Oct. 16, 1980), p. 14.

17. On Ryan's fall from grace as the defender of Quebec against Ottawa: Michel Roy, "L'unanimité nécessaire," *Le Devoir* (Nov. 10, 1980), p. 6, and "Un compromis acceptable," *Le Devoir* (Nov. 15, 1980), p. 18, fustigated Ryan. Ten days later Léon Dion lamented that Ryan was so hungry for power that he would support the federal position, which had just undermined his own: "Une triste journée pour le Québec et le Canada," *Le Devoir* (Nov. 25, 1980).

On the 1981 Quebec election and Claude Ryan's self-immolation: Bergeron, *Notre miroir*, p. 261. The Parti Québécois won its highest share of the popular vote, 49 per cent, and 80 of the National Assembly's 112 seats.

18. Quebec reactions to Lévesque's concessions to the Gang of Eight: Jean-Pierre Proulx, "Les virages du PQ," *Le Devoir* (June 15, 1981), p. 12; Louis O'Neill, a Péquiste MNA, "Les abracadabras de l'étapisme et l'avenir du pays," *Le Devoir* (July 10, 1981), p. 7; and Jean-Louis Roy, "Un risque historique," *Le Devoir* (Aug. 22, 1981), p. 10.

19. On Trudeau's basic strategy: Quote from transcript of an

interview with Jack Webster, on CHAN-TV, Vancouver, Nov. 24, 1981, p. 8.

Exchange between Trudeau and Lévesque: Authors' interview with Michael Kirby, Feb. 26, 1986; and G. Fraser, *PQ*, p. 295.

20. Daniel Latouche on the anglophone premiers: *The Champions, Part III*.

Lévesque quote: Authors' interview, Dec. 12, 1986.

21. Lévesque's statement about Trudeau: Authors' interview with René Lévesque, Oct. 21, 1981.

22. Remillard, *Le rapatriement*, p. 158.

23. Trudeau quote: *The Champions, Part III*.

24. Lévesque quote: Authors' interview, Dec. 12, 1986.

25. Names of ministers and aides: Sheppard and Valpy, *National Dream*, p. 292.

Trudeau quote: Conversation with the authors, Dec. 11, 1986.

26. Lord Carrington's report: Authors' interview with Mark MacGuigan, July 10, 1990.

27. Trudeau quote: Conversation with the authors, Dec. 11, 1986.

28. Trudeau quote: Conversation with the authors, June 6, 1985.

29. "On voyait bien que ça passait de quoi, mais ça ne servait à rien de lui en parler," said one top Québécois functionary, expressing his fellow bureaucrats' views that night. Confidential interview.

30. Sterling Lyon, who was back in Manitoba, fruitlessly campaigning to maintain his majority, had been reached by Peter Lougheed that morning and persuaded to sign on lest he be the sole anglophone dissident in a "gang of two" with Lévesque.

The final document that became the Constitution Act, 1982, included further equality rights for women and treaty rights for native people, offered fiscal compensation if Quebec opted out of amendments in the fields of culture and education, and made the application to Quebec of some of the charter's minority-language education rights subject to endorsement by the Assemblée nationale.

31. Two other premiers, Paul Sauvé (1959–60) and Antonio Barrette (1960), held office too briefly to become significant players in the Quebec–Ottawa constitutional games.
    Lévesque–Johnson exchange: Authors' interview with Pierre-Marc Johnson, Mar. 18, 1986.

32. Bombardier quote: Authors' interview, June 2, 1985.

BIBLIOGRAPHY

Adelman, Howard, "Clark and the Canadian Embassy in Israel," *Middle East Focus* 2, no. 6 (Mar. 1980), pp. 6–18.

Archibald, Clinton, "Corporatist Tendencies in Quebec," in Alain G. Gagnon, ed., *Quebec: State and Society* (Toronto: Methuen, 1984), pp. 353–64.

Arnopoulos, Sheila McLeod, and Dominique Clift, *The English Fact in Quebec* (Montreal: McGill-Queen's University Press, 1980).

Axworthy, Thomas S., "Of Secretaries to Princes," *Canadian Public Administration* 31, no. 2 (Summer 1988), pp. 247–64.

Axworthy, Thomas S., "Renewal of the Liberal Party: Suggestions for a Program," issued by the Office of the Leader of the Opposition, Ottawa, Nov. 12, 1979.

Axworthy, Thomas S., and Pierre Elliott Trudeau, *Towards a Just Society: The Trudeau Years* (Markham, Ont.: Viking, 1990).

Bakvis, H., and W.A. Chandler, eds., *Federalism and the Role of the State* (Toronto: University of Toronto Press, 1987).

Banting, Keith, ed., *State and Society: Canada in Comparative Perspective* (Toronto: University of Toronto Press, 1986).

Batten, Jack, *Robinette: The Dean of Canadian Lawyers* (Toronto: Macmillan of Canada, 1984).

Becker, Ernest, *The Denial of Death* (New York: Free Press, 1973).

Bélanger, André-J., *Ruptures et constantes: quatre idéologies du Québec en éclatement: La Relève, la JEC, Cité libre, Parti pris* (Montreal: Hurtubise HMH, 1977).

Bergeron, Gérard, *Notre miroir à deux faces* (Montreal: Québec/ Amérique, 1985).

Bergeron, Gérard, and Réjean Pelletier, eds., *L'État du Québec en devenir* (Montreal: Boréal Express, 1980).

Berkowitz, S.D., "Forms of State Economy and the Development of Western Canada," *Canadian Journal of Sociology* 4, no. 3 (Summer 1979), pp. 287–312.

Bernier, Gérard, and Robert Boily with Daniel Salée, *Le Québec en chiffres de 1850 à nos jours* (Montreal: La Grétsé, 1986).

Black, Conrad, *Duplessis* (Toronto: McClelland and Stewart, 1977).

Boivin, Jean, "Labour Relations in Quebec," in John Anderson and Morley Gunderson, eds., *Union-Management Relations in Canada* (Don Mills, Ont.: Addison-Wesley, 1982), pp. 422–454.

Bombardier, Denise, *L'enfance à l'eau bénite* (Paris: Éditions du Seuil, 1985).

Boschette, Anna, *Sartre and Les Temps Modernes* (Evanston, Ill.: Northwestern University Press, 1988).

Bourassa, André G., *Surrealism and Quebec Literature: History of a Cultural Revolution* (Toronto: University of Toronto Press, 1984).

Bourassa, André-G., and Gilles Lapointe, *Refus global et ses environs* (Montreal: L'Hexagone, 1988).

Bourgault, Jacques, and Stéphane Dion, "Governments Come and Go, But What of Senior Civil Servants? Canadian Deputy Ministers and Transitions in Power (1967–1987)." Paper presented to the Canadian Political Science Association, June 1988.

Breslin, Catherine, "The Other Trudeaus," *Chatelaine* (Sept. 1969), pp. 32–33, 108–111; (October 1969), pp. 42, 78–87.

Breton, Albert, "The Economics of Nationalism," *Journal of Political Economy* 72, no. 4 (Aug. 1964), pp. 376–86.

Breton, Raymond, "The Production and Allocation of Symbolic Resources: An Analysis of the Linguistic and Ethnocultural Fields in Canada," *Canadian Review of Sociology and Anthropology* 21, no. 2 (May 1984), pp. 123–44.

Breton, Raymond, and Albert Breton, "Le séparatisme ou le respect du statu quo," *Cité libre* 46 (Apr. 1962), pp. 17–28.

Brimelow, Peter, *The Patriot Game: National Dreams and Political Realities* (Toronto: Key Porter, 1986).

Brodie, Janine, *The Political Economy of Canadian Regionalism* (Toronto: Harcourt, Brace, Jovanovich, 1990).

Brown, Craig, "The Nationalism of the National Policy," in Peter Russell, ed., *Nationalism in Canada* (Toronto: McGraw-Hill, 1966), pp. 155–63.

Brunelle, Dorval, *Les trois colombes: Essai* (Montreal: VLB, 1985).

Cahill, Jack, *John Turner: The Long Run* (Toronto: McClelland and Stewart, 1984).

Cairns, Alan, *From Interstate to Intrastate Federalism* (Kingston, Ont.: Institute of Intergovernmental Relations, Queen's University, 1979).

Cairns, Alan, "The Governments and Societies of Canadian Federalism," *Canadian Journal of Political Science* 10, no. 4 (December 1977), pp. 695–726.

Cairns, Alan, "The Other Crisis of Canadian Federalism," *Canadian Public Administration* 22 (Summer 1979), pp. 175–95.

Cairns, Alan, "Recent Federalist Constitutional Proposals: A Review Essay," *Canadian Public Policy* no. 5 (Summer 1979), pp. 348–65.

Cairns, Alan, and Cynthia Williams, eds., *Constitutionalism, Citizenship and Society in Canada* (Toronto: University of Toronto Press, 1985).

Callwood, June, "Margaret's First Hurrah," *Maclean's* (Aug. 1974), pp. 4, 6–7.

Cameron, David, *Regionalism and Supranationalism* (Montreal: Institute for Research on Public Policy, 1981).

Cameron, Stevie, "Maggie: Happy at Last," *Chatelaine* (June 1985), pp. 56–57, 98, 106–110.

Cameron, Stevie, *Ottawa Inside Out* (Toronto: Key Porter, 1989).

Camp, Dalton, *Points of Departure* (Toronto: Deneau and Greenberg, 1979).

Canada, Department of External Affairs, *Foreign Policy for Canadians* (Ottawa: Queen's Printer, 1970).

Canada, Task Force on National Unity, *A Future Together* (Hull, Que.: Supply and Services, 1979).

Canadian Annual Review of Politics and Public Affairs, John Saywell, ed. (1972–78), R.B. Byers, ed. (1978–86) (Toronto: University of Toronto Press, annual).

Carrier, André, "L'idéologie politique de la revue *Cité libre*," *Canadian Journal of Political Science* 1, no. 4 (Dec. 1968), pp. 414–28.

Carty, R. Kenneth, and W. Peter Ward, eds., *Entering the Eighties: Canada in Crisis* (Toronto: Oxford University Press, 1980).

Casgrain, Thérèse F., *A Woman in a Man's World*, translated by Joyce Marshall (Toronto: McClelland and Stewart, 1972).

Chandler, Marsha A., "State Enterprise and Partisanship in Provincial Politics," in K.J. Rea and Nelson Wiseman, eds., *Government and Enterprise in Canada* (Toronto: Methuen, 1985), pp. 266–80.

Chandler, Marsha A., and William M. Chandler, *Public Policy and Provincial Politics* (Toronto: McGraw-Hill, 1979).

Charney, Ann, "Growing Up Private," *Maclean's* (Feb. 1972), p. 26.

Charron, Claude, *Désobéir!* (Montreal: VLB, 1983).

Chrétien, Jean, *Straight from the Heart* (Toronto: Key Porter, 1985).

Clarkson, Stephen, "The Defeat of the Government, the Decline of the Liberal Party, and the (Temporary) Fall of Pierre Trudeau," in Howard R. Penniman, ed., *Canada at the Polls, 1979 and 1980: A Study of the General Elections* (Washington, D.C.: American Enterprise Institute, 1981), pp. 152–89.

Clarkson, Stephen, *An Independent Foreign Policy for Canada?* (Toronto: McClelland and Stewart, 1968).

Clarkson, Stephen, "Pierre Trudeau and the Liberal Party: the Jockey and the Horse," in Howard R. Penniman, ed., *Canada at the Polls: The General Election of 1974* (Washington, D.C.: American Enterprise Institute, 1975), pp. 57–89.

Cohen, Lenard, Patrick Smith, and Paul Warwick, *The Vision and the Game: Making the Canadian Constitution* (Calgary: Detselig, 1987).

Coleman, William D., "The Class Bases of Language Policy in Quebec, 1949–1983," in Alain Gagnon, ed., *Quebec: State and Society* (Toronto: Methuen, 1984), pp. 388–409.

Coleman, William D., *The Independence Movement in Quebec, 1945-1980* (Toronto: University of Toronto Press, 1984).

"The Constitution: Day of Decision," *Globe and Mail* (Sept. 29, 1981), special section, pp. D1–6.

Cook, Ramsay, *The Maple Leaf Forever* (Toronto: Macmillan of Canada, 1966).

Copps, Sheila, *Nobody's Baby* (Toronto: Deneau, 1986).

Courchene, Thomas, *Ottawa and the Provinces: The Distribution of Money and Power* (Toronto: Ontario Eonomic Council, 1985).

Courtney, John C., "Campaign Strategy and Electoral Victory: The Progressive Conservatives and the 1979 Election," in Howard R. Penniman, ed., *Canada at the Polls, 1979 and 1980: A Study of the General Elections* (Washington, D.C.: American Enterprise Institute, 1981), pp. 121–51.

Craven, Paul, and Tom Traves, "The Class Politics of the National Policy, 1872–1933," *Journal of Canadian Studies* 14, no. 3 (Autumn 1979), pp. 14–38.

Dales, J.H., *The Protective Tariff in Canada's Development* (Toronto: University of Toronto Press, 1966).

Davey, Keith, *The Rainmaker: A Passion for Politics* (Toronto: Stoddart, 1986).

De Gaulle, Charles, *Le fil de l'épée* (Paris: Berger-Leurault, 1944).

Desbarats, Peter, *René: A Canadian in Search of a Country* (Toronto: McClelland and Stewart, 1976).

Djwa, Sandra, *The Politics of the Imagination: A Life of F.R. Scott* (Toronto: McClelland and Stewart, 1986).

Doern, Bruce, and Richard Phidd, *Canadian Public Policy: Ideas, Structure, Process* (Toronto: Methuen, 1983).

Doern, Bruce, and Glen Toner, *The Politics of Energy: The Development and Implementation of the NEP* (Toronto: Methuen, 1985).

Donner, Arthur W., *Financing the Future: Canada's Capital Markets in the Eighties* (Ottawa: Canadian Institute for Economic Policy, 1982).

Dufour, Christian, *Le défi québécois* (Montreal: Hexagone, 1989).

Dupont, Pierre, *How Lévesque Won: The Story of the PQ's Stunning Election Victory* (Toronto: Lorimer, 1977).

Dupré, Stefan, "Reflections on the Workability of Executive Federalism," in Richard Simeon, ed., *Intergovernmental Relations* (Toronto: University of Toronto Press, 1985), pp. 1–32.

Eayrs, James, *Indochina: Roots of Complicity* (Toronto: University of Toronto Press, 1983). *In Defence of Canada*, vol. 5.

Elkins, David, and Richard Simeon, eds., *Small Worlds: Provinces and Parties in Canadian Political Life* (Toronto: Methuen, 1980).

English, John, "The 'French Lieutenant' in Ottawa," in R. Kenneth Carty and W. Peter Ward, eds., *National Politics and Community in Canada* (Vancouver: University of British Columbia Press, 1986), pp. 184–200.

Erikson, Erik H., *Identity, Youth and Crisis* (New York: Norton, 1968).

Finkel, Alvin, *The Social Credit Phenomenon in Alberta* (Toronto: University of Toronto Press, 1989).

Fotheringham, Allan, *Malice in Blunderland* (Toronto: Key Porter, 1982).

Fowke, V.C., *The National Policy and the Wheat Economy* (Toronto: University of Toronto Press, 1957).

Fraser, Graham, *PQ: René Lévesque and the Parti Québécois in Power* (Toronto: Macmillan of Canada, 1984).

Fraser, Sylvia, "The Private Trudeau," *Star Weekly* (June 29, 1968), pp. 2–7.

Fremon, Celeste, "Margaret Trudeau," *Playgirl* (Sept. 1979), pp. 34–37, 88–91, 104, 115–20, 124.

Fussell, Paul, *Wartime: Understanding and Behavior in the Second World War* (New York: Oxford University Press, 1989).

Gagnon, Alain, "The Evolution of Political Forces in Quebec: The Struggle for Supremacy," in Alain Gagnon, ed., *Quebec: State and Society* (Toronto: Methuen, 1984), pp. 262–84.

Gagnon, Lysiane, *Chroniques politiques* (Montreal: Boréal Express, 1985).

Gaudet, Gérard, "Forces Underlying the Evolution of Natural Resource Policies in Quebec," in Carl E. Beigie and Alfred O. Hero, Jr., eds., *Natural Resources in U.S.-Canadian Relations*, vol. 1 (Boulder, Col.: Westview Press, 1980), pp. 247–65.

Gérin-Lajoie, Paul, *Constitutional Amendment in Canada* (Toronto: University of Toronto Press, 1950).

The Goldfarb Report: An Annual Canadian Marketplace Analysis (Toronto: Goldfarb Consultants, annual).

Goodman, Eddie, *Life of the Party* (Toronto: Key Porter, 1988).

Gordon, Walter, *A Political Memoir* (Toronto: McClelland and Stewart, 1977).

Gossage, Patrick, *Close to the Charisma: My Years Between the Press and Pierre Elliott Trudeau* (Toronto: McClelland and Stewart, 1986).

Graham, Ron, *One-Eyed Kings: Promise and Illusion in Canadian Politics* (Toronto: Collins, 1986).

Granatstein, J.L., *Canada 1957-1967: The Years of Uncertainty and Innovation* (Toronto: McClelland and Stewart, 1986).

Granatstein, J.L., *The Ottawa Men* (Toronto: Oxford University Press, 1982).

Great Britain, House of Commons, Foreign Affairs Committee, *British North America Acts: The Role of Parliament*, vol. I (London: Her Majesty's Stationery Office, 1981).

Greene, Ian, *The Charter of Rights* (Toronto: Lorimer, 1989).

Grosser, Alfred, *Affaires extérieures: La politique de la France 1944-1984* (Paris: Flammarion, 1984).

Grube, John, *Bâtisseur de pays: Étude sur le nationalisme au Québec* (Montreal: Éditions de l'Action Nationale, 1981).

Guindon, Hubert, *Quebec Society: Tradition, Modernity, and Nationhood* (Toronto: University of Toronto Press, 1988).

Gwyn, Richard, *The Northern Magus* (Toronto: McClelland and Stewart, 1980).

Gwyn, Sandra, "Inside the Tory Takeover," *Saturday Night* (Sept. 1979), pp. 17–24.

Gzowski, Peter, "Portrait of an Intellectual in Action," *Maclean's* (Feb. 24, 1962), pp. 23, 29–30.

Haggart, Ron, and Aubrey Golden, *Rumours of War* (Toronto: New Press, 1971).

Harrison, W.E.C., *Canada in World Affairs 1949 to 1950* (Toronto: Oxford University Press, 1957).

Hay, John, "Final Justice, Seen to be Done," *Maclean's* (May 11, 1981), pp. 21–22.

Hellman, John, *Emmanuel Mounier and the New Catholic Left: 1930-1950* (Toronto: University of Toronto Press, 1981).

Hockin, Thomas, *Apex of Power* (Scarborough, Ont.: Prentice-Hall, 1971).

Houle, François, "Economic Strategy and the Restructuring of the Fordist Wage-Labour Relationship in Canada," *Studies in Political Economy* no. 11 (Summer 1983), pp. 127–48.

Hoy, Claire, *Bill Davis* (Toronto: Methuen, 1985).

Hudon, Raymond, "Quebec, the Economy and the Constitution," in Keith Banting and Richard Simeon, eds., *And No One Cheered* (Toronto: Methuen, 1983), pp. 133–53.

Hustak, Allan, *Peter Lougheed* (Toronto: McClelland and Stewart, 1979).

Iglauer, Edith, "Prime Minister/Premier Ministre," *The New Yorker* (July 5, 1969), pp. 36–60.

Ignatieff, Michael, "The Longest Shadow," *Saturday Night* (Oct. 1987), pp. 25–32.

Ilkenberry, G. John, "The Irony of State Strength: Comparative Responses to the Oil Shocks in the 1970s," *International Organization* 40, no. 1 (Winter 1986), pp. 105–37.

Jenkins, Barbara, "Reexamining the 'Obsolescing Bargain': A Study of Canada's National Energy Program," *International Organization* 40, no. 1 (Winter 1986), pp. 139–65.

Johnson, Daniel, *Égalité ou indépendance* (Montreal: Éditions de l'Homme, 1965).

Johnston, Donald, *Up the Hill* (Montreal: Optimum, 1986).

Johnston, Donald, ed., *With a Bang, Not a Whimper: Pierre Trudeau Speaks Out* (Toronto: Stoddart, 1988).

Jung, Carl, *The Essential Jung*, selected and introduced by Anthony Storr (Princeton, N.J.: Princeton University Press, 1983).

Jung, Carl, and Marie-Louise von Franz, *Man and His Symbols* (New York: Doubleday, 1964).

Keating, Tom, and Don Munton, eds., *The Provinces and Canadian Foreign Policy* (Toronto: Canadian Institute of International Affairs, 1985).

Kent, Tom, *A Public Purpose* (Kingston and Montreal: McGill-Queen's University Press, 1988).

Kirby memorandum: *See* "Report to Cabinet on Constitutional Discussions."

Koch, Eric, *Inside This Hour Has Seven Days* (Toronto: Prentice-Hall, 1986).

Kome, Penney, "Anatomy of a Lobby," *Saturday Night* (Jan. 1983), pp. 9–11.

Krause, Robert, and Lawrence Leduc, "Voting Behaviour and Electoral Strategies in the Progressive Conservative Leadership Convention of 1976," *Canadian Journal of Political Science* 12, no. 1 (March 1979), pp. 97–135.

Kübler-Ross, Elisabeth, *On Death and Dying* (New York: Macmillan, 1969).

La Forest, Gerard V., *Natural Resources and Public Property Under the Canadian Constitution* (Toronto: University of Toronto Press, 1977).

Latouche, Daniel, *Canada and Quebec, Past and Future: An Essay* (Toronto: University of Toronto Press, 1986).

Laurendeau, André, *Journal* (Montreal: VLB, 1990).

Laxer, Gordon, "The Political Economy of Aborted Development: The Canadian Case," in Robert Brym, ed., *The Structure of the Canadian Capitalist Class* (Toronto: Garamond, 1985), pp. 67–102.

Laxer, James, *Oil and Gas* (Toronto: Lorimer, 1983).

Laycock, David, *Populism and Democratic Thought in the Canadian Prairies, 1910-1945* (Toronto: University of Toronto Press, 1990).

Le Moyne, Jean, *Convergence: Essays from Quebec* (Toronto: Ryerson, 1966).

Letourneau, Reginald S., *Inflation: The Canadian Experience* (Ottawa: The Conference Board, 1980).

Levant, Victor, *Quiet Complicity: Canadian Involvement in the Vietnam War* (Toronto: Between the Lines, 1986).

Lévesque, René, *Memoirs* (Toronto: McClelland and Stewart, 1986).

Lévesque, René, *An Option for Quebec* (Toronto: McClelland and Stewart, 1968).

Levinson, Daniel J., et al., *The Seasons of a Man's Life* (New York: Ballantine Books, 1978).

Levitt, Joseph, *Henri Bourassa on Imperialism and Bi-Culturalism, 1900-1918* (Toronto: Copp Clark, 1970).

Lipset, Seymour, "Democracy in Alberta," in John Courtney, ed., *Voting in Canada* (Toronto: Prentice-Hall, 1967), pp. 182–85.

Long, J.A., and P.Q. Quo, "Alberta: One Party Dominance," in Martin Robin, ed., *Canadian Provincial Politics: The Party System of the Ten Provinces* (Scarborough, Ont.: Prentice-Hall, 1972), pp. 1–26.

McCall-Newman, Christina, *Grits: An Intimate Portrait of the Liberal Party* (Toronto: Macmillan of Canada, 1982).

MacDonald, L. Ian, *From Bourassa to Bourassa: A Pivotal Decade in Canadian History* (Montreal: Harvest House, 1984).

MacDonald, L. Ian, *Mulroney: The Making of the Prime Minister* (Toronto: McClelland and Stewart, 1984).

MacGregor, Roy, "Maggie, the 'T' That Dares to be Known by Taste Alone," *Today* (Apr. 10, 1982), p. 7.

Machiavelli, Niccolo, *The Prince*, translated by Leo Paul S. de Alvarez (Irving, Tex.: University of Dallas Press, 1980).

McKenzie, R.T., *British Political Parties: The Distribution of Power Within the Conservative and Labour Parties* (London: Heinemann, 1955).

MacLaren, Roy, *Honourable Mentions: The Uncommon Diary of an M.P.* (Toronto: Deneau, 1986).

McLuhan, Marshall, "The Story of the Man in the Mask," review of Pierre Trudeau's *Federalism and the French Canadians* in *New York Times Book Review* (Nov. 17, 1968), pp. 36–38.

MacMillan, C. Michael, "Language Rights, Human Rights and Bill 101," *Queen's Quarterly* 90, no. 2 (Summer 1983), pp. 343–61.

McMurtry, Roy, "The Search for a Constitutional Accord – A Personal Memoir," *Queen's Law Journal* 8, nos. 1/2 (Fall 1982/ Spring 1983), pp. 28–73.

Macpherson, C.B., *Democracy in Alberta: Social Credit and the Party System* (Toronto: University of Toronto Press, 1962).

McRoberts, Kenneth, *Quebec: Social Change and Political Crisis*, 3rd ed. (Toronto: McClelland and Stewart, 1988).

McRoberts, Kenneth, "Unilateralism, Bilateralism and Multilateralism: Approaches to Canadian Federalism," in Richard Simeon, ed., *Intergovernmental Relations* (Toronto: University of Toronto Press, 1985), pp. 71–129.

McWhinney, Edward, *Canada and the Constitution, 1979-1982: Patriation and the Charter of Rights* (Toronto: University of Toronto Press, 1982).

McWhinney, Edward, *Quebec and the Constitution: 1960-1978* (Toronto: Lorimer, 1978).

Martin, Patrick, Allan Gregg, and George Perlin, *Contenders: The Tory Quest for Power* (Scarborough, Ont.: Prentice-Hall, 1983).

Martin, Paul, *A Very Public Life*, vol. II (Toronto: Deneau, 1985).

Maslove, Allan M., Michael J. Prince, and G. Bruce Doern, *Federal and Provincial Budgeting* (Toronto: University of Toronto Press, 1986).

Mathie, William, "Political Community and the Canadian Experience: Reflections on Nationalism, Federalism, and Unity," *Canadian Journal of Political Science* 12, no. 1 (Mar. 1979), pp. 3–20.

Meekison, J.P., "The Amending Formula," *Queen's Law Journal* 8, nos. 1–2 (Fall 1982/Spring 1983), pp. 99–122.

Meekison, J.P., R.J. Romanow, and W.D. Moull, *Origins and Meaning of Section 92A: The 1982 Constitutional Amendment on Resources* (Montreal: Institute for Research on Public Policy, 1985).

Meisel, John, "Howe, Hubris, and '72: An Essay on Political Elitism," in his *Working Papers on Canadian Politics* (Montreal: McGill-Queen's University Press, 1973).

Meisel, John, "The Larger Context: The Period Preceding the 1979 Election," in Howard R. Penniman, ed., *Canada at the Polls, 1979 and 1980: A Study of the General Elections* (Washington, D.C.: American Enterprise Institute, 1981), pp. 24–54.

Michels, Robert, *Political Parties: A Sociological Study of the Oligarchical Tendencies of Modern Democracy*, reprint (New York: Dover, 1959).

Milne, David, *The New Canadian Constitution* (Toronto: Lorimer, 1982).

Milne, David, *Tug of War: Ottawa and the Provinces Under Trudeau and Mulroney* (Toronto: Lorimer, 1986).

Milner, Henry, "Quebec Educational Reform and the Protestant School Establishment," in Alain Gagnon, ed., *Quebec: State and Society* (Toronto: Methuen, 1984), pp. 410–25.

Minifie, James, *Peacemaker or Powder-Monkey: Canada's Role in a Revolutionary World* (Toronto: McClelland and Stewart, 1960).

Monière, Denis, *Le développement des idéologies au Québec des origines à nos jours* (Montreal: Québec/Amérique, 1977).

Morin, Claude, *L'art de l'impossible: La diplomatie québécoise depuis 1960* (Montreal: Boréal, 1987).

Morin, Claude, *Lendemains piégés: Du référendum à la "nuit des longs couteaux"* (Montreal: Boréal, 1988).

Morin, Claude, *Quebec Versus Ottawa: The Struggle for Self-Government, 1960-1972* (Toronto: University of Toronto Press, 1976).

Mounier, Emmanuel, "Christian Faith and Civilization," *Cross Currents* 1, nos. 1–4 (1950–51), pp. 3–23. Translated by Erwin W. Geissman.

Murphy, Rae, Robert Chodos, and Nick Auf der Maur, *Brian Mulroney: The Boy from Baie-Comeau* (Toronto: Lorimer, 1984).

Nardocchio, Elaine F., *Theatre and Politics in Modern Quebec* (Edmonton: University of Alberta Press, 1986).

Naylor, R.T., *The History of Canadian Business, 1867-1914* (Toronto: Lorimer, 1975).

Newman, Christina, "The New Power in the New West," *Saturday Night* (Sept. 1976), pp. 17–25.

Newman, Christina, "Politicizing Pierre," *Maclean's* (Oct. 1974), pp. 36–42.

Newman, Peter, "Reflections on a Fall from Grace," *Maclean's* (Jan. 1973), pp. 21–23, 64–67.

Norrie, Kenneth, Richard Simeon, and Mark Krasnick, *Federalism and the Economic Union in Canada* (Toronto: University of Toronto Press, 1986).

Nurgitz, Nathan, and Hugh Segal, *No Small Measure: The Progressive Conservatives and the Constitution* (Ottawa: Deneau, 1983).

O'Hara, Jane, "Bedtime Story," *Maclean's* (Dec. 3, 1979), pp. 26–28.

Parti libéral du Québec, Commission constitutionnelle, *Une nouvelle fédération canadienne* (Montreal: Parti libéral du Québec, 1980). [Beige Paper.]

Paterson, Sheena, and Mary C. McEwan, "Margaret Trudeau's Struggle for Identity," *Chatelaine* (Aug. 1977), p. 91.

Payette, Lise, *Le pouvoir? Connais pas!* (Montreal: Québec/Amérique, 1982).

Peacock, Donald, *Journey to Power* (Toronto: Ryerson, 1968).

Pearson, Lester B., *Federalism for the Future: A Statement of Policy by the Government of Canada* (Ottawa: Queen's Printer, 1968).

Pearson, Lester B., *Mike: The Memoirs of Lester B. Pearson*, vol. 3 (Toronto: University of Toronto Press, 1975).

Pelletier, Gérard, *The October Crisis*, translated by Joyce Marshall (Toronto: McClelland and Stewart, 1971).

Pelletier, Gérard, *Years of Choice: 1960-1968*, translated by Alan Brown (Toronto: Methuen, 1987).

Pelletier, Gérard, *Years of Impatience: 1950-1960*, translated by Alan Brown (Toronto: Methuen, 1984).

Perlin, George C., *The Tory Syndrome: Leadership Politics in the Progressive Conservative Party* (Montreal: McGill–Queen's University Press, 1980).

Phillips, Paul, "The National Policy Revisited," *Journal of Canadian Studies* 14, no. 3 (Fall 1979), pp. 3–13.

Pickersgill, J.W., *My Years with Louis St. Laurent: A Political Memoir* (Toronto: University of Toronto Press, 1975).

Pinard, Maurice, and Richard Hamilton, "The Class Bases of the Quebec Independence Movement," *Ethnic and Racial Studies* 7, no. 1 (Jan. 1984), pp. 19–54.

Pinard, Maurice, and Richard Hamilton, "Le référendum québécois," *Policy Options/Options Politiques* 2, no. 4 (Sept.-Oct. 1981), pp. 39–44.

Porter, John, *The Vertical Mosaic* (Toronto: University of Toronto Press, 1965).

Powe, B.W., *The Solitary Outlaw* (Toronto: Lester and Orpen Dennys, 1987).

Pratt, Larry, "The State and Province-Building: Alberta's Development Strategy," in Leo Panitch, ed., *The Canadian State: Political Economy and Political Power* (Toronto: University of Toronto Press, 1977), pp. 133–62.

"President Charles de Gaulle's News Conference, Nov. 27, 1967," *Atlantic Community Quarterly* 5, no. 4 (Winter 1967–68), pp. 613–18.

Pross, Paul, *Group Politics and Public Policy* (Toronto: Oxford University Press, 1986).

Pross, Paul, and Susan McCorquodale, *Economic Resurgence and the Constitutional Agenda: The Case of the East Coast Fisheries* (Kingston, Ont.: Institute of Intergovernmental Relations, Queen's University, 1987).

Quebec, Gouvernement du Québec, *Quebec-Canada: A New Deal* (Quebec City: Éditeur officiel, 1979).

Quinn, Herbert F., *The Union Nationale: A Study in Quebec Nationalism* (Toronto: University of Toronto Press, 1963).

Radwanski, George, *Trudeau* (Toronto: Macmillan of Canada, 1977).

Rayside, David, "Federalism and the Party System: Provincial and Federal Liberals in the Province of Quebec," *Canadian Journal of Political Science* 11, no. 3 (Sept. 1978), pp. 499–528.

Remillard, Gil, *Le rapatriement de la constitution* (Montreal: Québec/Amérique, 1985). *Le fédéralisme canadien*, vol. II.

Renaud, Marc, "New Middle Class in Search of Social Hegemony," in Alain Gagnon, ed., *Quebec: State and Society* (Toronto: Methuen, 1984) pp. 150–85.

"Report to Cabinet on Constitutional Discussions, Summer 1980, and the Outlook for the First Ministers Conference and Beyond." [Kirby memorandum.] Prepared ... under the direction of FPRO and the Department of Justice. August 30, 1980. Library of Parliament, Ottawa.

Resnick, Philip, *Letters to a Québécois Friend* (Montreal: McGill-Queen's University Press, 1990).

Richards, John, and Larry Pratt, *Prairie Capitalism: Power and Influence in the New West* (Toronto: McClelland and Stewart, 1979).

Riley, Susan, *Political Wives: The Lives of the Saints* (Toronto: Deneau, 1987).

Roberts, John, *Agenda for Canada: Towards a New Liberalism* (Toronto: Lester and Orpen Dennys, 1985).

Robertson, Gordon, "Our Other National Sport," *Policy Options/ Options Politiques* 1, no. 3 (June–July, 1980), p. 8.

Romanow, Roy, John Whyte, and Howard Leeson, *Canada ... Notwithstanding: The Making of the Constitution 1976-1982* (Toronto: Carswell/Methuen, 1984).

Ross, Douglas A., *In the Interests of Peace: Canada and Vietnam* (Toronto: University of Toronto Press, 1984).

Rostand, Edmond, *Cyrano de Bergerac*, translated by Brian Hooker (New York: Bantam Books, 1950).

Rotstein, Abraham, ed. *Power Corrupted: The October Crisis and the Repression of Quebec* (Toronto: New Press, 1971).

Roy, Jean-Louis, *Le choix d'un pays: Le débat constitutionnel Québec-Canada 1960-1967* (Montreal: Leméac, 1978).

Rumilly, Robert, *Histoire d'Outremont 1885-1975* (Montreal: Leméac, 1975).

Russell, Peter, *The Judiciary in Canada: The Third Branch of Government* (Toronto: McGraw-Hill, 1987).

Russell, Peter, "The Political Purposes of the Canadian Charter of Rights and Freedoms," *Canadian Bar Review* 61, no.1 (Mar. 1983), pp. 30–54.

Russell, Peter, "The Supreme Court Decision: Bold Statescraft Based on Questionable Jurisprudence," in Peter Russell et al., *The Court and the Constitution* (Kingston, Ont.: Institute of Inter-governmental Relations, Queen's University, 1982).

Sargent, William, *Battle for the Mind* (London: Pan Books, 1970).

Saywell, John, "Introduction," in Pierre Elliott Trudeau, *Federalism and the French Canadians* (Toronto: Macmillan of Canada, 1968).

Schiffer, Irvine, *Charisma: A Psychoanalytic Look at Mass Society* (New York: Free Press, 1973).

Sennett, Richard, *Authority* (New York: Knopf, 1980).

Shaffer, Ed, *Canada's Oil and the American Empire* (Edmonton: Hurtig, 1983).

Shain, Merle, "Settling Up Sober," *Maclean's* (Feb. 1972), p. 29.

Sharp, Daryl, *The Secret Raven* (Toronto: Inner City, 1980).

Sheppard, Robert, and Michael Valpy, *The National Deal: The Fight for a Canadian Constitution* (Toronto: Fleet, 1982).

Shugarman, David P., and Reg Whitaker, eds., *Federalism and Political Community: Essays in Honour of Donald Smiley* (Peterborough, Ont.: Broadview Press, 1989).

Simeon, Richard, *Federal-Provincial Diplomacy* (Toronto: University of Toronto Press, 1972).

Simeon, Richard, "Regionalism and Canadian Political Institutions," in J. Meekison, ed., *Canadian Federalism: Myth or Reality* (Toronto: Methuen, 1977), pp. 292–304.

Simeon, Richard, ed., *Must Canada Fail?* (Montreal: McGill-Queen's University Press, 1977).

Simeon, Richard, and Ian Robinson, *State, Society, and the Development of Canadian Federalism* (Toronto: University of Toronto Press, 1990).

Simpson, Jeffrey, *Discipline of Power: The Conservative Interlude and the Liberal Restoration* (Toronto: Macmillan of Canada, 1980).

Singer, June, *Boundaries of the Soul: The Practice of Jung's Psychology* (Garden City, N.Y.: Anchor, 1972).

Smiley, Donald, *Canada in Question: Federalism in the Eighties* (Toronto: McGraw-Hill, 1980).

Smiley, Donald, *The Canadian Political Nationality* (Toronto: Methuen, 1967).

Smiley, Donald, *The Federal Condition in Canada* (Toronto: McGraw-Hill Ryerson, 1987).

Smiley, Donald, and R. Watts, *Intrastate Federalism in Canada* (Toronto: University of Toronto Press, 1985).

Smith, David, *The Regional Decline of a National Party: Liberals on the Prairies* (Toronto: University of Toronto Press, 1981).

Smith, Denis, *Bleeding Hearts, Bleeding Country* (Edmonton: Hurtig, 1971).

Smith, Denis, *Gentle Patriot* (Edmonton: Hurtig, 1973).

Snider, Norman, *The Changing of the Guard: How the Liberals Fell from Grace and the Tories Rose to Power* (Toronto: Lester and Orpen Dennys, 1985).

Speirs, Rosemary, *Out of the Blue: The Fall of the Tory Dynasty in Ontario* (Toronto: Macmillan of Canada, 1986).

Steed, Judy, *Ed Broadbent: The Pursuit of Power* (Markham, Ont.: Viking, 1988).

Stevens, Geoffrey, *Stanfield* (Toronto: McClelland and Stewart, 1973).

Stevenson, Garth, "Canadian Regionalism in Continental Perspective," *Journal of Canadian Studies* 15, no. 2 (Summer 1980), pp. 16–28.

Stevenson, Garth, *Unfulfilled Union: Canadian Federalism and National Unity*, 3rd ed. (Toronto: Gage, 1989).

Stewart, Sandy, *Here's Looking at Us: A Personal History of Television in Canada* (Toronto: CBC Enterprises, 1986).

Stewart, Walter, *Shrug: Trudeau in Power* (Toronto: New Press, 1971).

Sullivan, Martin, *Mandate '68* (Toronto: Doubleday, 1968).

Swift, Jamie, *Odd Man Out: The Life and Times of Eric Kierans* (Vancouver: Douglas & McIntyre, 1988).

Taylor, Charles, *Snow Job: Canada, the United States and Vietnam (1954 to 1973)* (Toronto: Anansi, 1974).

Thomas, L.G., *The Liberal Party in Alberta: A History of Politics in the Province of Alberta, 1905-1921* (Toronto: University of Toronto Press, 1959).

Thomson, Dale C., *Jean Lesage and the Quiet Revolution* (Toronto: Macmillan of Canada, 1984).

Thomson, Dale C., *Louis St. Laurent, Canadian* (Toronto: Macmillan of Canada, 1967).

Thomson, Dale C., *Vive le Québec libre* (Toronto: Deneau, 1988).

Toner, Glen, and François Bregha, "The Political Economy of Energy," in Michael Whittington and Glen Williams, eds., *Canadian Politics in the 1980s* (Toronto: Methuen, 1981), pp. 105–36.

Tremblay, Louis-Marie, "L'évolution du syndicalisme dans la révolution tranquille," *Relations industrielles* 22, no. 1 (Jan. 1967), pp. 86–97.

Trofimenkoff, Susan Mann, *The Dream of Nation: A Social and Intellectual History of Quebec* (Toronto: Gage, 1983).

Trudeau, Margaret, *Beyond Reason* (New York: Paddington Press, 1979).

Trudeau, Margaret, *Consequences* (Toronto: Seal Books, 1982).

Vaillant, George E., *Adaptation to Life* (Boston: Little, Brown, 1977).

Vallières, Pierre, *The Assassination of Pierre Laporte* (Toronto: Lorimer, 1977).

Vastel, Michel, *Trudeau le Québécois* (Montreal: Éditions de l'Homme, 1989).

Veilleux, Gérard, *Les Relations intergouvernementales au Canada 1867-1967* (Montreal: Presses de l'Université du Québec, 1971).

Vidal, Gore, *At Home: Essays 1982-1988* (New York: Vintage Books, 1990).

Von Franz, Marie-Louise, *Puer Aeternus*, 2nd ed. (New York: Sigo Press, 1981).

Von Riekhoff, Harald, *NATO: Issues and Prospects* (Toronto: Canadian Institute of International Affairs, 1967).

Wade, Mason, *The French Canadians, Volume Two: 1911-1967*, rev. ed. (Toronto: Macmillan of Canada, 1968).

Wearing, Joseph, *The L-Shaped Party: The Liberal Party of Canada: 1958-1980* (Toronto: McGraw-Hill, 1981).

Weber, Max, *From Max Weber: Essays in Sociology*, H.H. Gerth and

C. Wright Mills, eds. (New York: Oxford University Press, 1946).

Weber, Max, *The Sociology of Religion* (Boston: Beacon Press, 1964).

Westell, Anthony, *Paradox: Trudeau as Prime Minister* (Scarborough, Ont.: Prentice-Hall, 1972).

Whelan, Eugene, with Rick Archbold, *Whelan* (Toronto: Irwin, 1986).

Whitaker, Reginald, *The Government Party: Organizing and Financing the Liberal Party of Canada, 1930-58* (Toronto: University of Toronto Press, 1977).

Wilkinson, Bruce, "Canada's Resource Industries: A Survey," in John Whalley, ed., *Canada's Resource Industries and Water Export Policy* (Toronto: University of Toronto Press, 1986), pp. 1–159.

Wiseman, Nelson, "The Pattern of Prairie Politics," *Queen's Quarterly* 88, no. 2 (Summer 1981), pp. 298–315.

Wiseman, Sylvia, and Peter Scott, "March on Quebec," *The Nation* (Mar. 13, 1954), pp. 217–18.

Wood, David G., *The Lougheed Legacy* (Toronto: Key Porter, 1985).

Woods, Shirley E., *Her Excellency Jeanne Sauvé* (Toronto: Macmillan of Canada, 1986).

Zolf, Larry, *Dance of the Dialectic* (Toronto: James Lewis and Samuel, 1973).

Zolf, Larry, *Just Watch Me* (Toronto: Lorimer, 1984).

WORKS BY PIERRE ELLIOTT TRUDEAU

"Politique fonctionelle," *Cité libre* 1 (June 1950), pp. 20–24.

"Politique fonctionnelle – II," *Cité libre* 2 (1951), pp. 25–29.

"De libro, tributo . . . et quibusdam aliis" [About a book, taxes and certain other matters], *Cité libre* 10 (Oct. 1954), pp. 1–16. [Reprinted in *Federalism and the French Canadians* (Toronto: Macmillan of Canada, 1968), pp. 63–78.

Mémoire . . . à la Commission royale d'enquête sur les problèmes constitutionnels, 2nd ed. (Montreal: Fédération des Unions industrielles du Québec, 1955).

"Les octrois fédéraux aux universités," *Cité libre* 16 (Feb. 1957), pp. 9–31. [Translated as "Federal Grants to Universities" and reprinted in *Federalism and the French Canadians* (Toronto: Macmillan of Canada, 1968), pp. 79–102.]

"Some Obstacles to Democracy in Quebec," *Canadian Journal of Economics and Political Science* 24, no. 3 (Aug. 1958), pp. 297–311. [Reprinted in *Federalism and the French Canadians* (Toronto: Macmillan of Canada, 1968), pp. 103–23.]

"L'élection du 22 juin 1960," *Cité libre* 29 (Aug.-Sept. 1960), p. 4.

"L'aliénation nationaliste," *Cité libre* 35 (Mar. 1961), pp. 3–5.

"De l'inconvénient d'etre catholique," *Cité libre* 35 (Mar. 1961), pp. 20–21.

"Note sur le parti cléricaliste," *Cité libre* 38 (June/July 1961), p. 23.

"The Practice and Theory of Federalism," in Michael Oliver, ed., *Social Purpose for Canada* (Toronto: University of Toronto Press, 1961), pp. 371–93.

"La nouvelle trahison des clercs," *Cité libre* 46 (Apr. 1962), pp. 3–16.

"Les progrès d'illusion," *Cité libre* 47 (May 1962), pp. 1–2.

"L'homme de gauche et les élections provinciales," *Cité libre* 51 (Nov. 1962), pp. 3–5.

"Pearson ou l'abdication de l'esprit," *Cité libre* 56 (Apr. 1963), pp. 7–12.

"We Need a Bill of Rights, Not a New Version of the BNA Act," *Maclean's* (Feb. 8, 1964), p. 24.

"Les séparatistes: des contre-révolutionnaires," *Cité libre* 67 (May 1964), pp. 2–6.

[With others] "Manifeste pour une politique fonctionnelle," *Cité libre* 67 (May 1964), pp. 11–17.

[With others] "An Appeal for Realism in Politics," *The Canadian Forum* (May 1964), pp. 29–33.

[With Gérard Pelletier] "Pelletier et Trudeau s'expliquent," *Cité libre* 80 (Oct. 1965), pp. 3–5.

"Federalism, Nationalism and Reason," in P.A. Crepeau and C.B. Macpherson, eds., *The Future of Canadian Federalism* (Toronto: University of Toronto Press, 1965), pp. 16–35. [Reprinted in *Federalism and the French Canadians* (Toronto: Macmillan of Canada, 1968), pp. 182–203.]

"In Defence of Federalism," in Paul Fox, ed., *Politics: Canada* (Toronto: McGraw-Hill, 2nd ed., 1966), pp. 107–12. Translated by Fox from "Le réalisme constitutionnel," speech given by Trudeau on March 26, 1966, in Quebec City.

"A Constitutional Declaration of Rights" (speech given Sept. 4, 1967), in *Federalism and the French Canadians* (Toronto: Macmillan of Canada, 1968), pp. 52–60.

A Canadian Charter of Human Rights (Ottawa: Queen's Printer, January 1968).

"Quebec and the Constitutional Problem," in his *Federalism and the French Canadians* (Toronto: Macmillan of Canada, 1968), pp. 3–51.

Approaches to Politics, translated by I.M. Owen (Toronto: Oxford University Press, 1970). Prefatory note by Jacques Hébert.

Conversations with Canadians (Toronto: University of Toronto Press, 1972).

[As editor] *The Asbestos Strike*, translated by James Boake (Toronto: James, Lewis and Samuel, 1974).

[With Thomas S. Axworthy] *Towards a Just Society: The Trudeau Years* (Markham, Ont.: Viking, 1990).

Speeches

These transcripts are in the Library of Parliament.

"Translation of the Transcript of an Address to the Chamber of Commerce in Montreal on May 2, 1980."

"Prime Minister's Remarks at Maple Leaf Gardens Rally in Toronto," May 9, 1979.

"Prime Minister's Remarks at Sheraton Mount-Royal Hotel in Montreal, P.Q." May 10, 1979.

"Prime Minister's Remarks at Confederation Luncheon, Toronto, Ontario," May 11, 1979.

"Transcript of a Speech Given by the Right Honourable Pierre Elliott Trudeau at the Paul Sauvé Arena in Montreal on May 14, 1980."

"Statement by the Prime Minister in Response to the Quebec Referendum Vote," May 20, 1980.

LIST OF INTERVIEWS

In the course of our research, several hundred people talked to us specifically in connection with the events described in the two volumes of *Trudeau and Our Times*, many of them more than once and some as often as a dozen times. These books also draw on other interviews conducted during long careers spent writing about Canadian politics, in particular work done for Christina McCall's *Grits: An Intimate Portrait of the Liberal Party* and Stephen Clarkson's *Canada and the Reagan Challenge*. In addition, we benefitted from scores of seminars or lectures given by colleagues and dozens of speeches made by analysts and protagonists of the events under consideration here.

The book's chief protagonist, Pierre Elliott Trudeau, made a considered decision on leaving public office not to be interviewed formally about his prime ministership. He was kind enough, however, to discuss some of our ideas in a number of conversations, and in deference to his wishes, these are sparingly quoted in the text and cited in the notes. Half a dozen on-the-record interviews he granted the authors as individuals during his incumbency were also vital to our understanding of the Trudeau era.

A few interviewees, mostly public servants, requested anonymity and their names are not mentioned here or cited in the notes. What follows is a list, organized by region or country, of those who were willing to be named. We are profoundly grateful to all of them for their help.

Atlantic Canada

Cyril J. Abery
Hermann Bakvis
Leo Barry
Coline Campbell
Richard Cashin
Jim Cowan
Leslie Dean
Brian Flemming
Dale Godsoe
Gerry Godsoe
Richard Hatfield
Tom Kent
Eric Kierans
Susan McCorquodale
Alexa McDonagh
D.A. (Sandy) MacLean
David Mann
David Milne
Jim Morgan
William Morrow
Paul Pross
William Rompkey
Gordon Slade
Barry Toole
Clyde Wells
William Wells
Rick Williams

Ontario

Michael J. Adams

Alan Alexandroff
Rick Alway
Doris Anderson
Ronald Anderson
Gordon Ashworth
Paul Audley
Carl Beigie
Joel Bell
Claude Bissell
Conrad Black
Vince Borg
Sandford Borins
Albert Breton
Raymond Breton
Libby Burnham
Rod Byers
Milli Caccia
David Cameron
Tony Clement
Geoff Conway
Ramsay Cook
James Coombs
Jim Coutts
David Crane
John Crossley
Joe Cruden
Barney Danson
Donna Dasko
Dorothy Davey
William Davis
Wendy Dobson
Gordon Dryden
J. Stefan Dupré
Mary Eberts

Hershell Ezrin
Susan Fish
Douglas Fisher
Gordon Floyd
Jim Foulds
Ursula Franklin
Royce Frith
Northrop Frye
Alastair Gillespie
John Godfrey
Martin Goldfarb
Myron Gordon
Walter Gordon
Patrick Gossage
Charlotte Gray
Nigel Gray
Allan Gregg
Krystyne Griffin
John Grube
Anthony Hampson
John Harbron
Kenneth Hare
Jack Hart
Doug Hartle
Freda Hawkins
Jack Heath
Peter Herrndorf
David Hilton
John Holmes
Beland Honderich
Chaviva Hosek
Alison Ignatieff
George Ignatieff
Hal Jackman
Al Johnson
Patrick Johnston
Richard Johnston
Bruce Kidd

Tom Kierans
Brian King
Michael Kirby
John Kirton
Robert Laxer
Fred Lazar
Larry Leduc
Douglas LePan
Stephen Lewis
Seymour Martin Lipset
James Lorimer
Theodore Lowi
Donald C. MacDonald
Donald S. Macdonald
William Macdonald
Kenneth McRoberts
Michael Mandel
Patrick Martin
John Meisel
Stanley Meisler
Ross Milne
Edward Neufeld
Peter Nicholson
Martin O'Connell
Bernard Ostry
Sylvia Ostry
Frank Peers
Norman Penner
Michael Perley
George Perlin
Heather Peterson
James Peterson
Bob Rae
James Reed
Peter Regenstreif
Patrick Reid
Grant Reuber
John Robarts

John Roberts
John J. Robinette
Kathryn Robinson
Malka Rosenberg
Abraham Rotstein
Diana Royce
Janice Rubin
Peter Russell
Gordon Ryan
Ed Safarian
Rick Salutin
Stephen Schrybman
Ian Scott
Robin Sears
Gordon Sedgwick
Hugh Segal
John Sewell
John Shepherd
Robert Sheppard
David Shugarman
Richard Simeon
Sonja Sinclair
Donald Smiley
Mark Starowicz
Geoffrey Stevens
E.E. Stewart
Norman Stewart
Barbara Sullivan
Ethel Teitelbaum
Ann Tomlinson
John Turner
Boyd Upper
Peter Van Loan
Peter Warrian
Mel Watkins
Lorraine Weinrib
Reg Whitaker
David Wolfe

Donnie Wright
Christine Yankou

Ottawa/Hull and the National Capital Region

David Ablett
Rick Anderson
Hazen Argue
Norm Atkins
Jack Austin
Lloyd Axworthy
Tom Axworthy
Maude Barlow
Louis Berlinguet
Robert Bertrand
Jean-Jacques Blais
Jean Sutherland Boggs
David Bond
Gerald Bouey
Herb Breau
François Bregha
James Bruce
Robert Bryce
Ron Bulmer
Charles Caccia
Kenneth Calder
Iona Campagnolo
Duncan Cameron
Gerry Caplan
Margaret Catley-Carlson
Alf Chaiton
Denise Chong
Edmund Clark
Ian D. Clark
Joseph Clark
M.A. (Mickey) Cohen

David Collenette
Arthur Collin
J.P. Connell
David Crenna
Marshall Crowe
Mark R. Daniels
Keith Davey
Pierre De Bané
D.B. Dewar
G.H. Dewhirst
Jim de Wilde
Linda Diebel
Peter Dobell
David Dodge
Bernard Drabble
Kenneth Dye
Percy Eastham
C.G. Edge
David Elder
Judy Erola
Gordon Fairweather
James Fleming
Eugene Forsey
Robert Fowler
Ross Francis
Alastair Fraser
Claude Frenette
Daniel Gagnier
Rosé Gagnier
Linda Geller-Schwartz
Jacques Gérin
Fred Gibson
Philip Dean Gigantes
Audrey Gill
Eddie Goldenberg
Len Good
Allan Gotlieb
Joseph Gough

Alain Gourd
John Grace
Jerry Grafstein
Herbert Gray
Roberto Gualtieri
Reeves Haggan
A.L. Halliday
David Halton
James Harlick
Michael Harris
Michael Hatfield
Ivan Head
Paul Heinbecker
Jane Heintzman
Ralph Heintzman
Paul Henry
Raymond Hession
Abby Hoffman
Lawson Hunter
James Hurley
Glenn Jenkins
Pauline Jewett
Ted Johnson
Donald Johnston
Pierre Juneau
Naim Kattan
Michael Kelly
Colin Kenny
Jeremy Kinsman
David Kirkwood
Bill Knight
Arthur Kroeger
Huguette Labelle
Robert Latimer
Nate Laurie
Jeanne Laux
Romeo LeBlanc
William Lee

Claude Lemelin
Jean Le Moyne
Peter Lesaux
George Lindsey
Bruce Lister
Gaétan Lussier
David MacDonald
Flora Macdonald
Mary MacDonald
Allan J. MacEachen
Mark MacGuigan
Roy MacLaren
Norman McLeod
Charles McMillan
David Malone
J.L. Manion
Jean Marchand
Lorna Marsden
Robert Martin
Marcel Massé
Tim Maxwell
A.W. May
David Miller
Reid Morden
Nicole Morgan
Lowell Murray
Geoff O'Brian
Richard O'Hagan
Maureen O'Neil
Gordon Osbaldeston
James Page
Geoffrey Pearson
Maryon Pearson
Jean-Luc Pepin
Jack Pickersgill
Michael Pitfield
Timothy Porteous
George Post

Robert Rabinovitch
Victor Rabinovitch
Gerald Regan
Robert Richardson
Sean Riley
Gordon Robertson
Guy Rocher
Michel Rochon
Edward Rubin
James Rusk
Jeanne Sauvé
Anne Scotton
Blair Seaborn
Gerry Shannon
Mitchell Sharp
Leonard Shifrin
Jeffrey Simpson
Robert Slater
David Smith
Gordon Smith
Janet Smith
Stuart Smith
J.S. Stanford
Lloyd Stanford
Ian Stewart
John Stewart
Barbara Sulzenko
Harry Swain
John Swift
Andrew Szende
Donald Tansley
Roger Tassé
J.H. (Si) Taylor
Paul Tellier
John Terry
William Teschke
G.C.E. Theriault
Tamra Thomson

George Tough
Collette Trent
John Trent
Rick Van Loon
Michel Vastel
Gérard Veilleux
Manfred von Nostitz
Roger Voyer
Jean Wadds
Peter White
Barry Wilson
Helen Wilson
Ramsey Withers
Bernard Wood
Stephen Woolcombe
Torrance Wylie
Georgina Wyman
Maxwell Yalden

Quebec

Warren Allmand
Pierre Bastien
Louise Beaudoin
Monique Bégin
William Bennett
Pauline Bergeron
Louis Bernard
Yves Bérubé
Lise Bissonnette
Denise Bombardier
Bernard Bonin
Rémi Bujold
Sheila Burke
Pierre Bussières
Gretta Chambers
Micheline Côté

Denis Dawson
Jean de Grandpré
Pierre Deniger
Peter Donolo
Louis Duclos
André Dufour
Claude Forget
Yves Fortier
Francis Fox
Graham Fraser
Joan Fraser
Richard French
Lysiane Gagnon
Jean Garon
Jean-Marie Gaul
Gérald Godin
Carl Goldenberg
Harold Gordon
Céline Hervieux-Payette
Raymond Hudon
Pierre-Marc Johnson
William Johnson
Serge Joyal
Jean-Paul L'Allier
Marc Lalonde
Gilles Lamontagne
Daniel Latouche
François Lebrun
Paule Leduc
Pierre Levasseur
Gérard D. Lévesque
René Lévesque
Edward Lumley
Eric Maldoff
Jean-Claude Malépart
Alain Marcoux
Louis Martin
Paul Martin, Jr.

Jean Meloche
Denis Monière
Claude Morin
Brian Mulroney
Michel Nadeau
Robert Norman
Jean Paré
Alec Paterson
John Payne
Gérard Pelletier
Normand Plante
James Robb
Jean-K. Samson
Charles Taylor
Dale Thomson
Monique Vallerand
Betty Zimmerman

Western Canada

Geoff Andrew
Jim August
Cam Avery
David Barrett
Robert Blair
Allan Blakeney
Doug Campbell
Wayne Clifford
A.F. (Chip) Collins
J.M. Cormack
Michael Decter
Louis Desrochers
Grant Devine
John Donner
Gary Duke
Jean Edmunds
Mark Eliesen

Leroy Fjordbotten
Robert Foulkes
Garde Gardom
Gordon Gibson
Clay Gilson
David Godfrey
Ellen Godfrey
Ralph Goodale
John Helliwell
Lou Hyndman
Dick Johnston
Myron Kanik
Howard Leeson
Merv Leitch
Peter Lougheed
Patrick McGeer
Helmut Mach
Norman Macmurchy
Allan Macpherson
Edward McWhinney
James Matkin
Peter Meekison
G.B. (Barry) Mellon
Michael Mendelson
Gerry Mercier
Harold Millican
Chris Mills
Grant Mitchell
Keith Mitchell
Don Munton
R.J. (Randy) Palivoda
Wilson Parasiuk
Lorne Parker
Howard Pawley
Kevin Peterson
Art Phillips
Hugh Planche
Larry Pratt

Doug Radke
Phil Resnick
Clarence Roth
Frances Russell
E.G. (Ed) Shaske
Melvin Smith
Norman Spector
William Stanbury
Lauris Talmey
Nick Taylor
Paul Thomas
Allan Tupper
Richard Vogel
Art Wakabayashi
David Walker
Michael Webb
Bruce Wilkinson
Robert Williams

France

Fred Bild
Maurice Couve de Murville
Martial de la Fournière
Xavier Deniau
Gilles Duguay
Bernard Garcia
Madeleine Gobeil
Alfred Grosser
Claude Julien
François de Laboulaye
Jean Lacouture
François Leduc
Jean de Lipkowski
Pierre Maillard
Pierre-Louis Mallen
Georges Many

Michel Prada
Claude Roquet
Maurice Schuman
Jean-Marie Soutou

Great Britain

Jonathan Aitken
Derek Day
Louis Delvoie
Roy Faibish
John Ford
George Foulkes
John Freeland
Ian Gilmour
Vivien Hughes
Bernard Ingham
Jonathan Manthorpe
James McKibbon
Roy McMurtry
Kevin McNamara
David Owen
Anthony Parry
Francis Pym
Nicholas Ridley
Gordon Wasserman
Tom Wells
Baroness Young

United States

Willis Armstrong
Roger J. Beland
Derek H. Burney
Stanton Cook
William Diebold

Barbara Ehrenreich
Max Field
David Gergen
Gary Hufbauer
Edith Iglauer
George Jaeger
Darel Johnson
Robert Johnstone
James Medas
Robert Montgomery
Frank Morgan
Peter Morici
Edward Nef
Thomas Nile

Myer Rashish
George Rejhon
Paul Heron Robinson, Jr.
John Rouse
Jacques Roy
Peter Scott
Bhabani Sen Gupta
Robert Shelley
Max Stucker
Peter Towe
Philip Trezise
Sandy Vogelgesang
Clayton Yeutter

ACKNOWLEDGEMENTS

During the six years the two volumes of this book were in progress a number of political-economy students worked on specific aspects of the research. We acknowledge with gratitude the contributions of Jeremy Adelman, David Angell, Peter Biro, Lisa Feld, Lisa Freeman, Neil Freeman, Rodney Haddow, Ashley McCall, Andrew Mitrovica, Janice Rubin, Aleksandr Shprintsen, Joana Superina, Anna Valerio, Ruthanne Wrobel, and Ann Xinidis. We would like to make special mention of Christopher Boyle and the extraordinary efforts he made during nearly two years as our research assistant.

We were also fortunate to have critiques of various parts of the manuscript by distinguished experts: Professor Kenneth McRoberts of York University, on the chapters touching on Quebec's political economy; the Hon. Claude Morin of the École nationale d'administration publique in Quebec City, on the relationship between Trudeau and Quebec politics; Dr. James Reed of the University of Toronto, on the psychoanalytical theory underlying the analysis in Part I; and Professor Peter Russell of the University of Toronto, on the constitutional details in Part II.

We owe a special debt of gratitude to Jean-Marie Gaul and Mme Suzette Trudeau Rouleau, the former for exhaustive efforts in ferreting out information from the archives of the municipality and parish of Outremont, and the latter for kindly making available to us previously unpublished photographs of her family.

Special thanks are also due to J. Stefan Dupré, former chair of the Department of Political Economy of the University of Toronto, for suggesting that we apply for scholarly funding; Robert Fulford, former editor of *Saturday Night* magazine, for his early enthusiastic encouragement of our collaboration; David Trick for help in tracking down government data and statistics and for reading the manuscript; Arthur Kroeger for advice on research into the problems of the Crow's Nest Pass Rate; Marsha Chandler, chair of the Department of Political Science of the University of Toronto, for her understanding and support while this project has been in progress; Jane Barrett, librarian at the Canadian Institute of International Affairs, for her help in unearthing elusive documents; Louis Delvoie of the Canadian High Commission in Great Britain for helping organize a week's interviewing in London; Fred Bild of the Canadian Embassy in France for helping organize a week's interviewing in Paris; Paul Chapin of the Canadian Embassy in the United States for help in arranging interviews in and around the Pentagon and the State Department in Washington; the staff of the Robarts Library, University of Toronto, for providing carrel space and the library's resources; and the Master and staff of Massey College for offering us a haven in the summer of 1989.

As our list of some 550 interviewees attests, we had direct access to most of the protagonists in the Quebec–Canada wars, and we want to acknowledge their willingness to share their insights, often in confidence, into the dramatic events of this period. We also want to pay tribute to the superb work in the field done by Robert Sheppard, Michael Valpy, Graham Fraser, and Jeffrey Simpson, four good journalists who flourished in the admirably open atmosphere of Richard J. Doyle's *Globe and Mail*, as well as to the consistently knowledgeable reporting of Robert McKenzie of the *Toronto Star* and the penetrating columns of Lysiane Gagnon in *La Presse* and Lise Bissonnette in *Le Devoir* and *The Globe and Mail*.

We are particularly grateful for many friends who lent us their good cheer, willing ears, and incisive advice over the years, especially Libby Burnham, Duncan Cameron, Sherrill Cheda, Marjorie Cohen, Daniel Drache, Patricia Dumas, Vera Frenkel, Elizabeth Gordon, Marion Harris, Mary Harrison, Alec Havrlant, Prue Hemelrijk, Bruce Kidd, Jeanne Laux, François Lebrun, Geoffrey and Jane O'Brian, Wanda and Richard O'Hagan, Alan Powell, Cranford Pratt, David Shugarman, Ethel Teitelbaum, Leonie Van Ness, Orlie and Bob Vincent, Mel Watkins, Helen Wilson, David Wolfe, and Betty Zimmerman.

It was our good fortune to have the professional advice of three mainstays of the Canadian publishing world: Barbara Czarnecki, who acted as our meticulous editor; Marian Hebb, who displayed supple skills as our lawyer; and Douglas Gibson, our publisher at McClelland and Stewart, who was unfailingly inventive, enthusiastic, and patient.

This project has benefitted from Social Sciences and Humanities Research Council grants in 1985–86; Summer Employment/Experience Development grants in 1984, 1987, and 1988, which permitted us to hire Jeremy Adelman, Rod Haddow, Ruthanne Wrobel, and Christopher Boyle; a number of small grants from the Humanities and Social Science Committee of the University of Toronto in 1986, 1987, 1988, and 1990; a Canada Council Non-Fiction Program grant in 1988–89; and support from the Ontario Arts Council in 1989. It also had the encouragement of the

Walter and Duncan Gordon Foundation, whose co-founder, Walter Lockhart Gordon, played such an important role in both our lives. Walter, *ubicumque es te salutamus*!

Finally, we want to thank our daughters for buoying us up during the long period that it took to research and write this work. Over and above the practical contribution of meals cooked and errands run, and the continuous moral support lovingly offered by Ashley McCall and Blaise and Kyra Clarkson, Blaise Clarkson drafted an appendix and acted as general reader; Kyra Clarkson wrote many letters and otherwise voiced her encouragement from phone booths all over Europe; and Ashley McCall devoted six months of a postgraduate year to the difficult job of acting as midwife during the last crucial period of Volume 1's delivery, taking particular responsibility for researching, arranging, and selecting the photographs, a job she did with great flair. Her optimism and quick wit made the book's completion possible and, on occasion, even pleasurable.

Toronto, July 1990   Stephen Clarkson
                                                     & Christina McCall

INDEX